Dian Parluhutan

The Implementation of Circumstancial Evidence pursuant to the European Union Competition Law, the German Cartel Law and the Indonesian Competition Law

Dian Parluhutan

The Implementation of Circumstancial Evidence pursuant to the European Union Competition Law, the German Cartel Law and the Indonesian Competition Law

Tectum Verlag

a.t.: Freie Universität Berlin, Diss., 2017
original title: Juridicial Analysis concerning Implementation of Circumstancial (Indirect) Evidence pursuant to The European Union (EU) Competition Law, The German Cartel Law and The Indonesia Competition Law Number 5/1999
Gefördert durch die Hanns-Seidel-Stiftung e.V.

The Deutsche Nationalbibliothek lists this publication in the Deutsche Nationalbibliografie; detailed bibliographic data are available on the Internet at http://dnb.d-nb.de

ISBN 978-3-8288-4127-7 (Print)
978-3-8288-7337-7 (ePDF)

British Library Cataloguing-in-Publication Data
A catalogue record for this book is available from the British Library.

ISBN 978-3-8288-4127-7 (Print)
978-3-8288-7337-7 (ePDF)

Library of Congress Cataloging-in-Publication Data
Parluhutan, Dian
The Implementation of Circumstancial Evidence pursuant to the European Union Competition Law, the German Cartel Law and the Indonesian Competition Law
336 pp.
Includes bibliographic references.

ISBN 978-3-8288-4127-7 (Print)
978-3-8288-7337-7 (ePDF)

1st edition 2019

Printed and bound in Germany.

Preface

This book provides analysis regarding the implementation of circumstantial (indirect) evidences, notably 'facilitating practices' and 'plus-factors' to prove cartel violations in the German and European Competition law's praxis as well as the Indonesian Competition law's practice. First and foremost, I would like to express my gratitude to Prof. Dr. iur. Dr. rer. pol. Dres. h.c. Franz Jürgen Säcker Hon.Ph.D.(PCCC) for his genuine motivation and fatherhood guidance as well as his staff at the *Institut für Energie- und Regulierungsrecht* Berlin. I would also to thank sincerely Dr. jur. Udin Silalahi, SH., LL.M, Lecturer at *Universitas Pelita Harapan* (UPH) for having inspired and encouraged me to finalize my doctoral research project. Particulary, I would like to thank *Studienförderung Ausland, Hanns-Seidel Stiftung* also Mr. John Riady for having supported my doctoral study in Germany. Furthermore, I would like to thank *Kanzlei* Linklaters LLP Berlin as well as Faculty of Law, State University St. Petersburg for supporting my study through professional and research fellowship experiences. Also, I am very thankful to the *Freie Universität Berlin's* Faculty of Law and International Office's staff members. Moreover, I would like to thank Jusuf Indradewa and Partners, Jakarta.

My deepest gratitude, however, I owe to my family and community-group's friends in Berlin-Potsdam and Jakarta, who showed the best support, unlimited patience, positivity and confidence to accomplish the doctoral research and this publication.

Karawaci, October 2019

Foreword

With delight I write this foreword, not only because Mr. Parluhutan has worked as a Lecturer under my leadership, but also because I believe that his book serves as a contribution to the development of teaching and research on the international business and competition law in Indonesia.

I genuinely hope this book will become a primer for academicians and practitioners to enrich and to foster their expertise in the field of Indonesian and international business and competition law in the contemporaneity and in the future.

Professor Dr. Bintan Saragih, SH
Dean Faculty of Law

Inhaltsverzeichnis

Chapter One Introduction

1.1 Research Background

On 5th March 2000 the Law of the Republic Indonesia Number 5 of 1999 concerning the Prohibition of Monopolistic Practices and Unfair Business Competition ("the Law Number 5/1999") was enacted by the Indonesian House of Representatives ("DPR"). Notwithstanding the polemics regarding necessity and appropriateness of the Law Number 5/1999, the proponents of it argued that the Law Number 5/1999 is profoundly important for establishing the economic democracy in Indonesia.[1] Indeed, Article 33 of the 1945 Indonesian Constitution mandates the attainment of economic democracy.[2]

Equally important, according *to Säcker and Lohse*, the Law Number 5/1999 purports, *inter alia*, to achieve the economic democracy. Put differently, the Law Number 5/1999 aims to promote further innovations, economic efficiencies as well as to increase consumers' welfare

---

1 M. U. Silalahi, *Fusionskontrolle in Indonesien gemäß Regierungsverordnung Nr. 27/1998 und Gesetz Nr. 5/1999 im Vergleich zur deutschen und europäischen Fusionskontrolle* (Friedrich-Alexander-Universität Erlangen, 2001) 55–57.

2 Article 33 of the 1945 Indonesian Constitution (4th Amendment, 2002). ‹http://www.unesco.org/education/edurights/media/docs/b1ba8608010ce0c48966911957392ea8cda405d8.pdf› accessed on 03 January 2019.
The concept of an economic democracy (*Wirtschaftsdemokratie*) is in contrast to the following systems of economy:
First, *Laissez-faire* (free fight liberalism), which refers to a system without the state regulatory intervention and depends largely on market mechanism.
Second, etatism system, which is characterised by the centralised state economic system and thus paralyses private economic activities.
Third, the economic concentration system, which ran through the certain groups (elite groups). See Silalahi, *Fusionskontrolle in Indonesien gemäß Regierungsverordnung Nr. 27/1998 und Gesetz Nr. 5/1999* (n 1) 33–55.

optimally.[3] Even more, *Silalahi* asserts that the Law Number 5/1999 serves as the economic constitutional-order (*Verfassung der Wirtschaftsordnung)* in the Indonesian national developments.[4]

Whereas the Law Number 5/1999 has been approximately for 17 years implemented, it encounters considerable difficulties to uncover (detect) and prosecute cartel infringement in Indonesia.[5] In fact, the Indonesian Commission for the Business Competition Supervision ("Komisi Pengawas Persaingan Usaha-KPPU"), as an independent authority established to supervise the application of the Law Number 5/1999, had been experiencing profound obstacles to implement the circumstantial (indirect) evidences the competition law enforcement proceedings against cartel. In fact, KPPU encountered difficulties and inconsistencies regarding the implementation of the circumstantial (indirect) evidences in the cement cartel,[6] airlines fuel surcharge cartel,[7] SMS telecommunication cartel,[8] soybean cooking oil cartel,[9] anti-hypertension pharmacy cartel[10] and the most recent is automotive tire cartel.[11]

---

3 Wolfgang Kartte and Knud Hansen in F. J. Säcker, et.al (eds.), *Law Concerning Prohibition of Monopolistic Practices and Unfair Business Competition* (GTZ-Katalis, 2001) 1–7. cf. *Säcker and Lohse* in F. J. Säcker, et.al (eds) (n 3) 117–122.

4 The concept of „*Verfassung der Wirtschaftsordnung*" in Indonesia requires also the economic reforms through the introduction Law Number 8 year of 1999 on Consumer Protection, the Law Number 10 year of 1998 on Banking Sector, and the Law Number 4 year of 1998 on Bankruptcy and Indonesian Commercial Court as the integrated economic reform package to ensure justice and legal certainty for all economic and business actors. M. U. *Silalahi*, (n 1) 55–60.

5 *M. U. Silalahi* and D. Parluhutan, 'Circumstantial Evidence in the Substantiation Mechanism against Cartel Infringements in Indonesia' (Jurnal Hukum Bisnis, Vol. 30/Nr. 2, 2011) 2–3.

6 KPPU Decision on the Industry Cement Cartel (Putusan Perkara No. 01/ KPPU-L/ 2010).

7 KPPU Decision on the Garuda Indonesia Airwarys (Persero) (Putusan Perkara No: 25/KPPU-I/2009).

8 KPPU Decision on the Short Message Service (SMS) Telecommunication Cartel (Putusan Perkara No.26/KPPU-I/2007).

9 KPPU Decision on the Cooking Oil Cartel (Putusan Perkara No.24/KPPU-I/2009).

10 KPPU Decision on the Pharmacy Cartel on Hypertension Amlodipine (Putusan Perkara No. 17/KPPU-I/2010).

11 KPPU Decision on the Bridgestone Tire Indonesia (Putusan KPPU No. 08/KPPU-I/2014 *juncto.* MARI Decision 221 K/Pdt.Sus-KPPU/2016).

According to the European Union Commission ("Commission"), cartel refers to:

> "Arrangement(s) between competing firms designed to limit or eliminate competition between them, with the objective of increasing prices and profits of the participating companies and without producing any objective countervailing benefits. In practice, this is generally done by fixing prices, limiting output, sharing markets, allocating customers or territories, bid rigging or a combination of these specific types of restriction. Cartels are harmful to consumers and society as a whole due to the fact that the participating companies charge higher prices (and earn higher profits) than in a competitive market."[12]

On the one hand, *Wollmann and Herzog* describe cartel as an agreement, decision of association of undertakings or concerted practices, which aim to restrict and distort competitions in a market.[13] On the other hand, the Indonesian Competition Law Number 5/1999, Article 11 stipulates:

> "An undertaking shall be prohibited to make agreements with their business competitors, with the intention of influencing prices by arranging production and/or marketing of a good and/or service, *which could result* in the occurrence of monopolistic practice and/or unfair business competition."

Taking into account the cartel characteristics, *Silalahi* contends that Competition Authorithy ("CA") will find difficulties in investigating and prosecuting cartels violation due to its secretive nature.[14] Regardless its collusive feature, cartels cause detrimental effects to the competition in a market, for instance increases of price and decreases of consumers' welfare.[15] For that reason, *Ruky* believes that cartel is a provide a most dangerous violation of competition law, because CA must be able to

12 EU Commission, *Glossary of terms used in the EU competition policy* (EU Publishing, 2003) 8–10.

13 Wollmann and Herzog, ‚Art. 101 (1) AEUV' in F. J. Säcker, et.al. (eds.), *Europäisches Wettbewerbsrecht (2. Aufl.). Münchener Kommentar europäisches und deutsches Wettbewerbsrecht (Kartellrecht): Kartellrecht, Missbrauchs- und Fusionskontrolle, Band 1 & Band 2* (CH Beck, 2015) 738–40.

14 *Silalahi, 'Circumstantial Evidence Dalam Memberantas Kartel Berdasarkan Hukum Persaingan Usaha' (UPH Law Faculty National Seminar Eradicating Cartel Practices in Indonesia: The Challenges of Indirect Evidence, Lippo Karawaci, 20th January 2012) 2.*

15 *Silalahi*, ibid. 3.

answer 'who commits cartels violation?'[16] Equally important, cartel frequently takes place in an oligopolistic market, in which business actors could be subject to the oligopolistic interdependence (conscious parallelism). At the same time, Adam Smith maintains that *„people of the same trade seldom meet together, even for merriment and diversion, but the conversation ends in a conspiracy against the public, or in some contrivance to raise prices"*.[17] On account of this reason, the investigation and prosecution of cartels violation prerequisite not only the direct evidence, but also the circumstantial (indirect) one.[18] In brief, the *circumstantial (indirect) evidence*s refers to "evidence which is appropriate to corroborate the proof of the existence of cartels by way of deduction, common sense, economic analysis or logical inference from the demonstrated facts."[19]

Whereas CA such as KPPU, is authorized to employ the circumstantial (indirect) evidence, KPPU must carefully apply the circumstantial (indirect evidence) due to following reasons.[20] First, KPPU must prevent the 'false positive' (type 1 error).[21] Second, KPPU must avoid the 'false negative' (type 2 error).[22] Accordingly, KPPU is subject to the procedural rules, such as proportionality and due process principles enshrined in the KPPU Regulation (Peraturan Komisi-Perkom) Number 1/2010 concering the Guidelines for Adjudication of competition infringement cases.[23] Thus, in the judicial practice of European competition law and German cartel law, the Competition Authorities are subject to the procedural law's principles in applying both of direct

---

16 *I.M. S. Ruky, 'Economic Evidence Dalam Pembuktian Kartel' (UPH Law Faculty National Seminar Eradicating Cartel Practices in Indonesia: The Challenges of Indirect Evidence, Lippo Karawaci, 20th January 2012) 1–2.*

17 *Silalahi*, ibid. 2.

18 *Silalahi* and D. Parluhutan,*'Circumstantial Evidence in the Substantiation Mechanism against Cartel Infringements in Indonesia' (n 5)* 3–5.

19 Organisation of Economic Developments and Cooperation (OECD), '*Prosecuting Cartel without Direct Evidence of Agreement: Policy Brief*' (OECD Secretariat, 2007) 5.

20 Ruky, *'Economic Evidence', (n 16) 3–8. See also* H. G. Kekevi, *'Can Economics Help Us with Cartel Detection?' (Presentation to the International Competition Network Cartel Workshop Lisbon, Portugal, 28th October, 2008) 2–5.*

21 *Ruky*, "*Economic Evidence*' (n 16) 3–8.

22 ibid. 5–7.

23 KPPU, ‹http://www.kppu.go.id/docs/SK/sk_1_2010.pdf, › accessed on 02th January 2019.

and circumstantial (indirect) evidences in order to prove a cartels offence. According to *Hofmann*, the principles are of highly importance and serve as the commonly accepted legal foundations of the European Union (EU) Law.[24] Indeed, Article 2 of Treaty on the Functioning of the European Union ("TFEU") provides:

> "The Union is founded on the values of respect for human dignity, freedom, democracy, equality, the rule of law and respect for human rights, including the rights of persons belonging to minorities. These values are common to the Member States in a society in which pluralism, non-discrimination, tolerance, justice, solidarity and equality between women and men prevail".[25]

Specifically, the European competition law as well as the German cartel law proceedings embrace the principle of *in dubio pro reo*, which literally means 'when in doubt, in favour of the accused' (the presumption of innocence).[26] Also, in the *Rhône-Poulenc* case the *Advocate General Vesterdorf* asserted the importance of procedural law principle in competition law cases, as follows:

> "Considerable importance must be attached to the fact that the competition cases of this kind (cartels) are in reality of a penal nature, which naturally suggests that *a high standard of proof is required (…). There must be a sufficient basis for the decision* and any reasonable doubt must be for the benefit of the applicants according to the principle of *in dubio pro reo*."[27]

In contrast, in the judicial practice of the Law Number 5/1999, there is a dubiousness in the implementation of circumstantial (indirect) evidence. Whilst KPPU has decided cartel infringement cases by applying the circumstantial (indirect) evidence, both of the competition law

24 *H. Hofmann, G. C. Rowe, A. Türk, Administrative Law and Policy of the European Union (1. publ., OUP, 2011) 27–30.*

25 Consolidated versions of the Treaty on European Union and the Treaty on the Functioning of the European Union – Consolidated version of the Treaty on the Functioning of the European Union – Protocols – Annexes – Declarations annexed to the Final Act of the Intergovernmental Conference which adopted the Treaty of Lisbon, signed on 13th December 2007 [Official Journal C 326, 26/10/2012 P. 0001–0390]

26 I. Lianos and C. Genakos, '*Econometric Evidence in EU Competition Law: An Empirical and Theoretical Analysis*' in I. Lianos and D. Geradin (eds.). *Handbook on European Competition Law: Enforcement and Procedure* (Edward Elgar Publishing, 2013) 7–10.

27 Lianos and Genakos, ibid.86 – 87.

practitioners and scholars in Indonesia object the KPPU's decision. For instance, they contend that the circumstantial (indirect) evidence creates contentious and overlapping impact to the existing evidentiary requirement rules, notably Article 184 (1) of the Indonesian Criminal Procedural Code ("KUHAP") and Article 1866 of the Indonesian Civil Code ("*Burgerlijk Wetboek*"or "KUHPerdata").[28] To date, by examining the KPPU's decision in an automotive cartels case, *Silalahi* indicates that there is an inconsistency in the application of circumstantial (indirect) evidence.[29]

While the implementation of circumstantial (indirect) evidence is profoundly important to ensure effective enforcement of the Law Number 5/1999, there has been deficit of scholarly works regarding the employment of circumstantial (indirect) evidence in Indonesia. Specifically, *Silalahi* and *Parluhutan* have introduced academic discourses on the circumstantial (indirect) evidence in accordance with jurisprudential development of the Law Number 5/1999.[30] Afterward, *Anggraini* highlighted the KPPU's practice in applying the circumstantial (indirect) evidence within cartels violation cases.[31] Accordingly, *Rizkiyana and Iswanto* recommend that KPPU must be empowered with broader investigative powers.[32]

---

28 The Indonesia Law Number 8 year of 1981 concerning the Indonesian Criminal Law Proceedings ("KUHAP") and The Indonesia Civil Code ("KUH Perdata") (30 April 1847, Staatsblad No. 23), Book III. Furthermore, this pros and cons of the implementation of circumstantial evidences were manifest in discussions between Indonesian scholars and practitioners on competition law. cf. R. Rizkiyana and V. Iswanto, 'Eradicating Cartel: The Use of Indirect Evidence' (UPH Law Faculty National Seminar "Eradicating Cartel Practices in Indonesia: The Challenges of Indirect Evidence", Lippo Karawaci, 20th January 2012) 5–10.

29 Faculty of Law Pelita Harapan University (FH-UPH), Seminar Publik "Eksaminasi Putusan Komisi Pengawas Persaingan Usaha No. 08/KPPU-I/2014 tentang Dugaan Pelanggaran Pasal 5 ayat (1) dan Pasal 11 Undang-undang No. 5 Tahun 1999. UPH Media, 'Public Seminar: Eksaminasi Putusan KPPU' (UPH News, 14th September 2015), ‹http://www.uph.edu/id/component/wmnews/new/2401.html›, accessed on 16th October 2015.

30 Silalahi and Parluhutan, '*Circumstantial Evidence in the Substantiation Mechanism*' (*n 5*), 2–7.

31 A. M. T. Anggraini, '*Penggunaan Bukti Ekonomi dalam Kartel Berdasarkan Hukum Pesaingan Usaha*' (Jurnal Hukum PRIORIS, Vol.3/Nr. 3, 2013) 1–5.

32 *Rizkiyana and Iswanto*, 'Eradicating Cartel' (n 28) 2–7.

Thereby, the dissertation attempts to perform holistic analysis concerning both of the normative (regulatory) framework of circumstantial (indirect) evidence as well as the judiciary practice of Competition Authorithy on circumstantial (indirect) evidence pursuant to the Indonesia Competition Law Number 5/1999 in comparison to the German Cartel Law and the European Union (EU) Competition Law.[33] Furthermore, by means of juridical comparison with the German Cartel Law and the EU Competition Law, the dissertation's endeavor is to examine the implementation of Leniency programme in order to eradicate cartels violations optimally. Equally important, this dissertation aims to provide recommendation for the improvement of the Law Number 5/1999 in accordance with the national middle-term 2015–2019.[34] Moreover, by taking into account the ASEAN Economic Community ("AEC"),[35] the Law Number 5/1999 shall be able to response against cross-borders anticompetitive practices, that is to say, cartel infringement.[36]

33 D. Geradin, A. L. Farrar, N. Petit, *EU Competition Law and Economics* (OUP, 2012) 321–322.

34 Explanation of the KPPU Chairman, M. Nawir Messi, (R. S. Pradana). ‹http://finansial.bisnis.com/read/20150127/9/395434/amandemen-uu- no.51999-soal-monopoli-tuntas-tahun-ini›, accessed on 12th March 2016.

35 ASEAN is the abbreviation of the Association of Southeast Asian Nations with currently 10 member countries: Indonesia, Singapore, Thailand, Malaysia, Brunei Darussalam, Phillipines, Vietnam, Myanmar, Laos PDR, Cambodia. By virtue of the ASEAN Concord II declared in Bali in 2003, the ASEAN countries have agreed to establish the ASEAN Economic Community ("AEC") by 2015 which will not only transform ASEAN into a region with free movement of goods, services, investment and skilled labour, and a freer flow of capital, but also it will create a highly competitive region that is fully integrated with the global economy. Thus, through the AEC the currently 10 ASEAN member states determine themselves to achieve the following core objectives gradually: First, the single market and production base. Second, the highly competitive economic region. Third, the region of equitable economic development. Fourth, the region fully integrated into the global and other regional economies. See also ASEAN Secretariat, 'ASEAN Economic Community Blueprint' (Jakarta 2015) ‹http://www.asean.org/asean-economic-community/› accessed on 12th March 2016.

36 *Silalahi*, 'The Role of Competition Law in Supporting the ASEAN Economic Integration' (Paper presentation on the ASEAN Competition Law Conference, Jakarta, July 2015) 3–5. See also A. Stephan, 'The Role of Competition Policy in Promoting the ASEAN Economic Community' (Presentation on the ASEAN Competition Conference, Bali, 2011) 6–10.

1.2 Discourse of Analysis

In order to provide systematic and sound expositions, this dissertation is structured as follows. After the introduction and structure of analysis have been exposed, the second part of dissertation analyses systematically both of conceptual and substantive regulatory frameworks of cartels prohibition in accordance with the European Union (EU) Competition Law, the German Cartel Law (*Gesetz gegen Wettbewerbsbeschränkungen- "GWB")* and the Indonesia Competition Law Number 5/1999. The second part describes the following substances: (1) cartels in an oligopolistic market by taking into consideration the 'oligopolistic interdependence' (conscious parallelism) therein, (2) analysis of he statutory elements of cartels prohibition, (3) the application of cartels prohibition according to theEU Competition and German Cartel Law, both in terms of horizontal and vertical applications, (4) the substantial matter in the German Cartel Law, notably "hub-and-spoke cartels"and interpretative rule, (5) the cartel prohibition according to the Law Number 5/1999 and the KPPU's Regulation and guideline on cartels prohibition. Afterwards, the third part of dissertation will describe the procedural framework of cartels prohibition in accordance with the EU Competition Law, the German Cartel Law and the Law Number 5/1999. Specifically, this part devotes with the following matters regarding cartel prohibition enforcement proceeding: (1) the guiding procedural principles of European Competition and German Cartel Law, for instance legality, presumption of innocence (in dubio pro reo), the protection of fundamental human rights, (2)Sthe stages of cartel prohibition enforcement procedure in the EU, notably the administrative procedure, which is then followed by the judiciary proceedings, (3) the guiding principle and rule concerning evidentiary requirement, notably, the burden and standard of proof as well as evaluation and categorization of evidences, (4) the recognised cartel *enforcement proceedings in Germany, namely, the Administrative Procedure (Verwaltungsverfahren)*, the *Imposition of Fines (Bußgeldverfahren) and the Civil Litigation Process (Bürgerliche Streitigkeiten Verfahren)*, (5) the evidentiary requirement in Indonesia legal system and the Law Number 5/1999, specifically the judge conviction theory (*conviction intime*), positive law theory (*positief wettelijke bewijstheorie*), restricted judge conviction theory (*conviction raisonee*) and negative law theory (*negatief wettelijke*). Furthermore, the third part's last section, provides comprehensive discussions and analysis concerning the evidentiary rules' implementation as well as the implementation of indirect (circumstantial) evidences. In addition, the application of "Plus factors" or "parallelism plus" in accordance with the European Competition and the German Cartel Laws in conjunctions with the United States (US) Antitrust law as well as the Law Number 5/1999 are to be explained.

Afterwards, the fourth part of the dissertation primarily explains, not only the conceptual and normative aspect of the circumstantial (indirect) evidence, but also the judiciary practices in the EU, Germany and Indonesia with respect to the indirect (circumstantial) evidences, which comprises: the Decision of KPPU and the Judgement of Indonesian Supreme Court (MARI) concerning the Automotive Tire Cartel, the Decision of KPPU on the Cement, the Decision of KPPU on the Short Message Service (SMS) Telecommunication, the Decision of KPPU on the Amlodipine Anti-Hypertension Pharmaceutical Cartels. In addition, the EU Competition and German Cartel Laws' precedents, such as *Bundesverband der Arzneimittel-Importeure v Commission of the European Communities* (Bayer Adalat Cartel) and '*Toshiba Court v European Union Commission*' (Gas Insulated Switchgear-GIS Cartel) in the years of 2004 and 2017. Eventually, the fifth part of the dissertation provides the conclusion and feasible recommendations concerning the implementation of circumstantial (indirect) evidence, notably in the Indonesia Competition Law, by means of the juridical comparisons with the EU Competition Law and the German Cartel Law, in order to substantially improve the Competition Law Number 5/1999 within the perspective of regional economic integration in the Association of the South East Asian Nations (ASEAN) respectively.

Chapter Two The Cartel Prohibition Pursuant to the European Union (EU) Competition and the German Cartel Laws and the Law Number 5/1999

2.1 The Cartels Prohibition

2.1.1 Conceptual Framework

According to the Black's Law Dictionary a cartel is defined as:

> "A combination of producers or sellers that joint together to control a product's production or prices or an association of firms with common interests, seeking to prevent extreme or unfair competition, allocate markets or share knowledge."[37]

Whereas the EU Commission defines cartel, as follows:

> "Arrangement(s) between competing firms designed to limit or eliminate competition between them, with the objective of increasing prices and profits of the participating companies and without producing any objective countervailing benefits. In practice, this is generally done by fixing prices, limiting output, sharing markets, allocating customers or territories, bid rigging or a combination of these specific types of restriction. Cartels are harmful to consumers and society as a whole due to the fact that the participating companies charge higher prices (and earn higher profits) than in a competitive market."[38]

---

37 B. A. Gardner (ed.), *Black's Law Dictionary* (7th Edition, West Group Publishing, 2000) 205–207.

38 EU Commission, 'Glossary of terms used in the EU competition policy' *(Commission*, 2003) 8–10. cf. Rizkiyana and Iswanto, 'Eradicating Cartel' (n 28) 5–7.

Moreover, the *Organisation of Economic Cooperation and Development* (OECD) provides definition of cartels:

> "A cartel is formal agreement among firms in an olygopolistic industry. Cartel members may agree on such matters as prices, total industry output, market shares, allocation of customers, allocation of territories, bid rigging, establishment of common sales agencies, and the division of profits or combination of these".[39]

In other words, a cartel practice takes place whenever two or more undertakings agreed thorough written or tacit concords to reduce the internal competition and thus to increase each undertaking economic position through cartel in the relevant market.[40] Historically, the term cartel derived from the Latin word 'charta' meaning written certified claim or entitlement. Initially in the year of 1883, the term cartel was introduced by *Friedrich Kleinwächter* in terms of a contract with the written certified claims between the contracting parties which promised not to compete against each other in a respective market.[41] The first modern definition of cartels could be found in the United States Antitrust Law, Sherman Act 1980 Section 1, whereas in Germany the term cartel was for a first time stipulated in the Section 1 *Kartellverordnung (KartVO 1923)* which prescribed none of prohibition. According to Section 4 KartVO 1923, *Der deutsche Reichwirtschaftsminister* was only authorized to file a petition to the *Kartellgericht* in order to rescind and to unallow certain cartel practice. For the first time, through the enactment of the GWB in 1957 the cartel prohibition principle was introduced in Germany.[42]

Furthermore, according to *Wollmannn and Herzog*, agreements, decisions of association of undertakings or concerted practices, whose aims to restrict or to distort the competitions in market are known as cartels. Accordingly, such collusive practices have been widely subject

39 R. S. Khemani and D. M. Shapiro, 'Glossary of industrial Organitation Economics and Competition Law' (OECD, Paris, 1996), 7.

40 K. W. Lange and T. W. Preis (eds.), *Einführung in das europäische und deutsche Kartellrecht Einführung (Verlag Recht und Wirtschaft in Deutscher Fachverlag GmbH, 2. Aufl. 2011), 24–25.*

41 *H. P. Schwintowski, Wettbewerbs-und Kartellrecht* (5. Auflage, C. H.Beck, 2012) 2–10.

42 Lange and Preis (eds.), *Einführung in das europäische und deutsche Kartellrecht Einführung* (n 40), 19–20.

to *Per-se Illegal* rule.[43] The European (EU) Competition Law provides elaboration of cartels agreement in the Article 101 TFEU, in particular hardcore cartels.[44]

The European Commission has a strong opposition against cartels and considers that detection and deterrence of cartels practice would be a central and primary concern of the EU Competition Law enforcement. This stance had been reflected in following statements of the former Commissioner on Competition Policy:

> "Fighting cartels is one of the most important areas of activity of any competition authority and a clear priority of the Commission. Cartels are cancers on the open market economy, which forms the very basis of our Community. By destroying competition, they cause serious harm to our economies and consumers. In the long run cartels also undermine the competitiveness of the industry involved, because they eliminate the pressure from competition to innovate and achieve cost efficiency."

In the words of Adam Smith there is a "tendency for competitors to conspire". This tendency is of course driven by the increased profits that follow from colluding rather than competing. We can only reserve this tendency through effective enforcement that creates effective deterrence. The risk of being uncovered and punished must be higher than the probability of earning extra profits form successful collusion.

Cartels differ from most other forms of restrictive agreements and practices by being "naked". They serve to restrict competition without producing any objective countervailing benefits. In contrast, a joint venture between competitors, for example, while restricting competition may at the same time produce efficiencies such as economies of scale or quicker product innovation or development. In these cases, a proper analysis requires that the positive and negative effects are balanced against one another. This is not so with cartels. In cartels the positive side of the equation is zero.

Cartels, therefore, by their very nature eliminate or restrict competition. Companies participating in a cartel produce less and earn higher profits. Society and consumers pay the bill. Resources are misallo-

---

43 Wollmann and Herzog in F.J. Säcker, et.al (eds) (n 13) 742–747.

44 Emmerich 'Art. 101 Abs. 1 AEUV' in U. Immenga und E. J. Mestmäcker, *Wettbewerbsrecht Band 1/Teil 1 Kommentar zum Europäischen Kartellrecht* (5 Aufl, CH. Beck, 2012) 198–222.

cated and consumer welfare is reduced. It is therefore for good reasons that cartels are almost universally condemned. Of all restrictions of competition, cartels contradict most radically the principle of a market economy based on competition, which constitutes the very foundation of the Community.'[45]

Moreover, it is clear nowadays, that Competition Authorities worldwide agree, that one of the most important goal of competition law is to uncover (detect), punish, prevent and eradicate the operation of cartels, notably the 'hardcore cartels'. According to the OECD Recommendation concerning Effective Action Against Hard-Core Cartels, a hardcore cartel is defined as:

> "an anti-competitive agreement, anti-competitive concerted practice, or anti-competitive arrangement by competitors to: *(1) fix prices, (2) make rigged-bids (collusive tender), (3) establish output restrictions or Quota, or (4) share or divide markets by allocating customers, suppliers, territories or lines of commerces*."[46]

In the Indonesian Competition Law, prohibitions against cartels practices are explicitly regulated in Article 11 of the Law Number 5/1999 and the Competition Law Commission Regulation (Perkom) No. 4/2011.[47]

45 EU Commission, 'XXXIst Report on Competition Policy.' ‹http://ec.europa.eu/competition/publications/annual_report/2001/competition_policy_en.pdf› accessed on 19th October 2015. See also M. Jephcott, *Law of Cartels* (Jordans Publishing, 2011), 21–25.

46 A. Jones and B. Sufrin, *EU Competition Law: Text, Cases and Materials* (5th ed, OUP, 2018), 667–668.

47 Article 11 of the Competition Law Number 5/1999 stipulates: "Undertakings are prohibited from making a ny agreements with their competitors with the intention to influence the price by determining production and/or marketing of goods and/or services that can result in monopolistic practices and/or unfair business competition."
Whereas the Competition Commission (KPPU) Regulation Number 4/2011 provides: "[…] cooperation of a number of competing undertakings to coordinate their activities in order to control the volume of production and the prices of goods and or services to gain a profit above reasonable profit."

2.1.2 Cartels and The Oligopolistic Interdependence

A collusion (collusive agreement) rests on the dynamic interaction between firms or undertakings, that is to say, firms or companies condition their future behavior in the market on the current behaviour of competitors. This type of dynamic interaction allows firms to maintain prices at levels close to monopoly prices and significantly above what unilateral conduct alone would allow.[48] Interestingly, several following factors have been established to be of relevance to create a collusion (cartels): First, firms have to reach terms of coordination between them. Second, firms are to monitor compliance to a collusion. Third, firms are able to threaten timely retaliation. Fourth, firms can limit the reactions by outsiders.[49]

Taking into consideration the market characteristics, cartels can be found frequently in an oligopolistic market.[50] According to *Silalahi, an* oligopolistic market refers to economic circumstances whereby there are merely few business actors having approximately equal market shares on the relevant market.[51] Further, OECD defines an oligopolistic market, as follows:

---

48 H. W. Friederiszick, F. P. Maier-Rigaud, 'The Role of Economics in Cartel Detection in Europe' in D Schmidtchen, M. Albert and S. Voigt (eds.), *The More Economic Approach in European Competition Law* (Mohr Siebeck, 2007), 182–183.

49 ibid. See also S. Bishop and M. Walker, *The Economics of EC competition Law: Concepts, Application and Measurement* (3rd Ed, Sweet & Maxwell, 2011), 3–306, 5–001, 5–007.

50 Silalahi, 'Circumstantial Evidences' (n 14), 3–7.

51 Furthermore, as regards to the oligopolistic market, Sullivan argues that 'an industry is oligopolistic when so large a share of its total output in the hands of so few relatively large firms that a change in the output of any of these firms will discernibly affect the market price. Theoretically, in the economic and business sphere there are several types of market, which range from a perfectly competitive market to a monopolistic market. Further, from the perspective of market parameter such as 'workable competition', the oligopoly market situates between the perfectly competitive market and the monopolistic market. On the one hand, in the monopolistic market, business actors act as the monopolist, possess a maximum market power and a full control to stipulate prices and outputs above the competitive level. On the contrary, in the perfectly competitive market there isa large number of sellers and buyers, who each sell or buy a relatively small quantity of homogenous products, free entry into and exit of the market and perfect information. Consequently, there are no one business actors in this market who possess any market power which can finally lead prices to equal marginal costs. S. Stroux, 'Economics of

> "An oligopoly is a market characterised by a small number of firms who realize they are interdependent in their pricing and output policies. The number of firms is small enough to give each firm some market power."[52]

Accordingly, two types of an oligopoly market could be identified: on the one hand a symmetric oligopolistic market and, on the other hand, an asymmetric oligopolistic market.[53]

As far as the characteristic of an oligopolistic market is concerned, the so-called "parametric interdependence" is an important one. This means, each firm in an oligopoly market is aware of existing mutual reactive dependences and considers strategically market reactions of the competitors in order to make a business decision.[54] With regard to an oligopolistic market, hitherto there are two school of thoughts for analysing interaction between firms on an oligopoly market.[55] In other words, within an oligopolistic market there is a so-called 'oligopolistic

---

Oligopoly: An Introduction for Lawyer' (European University Institute Florence Working Paper No 2002/6, Florence) 1. cf. S. Stroux, *US and EC Oligopoly Control* (Kluwer Law, 2009) 10–12.

52 OECD, *Glossary of Statistical Terms* (OECD Publisher, 2008), 378–380.

53 According to OECD, a symmetric oligopolistic market is defined as follows: "When all firms are of (roughly) equal size, the oligopoly is said to be symmetric." Whereas an asymmetric oligopolistic market is "When this is not the case, the oligopoly is asymmetric." ibid.

54 R. Brütsch, *Parallelverhalten im Oligopol als Problem des schweizerischen Wettbewerbsrecht* (1.Aufl, Stämpfli Verlag AG, 2003), 9–12.

55 "First, the structuralists. The Structuralist or Harvard school, basing itself on the Structure-Conduct-Performance (SCP) Paradigm, retains that when the Structure of the market is concentrated, the Conduct, namely the way of competing, of the few competitors present in the market is interdependent, which leads to a performance of decreased output and supra-competitive prices, leading to supra-competitive profits. The Structuralists in their studies thus retain that concentration almost inevitably leads to supra-competitive pricing due to the adapation of oligopolists each other's behavior. However, the adequacy of many studies has, subsequently, been disputed by scholars of the Behaviouralists' school and the soundness of result of empirical research confirming the link between market structure and profits levels have been questioned.
Relying on the fact that each oligopolist is aware of this fact, price-cutting may not occur, and the market as a whole can maintain supra-competitive price without the need for a formal or tacit agreement. This 'theory of interdependence', however, gives no explanation on how the supra-competitive pricing is reached.
Second, the Behaviouralist. The behaviouralist of Chicago School, in contrast, challenged the Structural school's view, that supra competitive pricing in oligopolistic market is virtually inevitable, as they blame supra-competitive pricing on be-

interdependence' phenomenon. Due to the characteristics of an oligopoly market, companies or firms would not compete against one another in terms of price and thus have insignificant incentives to compete in other ways whatsoever. Accordingly, these firms (oligopolists) could gain supra-competitive profits, without even committing an agreement or concerted practice, which are prohibited by the Antitrust law.[56] Put differently, market circumstances contribute to interdependent market reactions between business actors in an oligopoly market. Hence, business actors would be able to exercise the market power even without having to enter into an explicit collusive agreement.[57] Competition law and economics scholar, *Posner*, had studied and thus identified this phenomenon as "conscious paral-

---

havioural factors. Their ideas are based on neo-classical price theory and focus exclusively on allocative efficiency. Building upon Stigler's seminar article 'Theory of Oligpoly' of 1964, the Behaviouralist sustain that, in a concentrated market, as in an unconcentrated market, a concencus level of pricing needs to be reached, the adherence thereto monitored, and secret price cutting needs to be prevented by detecting punishing deviations of the consensus-pricing. Stigler suggested that the greatest obstacle to collusion, in absence of entry, would be what he characterised as 'secret price cutting'. Altough they recognize that concentration is an important and necessary condition for oligopolists to collude, they argue that other factors on the market, such as the existence of countervailing buyer's and presence of barriers to entry can inhibit collusion from coming into existence. Furthermore, the threat of punishment must be such as to constitute a stabilising factor of collusion.
Furthermore, behavioural scholars point out that market structure should not be taken exclusively exogenously determined, but at least partially also influenced endogenously. Large companies should not be condemned per se as they can be the result of superior efficiency. They thus maintain that SCP model of the Sturturalists also works the other way around: market structure is determined by the performance of firms, and should not be attacked because firms have succeded. Stroux, *US and EC Oligopoly Control*, p.10 – 15.

56 R. Whish and D. Bailey, *Competition Law* (9th Ed., OUP, 2011), 560–562.

57 The interdependent market reactions on the oligopolistic market can be described as follows:
Accordingly, there has been insignificant competition in terms of quality between the business actor and other competitors in a relevant market. Moreover, the business actors largely shall, without explicit communication, coordinate their commercial behaviours to align and to set their prices at supra-competitive levels with the other competitors. Thus, as a rational response, the business actors become reactive to other competitors such as by monitoring the behaviors of other competitors, notably the price reductions to prevent the withdrawal of their consumers. Consequently, whenever a business actor or the market leader increases the prices, other business actors will also increase the prices and *vice versa*. In the oligopolistic

lelism", "tacit collusion", or "oligopolistic interdependence".[58] Moreover, it has been argued that game theory supports the oligopolistic interdependence.[59]

With regard to cartels and the oligopolistic interdependence (conscious parallelism), by considering the market characteristics, cartels can be found frequently in an oligopoly market.[60] According to *Silalahi, an* oligopolistic market refers to economic circumstances whereby there are merely few business actors having approximately equal market shares on the relevant market.[61] Further, OECD defines an oligopolistic market as follows:

> "An oligopoly is a market characterized by a small number of firms who realize they are interdependent in their pricing and output policies. The number of firms is small enough to give each firm some market power."[62] Accordingly, two types of an oligopoly market could be identified: *First*, a symmetric oligopolistic market. *Second*, an asymmetric oligopolistic market."[63]

---

market, thus the business actors acknowledge their interdependences and the most efficient commercial action is to set their prices at the profit-maximizing level, which requires necessarily none of previous explicit agreements. Moreover, from the consumers' perspective whenever they demand for the homogenous product they are not bound to certain suppliers but are freely able to purchase the products from the available business actors in the market. Hence, in the oligopolistic market frequently occurs the '*consciously parallel conduct*', which not automatically indicates the prohibited collusive practice. According to *Bishop, Walkers and Bakers*, the concept of 'market power' refers to 'the ability of a firm or group of firms to raise prices, through the restriction of output and maintain them for a significant period of time above the level that would prevail under the competitive conditions and thereby to enjoy increased profits from the action. cf. L.O. Blanco, Market Power in EU Antitrust Law (1st Ed, Hart Publishing, 2011), 20–23.

58 T. Körber, 'Antitrust Law' (ZWeR 2003) 373. See also Silalahi, 'Circumstantial Evidence' (n 14) 3–7.

59 All firms on an oligopoly market would have to maximize profits: profits are greater in monopolistic markets in which output is suppressed. These firms recognize their interdependence as well as their own interest. cf. Whish and Bailey, (n 56) 567.

60 Silalahi, (n 14) 3–7.

61 ibid.

62 OECD Glossary, (n 52) 378.

63 According to OECD, a symmetric oligopolistic market is "When all firms are of (roughly) equal size, the oligopoly is said to be symmetric." Whereas an asymmetric oligopolistic market is "When this is not the case, the oligopoly is asymmetric." ibid. 378–10.

With regard to the oligopolistic market, *Sullivan* argues, as follows:

> "an industry is oligopolistic when so large a share of its total output in the hands of so few relatively large firms that a change in the output of any of these firms will discernibly affect the market price."[64]

Theoretically, in the economic and business sphere there are several types of markets, which range from a perfectly competitive market to a monopolistic market. Further, from the perspective of a market parameter such as 'workable competition', the oligopoly market is situated between the perfectly competitive market and the monopolistic market. On the one hand, in the monopolistic market, business actors act as the monopolist, possess a maximum market power and a full control to stipulate prices and outputs above the competitive level. On the other hand, in the perfectly competitive market there are a large number of sellers and buyers, who each sell or buy a relatively small quantity of homogenous products, but have free entry into and exit of the market and perfect information. Consequently, there are no business actors in this market who possess any market power which can finally lead prices to equal marginal costs.[65]

As far as the characteristic of an oligopolistic market is concerned, the oligopolistic interdependence is an important one. That is to say, each firm in an oligopoly market is aware of existing mutual reactive dependences and considers strategically market reactions of the competitors in order to make business decisions.[66] With regard to an oligopolistic market, up to now there are two school of thoughts for analyzing interaction between firms on an oligopoly market.[67]

---

64 L A. Sullivan, *Handbook of The Law Of Antitrust.* (West Publishing Company. 1977), 331.

65 Stroux, 'EU US Oligopoly', (n 51).

66 Brütsch, *Parallelverhalten in Oligopol,* (n 54) 9–12.

67 "First, the structuralists. The Structuralist or Harvard school, basing itself on the Structure-Conduct-Performance (SCP) Paradigm, retains that when the Structure of the market is concentrated, the Conduct, namely the way of competing, of the few competitors present in the market is interdependent, which leads to a performance of decreased output and supra-competitive prices, leading to supra-competitive profits. The Structuralists in their studies thus retain that concentration almost inevitably leads to supra-competitive pricing due to the adapation of oligopolists each other's behavior. However, the adequacy of many studies has, subsequently, been disputed by scholars of the Behaviouralists' schooland the sound-

With regard to a firms' interaction in an oligopolistic market, it is necessarily important to understand the game theory, which serves as background of cartels practice. *Neumann and Morgenstern* introduced firstly this theory to enlighten dynamic interactions of an oligopolistic interdependence. Principally, game theory refers to efforts to search a combination of the strategies that represent the best strategy for every competitor or market player, who presumably seeks 'rational' decisions to maximize profits ("equilibria").[68] In other words, the game theory refers to the firms' interactions to collude or not to collude in order to achieve and maintain a collusive equilibrium in the market,[69] which can be schematised into a matrix, as follows:

ness of result of empirical research confirming the link between market structure and profits levels have been questioned.
Relying on the fact that each oligopolist is aware of this fact, price-cutting may not occur, and the market as a whole can maintain supra-competitive price without the need for a formal or tacit agreement. This 'theory of interdependence', however, gives no explanation on how the supra-competitive pricing is reached.
Second, the Behaviouralist. The behaviouralist of Chicago School, in contrast, challenged the Structural school's view, that supra competitive pricing in oligopolistic market is virtually inevitable, as they blame supra-competitive pricing on behavioural factors. Their ideas are based on neo-classical price theory and focus exclusively on allocative efficiency. Building upon Stigler's seminar article 'Theory of Oligpoly' of 1964, the Behaviouralist sustain that, in a concentrated market, as in an unconcentrated market, a concencus level of pricing needs to be reached, the adherence thereto monitored, and secret price cutting needs to be prevented by detecting punishing deviations of the consensus-pricing. Stigler suggested that the greatest obstacle to collusion, in absence of entry, would be what he characterized as 'secret price cutting'. Altough they recognize that concentration is an important and necessary condition for oligopolists to collude, they argue that other factors on the market, such as the existence of countervailing buyer's and presence of barriers to entry can inihibit collusion from coming into existence. Furthermore, the threat of punishment must be such as to constitute a stabilizing factor of collusion.
Furthermore, behavioural scholars point out that market structure should not be taken exclusively exogenously determined, but at least partially also influenced endogenously. Large companies should not be condemned per se as they can be the result of superior efficiency. They thus maintain that SCP model of the Stucturalists also works the other way around: market structure is determined by the performance of firms, and should not be attacked because firms have succeded. Stroux, *US and EC Oligopoly,* (n 51) 10–15.

68 ibid.

69 Jephcott and Martani, 'Law of Cartels', (n 45) 10–15.

		Firm B	
		Adhere	Deviate
Firm A	Adhere	A and B get € 7 Million	B gets € 6 Million, A gets € 2 Million
	Deviate	A gets € 6 Million, B gets € 2 Million	Both get € 4 Million

Explanations:

■ Cartels result

□ Non-collusion result

Currently, the non-cooperative game theory has been generally accepted as an appropriate approach to analyze dynamic interactions of firms in an oligopolistic market, whereby this theory postulates that each firm's independent choice for a best strategy would result in an equilibria, which is non-cooperatively optimal given the other firms' similarly calculated optimal strategies in an oligopolistic market.[70]

Furthermore, it should be bore in mind that within an oligopolistic market there is a so-called "oligopolistic interdependence" phenomena. Due to the characteristics of an oligopoly market, firms would not compete with one another in terms of price and thus have insignificant incentives to compete in other ways whatsoever. Accordingly, these firms (oligopolists) could be able to gain supra-competitive profits without even committing an agreement or concerted practice, which is prohibited by the law.[71] In other words, market circumstances contribute to interdependent market reactions between business actors in an oligopoly market. Hence, business actors would be able to exercise the market power even without having to enter into an explicit collu-

70 Stroux, *US and EC Oligopoly Control,* (n 51) 13.
71 Whish and Bailey, (n 56) 560–561.

sive agreement.[72] *Posner*, had studied and thus identified this phenomenon as 'conscious parallelism', 'tacit collusion' or 'oligopolistic interdependence'.[73] Moreover, it has been argued that game theory supports the oligopolistic interdependence.[74]

Nevertheless, the theory of an oligopolistic interdependence is subject to theoretical criticisms, which are: (1) the oligopolistic interdependence theory would overstate the interdependence of firms in an oligopoly market; (2) the oligopolistic interdependence exhibits a very simplistic picture of real-life market; (3) the oligopolistic interdependence theory could not explain why in some oligopolistic markets competition is intense. (4) the oligopolistic interdependence theory could not satisfactorily explain why the firms could gain supra-com-

---

72 The interdependent market reactions on the oligopolistic market can be described as follows:
Accordingly, there has been insignificant competition in terms of quality between the business actors and other competitors in a relevant market. Moreover, business actors largely shall, without explicit communication, coordinate their commercial behaviours to align and to set their prices at supra-competitive levels with the other competitors. Thus, as a rational response, the business actors become reactive to other competitors such as by monitoring the behaviours of other competitors, notably the price reductions to prevent the withdrawal of their consumers. Consequently, whenever a business actor or the market leader increases the prices, other business actors will also increase the prices and *vice versa*. In the oligopolistic market, thus the business actors acknowledge their interdependences and the most efficient commercial action is to set their prices at the profit-maximizing level, which requires necessarily none of the previous explicit agreements.
Moreover, from the consumers' perspective whenever they demand for the homogenous product, they are not bound to certain suppliers but are freely able to purchase the products from the available business actorson the market. Hence, in the oligopolistic market frequently the '*consciously parallel conduct*' occurs, which not automatically indicates the prohibited collusive practice.
According to *Bishop, Walkers and Bakers*, the concept of 'market power' refers to 'the ability of a firm or group of firms to raise prices, through the restriction of output and maintain them for a significant period of time above the level that would prevail under the competitive conditions and thereby to enjoy increased profits from the action. See Blanco, *Market Power (n 57)*, 20–23.

73 Körber, (n 58). cf. Silalahi, 'Circumstantial Evidence' (n 14) 5–7.

74 All firms on an oligopoly market would have to maximize profits: profit is greater in monopolistic markets in which output is suppressed. These firms recognize their interdependence as well as their own interest. cf. Whish and Bailey, *Competition Law, (n 56)* 564–565.

petitive profits without committing a collusive agreement or concerted practice.[75]

Hence, it could be inferred that within an oligopolistic market, there would be two possible outcomes of firms' interaction, notably: collusive agreement or cartels and conscious parallelism. Whilst the former is strictly prohibited and subject to penal sanctions, the latter is permitted.[76] Based upon the explanations above, in an oligopolistic market there are four possibilities of the price formations, which are: cutthroat competition, cooperation, price-rigging and price leadership.[77]

Arguably, there are certain market characteristics, facilitating and stabilizing collusion of firms in an oligopolistic market. According to *Shapiro*, these market characteristics are often called as 'topsy-turvy' principle of collusion: 'anything [...] that makes more competitive behaviour feasible or credible actually promotes collusion'.[78] The non-exhaustive list of market characteristics enhancing and/or stabilizing (tacit) collusion encompasses, as follows: (1) number of competitors, (2) market concentration, (3) homogeneity of suppliers, (4) countervailing competitive power,(5) market entry arriers, (6) countervailing buyer's power, (7) prduct homogeneity, (8) multi-market contacts, (9) demand variation, (10) transaction characteristics, (11) transparency.[79]

Posner provides, however, a more sophisticated economic approach to detect and to substantiate collusion in a relevant market, which are is: First, involvement of identifying markets in which conditions are propitious for the emergence of collusion. Second, involvement of determining whether there really is collusive pricing in any of those markets. This economic approach is to be employed to achieve the following main goals: On the one hand, to facilitate law enforcers to concentrate their resources in markets where those resources are likely to be employed most productively. On the other hand, to enable ambiguous conduct to

75 ibid.

76 Joined cases 40 to 48, 50, 54 to 56, 111, 113 and 114-73, *Coöperatieve Vereniging "Suiker Unie" UA and others v Commission of the European Communities*. European Court Reports 1975 -01663.

77 Nörbert Boing, ‹http://www.zum.de/Faecher/kurse/boeing/udb/› accessed 9th February 2015.

78 Stroux, *US and EC Oligopoly Control*, (n 51) 27–30.

79 ibid.

be evaluated.[80] Moreover, according to Posner, the following factors could facilitate collusive practices in an oligopolistic market, which are: (1) market concentrated on the selling side, (2) no fringe of small sellers, (3) inelastic demand at competitive price, (4) entry takes a long time, (5) buying side of market unconcentrated, (6) standard product, (7) non-durable product, (8) the principal firms sell at the same level, (9) price competition more important than other forms of competition, (10) high ratio of fixed to variable costs, (11) similar cost structures and production processes, (12) demand static or declining over time, (13) prices can be changed quickly, (14) sealed bidding, (15) market is local, (16) cooperative practices, (17) the industry's antitrust "record".[81]

2.2 Cartel Prohibitions pursuant to the European Union (EU) Competition Law

2.2.1 Background and Objective

The European (EU) Competition Law refers to a set of rules, serving both of the envisaged economic and integration purposes, which systematically are enshrined in the legal instruments: First, treaty laws; whereby these rules are embodied in Title VII, Chapter I of the Treaty on Functioning of European Union ("TFEU"). Second, secondary laws; whereas these rules can be found in Council Regulations and Commission Regulations. Third, case laws (jurisprudences or precedents), whose substances consist of: 1) decisional practice of the Commission; 2) case-laws (jurisprudence) of the European Courts; 3) national case-laws.[82]

80 *Posner* further gives an example: in a market in which conditions are favourable to collusion an exchange of price information may be persuasive evidence of collusive pricing, while in a market in which conditions are unfavourable the same exchange may be no evidence of collusive behaviour at all, may be, in fact, a procompetitive feature of the market. cf. R. Posner, *Antitrust Law,* (2nd Ed., University of Chicago Press, 2001.), 20–27.

81 ibid.

82 Geradin, Farrar, Petit, EU Competition, (n 33) 25–27.

Principally, with respect to the objectives of the EU Competition laws, the Commission stipulates that:

> "The objective of Article 101 TFEU is to protect competition on the market as a means of enhancing consumer welfare and of ensuring an efficient allocation of resources. Competition and market integration serve these ends since the creation and preservation of an open single market promotes an efficient allocation of resources throughout the Community for the benefit of consumers."

Equally important, according to *Säcker,* the legal policy of the competition law shall prudently take into consideration three main arguments: Firstly, the competition law to establish socio-economic freedoms and fair competitions in the society. Secondly, the employment of efficiency enhancements as justification grounds. Thirdly, the economic limit for applying competition instruments for the prosperity policy.[83] With regard to the notion of socio-economic freedoms and fair competition, the provisions of Article 119 TFEU in conjunctions with the Protocol Number 27 of TEU concerning internal market and competition stipulate the envisaged goal of economic freedom and a system of free competition.[84] These provisions state that for the purposes set out in Article 3 TFEU, the activities of the Member States and of the EU shall include the adoption of an economic policy based on the internal market and conducted in accordance with the principle of an open market economy with free competition. Furthermore, the principle of open markets with free competition acknowledge the fundamental role of the market and of competition in guaranteeing consumer welfare, encouraging the optimal allocation of resources and granting to economic agents the appropriate incentives to pursue productive efficiencies, qualities and innovations.[85] This fundamental principle has thus been concretised in the provisions of Articles 101 until109 of TFEU which

83 Säcker, ‚Die rechtspolitischen Grundlagen des Wettbewerbsrechts' in F.J. Säcker, et.al. (eds.) (n 13) 8-21

84 Häde, ‚*AEUV Art. 119 [Wirtschafts- und Währungsunion]*' in C. Calliess and M. Ruffert, EUV/AEUV: *Der Verfassungsrecht der EU mit Europäischer Grundrechtcharta* (5. Aufl., CH Beck, 2016)

85 A. D. Chirita, *The German and Romanian Abuse of Market Dominance in the Light of Article 102 TFEU*, (Nomos Verlag, 2001), 33–34. cf. M. Monti, 'European Competition Policy fort eh 21st Century', in B. E. Hawk (ed.), *International Antitrust Law & Policy* (Fordham Competition Law 2000), 257.

prescribe the rules on competition.[86] Principally, these provisions aim further to achieve the market integration for the purpose of competition, whereas the competitions are not distorted and economic freedom-based competitions exist in the EU. Indeed, these envisaged purposes shall have priority over the other policy objectives, for example the scientific and technological goals in Article 3 (3) TFEU.[87]

2.2.2 Statutory Element of the Cartel Prohibition of Article 101 TFEU

In principle, the statutory elements of cartels prohibition are enshrined in Article 101 (1) TFEU, which stipulates:

> ***Article 101 (1) (formerly Art. 81(1) EC; ex Art. 85)***
> 1. *The following shall be prohibited as incompatible with the internal market: all agreements between undertakings, decisions by associations of undertakings and concerted practices which may affect trade between Member States and which have as their object or effect the prevention, restriction or distortion of competition within the internal market, and in particular those which:*
> (a) *directly or indirectly fix purchase or selling prices or any other trading conditions;*
> (b) *limit or control production, markets, technical development, or investment;*
> (c) *share markets or sources of supply;*
> (d) *apply dissimilar conditions to equivalent transactions with other trading parties, thereby placing them at a competitive disadvantage;*
> (e) *make the conclusion of contracts subject to acceptance by the other parties of supplementary obligations which, by their nature or according to commercial usage, have no connection with the subject of such contracts.*

By virtue of the Article 101 TFEU, according to *Wollmann and Herzog*, agreements, decisions of association of undertakings or concerted practices whose aims are to restrict or to distort the competitions in market are known as "cartels". Accordingly, such collusive practices have been widely subject to *Per-se Illegal* rule.[88] The example catalogues of Article 101 (1) alphabets (a) until (e) elaborate cartels in practice and

86 Säcker, et.al, *Europäisches Wettbewerbsrecht*, (n 13) 8–10.
87 Chirita, (n 85) 31–3.
88 Wollmann and Herzog (n 13) 742–745.

thus imply that the enumerated cartels hardly fulfill the legal exemptions of Article 101 (3) TFEU.

In addition, practices of cartels could manifest in four typologies of horizontal agreements: (1) an agreement on prices and trade conditions[89] (2) an agreement on limitation of production and/or sales,[90] (3)

89 The provision of Article 101 (1) TFEU strictly prohibits direct or indirect agreements to fix prices and other trade requirements. Put differently, this provision prohibits every obstruction to the freedom of undertakings pertaining the prices and other trade requirements. These cartels practices include: (1) fixation of prices, price objective, price increase, target price, minimum sale prices, recommended price, price structuring principles; (2) setting the purchase price paid by processors to suppliers; (3) dividing customers in several categories and applying jointly differentiated prices; (4) deciding not to offer discounts, reaching agreements on maximum discounts or reducing the discounts to consumers; (5) adopting mathematical methods for calculating and establishing minimum common sales prices; (6) engaging in dumping prices, selling below published prices; (7) establishing compensation system for balancing revenues resulting from domestic sales and export sales. However, according to Geradine *et.al,* in this type of cartels, there are additional agreements, which have the function to ensure that the pursued agreement operates as planned. For example, setting up a timetable for pricing announcements, to ensure effective function of the main pursued agreement. Besides, an agreement on regular price reporting obligation is considered as additional agreement. According to the Article 101 TFEU these agreements are illegal. Equally important, this type of cartels practice encompasses an agreement relating to the terms and conditions under which product/ services are supplied. Thus, this agreement eliminates competitions on qualities of the competitors' products. In the Trans-Atlantic Conference Agreement (TACA) case, the Commission considered the joint service contract between marine shipping and cargo companies has restrictive effects to competition on price and trading terms. See Geradin, Farrar, Petit, *EU Competition* (n 33) 400.

90 According to Wollmann and Herzog, this cartels practice refers to restriction or controlling over production, sales, technological innovations or investments. Thus, the artificial shortages of products' supplies on a market have similar detrimental effects to competition just like the direct price fixing. Further, the limitation of production and/or sales can be committed through: First, to limit output directly, at the production level, by means of quotas to each cartel member. Second, to limit output indirectly, at the distribution level, by reducing product supplies to customers. The Courts of Justice of the EU have dealt with such cartel's practices in the Quinine Cartel case, involving price raising through the output restriction. In the Zinc Phosphate case, the cartelists made initial market share and they were obliged to obey this market share and thus sales quotas were set-up in the European level. Further, a monitoring system was also made between the cartels members to detect deviation form cartels agreement and impose punishment. Moreover, *Wolman and Herzog* stated that 'restrictions of production' encompasses every limitation of service portfolios (range).

an arrangement to allocate market or supply sources,[91] (4) discriminations,[92] (5) coupling (Koppelung).[93]

Equally important, *Tobler* describes three main normative elements of the cartel prohibition of Article 101 (1) TFEU, encompassing: First, 'agreements between undertakings, decisions by association of under-

---

Also, this includes information exchange agreement on prices and quantity delivered. Moreover, as to limitation or control of markets, in the BP Kemi case, the Commission was of the opinion that 'when a major buyer undertakes, for certain period, to purchase all required quantities of a product from the single manufacturer, this will prevent other manufacturers of same product from supplying the large buyer. These cartels have an anticompetitive effect, namely a single branding, to foreclose wholly supplies between large firms. Wollmann and Herzog (n 13) 744–750.

91 This type of cartels, according to Wollmann and Herzog, comprises limitation or controlling over a geographical market, producers, economic (commercial) branches or customer groups. Thereby, these collusive practices cause relevant market partitioning amongst the competitors. Thus, these practices bring anticompetitive effects similar to an artificial monopolization. According to Geradine, et.al, this type of cartels frequently manifest in the form of a reciprocal grant of territorial exclusivities. In the Peroxygen case, the Commission imposed severe fines to European peroxygen manufacturers due to market sharing agreement under 'domestic market'rule, whereby they agreed not to sell products on each other's domestic market. Besides, these collusive practices can emerge in the non-geographic market sharing and bid-rigging (collusive tendering). However, under the ancillary agreement concept, this practice could be to some extent allowed, subject to the Commission Notice on Ancillary restraint.

92 According to Wollmann and Herzog, this type of cartels refers to the agreement, whereby the parties impose differing trading conditions (requirements) against other undertakings, yet for the equivalent (homogeneous) product. This type of cartels causes discriminative impact to other undertakings in the market. Primarily, the main goal of this collusive agreement is to restrict or hinder competitions either on the up- or downstream markets. ibid.
Equally important, according to Geradine, this cartels practice include collective boycott strategies, which aim to punish or eliminate a customer, supplier or competitor deemed as undesirable as well as to force unilaterally an undertaking for doing certain desired market conducts. In the case of Belgian Wallpaper, the Commission penalized the Belgian association of wallpaper companies because its members unilaterally stopped supplies to an independent wholesaler rejecting to the uniform pricing policy set up by the association. Geradine, Farrar, Petit (n 33) 406.

93 According to Wollmann and Herzog, collective coupling agreements take place whenever one party to the contract requires the other parties to accept additional commercial enforcements, which have none of correlations both to the contract and to commercial customs. Accordingly, the producing undertakings have to bear burdens because of blockades of sales chain. Besides, the undertakings having market power are able to level-up prices above the competitive price and thus to expel other competitors from relevant markets. Wollmann and Herzog (n 13) 747.

takings and concerted practices' (three categories of conduct between undertakings). Second, 'which may affect trade between Member States (inter-state or internal market element). Third, 'which have as their object or effect the prevention, restriction or distortion of competition' (competition element).[94]

Equally important, Säcker and Wolf systematically conclude that the following testing scheme will guide the analysis of the Article 101 (1) TFEU, encompassing: First, the concept of undertakings, second, agreements third, coordination between remaining independent undertakings, fourth, appreciable restrictions of competition and fifth, inter-states clause.[95]

2.2.2.1 The Undertaking and Association of Undertakings

Whilst the EU Treaties do not provide an exact meaning of undertakings in terms of competition law, the Court of Justice in *Höfner* stipulated as follows: "[i]n the context of competition law [...] the concept of an undertaking, encompasses every entity engaged in an economic activity, regardless of the legal status of the entity or the way in which it is financed." Nevertheless, the term 'economic activity' remained unclear, until the European competition case-laws settled the meaning of economic activity under Article 101 (1) TFEU,[96] which are as follows: First, an activity which offers goods and/or services on a market.[97] Second, an activity having potential to generate profits. Third, an activity which bears financial risk. Hence, the concept of undertaking in Article 101 TFEU is a functional one, that is to say 'it focuses on the nature of activity being carried out by the entity concerned rather than its institutional status.[98] In other words, the term 'undertakings' would be interpreted broadly.[99] Subsequently, the Court of Justice in *Wouters*

94 C. Tobler, J. Beglinger, W. Geursen, *Essential EU Competition Law in Charts – a field manual* (HVG-ORAC 2011) 23–25.
95 F. J. Säcker and M. Wolf, *Kartellrecht in Fällen* (Valen Jura, 2010) 295–297.
96 K. Arvidsson, 'Re-Use of PSI and the Undertaking Concept in the EU Competition Law' (LL. M Thesis Law Faculty Stockholm University, 2014) 21–24.
97 Jones and Surfin, (n 46) 141–169.
98 Whish and Bailey, *Competition Law,* (n 56) 86.
99 Hengst in Langen and Bunte, *Kartellrecht Kommentar: Europäisches Kartellrecht (12. Aufl. Luchterhand Verlag, 2014),* 49–50.

case ruled out, that entity which performs tasks for the public interests is not subject to Article 101 (1) TFEU.[100]

Further, with regard to undertakings, the concept of single economic entity is of main importance. According to this concept, whenever there are two or more undertakings in the market having distinct legal personalities, notably the parent and subsidiary, yet they enjoy no economic independence, belong to the same concern, and form an economic unit within which the subsidiary has no real freedom to determine its course of action on the market, thus they are considered as a single economic entity. Consequently, the agreements between the parent and the subsidiary constitute a truly unilateral behavior of undertaking and thus escape the ambit of cartel prohibition of Article 101(1) TFEU, unless those undertakings hold a dominant position and abuse the position in the market. This stance had been confirmed by the General Court (GC) in the Viho case, stipulating as follows:

> *"Where, as in this case, although having separate legal personality, does not freely determine its conduct on the market but carries out the instructions given to it directly or indirectly by the parent company by which it is wholly uncontrolled, Article [101 (1) TFEU] does not apply to the relationship between the subsidiary and the parent company with which it forms an economic unit."*[101]

Furthermore, under the EU Competition law the existence of a single economic unit is presumed provided that the parent company owns 100 per cent of the shares or its subsidiary.[102]

Moreover, in the analysis of Article 101 TFEU the term 'association of undertakings' is an important element, whereby this term is conceived as an organisational entity whose members are undertakings, as stipulated in Article 101 (1) TFEU, and thus represents the economic interests of its member.[103] Whether the 'association of undertakings' strive to reach their own business profits or not, is not relevant in this respect.[104] In *Wouters v.Alegmenen Raad van de Nederlandse Order van Advocaaten*, the ECJ reiterated that an 'association of

100 Whish and Bailey, (n 56) 84.
101 Geradin, Farrar, Petit, EU Competition Law, (n 33) 27–29.
102 *Jones and Sufrin*, EU Competition Law, (n 46) 142–144.
103 de Bonett in Schulte and Just, *Kartellrecht*: GWB, Kartellvergaberecht, EU-Kartellrecht (1.Aufl. Carl Heymanns Verlag, 2012), 408–410.
104 ibid.

undertakings encompasses of undertakings of the same general type and makes itself responsible for representing and defending their common interests *vis-à-vis* other economic operators, government bodies and the public in general'.[105]

With regard to the 'association of undertakings' the EU Competition law adopts functional approach which 'seeks to prevent undertakings from being able to evade the rules on competition on account simply of the form in which they coordinate their conduct on the market. To ensure that this principle is effective, Article 101 (1) TFEU covers not only direct methods of coordination conduct between undertakings (agreements and concerted practices) but also institutionalised forms of cooperation, that is to say, situations in which economic operators act through a collective structure or a common body.[106] Furthermore, the ECJ asserted that, whether a decision of 'association of undertakings' has been endorsed by public authority or generated by association whose members are appointed by the government, namely having a statutory function, does not preclude the application of prohibition rules of Article 101(1) TFEU. Hence, in *Wouters v.Alegmenen Raad van de Nederlandse Order van Advocaaten* the ECJ affirmed that the Netherland Bar Association, which is governed by public law, in adopting a professional regulation as to prohibition of certain multi-disciplinary partnerships for its members, had indeed practiced economic activity, instead of practicing the powers of public authority.[107] In sum, it can be outlined that, irrespective its legal forms, 'association of undertakings' comprises: First, a trade association, serving as forum for exchanging commercial and strategic information for the mutual cooperation and benefits of the involved undertakings. Second, agricultural cooperatives, that is established by farmers. Third, a body set up by statute for public function provided it serves the trading interests of its members. Fourth, a professional association, albeit it is regulated by a public law statue.[108]

---

105 *Jones and Surfin, (n 46)* 341

106 ibid.

107 Whish and Bailey, Competition Law, (n 56) 92. cf. *Jones and Surfin*, (n 46) 146–147.

108 ibid.

2.2.2.2 The Existence of Agreements ("Concurrence of Wills")

According to Herrmann and Paschke, in the analytical framework of cartels prohibition pursuant to Article 101 (1) TFEU, the concept of "agreements" comprises contracts, decisions of associations of undertakings and concerted practices.[109] Moreover, according to Jones and Surfin, in EU competition law, the ECJ has provided a liberal interpretation as to the term 'agreement', whereas 'agreement' principally refers to the existence of a concurrence of wills between minimally two undertakings'.[110] In practice, however, the concurrence of wills emerges in three different forms, which are: agreements, decision by the association of undertakings, and concerted practice.[111] In the case of *T-Mobile Netherlands and others*, the ECJ reiterated that these three forms of collusion are distinguishable from each other merely by their intensity and the forms in which they manifest themselves.[112] Further, with regard to these three forms of collusion, the ECJ in the case of *Commission v Anic Partecipazoni* explicitly stated the aim is to have the prohibitions of that article catch different forms of coordination and collusion between undertakings. Accordingly, a precise characterisation of the nature of the cooperation at issue in the main proceedings is not liable to alter the legal analysis to be carried out under Article [101 TFEU].[113]

2.2.2.2.1 'Agreements'

In the EU Competition Law, the term 'agreement' refers primarily to parallel conduct, by which two or more undertakings/associations of undertakings take part to voice collective intentions, so that minimally one undertaking/association of undertaking conduct in specific man-

109 Hermann and Paschke in F. J. Säcker *et.al*, (n 13) 692.

110 *Jones and Sufrin*, (n 46) 142–143. See also Joined Cases C-2/01 P and C-3/01 P BAI and Commission v Bayer Adalat 2004 I-00023, paras. 18, 97–98.

111 de Bonett (n 103) 772.

112 *Jones and Sufrin*, (n 46), 4. See also Case C-8/08 T-*Mobile Netherlands BV, KPN Mobile NV, Orange Nederland NV and Vodafone Libertel NV v Raad van bestuur van de Nederlandse Mededingingsautoriteit*. 2009 I-04529, paras. 23-ff.

113 Jones and Surfin (n 46) 141. See alo Case C-49/92 P. Commission of the European Communities v Anic Partecipazioni SpA. 1999 I-04125.

ner on the market.[114] In the case of *Bayer AG v. Commission*, the GC argued that, the term 'agreement' in the context of Article 101 (1) TFEU 'centres around the existence of concurrence of wills between at least two parties, the form in which it is manifested being unimportant as long as it constitutes the faithful expression of the parties' intention.'Further, the GC asserted that proof of agreement pursuant to Article 101(1) TFEU must be established upon 'the existence of the subjective element that characterises the very concept of the agreement, that is to *say, a concurrence of wills* between economic operators on the implementation of a policy, the pursuit of an objective, or the adoption of a given line of conduct on the market'.[115] Further, in the case of *Montedipe SpA v. Commission,* the CFI stipulated that for the existence of agreement under Article 101(1) TFEU it is sufficient that the undertakings in question should have expressed their joint intention to conduct themselves on the market in a specific way. For example, whenever there are common intentions between the undertakings to achieve price and sales volume targets.[116] Conversely, in the event one party to agreement conducts self-imposed restriction on the market, whereas this self-imposed restrictions arenot part of common intentions prescribed in the agreement between undertakings, thus there is no agreement in the sense of Article 101 (1) TFEU.[117]

In the case of *Volkswagen and AC-Treuhand*, it has been established, that in application of Article 101(1) TFEU toward the prohibited 'agreement', proving the existence of *concurrence of wills* becomes the primary prerequisite, irrespective the forms and legal qualifications of agreements.[118] Consequently, in substantiating the existence of the 'agreement' mentioned above, the Commission must base upon the direct or indirect finding of a concurrence of wills between undertakings

114 de Bonett (n 103) 776.

115 *Jones and Sufrin*, (n 46) 142–143. See also Joined Cases C-2/01 P and C-3/01 P BAI and Commission v Bayer Adalat 2004 I-00023, paras. 18, 97–98.

116 de Bonett (n 103) 777.

117 ibid. 776. See also T-419/03 – Altstoff Recycling Austria AG v European Commission. 2011 II-00975.

118 Lober in Schulte and Just (n 103) *Kartellrecht*,776–777. See also Case C-74/04 P Commission of the European Communities v Volkswagen AG [2003] ECR II-5141. cf. Case T-99/04 AC-Treuhand AG v Commission of the European Communities 2008 II-01501.

or associations of undertakings, which constitute the faithful expression of the parties' intention.[119]

Furthermore, based upon the jurisprudence of EU Competition law pertaining the term 'agreement', Article 101 (1) TFEU encompasses not only written and oral agreements, but also implicit consensus, whose substantiation, however, poses profound difficulties.[120] In other words, the term 'agreement' under Article 101 (1) TFEU reaches a wide scope of 'concurrences of wills', irrespective of their status under respective national laws, their intentions to be legally binding or not, their contents which stipulate sanctions or not. In elaborative way, the term 'agreement' of Article 101(1) TFEU captures among others, but is not limited to: First, 'gentlemen's agreements',[121] second, standard conditions of sale,[122] third, trade association rules,[123] fourth, agreements entered into to settle disputes,[124] fifth, 'good neighbouring rules' or 'certain rules of game which it is in the interests of all of us to follow',[125] sixth, a terminated agreement whose effects remain existing after the termination period[126] and seventh, agreements which are endorsed of consented by national law or which take into effect after consultation with the national authorities.[127] In other words, these latter 'agreements' receive no immunity from prohibition of Article 101(1) TFEU.[128] Subsequently, in the case of Industrial and Medical Gases, the Commission avowed that, whether the undertakings or associations of undertakings defended that they never intended to implement or to adhere to the agreement's terms, did not regrettably, any justification value under prohibition rules of Article 101(1) TFEU.[129]

---

119 *Jones and Surfin, EU Competition Law*, p. 142. See Case C-338/00 P, Volkswagen AG v. Commission [2003] ECR I-9189.
120 de Bonett, in Schulte and Just, *Kartellrecht*, 77.
121 Hengst in Langen and Bunte, *Kartellrecht Kommentar*, 77.
122 ibid.
123 Jones and Surfin, (n 46) 142–145.
124 ibid.
125 Hengst in Langen and Bunte, (n 99) 77.
126 ibid.
127 *Jones and Surfin (n 46) 142–145.*
128 de Bonett, in Schulte and Just, (n 103) 77.
129 *Jones and Surfin, (n 46)* 143.

Subsequently, in respect of 'agreements' prescribed by Article 101(1) TFEU, the ECJ falsified the existing tenet that Article 101(1) TFEU is inapplicable to agreements between undertakings operating at different levels of economy or in separate markets. In the case of *Consten and Grundig v. Commission*, however, the ECJ has indeed reiterated, that the provision of Article 101(1) frames that a distinction between horizontal and vertical agreements should be drawn.[130] With regard to collective bargaining agreements, ensuing the decision of the ECJ in the case of *Albany International BV v. Stichting Bedrijfspensioenfonds Textielindustrie*, it has been held that Article 101(1) TFEU does not catch collective agreements between workers and employers, whose objective is to improve conditions of work and employment. The ECJ reckons that one of the main purposes of the EU Treaty is to achieve a high level of employment and social protection. In a more elaborative assessment, in the case of *Polypropylene*, the ECJ has emphasised that cartels' practice, which consists of a whole complex of arrangements and which are based upon common and detail plan, constitutes a single continuing agreement and thus subject to prohibition of Article 101(1) TFEU.[131] Accordingly, *in the case of PVC II*, it is reiterated that, whenever undertakings had been party to collusive schemes, arrangements and measures within a regular meeting's framework and the involved undertakings reach sufficient consensus to limit or likely to limit their commercial independency on the market, thus these collusive schemes, arrangements and measures constitute agreement under Article 101(1) TFEU.[132] Hence, the existence of a legally binding agreement does not required to be proved.

130 ibid. 150.

131 ibid. 147.

132 Joined cases C-238/99 P, C-244/99 P, C-245/99 P, C-247/99 P, C-250/99 P to C-252/99 P and C-254/99 P.
Limburgse Vinyl Maatschappij NV (LVM) (C-238/99 P), DSM NV and DSM Kunststoffen BV (C-244/99 P), Montedison SpA (C-245/99 P), Elf Atochem SA (C-247/99 P), Degussa AG (C-250/99 P), Enichem SpA (C-251/99 P), Wacker-Chemie GmbH and Hoechst AG (C-252/99 P) and Imperial Chemical Industries plc (ICI) (C-254/99 P) v Commission of the European Communities. 2002 I-08375.

2.2.2.2.2 Decisions by Association of Undertakings

In business practice, the existence of concurrence of wills between undertakings might manifest in decision by association of undertakings as well. In other words, the association of undertakings serves as a medium for undertakings under its auspices, so that they are able to commit cartels practice and coordinate their corporate actions on certain market. In particular, when there is a large number of undertakings engaging in similar business on the market, thus association of undertakings becomes very crucial to establish collusive practices. Article 101 (1) TFEU therefore catches decisions by associations of undertakings in order to prevent the use of association as a vehicle to coordinate and promote collusive practices. In the precedent of the ECJ, decision of undertaking falls under Article 101 (1) TFEU, provided Articles of Association required its members to regard association's decisions as binding ones. Indeed, even recommendations of association can be subject to prohibition of Article 101(1) TFEU, whenever these recommendations contain specific concurrence of wills of the undertakings to behave specifically on the market. The precedents of EU competition law has broadly interpreted the term'decisions of associations of undertakings', so that it captures every conduct to conclude a collusive arrangement between undertakings members of the association, which achieved through resolutions of association, recommendations, the operation of certification schemes, or through the association's article of incorporations. Furthermore, in the case of *Certificatie Krannverhuurbedrijf and the Federatie van Nederlandse Krannverhuurbedrijven v. Commission*, the ECJ reasserted that the term 'decision' of Article 101 (1) TFEU catches certification schemes issued by association, whose objective is to block non-member undertakings to penetrate the domestic market of the association's members. In other words, Article 101 (1) TFEU prohibits more informal methods of coordinating members' business actions.

Equally important, decisions by the association of undertakings, in the development of EU Competition Law, the Court of Justice and the Commission have applied a so-called non formalist approach towards the decisions taken by the association of undertakings. This means the term agreement of Article 101 (1) TFEU comprises not only all agreements within the framework of collective or representative bodies like trade association, but also a circular, a recommendation, or even an email can constitute the decision by the association of undertakings. For instance, in the case of *Wouters* the Court of Justice ruled out that the recommendation of National Bar Association in Netherlands constitutes the decision by the association of undertakings.[133]

2.2.2.2.3 'Concerted Practices'

In the *Dyestuffs* case, the Court of Justice of the EU explains the meaning of concerted practices as 'a form of coordination between undertakings' which, without having reached the stage where an agreement properly so-called has been concluded, knowingly substitutes practical cooperation for the risks of competition.[134] Subsequently, in the *Suiker Unie* case, the Court of Justice of the EU elaborated that, in terms of coordination or cooperation, 'the working out of an actual plan' is not required.[135] In the case of *T-Mobile Netherlands v. Raad van bestuur van de Nederlandse Mededingingsautoriteit*, the Court of Justice of EU explained:

> "Article 101 (1) TFEU strictly precluded any direct or indirect contact between such operators, the object or effect whereof is either to influence the conduct on the market of an actual or potential competitor or to disclose to such a competitor the course of conduct which they themselves have decided to adopt or contemplate adopting on the market.[136]

Accordingly, it can be inferred that the followings are elements of the concerted practices thereof: Firstly, the existence of mental consensus between the undertakings to replace competition with practical cooperation on a market. Secondly, the consensus can be both verbal and non-verbal. Thirdly, the consensus originated either from direct or in-

133 Hengst, in Langen and Bunte, (n 99) 34–39. See also Geradin, Farrar and Petit, (n 33) 32–35.

134 Case 48–69 Imperial Chemical Industries Ltd. v Commission of the European Communities, ECLI:EU:C:1972:70, paras. 121-et.seq.

135 Joined cases 40 to 48, 50, 54 to 56, 111, 113 and 114–73, *Coöperatieve Vereniging "Suiker Unie" UA and others v Commission of the European Communities*, European Court Reports 1975 -01663, paras. 173–174.

136 Case C-8/08 T-Mobile Netherlands v. Raad van bestuur van de Nederlandse Mededingingsautoriteit [2009] ECR I-4529, [2009] 5 CMLR 1701, para 26.

direct undertaking's communications.[137] Further, an undertaking's unilateral measure is not subject to the concerted practices prohibition.[138] In addition, the Court of Justice of the EU in the *Polypropylene* case, exposed that the concerted practices encompass every form of market behaviour coordination, which leads to intended or envisaged collaboration of the undertakings for the purpose of eliminating risks of competition on a market.[139]

From the praxis of European Competition law, the prohibition of concerted practices serves two function consecutively. Firstly, the concerted practices can be proved by means of a series of 'indirect (circumstantial) evidences' before the Court. Subsequently, the concerted practice is merely seen as a part of the complex and continuous anti-competitive practices on a market, which consist of agreements, decisions of undertakings' association and the concerted practices itself.[140]

Furthermore, *Emmerich* asserts, that the concerted practices prohibition serves two consecutive functions. Initially, this prohibition enlarges the application of Article 101 para. 1 TFEU to the whole kind of market coordination of undertakings, having not fulfilling elements of agreements and/or decisions of undertakings' association. Subsequently, this prohibition would serve as the catchall element, whereby whatsoever form of market conduct coordination between undertakings could be proved.[141]

With respect to the joint classification of agreements and 'concerted practices' the Court of Justice of EU in the *PVC* case, confirming the Commission's stance, that

> "In the context of a complex infringement which involves many producers seeking over a number of years to regulate the market between them the Commission cannot be expected to classify the infringement precisely, for each undertaking and for any given moment, as in any event both those forms of infringement are covered by Article [101] of the Treaty."

137 Whish and Bailey, (n 56) 115.

138 According to Lettl, this undertaking unilateral measures would be subject to Article 102 TFEU. T. Lettl, Kartellrecht (3. Aufl.CH. Beck, 2016), 36–37.

139 Case T-8/89 DSM NV v the Commission (Polypropylene) [1991] ECR II-1833, para. 158.

140 Emmerich in Immenga and Mestmäcker, *Wettbewerbsrecht,* (n 44) 188.

141 ibid. 189.

Hence, the notion of agreements, decisions of undertakings association and the concerted practices could be viewed as the continuum of infringements against Article 101 (1) TFEU.[142] The distinctive factor of respective violations abovementioned is the evidentiary aspect.[143]

2.2.2.2.3.1 'Conscious Concertation'

The term 'concertation' includes every concerted action whatsoever, both of written or oral concertation as well as both of expressly and implied concertation. In the case of *Imperial Chemical Industries Ltd. v Commission of the European Communities* ("ICI case"), the ECJ in its Judgement asserted the concept of 'concerted practices':

> "Article 85 draws distinction between the concept of "concerted practices" and that of "agreements between undertakings" or of "decisions by association of undertakings"; the object is to bring within the prohibition of that article a form of coordination between undertakings wich, without having reached the stage where an agreement properly so-called has been concluded, knowingly substitutes practical cooperation between them for the risk of competition".[144]

In conjunction with 'concertation', the Court of Justice of the EU in the *Suiker Unie* case explicitly mandated the undertaking's independence postulate *(Selbständigkeitspostulat)*, which further reiterated by the ECJ decided in *the T-Mobile Netherlands* case:

> "While it is correct to say that this requirement of independence does not deprive economic operators of the right to adapt themselves intelligently to the existing or anticipated conduct of their competitors, it does, *none the less, strictly preclude any direct or indirect contact between such operators by which an undertaking may influence the conduct on the market of its actual or potential competitors or disclose to them its decisions or intentions concerning its own conduct on the market where the object or effect of such contact is to create conditions of competition which do not correspond to the normal conditions of the market in question, regard being had to the nature of the products or services offered, the size and number of the undertakings involved and the volume of that market* (see, to that effect, *SuikerUnie and Others* v *Commission*, paragraph 174; *Züchner*, paragraph 14; and *Deere* v *Commission*, paragraph 87)."[145]

142 ibid.
143 ibid.
144 Emmerich in Immenga and Mestmäcker, Wettbewerbsrecht, (n 44) 188.
145 Suiker Unie, (n 135) para. 173. Para. 33 of the Judgement. cf. Letl (n 138) 37–39.

Subsequently, the Court's arguments abovementioned has been confirmed again in the Dole Food case, whereby the concerted practices prohibition does not deprive an undertaking's right to adapt itself intelligently to the market conducts of competing undertakings.[146]

Whereas an undertaking had participated in a meeting or a series of meetings, whose intentions was to create cartels on a market, thus this undertaking is to be deemed as the cartels' participant. Nonetheless, this proposition is refutable, whenever an undertaking can prove that it had explicitly asserted an opposition before other participants against the envisaged cartels, as the Court of Justice vividly accentuated in the Aarlborg Portland Cement case:

> "any regular participant at a meeting at which an anticompetitive agreement is concluded will be taken to have participated in that agreement, unless it can establish that the undertaking did not have any competitive intention when it attended the meeting, and that the other participants were aware of this. It appears, therefore, that the participants tacitly accept an offer to collude by not publicly distancing themselves further from the agreement. It is no defence that the participant did not put the initiatives into effect and evidence of prices or other behavior not reflecting those discussed at the meeting would not be sufficient to prove that it had not participated in the scheme."[147]

Furthermore, the Court of Justice of EU underlines the threshold of an undertaking's participation in the cartel purposive meetings, as follows:

> "According to settled case-law, it is sufficient for the Commission to show that the undertaking concerned participated in meetings at which anti-competitive agreements were concluded, without manifestly opposing them, to prove to the requisite standard that the undertaking participated in the cartel. Where participation in such meetings has been established, it is for that undertaking to put forward evidence to establish that its participation in those meetings was without any anti-competitive intention by demonstrating that it had indicated to its competitors that it was participating in those meetings in a spirit that was different from theirs (see

146 Case C-286/13 P *Dole Food Company, Inc. and Dole Fresh Fruit Europe v European Commission*. para.120.

147 Joined cases C-204/00 P, C-205/00 P, C-211/00 P, C-213/00 P, C-217/00 P and C-219/00 P. *Aalborg Portland A/S (C-204/00 P), Irish Cement Ltd (C-205/00 P), Ciments français SA (C-211/00 P), Italcementi – Fabbriche Riunite Cemento SpA (C-213/00 P), Buzzi Unicem SpA (C-217/00 P) and Cementir – Cementerie del Tirreno SpA (C-219/00 P) v Commission of the European Communities*.2004 I-00123. paras. 79–80.

Case C-199/92 P Hüls v Commission [1999] ECR I-4287, paragraph 155, and Case C-49/92 P Commission v Anic [1999] ECR I-4125, paragraph 96).

The reason underlying that principle of law is that, having participated in the meeting without publicly distancing itself from what was discussed, the undertaking has given the other participants to believe that it subscribed to what was decided there and would comply with it.

The principles established in the case-law cited at paragraph 81 of this judgment also apply to participation in the implementation of a single agreement. In order to establish that an undertaking has participated in such an agreement, the Commission must show that the undertaking intended to contribute by its own conduct to the common objectives pursued by all the participants and that it was aware of the actual conduct planned or put into effect by other undertakings in pursuit of the same objectives or that it could reasonably have foreseen it and that it was prepared to take the risk (Commission v Anic, paragraph 87)."[148]

In similar arguments, *Ghezzi and Maggiolino* argue:

> "what neutralizes the evil of solicitation to collude is that rivals take (genuine) public distance from, or manifest their opposition to, the gained information. Since cartels' likehood is seriously undermined when competitors do not give their rivals reasons to believe that they are intended to subscribe the invitation and comply with it, only rivals's clear statement that they do not wish to receive strategic date, or that they do not want to particpate in the cartel, or in meetings of a professional asscoiation which served as a veil for unlawful concerted actions, are the quite essential tools to exclude concertation."[149]

2.2.2.2.3.2 'Subsequent Market Conduct'

Not only the concertation and the causality, concerted practices prerequisites also the subsequent implementing market behaviour or conducts. As it had been asserted in the case *Hüls AG v Commission*, the ECJ argued that:

---

148 ibid. paras.81 – 85. See also Van Bael and Bellis, *Competition Law of the European Communitie (5th Ed. Kluwer Law International, 2009), 40.*

149 Van Bael and Bellis, *Competition Law of the European Community*, 5th Edition (Wolters Kluwer, Hague,2010), p. 25–33.

> "It follows, first, that the concept of a concerted practice, as it results from the actual terms of Article 81(1) EC, implies, besides undertakings' concerting with each other, subsequent conduct on the market, and a relationship of cause and effect between the two."[150]

2.2.2.2.3.3 'Causality'

In the case *Hüls AG v. Commission*, the Court of Justice confirmed that:

> "However, subject to proof to the contrary, which the economic operators concerned must adduce, the presumption must be that the undertakings taking part in the concerted action and remaining active on the market take account of the information exchanged with their competitors for the purposes of determining their conduct on that market. That is all the more true where the undertakings concert together on a regular basis over a long period, as was the case here, according to the findings of the Court of First Instance."[151]

In the case of T-Mobile Netherlands, the Court of Justice reiterated:

> "In the light of the foregoing considerations, the answer to the second question must be that, in examining whether there is a causal connection between the concerted practice and the market conduct of the undertakings participating in the practice – a connection which must exist if it is to be established that there is concerted practice within the meaning of Article 81(1) EC – the national court is required, subject to proof to the contrary, which it is for the undertakings concerned to adduce, to apply the presumption of a causal connection established in the Court's case-law, according to which, where they remain active on that market, such undertakings are presumed to take account of the information exchanged with their competitors."

Nevertheless, the causality presumption between the 'concertation' and subsequent market conduct is subject to rebuttal. In the *T-Mobile Netherlands* case, the ECJ argued:[152]

> "Vodafone, T-Mobile and KPN essentially take the view that it cannot be inferred from Commission v Anic Partecipazioni or Hüls that the presumption of a causal connection is applicable in all cases. In their view, that presumption should be applied only in cases in which the facts and circumstances are the same as those in those cases. In essence, they sub-

150 Case C-199/92 P Hüls AG v Commission of the European Communities, 1999 I-04287, para. 161. cf. Lettl, Kartellrecht, 38.

151 ibid. para. 156.

152 T-Mobile Netherlands (n 136) para.55 cf. Jones and Sufrin (n 46) 550.

mit that it is only where the undertakings concerned meet on a regular basis, in the knowledge that confidential information has been exchanged in the course of previous meetings, that those undertakings can be presumed to have been guided in their market conduct on the basis of the concerted action. Moreover, they consider that it is irrational to take the view that an undertaking should base its market conduct on information exchanged in the course of just one meeting, in particular where, as in the case in the main proceedings, the meeting has a legitimate purposen the other hand, the Netherlands Government and the Commission submit that it is evident from the case-law, the *Commission v AnicPartecipazioni and Hüls*, that the presumption of a causal connection is not dependent on the number of meetings which gave rise to the concerted action. They observe that such a presumption is justified if the contact which took place, due being had to its context, content and the frequency with which it occurred, is sufficient to result in coordination of conduct on the market that is capable of preventing, restricting or distorting competition within the meaning of Article 81(1) EC and if, moreover, the undertakings concerned remain active on the market."

2.2.2.2.3.4 The Concerted Practices' Main Instruments

In the praxis of Competition law, the information exchanges have been the primary instrument for the concerted practice. By means of an exchange of information, an undertaking would be capable to eliminate uncertainties as to the reactions and responses of competitors on the market.[153] Basically, the information exchange can be found as a general practice in many competitive markets. Accordingly, the Guidelines on Horizontal Cooperation Agreements denotes:

> "Competitors cannot compete in a statistical vacuum: the more information they have about market conditions, the volume of demand, the level of capacity that exists in an industry and the investment plans of rivals, the easier it is for them to make rational and effective decisions on their production and marketing strategies. Competitors may benefit, without harming their customers, by exchanging information on matters such as methods of accounting, stock control, book-keeping or the draftsmanship of standard-form contracts."[154]

Emmerich further explains, that the information exchange serves, at the same time, not only to inform other competitors as to planned and

153 Emmerich in Immenga and Mestmäcker, Wettbewerbsrecht, (n 44) R. 89–90.

154 Slaughter and May, 'The EU Competition Rules on Horizontal Agreements: A Guide to the Assessment of Horizontal Agreements', (Guidelines, June 2016), 8–10.

envisaged conducts (behaviour) on the market, but also to obtain exposure as to the future conducts (behaviour) of other competitors on the market.[155] In the legal practices, the exchange of information can occur either directly or through third party. The information exchange could pertain actual market data or future market information as well as the relevant to competition data.[156] On the market, the information exchanges could take place through several occasions. Firstly, the information is being exchanged directly between competitors, secondly, indirectly through a common focal point, such as a trade association, thirdly, through a third party, such as a market research institution or the retailers or suppliers.[157]

In the praxis of European Competition law, the Commission distinguishes between two categories of information exchanges: (1) information exchanges, which are neutral to competition; and (2) information exchanges, restricting competitions on the market.[158] Whereas the exchanges of information regarding aggregated corporate data according to statistical customs and anonymous is classified under the first category; the information exchanges concerning individualised and strategic data on volumes and prices of a product is to be classified as the latter category.[159]

155 Emmerich in Immenga, Mestmäcker, (n 44) R. 89–90.

156 C. Sadler, ‚*Informationsaustausch zwischen Unternehmen Die Rechtslage in der EU und in Deutschland*' (Studienvereinigung Kartellrecht, 12. Juni 2015), 3 -5.

157 Commission, 'Guidelines on the applicability of Article 101 of the Treaty on the Functioning of the European Union to horizontal co-operation agreements' (Text with EEA relevance) COM 2011/C 11/01, para. 55.

158 ibid. paras. 55–59. cf. Emmerich in Immenga and Mestmäcker, (n 44), 272–273.

159 With regard to the first category:
„Exchanges of genuinely aggregated data, where the recognition of individualised ompany level information is sufficiently difficult, are much less likely to lead to restrictive effects n competition than exchanges of company level data. Collection and publication of aggregated market data (such as sales data, data on capacities or data on costs of inputs and components) by a trade organisation or market intelligence firm may benefit suppliers and customers alike by allowing them to get a clearer picture of the economic situation of a sector. Such data collection and publication may allow market participants to make better-informed individual choices in order to adapt efficiently their strategy to the market conditions. More generally, unless it takes place in a tight oligopoly, the exchange of aggregated data is unlikely to give rise to restrictive effects on competition. onversely, the exchange of individualised data facilitates a common understanding on the market and punish-

Hence, the exchange of information can constitute the concerted practices if it reduces strategic uncertainties about the competitors' conduct on a market, leading to facilitation of cartels.[160]

2.2.2.2.3.5 The Concerted Practices and the Facilitating Practices

In practice, cartels, occurring through collusive agreements and/or the concerted practices, take place due to the following factors, which are: First, the existence of direct or indirect inter-firm contacts and second, the intention or effect of influencing the market conducts of undertakings concerned.[161] Furthermore, in the tacit collusion, the following components must be present to establish a cartel: 1. Firms have to reach terms of coordination; 2. They need to monitor compliance; 3. It is important for them to threaten timely retaliation and 4. to limit the reactions by outsiders.

ment strategies by allowing coordinating companies to single out a deviator or entrant. Nevertheless, the possibility cannot be excluded that even the exchange of aggregated data may facilitate a collusive outcome in markets with specific characteristics. Namely, members of a very tight and stable oligopoly exchanging aggregated data who detect a market price below a certain level could automatically assume that someone has deviated from the collusive outcome and take marketwide retaliatory steps. In other words, in order to keep collusion stable, companies may not always need to know who deviated, it may be enough to learn that 'someone' deviated. Whereas regarding the second category:

The exchange between competitors of strategic data, that is to say, data that reduces strategic uncertainty in the market, is more likely to be caught by Article 101 than exchanges of other types of information. Sharing of strategic data can give rise to restrictive effects on competition because it reduces the parties' decision-making independence by decreasing their incentives to compete. Strategic information can be related to prices (for example, actual prices, iscounts, increases, reductions or rebates), customer lists, production costs, quantities, turnovers, sales, capacities, qualities, marketing plans, risks, investments, technologies and R&D programmes and their results. Generally, information related to prices and quantities is the most strategic, followed by information about costs and demand. However, if companies compete with regard to R&D it is the technology data that may be the most strategic for competition. The strategic usefulness of data also depends on its aggregation and age, as well as the market context and frequency of the exchange.

See COM 2011/C 11/01, paras. 86 and 89. cf. Zimmer in Immenga and Mestmäcker, Wettbewerbsrecht, (n 44) 272–73.

160 Slaughter and May, (n 154) 8–10.

161 Van Bael and Bellis, *Competition Law,* (n 148) 38–50.

In the oligopolistic market structure, there are the so-called "facilitating practices" (facilitating mechanisms or devices), which could bring two effects: First, the contribution for the prompting factors abovementioned and second, making easier for the formation of cartels.[162]

On the one hand, according to *Page*, the facilitating practices refer to mechanisms that enhance rival firms' ability to closely monitor arrangements on the key terms of a collusion and to detect and thus penalize deviating firms or cheaters.[163] These include price reporting systems, preannouncements of price changes, most favoured customers clauses, meeting competition clauses, basing (delivered) point pricing and an industry-wide resale price maintenance.[164] Further, the facilitating practices are part of oligopolistic behaviour, which is useful for the competition analysis.[165] On the other hand, *Hovenkamp* adds that the facilitating practices exist whenever "Firms [....] agree among themselves, either explicitly or tacitly, to engage in certain practices that will make collusion easier".[166]

Equally important, the OECD defines a facilitating practice as one that "makes it easier for parties to coordinate price or other behaviour in an anticompetitive way".[167] Furthermore, the facilitating practices are divided into two categories: First, the facilitating practices which facilitate agreement on the central provisions of price or output.[168] Second, the

162 W. H. Page 'Facilitating Practices and Concerted Action Under Section 1 of the Sherman Act' (Antitrust Law and Economics Journal, University of Florida – Levin College of Law, 2008) ‹https://papers.ssrn.com/sol3/papers.cfm?abstract_id=1117667›, accessed 22.October 2018.

163 ibid. 3–8.

164 ibid. 3–8.

165 ibid. 25.

166 H. Hovenkamp, Federal Antitrust Law Policy: The Law of Competition and Its Practice (West Publishing Company,1994) 171.

167 According to the OECD:
These (facilitating practices) agreements can channel competition and thus limit the ways in which firms engage in nonprice or quality competition as a way of cheating on a price agreement. Expressed differently, one mechanism facilitates making an initial agreement on price, and the other tends to protect a price agreement that has already been reached. Regardless of its specific type, any facilitating agreement may produce anticompetitive effects, or efficiencies, or both." See OECD, 'Facilitating Practices in Oligopolies' (OECD Secretariat, 2007) 9–11.

168 This includes for example agreements thatexchange plans on future prices, or take factory downtime. ibid.

facilitating practices that restrict competition on the market collaterally as to non-price parameters.[169] In other words, there are facilitating practices that foster an initial collusion on prices as well as the practices which protect a price agreement already achieved.[170] Furthermore, according to *Hylton* the facilitating practices or facilitating mechanisms refer to mechanisms which make collusion more effective by serving one or more of the following functions: First, to establish a methodology for monitoring compliance. Second, to enable parties to enforce compliances and to cover collusion from a public view.[171]

According to OECD, the facilitating practices can be categorised into two main types, namely: (1) the practices facilitating the formation of price cartels as well as (2) the practices maintaining the prevailment of cartelised prices.[172] The plan for data dissemination is the example of facilitating mechanisms. Nevertheless, the data dissemination plan could constitute cartels or concerted practices, provided it is a 'necessary and sufficient' element for a price-fixing cartel. It must be bore in mind that the data dissemination plan would not only facilitate cartels but could also facilitate other less harmful or even beneficial results at the end.[173]

In different perspectives, *Grillo* explains that the facilitating practices refer to:

> "a behavioral attitude other than the one that merely guarantees strategic equilibrium co-ordination, which contribute to a number of typical artifices that characterise the organization of actual oligopolies, provided economic analysis supports the theoretical conclusion that such "artifices" can only be normally understood as social mechanisms intended to ease the collusive maximization of the industry joint profits."[174]

Nevertheless, the facilitating practices are subject to careful and prudent analysis by the Competition Authorities, whether these practices would

169 ibid.
170 ibid.
171 K. Hylton, Antitrust Law: Economic Theory and Common Law Evolution (Cambridge University Press, 2011) 144.
172 OECD, 'Facilitaing Practices' (n 167), 2.
173 ibid. 144.
174 M. Grillo, 'Collusiong and Facilitating Practices' (European Journal of Law and Economics, Kluwer Academic Publishing 2002) 151–169.

result in the anticompetitive effects, procompetitive effects or both of them.[175] Accordingly, the OECD argued for the following opinions:

> "The agencies assess facilitating practices in light of their individual purposes and effects. Sometimes facilitating practices may decrease competition, through such mechanisms as reducing the number of bidding variables on which the colluding firms would have to reach agreement, or helping to monitor defections from such an agreement. In other respects, however, the same practices may help to bring about beneficial efficiencies. The reduction in bidding variables may facilitate collusion, but also can help buyers to make head-to-head price comparisons, and in that respect may tend to make a market more competitive rather than less. Similarly, mechanisms to monitor defections may also tend to make prices and bidding more transparent, which under some conditions may induce greater competitive efforts by other firms. Given these complexities, the agencies must attempt to balance the procompetitive and anticompetitive effects of changes to facilitating practices that would be caused by any enforcement actions." [176]

Particularly important, in the US Antitrust law practice, facilitating practices serve as "circumstantial evidence" of a collusive agreement. In other words, the US Competition Authorities can merely:

> "use the evidence on the facilitating practices (or even on an agreement the content of which is the facilitating practice) to detect the main agreement, in which the undertakings reached a meeting of minds to commit cartel or concerted practices.[177]"

Subsequently, the facilitating practices under the cartel prohibition, could manifest in an adoption of rivals' practices by an express agreement as well as an adoption of the practices by means of parallel conduct on a market.[178] In particular as to the adoption of facilitating practices, that are accompanied by the market parallel conduct, the Competition Authority must pay rigorous analysis in order to judge the existence of an collusive agreement (cartels). As a matter of fact, the Competition Authority cannot immediately infer the existence of cartels because of the existence of facilitating practices and a market parallel conduct. Put differently, the US Court's evidentiary rule is of opinion that "facilitating practices (devices)" are not necessarily sufficient under the law to

175 OECD, Roundtable on Facilitating Practices in Oligopolies (2007), p. 2
176 *ibid.*, p. 2.
177 M. Grillo (n 174) 159–60.
178 W. Page (n 162) 29.

constitute a "plus factor".[179] Consequently, the Court would not conclude the existence of a collusive agreement only by seeing, at the first snapshot, the presence of parallel pricing that is accompanied by facilitating practices.[180] In the US Court's case decision it is stated that: "facilitating devices" are not necessarily sufficient under the law to constitute a "plus factor".

There are two reasons supporting this argument: First, there could be an independent justification for a firm to adopt practices facilitating coordinated prices. Second, a parallel adoption of the facilitating practices by competing firms will not preclude the possibility that each firm acted independently on the market.[181]

Hence, the US Antitrust scholar, Page, argues that the analysis of facilitating practices and parallel conduct must take into account the following elements, which are: (1) a definition of an agreement; (2) mutual communication between firms regarding a reliance and an intent to collude.[182] Further, the facilitating practices must be accompanied by inter-firm communications and supporting evidences to conclude, based on the nature and substances of communication, that the firms have a concertation of wills to collude on the market.[183]

In practice of the US Antitrust Law and subsequently in the European Competition Law, the 'facilitating devices'have been developed. Basically, these are arrangements or practices which can be construed as helping firms in at least one of the 4 steps to stable, successful tacit collusion: defining the possible agreements; focusing upon one; preserving it and providing for credible effective punishment.[184] These practices, encompass, among others, as follows:

2.2.2.2.3.5.1 Information Exchanges

In practice of European Competition Law and US Antitrust law, the information exchange could occur through several scenarios. First,

179 ibid.
180 W. Page (n 162) 30.
181 ibid. 33.
182 ibid. 30
183 ibid.
184 T. Frazer and M. Waterson, *Competition Law and Policy: Cases, Materials and Commentary* (Prentice Hall Publishing, 1994) 78–80.

direct sharing of data between competing undertakings. Second, by means of a common agency, such as trade associations. Third, through the third party, such as a market research organisation. Fourth, by means of the undertakings' suppliers or retailers.[185] Equally important, by the context, one can distinguish information exchange through agreements, decisions of association of undertakings and concerted practices whereby their main goal is the exchange of information itself. Moreover, information exchange serves only as a part of whole horizontal cooperation agreement, such as the parties in production agreement share certain information on costs or in the Research and Development agreement. Consequently, each of these information exchanges require contextual assessment of the horizontal cooperation agreement.[186]

Furthermore, the EU Competition Law acknowledges the possible procompetitive and anticompetitive effects of information exchange in the market. From the procompetitive aspect, information exchange may solve problems of information asymmetries, leading to various efficiencies gains. Moreover, undertakings could increase efficiencies by means of benchmarking towards other undertakings' best practices. In addition, undertakings are able to save costs by reducing their inventories, enabling quicker delivery of perishable products to consumers. Besides, the consumers can reap benefits directly by diminishing costs of search and improving choice.[187] From the anticompetitive aspect, information exchange could lead to restriction of competition, whenever the information exchange involves so-called 'strategic information exchange'. This, however, depends largely both on the market characteristics (such as concentration, transparency, stability, symmetry, complexity) and the types of exchanged information, capable of modifying the market's circumstances. Most important, information exchange between undertakings could constitute cartels practice, whereby the exchanged information facilitates collusion by means of monitoring the participating

185 ibid.
186 The Commission Guidelines on Horizontal Cooperation Agreement of 2010, para 57.
187 The Commission Guidelines on Horizontal Cooperation Agreement of 2010, para 58.

undertakings; that is to say, whether the undertakings obey the cartels practices terms or not.[188]

Moreover, communication of information among competitors may constitute an agreement, a concerted practice, or a decision by an association of undertakings with the object of fixing, in particular, prices or quantities. Those types of information exchanges will normally be considered and be penalized as cartels. Information exchange may also facilitate the implementation of a cartel by enabling companies to monitor whether the participants comply with the agreed terms. Those types of exchanges of information will be assessed as part of the cartel.

As has been noted, under the prohibition rule of Article 101 (1) TFEU, information exchange could trigger restriction of competitions in the market. As a result, the Commission explicitly indicates two anti-competitive concerns with regard to information exchange, provided the agreements, decisions of association of undertakings concerted practices have been existing before. These concerns comprise: First, the collusive outcome[189] and second, the anticompetitive foreclosure.[190] As far as the collusive outcome is concerned, the Commission Guidelines on Horizontal cooperation agreement reiterates that information exchange facilitates collusive practices by conducing artificial transparency on the market, whereas these illegal practices could result from three main channels, which are: First through the information exchange, whereas undertakings caneasily reach collusive deals over competition parameters, such as prices and product quantity, even without involving explicit agreement. Also, the information exchange could reduce uncertainties as to the future circumstances in the market by generating the mutually consistent business expectations amongst undertakings. Equally important, the Commission emphasises that the information exchange concerning future conducts will be largely against the prohibition rule of Article 101 (1) TFEU.

Second information exchange facilitates anticompetitive practices by increasing the internal stability of collusive outcomes in the market; that is to say, the undertakings are able to monitor and thus punish other

188 The Commission Guidelines on Horizontal Cooperation Agreement of 2010, para 59.
189 The Commission Guidelines on Horizontal Cooperation Agreements, paras. 65–68.
190 The Commission Guidelines on Horizontal Cooeration Agreements, paras. 69–71.

participating undertakings whenever they deviate or disobey the cartels agreement by means of retaliating measures.

Third, information exchange facilitates an increase as to the external stability of a collusive outcome on the market. Thus, the colluding undertakings could monitor other undertakings, notably when and where they will enter the market, in order to target the new entry undertakings. At the same time, this restrictive practice relates largely to foreclosure effects in the market. The Commission believes that both of exchanges of present and past information constitute a monitoring mechanism abovementioned. Furthermore, as regards to the anticompetitive foreclosure effect, the Commission hypothesises that information exchange leads to foreclosure effects both to the undertakings engaging in the same relevant market as well as the third parties in a related market.[191]

With regard to the competition assessment of information exchanges, the EU Competition law prerequisites that comprehensive analysis concerning restrictions of competition either 'by objects' or 'by effects' must be performed. In the analysis of restriction of competition by object, the Commission will particularly take into account: First, the legal and economic contexts in which the exchange takes place. Second, whether the exchange, by its very nature would lead to restrictions of competition. Moreover, the Commission argues that "Exchanging information on companies' individualised intentions concerning future conduct regarding prices or quantities is particularly likely to lead to a collusive outcome." Finally, the Commission concludes that "informa-

191 According to Commission Guidelines on Horizontal Cooperation Agreements, regarding foreclosure effects in the same relevant market.
This can occur when the exchange of commercially sensitive information places unaffiliated competitors at a significant competitive disadvantage as compared to the companies affiliated within the exchange system. This type of foreclosure is only possible if the information concerned is very strategic for competition and covers a significant part of the relevant market." On the other hand, the Commission asserted as to foreclosure effects to third parties:? "This can occur when the exchange of commercially sensitive information places unaffiliated competitors at a significant competitive disadvantage as compared to the companies affiliated within the exchange system. This type of foreclosure is only possible if the information concerned is very strategic for competition and covers a significant part of the relevant market." The Commission Guidelines on Horizontal Cooperation Agreements, para. 70–71.

tion exchanges between competitors of individualized data regarding intended future prices or quantities should therefore be considered a restriction of competition by object." Consequently, this kind of information exchange, according to the Commission, will hardly fulfill the legal exemptions pursuant to Article 101 (3) TFEU. Whereas the horizontal agreement contains restriction of competition by objects, the Competition Authorities do not have to conduct analysis over restriction of competition by effect.[192]

According to the Commission, as to the latter elements:

> "The likely effects of an information exchange on competition must be analysed on a case-by-case basis as the results of the assessment depend on a combination of various case specific factors. The assessment of restrictive effects on competition compares the likely effects of the information exchange with the competitive situation that would prevail in the absence of that specific information exchange. For an information exchange to have restrictive effects on competition within the meaning of Article 101(1), it must be likely to have an appreciable adverse impact on one (orseveral) of the parameters of competition such as price, output, product quality, product variety or innovation. Whether or not an exchange of information will have restrictive effects on competition depends on both the economic conditions on the relevant markets and the characteristics of information exchanged."[193]

Nevertheless, it should be bore in mind, that in conducting analysis over restriction of competition by effects, the Commission suggests that several key market characteristics must be carefully scrutinised.[194] Moreover, the market conditions should be analised carefully at first before information exchange takes place. Most important, the market characteristics encompass the following aspects:[195] First, transparen-

192 ibid.

193 The Commission Guidelines on Horizontal Cooperation Agreements, para. 75.

194 The Commission Guidelines on Horizontal Cooperation Agreement, paras. 77–85.

195 The Commission Guidelines on Horizontal Cooperation Agreement, para. 77–85. See Geradin, et.al, p.431–2.

cy,[196] second, concentration,[197] third, complexity,[198] fourth, stability,[199] fifth, symmetry[200] and sixth, possibility of retaliation.[201]

---

196 According to the Commission Guidelines on Horizontal Cooperation Agreement, para.77–8: Companies are more likely to achieve a collusive outcome in markets which are sufficiently transparent, concentrated, non-complex, stable and symmetric. In those types of markets companies can reach a common understanding on the terms of coordination and successfully monitor and punish deviations. However, information exchange can also enable companies to achieve a collusive outcome in other market situations where they would not be able to do so in the absence of the information exchange. Information exchange can thereby facilitate a collusive outcome by increasing transparency in the market, reducing market complexity, buffering instability or compensating for asymmetry. In this context, the competitive outcome of an information exchange depends not only on the initial characteristics of the market in which it takes place (such as concentration, transparency, stability, complexity etc.), but also on how the type of the information exchanged may change those characteristics

197 According to the Commission Guidelines on Horizontal Cooperation Agreement, para.79: Tight oligopolies can facilitate a collusive outcome on the market as it is easier for fewer companies to reach a common understanding on the terms of coordination and to monitor deviations. A collusive outcome is also more likely to be sustainable with fewer companies. With more companies coordinating, the gains from deviating are greater because a larger market share can be gained through undercutting. At the same time, gains from the collusive outcome are smaller because, when there are more companies, the share of the rents from the collusive outcome declines. Exchanges of information in tight oligopolies are more likely to cause restrictive effects on competition than in less tight oligopolies and are not likely to cause such restrictive effects on competition in very fragmented markets. However, by increasing transparency, or modifying the market environment in another way towards one more liable to coordination, information exchanges may facilitate coordination and monitoring among more companies than would be possible in its absence.

198 According to the Commission Guidelines on Horizontal Cooperation Agreement, para.80: Companies may find it difficult to achieve a collusive outcome in a complex market environment. However, to some extent, the use of information exchange may simplify such environments. In a complex market environment, more information exchange is normally needed to reach a common understanding on the terms of coordination and to monitor deviations. For example, it is easier to achieve a collusive outcome on a price for a single, homogeneous product, than on numerous prices in a market with many differentiated products. It is nonetheless possible that to circumvent the difficulties involved in achieving a collusive outcome on a large number of prices, companies may exchange information to establish simple pricing rules (for example, pricing points).

199 According to the Commission Guidelines on Horizontal Cooperation Agreement, para.81: Collusive outcomes are more likely where the demand and supply conditions are relatively stable (1). In an unstable environment it may be difficult for

Equally important, in performing legal analysis of restriction of competition by object, the Commission underlines the categorisation or characteristic of information being exchanged in the market. Principally, the Guidelines on Horizontal cooperation agreement acknowl-

---

a company to know whether its lost sales are due to an overall low level of demand or due to a competitor offering particularly low prices, and therefore it is difficult to sustain a collusive outcome. In this context, volatile demand, substantial internal growth by some companies in the market, or frequent entry by new companies, may indicate that the current situation is not sufficiently stable for coordination to be likely (2). Information exchange in certain situations can serve the purpose of increasing stability in the market, and thereby may enable a collusive outcome in the market. Moreover, in markets where innovation is important, coordination may be more difficult since particularly significant innovations may allow one company to gain a major advantage over its rivals. For a collusive outcome to be sustainable, the reactions of outsiders, such as current and future competitors not participating in the coordination, as well as customers, should not be capable of jeopardising the results expected from the collusive outcome. In this context, the existence of barriers to entry makes it more likely that a collusive outcome on the market is feasible and sustainable.

200 According to the Commission Guidelines on Horizontal Cooperation Agreement, para.82: A collusive outcome is more likely in symmetric market structures. When companies are homogenous in terms of their costs, demand, market shares, product range, capacities etc., they are more likely to reach a common understanding on the terms of coordination because their incentives are more aligned. However, information exchange may in some situations also allow a collusive outcome to occur in more heterogeneous market structures. Information exchange could make companies aware of their differences and help them to design means to accommodate for their heterogeneity in the context of coordination.

201 According to the Commission Guidelines on Horizontal Cooperation Agreement, para. 85: Overall, for a collusive outcome to be sustainable, the threat of a sufficiently credible and prompt retaliation must be likely. Collusive outcomes are not sustainable in markets in which the consequences of deviation are not sufficiently severe to convince coordinating companies that it is in their best interest to adhere to the terms of the collusive outcome. For example, in markets characterised by infrequent, lumpy orders, it may be difficult to establish a sufficiently severe deterrence mechanism, since the gain from deviating at the right time may be large, certain and immediate, whereas the losses from being punished small and uncertain, and only materialise after some time. The credibility of the deterrence mechanism also depends on whether the other coordinating companies have an incentive to retaliate, determined by their short-term losses from triggering a price war versus their potential long-term gain in case they induce a return to a collusive outcome. For example, companies' ability to retaliate may be reinforced if they are also interrelated by vertical commercial relationships which they can use as a threat of punishment for deviations.

edges 7 characteristics: First, strategic information,[202] second, market coverage,[203] third, aggregated or individualised information,[204] fourth, age of information,[205] fifth, frequency of the information exchange,[206] sixth, public or non-public information[207] and seventh, public or non-public exchange of information.[208]

2.2.2.2.3.5.2 Price Leadership

According to the Organisation for Economic Co-operation and Development (OECD), a price leadership:

> "refers to a situation where prices and price changes established by a dominant firm, or a firm are accepted by others as the leader, and which other firms in the industry adopt and follow."[209]

In Bain's analysis regarding price leadership 'in an oligopolistic market any independent price change by a single oligopolist tends to be read as an 'offer' by his rivals, and an acceptable reaction to the price change may be interpreted as an acceptance of the offer of the first firm. Thus, negotiation can perhaps take place through a series of public announcements rather than through a meeting of persons, and the meaning of true consensual action becomes vague'.[210]

According to *Markham*, there are three categories of a price leadership, which are:

First, a dominant price-leadership 'whereas one dominant competitor, the only firm large enough to significantly affect the market, imposes its prices upon the industry, and the other competitors follow,

202 The Commission Guidelines on Horizontal cooperation agreements, para. 86.
203 The Commission Guidelines on Horizontal cooperation agreements, para. 87–88.
204 The Commission Guidelines on Horizontal cooperation agreements, para. 89.
205 The Commission Guidelines on Horizontal cooperation agreements, para. 90.
206 The Commission Guidelines on Horizontal cooperation agreements, para. 91.
207 The Commission Guidelines on Horizontal cooperation agreements, para. 92–93.
208 The Commission Guidelines on Horizontal cooperation agreements, para. 94.
209 However according to Seaton and Waterson "*Price leadership* occurs when one firm makes a change in a *price* (or set of prices) that is followed within a *predetermined short period* by the other (more generally, another) firm making a *price* change of exactly the same monetary amount in the same direction on the *same product(s)*, and doing so *significantly more often than would be expected by chance*." Khemani and Shapiro, Glossary of Industrial Organisation Economics and Competition Law (n 39). Page?
210 Stroux, EC and US Oligopoly, (n 51) 28–29.

as they will have little to gain from diverging from the dominant firm's prices'.[211] Second, a barometric price leadership, whereas an undertaking as the leader is not dominant but is widely accepted as the best performing undertaking which is able to meet the demand and to adapt to evolving market conditions, such as cost increases.[212] Third, collusive price leadership, either explicit or tacit one, where the competitors commit themselves to adapt to price increases initiated by one of them, acting as the price leader.

2.2.2.2.3.5.3 Basing Point Pricing

This is a pricing system often encountered in industries, such as steel and cement, where transport costs are high relative to production costs and buyers and sellers are spatially dispersed. In one variant, manufacturing plants of each seller are designated as bases, and a 'base price' is set at each of them. There is also a standard table of transport charges. Then, a buyer at any given location will be quoted a price at the nearest base plus the standard charge for transporting the product from the base to the buyer's location.[213]

2.2.2.2.3.5.4 Most-Favoured Customer (MFC) Clauses in Buyer Seller Contracts

According to *Salop*, MFC and 'Meeting Competition' (MC) clauses in contracts between undertakings could facilitate collusion between buyers and sellers as well as between sellers.[214]

By definition, OECD explains the most favoured customer clause as:

> "a provision in a sales contract, under which the seller agrees to give the buyer the benefit of any more favourable contract terms that it may later negotiate with some other purchasers (the name itself is borrowed from international tariff negotiations). Under certain narrow circumstances

211 ibid.

212 According to Stigler, in the barometric price leadership, the barometric firm commands the adherence of rivals to this price only because, and to the extent that, its price reflects market conditions with tolerable promptness. R J. Deneckere and D Kovenock, 'Price Leadership' (Review of Economic Studies, Vol. 59/Nr. 1, OUP, 1992), 143–162.

213 Stroux, (n 51) 28–32. cf. L. Philips, *Basing Point Pricing, Competition and Market Integration* (European University Institute, 1992), 2–5.

214 Hylton, (n 171), 6–8.

> these clauses may tend to deter competitive price-cutting, and so may tend to facilitate the maintenance of cartel prices."[215]

In practice, the imposition MFN clause can result either in a benign and pro-competition impact, whereby a MFN clause warrants a buyer that if, when the contract is concluded or within some specified time period later, the seller makes a sale to another buyer at a lower price, then the buyer in question will also receive that lower price.[216]

Judge *Posner* argued that this clause "standard devices by which buyers try to bargain for low prices."[217]

On the other hand, a MFN clause can lead to an anticompetitive effect whereby it deters the undertakings participating in cartels from cheating. As the OECD describes "a classic problem faced by a cartel is that its members try to cheat on it. Most-favoured-nation clauses can reduce the incentive to cheat, by increasing the cost of cheating. The low price offered on a particular contract would then become, not just a one-time occasion when the cheater could gain some incremental sales volume, but rather an occasion for across-the-board revenue losses as many of the firm's contract prices are reset."[218]

Nevertheless, the assessment of anticompetitive impact is subject to the following factors, for example: (1) the contracts must be routinely used by most undertakings in certain industries as well as by the customers; (2) the clauses that were demanded or objected by the customers are pertinent.[219]

2.2.2.2.3.5.5 Governmental Action Encouraging the Facilitating Practices

According to OECD, the facilitating practices can be a manifested result of a governmental act or statute. In terms of durability and immunity to many feasible legal challenges, this governmental statute characterises cartels.

Whereby these facilitating practices had been originated from the legislative statute and the administrative board, they could take several

215 OECD, Roundtable on Facilitating Practices in Oligopolies (2007), 6.
216 ibid.
217 ibid.
218 ibid.
219 ibid.

forms: (1) restrictions on advertising and (2) the authorisation form competing firms to agree on prices.[220] Governmental statute encouraging the facilitating practices could result to and be prompted by anti-competitive reasons, such as lobbying of association of industries. Furthermore, the governmental statute facilitating practices are stripped-off from an immunity and thus subject to the antitrust law scrutiny, provided two situations emerge.

Accordingly, OECD explains these two situations:

> "First, if the state agency's actions were not clearly authorized by the state legislature – since the necessary authority must ultimately come from one of the state's constitutional branches. Second, if the scheme is not "actively supervised" by some part of the state government, to make the conduct truly the state's own. It is not yet entirely clear at what point a facilitating practice will create "private market power" for this purpose; nor it is entirely clear whether a state regulatory board, numerically dominated by members of the regulated profession, has enough private characteristics to require active supervision."[221]

2.2.2.3 Appreciable Restrictions of Competition and which have as their object or effect the prevention, restriction or distortion of competition"[222]

According to *Säcker and Molle*, within the practices of EU Competition Laws, although some agreements may restrict competition, these agreements could finally bring efficiencies enhancements and thus promote working competition. Accordingly, this occurs whenever a restrictive to competition accord is a part of the larger agreements, which serve only neutral economic purposes. Thus, to determine the procompetitive and anticompetitive effects of agreements abovementioned, the appreacibility or noticeability (*Spürbarkeitstest*) must take place.[223] Equally important, in the context of EU Competition law analysis, this thinking could correlate to the concept of "ancillary restraints", meaning: restriction on the parties to agreements, which initially appears restrictive to competition, but actually does not consti-

220 OECD, Roundtable on Facilitating Practices in Oligopolies (2007) 6.
221 OECD, Roundtable on Facilitating Practices in Oligopolies (2007). 9.
222 Säcker and Molle in F.J. Säcker (n 13) 718–720.
223 ibid.

tute the main goals of the agreements but is directly related to and necessary for the proper implementation of the genuine objectives envisaged by the agreements.[224]

Although different in nature, the concept of "Ancillary Restraints" corresponds to some extend to the concept of "Rule of Reason" in the US Antitrust laws. By comparison, the "Rule of Reason" refers to a legal approach in the competition law whereas the competition authorities and the courts make attempts to evaluate the pro-competitive effects of a restrictive business practice against the anti-competitive effects thereof for determining whether or not the practice should be prohibited.[225] Arguably, the implementation of the "Rule of Reason" has been dogmatically viewed as the balancing consideration effort in the light of the EU Competition laws' objectives, particularly towards the strict prohibition rule of Article 101 (1) TFEU.

Moreover, according to *Säcker and Molle*, the concept of weighing the pro-competitive and anti-competitive effects of certain agreements under the provisions of Article 101 (1) and (3) TFEU has been derived from the "Rule of Reason" concept in the US Antitrust laws.[226] In contrast to the Per se Illegal approach, "the Rule of Reason" concerns

---

224 Institute of Competition Law, 'Glossary of Competition Terms' ‹http://www.concurrences.com/Droit-de-la-concurrence/Glossaire-des-termes-de/?lang=en› accessed 24 March 2016.

225 Furthermore, according to the OECD:
"some market restrictions which prima facie give rise to competition issues may on further examination be found to have valid efficiency-enhancing benefits. For example, a manufacturer may restrict supply of a product in different geographic markets only to existing retailers so that they earn higher profits and have an incentive to advertise the product and provide better service to customers. This may have the effect of expanding the demand for the manufacturer's product more than the increase in quantity demanded at a lower price. The opposite of the rule of reason approach is to declare certain business practices per se illegal, that is, always illegal are per se illegal."
See Khemani and Shapiro (n 39) 77.

226 The US Antitrust laws introduced firstly in 1914 by the Sherman Act 1980 and thus complemented by the Clayton Act. In the same year, the Federal Trade Commission Act was enacted. Further, in 1936 the Clayton Act had been amended by the Robinson Patman Act, whereas the imporvemeents were limited to Article 2 of the Clayton Act. cf. A. F. Lubis and N. N. Sirait (eds), *Hukum Persaingan Usaha: Antara Teks and Konteks* (Gesellschaft für Technische Zusammenarbeit-GTZ, 2009), 55–80.

chiefly with the effects-based assessment over agreements or corporate conducts in order to determine whether the agreements or corporate actions in question are either to promote or to restrict competitions.[227]

Originally, the Rule of Reason concept has been introduced by the US Supreme Court in the landmark case of *Standard Oil and Co of N.J. v. United States* as regards an interpretation of the Sherman Act in the year of 1911. In this case, the main legal considerations of the judges were the wealth maximisations and satisfaction of consumer needs. Further, the judges argued that the main goal of the antitrust law was not to obstruct an efficiently established a joint company, but to prevent and reduce the business practices which eliminate competitions on markets. Thereby, the court must examine the following main factors to decide antitrust cases, namely, to decide whether an agreement will bring economic efficiencies and thus increase productions. Subsequently, whether an agreement will restrict competition and thus limit productions. Principally, the application of the "Rule of Reason" approach requires three-step examinations. Firstly, the existence of Perse illegal, secondly, the existence of intention or object of the parties to restrict competition and thirdly, the subsequent effects of an agreement to competition.[228]

Afterwards, in the case of *Chicago Board of Trade v. United States*, the US Supreme Court also imposed the "Rule of Reason" approach. In this case the court examined the economic effects of an agreement and impacts to competition. This examination encompassed: First, detrimental effects to competition from an agreement. Second, the existence of reasonable and legal justifications behind an agreement. Third, if the justifications exist, thus the court review restrictions in an agreement are necessary to achieve the aim of an agreement. Furthermore, the court performs two examinations separately: Firstly, whether an agreement restricts existing competition and secondly, the court will examine the impacts of an agreement in a comprehensive way. In this examination, for example, price deviations could be deemed as a restrictive effect. In this case, the judges applied the reasonableness test

227 ibid.
228 Säcker and Molle, in F.J Säcker et.al (n 13) 718–720.

to evaluate an allegedly anticompetitive agreement. Accordingly, the judge stated:

> "the legality of an agreement or regulation cannot be determined by so simple a test, as whether it restrains competition. Every agreement concerning trade, every regulation of trade, restrains. To bind, to restrain, is of their very essence. The true test of legality of whether the restraint imposed is such as merely regulates and perhaps thereby promotes competition or whether it is such as may suppress or even destroy competition. To determine that question the court must ordinarily consider the facts peculiar to the business [...]; its condition before and after the restraint was imposed; the nature of the restraint and its effect, actual and probable. The history of the restraint, the evil believed to exist, the reason for adopting the particular remedy, the purpose or end sought to be attained, are all relevant facts. This is not because good intention will save an achieved objectionable regulation or the reverse; but because knowledge of intent may help the court to interpret facts and to predict consequences."[229]

However, in the practice of the Antitrust laws, the application of "Rule of Reason" has both: an advantage and a disadvantage. On the one hand, the "Rule of Reason" introduces and utilises economic analysis by considering the efficiencies enhancements to determine accurately whether agreements or conducts in question have substantial effects to the competition. Further, this approach takes into account "economic values, that is, with the maximization of consumer want satisfaction through the most efficient allocation and use resources."[230] On the other hand, the "Rule of Reason" has also several drawbacks. Firstly, it prerequisites the comprehensive and sound knowledge in economics and industrial organisation theories in order to generate court decisions which are of a high quality. This problematic obstacle has hindered the courts in adjudicating the antitrust cases litigations. Secondly, in the application of the "Rule of Reason" before the courts, the applicant with his or her allegations must provide economic experts as well as documentary evidences from other competing firms, which are mostly difficult to obtain, for example in cartel cases.[231]

Furthermore, according to *Säcker and Molle*, the application of the "Rule of Reason" based approach in the provisions of Article 101 (1)

---

229 Lubis and Sirait (n 225), 68.
230 Lubis and Sirait (n 225), 66–70.
231 ibid. 70–72.

and (3) TFEU has impacts to the considerations of a normative relationship between the provisions of Article 101 (1) and (3) TFEU. Accordingly, the following aspects are to be take into account. First, the cartel administrative enforcement proceedings, whereas there are separate evidentiary proceedings under the Articles 101 (1) and (3) TFEU[232] and second, the normative interpretations.[233]

Equally important, as to the practice of the provisions of Article 101 (1) in conjunctions with Article 101 (3) TFEU, the Commission and the Court of Justice of the EU have adjudicated several related cases. First, Reuter/BASF case.[234]Second, DLG Case. Third, O2 (Germany) GmbH & Co OHG v Commission[235] Fourth, *Wouters v Algemene Raad van de Nederlandse Orde van Advocaten.*[236]

Initially, the case of *Reuter/BASF* was primarily concerned with the concept of ancillary restriction developed with regard to the transfer of business in the chemical sector. In this case Dr. Reuter, a chemical expert, assigned his entire business in the chemical sector to the BASF, a competing company in the similar sector, through an assignment

232 Accordingly, Säcker and Molle assert:
„Since the modernization of the antitrust proceedings the right above method legal arguments have no more meaning. With the abolition of the exemption monopoly Commission and the completed change from the system of exemptions for legal exception is the material unity of the Art. 101 has been implemented on a procedural level. The European legislator has indicated the fact that he abs the courts and antitrust authorities Dern of the Member States a direct application of Art. 101 (3) TFEU trusts and is prepared to accept the risk of inconsistent application of Community law. This risk is reduced by the adoption of guidelines by the Commission and the co-operation between the Commission and relevant institutions in the Member States in accordance with Art. 11–16 Regulation 1/2003. Decisive 101 para. 3 TFEU on procedural level remains the differentiation between the account-competitive moments under Art. 101 para. 1 and Art. But for the burden of proof under Article 2 of Regulation 1/2003." Säcker and Molle, in F.J Säcker (n 13) 720–734.

233 Säcker and Molle, in F.J Säcker et.al (n 13) 720–734.

234 76/743/EEC: Commission Decision of 26th July 1976 relating to a proceeding under Article 85 of the EEC Treaty (IV/28.996 – Reuter/BASF). cf. Hawk, EC Competition Law (n 85) 57.

235 Case T 328/03, General Court 2006, O2 (Germany) GmbH & Co. OHG v Commission of the European Communities.

236 Case C 309/99, J. C. J. Wouters, J. W. Savelbergh and Price Waterhouse Belastingadviseurs BV v Algemene Raad van de Nederlandse Orde van Advocaten, intervener: Raad van de Balies van de Europese Gemeenschap, 2002 I-01577.

agreement. This transfer agreement contained the non-competition clause imposed to Dr. Reuter. The Court of Justice was of the opinion that such a non-competition clause is necessary for the BASF and thus compatible with the competition law because technical knowledge constituted an important part of the value of the transferred undertakings. Thus, the court argued if Dr. Reuter competed against the BASF this could jeopardise the business value assigned to the BASF. The court opined that the non-compete clause was excessive in terms of the competition rules. First, the non-compete clause exceeds the period of five years. Second, it unnecessarily penetrates also the independent research and development of the other party.[237]

Subsequently, in the second case *Danks Lanbrugs Grovvareseklab (DLG) v. Gottrup Klim.*[238] The DLG was a Danish cooperative cooperation distributing farming supplies to its members, such as fertilisers and plant protection products with the lowest prices. However, in 1975 several former members of DLG established a national union of cooperative associations (LAG), engaging in the farming supplies. Thus, DLG changed its Article of Associations (AoA) in 1988 which requires the exclusion of farmers which were members of LAG. Further, DLG prohibited its members from buying farming supplies from other parties beside DLG in order to set up efficient prices for its members. Afterwards, the members of LAG challenged the AoA of DLG by arguing that the AoA was to restrict competition, notably as to the purchasing prohibition.[239] In the adjudication proceedings, the Court of Justice found that the DLG Articles of Association do not restrict competition and thus are necessary to achieve the goals of DLG. Equally important, in this case, the Court of Justice applied the concept of ancillary restriction to review the DLG AoA. Thus, the "Anciallary Restraints" concept requires none of weighing of positive and negative effects to competition. The application of them was limited to the determination

237 L. Ritter and W.D. Braun, European Competition Law: A Practitioner Guide (3rd. Ed. Kluwer Law International, 2004) 635. See also Commission, Decision 26th July 1976 relating to a proceeding under Article 85 of the EEC Treaty (IV/28.996 – Reuter/BASF) (76/743/EEC).

238 Case C-250/92. Gøttrup-Klim e.a. Grovvareforeninger v Dansk Landbrugs Grovvareselskab AmbA. See O. Odudu, The Boundaries of EC Competition Law: The Scope of Article 81 (OUP, 2006), 18.

239 A. Ezrachi, EU COmpetion Law (4th Ed. Bloomsbury Publishing PLC, 2014), 109.

whether in a specific context of a main non-restrictive transaction, a particular restriction is necessary and proportional to achieve the aims of main agreement. Accordingly, the Court of Justice in its decision stated as follows:

> *"A cooperative purchasing association is a voluntary association of persons established in order to pursue common commercial objectives. The compatibility of the statutes of such an association with the community rules on competition cannot be assessed in the abstract. It will depend on the particular clauses in the statutes and the economic conditions prevailing on the markets concerned. In a market where product prices vary according to the volume of orders, the activities of cooperative purchasing associations may, depending on the size of their membership, constitute a significant counterweight to the contractual power of large producers and make way for more effective competition.*
> *Where some members of two competing cooperative purchasing associations belong to both at the same time, the result is to make each association less capable of pursuing its objectives for the benefit of the rest of its members, especially where the members concerned, as in the case in point, are themselves cooperative associations with a large number of individual members. It follows that such dual membership would jeopardize both the proper functioning of the cooperative and its contractual power in relation to producers. Prohibition of dual membership does not, therefore, necessarily constitute a restriction of competition within the meaning of Article 85(1) of the Treaty and may even have beneficial effects on competition.*
> *Nevertheless, a provision in the statutes of a cooperative purchasing association, restricting the opportunity for members to join other types of competing cooperatives and thus discouraging them from obtaining supplies elsewhere, may have adverse effects on competition. So, in order to escape the prohibition laid down in Article 85(1) of the Treaty, the restrictions imposed on members by the statutes of cooperative purchasing associations must be limited to what is necessary to ensure that the cooperative functions properly and maintains its contractual power in relation to producers."* (paras 30–35)

Eventually, the Court stipulated:

> *"The answer to the second set of questions referred by the national court must therefore be that a provision in the statutes of a cooperative purchasing association, forbidding its members to participate in other forms of organized cooperation which are in direct competition with it, is not caught by the prohibition in Article 85(1) of the Treaty, so long as the abovementioned provision is restricted to what is necessary to ensure that the cooperative functions properly and maintains its contractual power in relation to producers."*[240]

---

240 ibid.

Third, O2 (Germany) GmbH & Co OHG v Commission.[241]O2 Germany GmbH and T-Mobile Deutschland GmBH (T-Mobile), two operators of digitial mobile telecommunication networks, conclude agreement on an infrastructure sharing agreements in Germany for the 3rd generation (3G) mobile communications. Following the notifications of the agreement, the Commission found no grounds for actions with respect to the site sharing agreement between the parties but raised concerns as to the compatibility of the provisions relating to national roaming between network operators with Article 101 (1) TFEU. In its decision the Commission granted exemption to the provisions for limited periods under Article 101 (3) TFEU. O2 appealed the decision to the General Court, contesting among other things, the finding that the provisions relating to national roaming restricted competition between operators.[242]

The General Court in examining this case applied the concept of the necessity to establish a counterfactual. This means, in determining whether an agreement has restrictive effects to competition, it is necessary to analyse what the position or circumstance would be in the absence of an agreement. Thus, the court required the careful examination of the counterfactual; whereas the Commission failed to perform the counterfactual analysis. Previously, the Commission issued the decision stating that the agreement between O2 and T-Mobile in Germany had the effect of restricting competition. However, according to the General Court, the Commission was not able to demonstrate what the position of O2 or T-Mobile, would have been if the agreement was absent. Further, the Commission failed to prove whether the agreement between O2 and T-Mobile could have restriction to competition effects in the 3G telecommunication sector in Germany.[243] Subsequently, the General Court arguably provides:

> "In order to assess whether an agreement is compatible with the common market in the light of the prohibition laid down in Article 81(1) EC, it is necessary to examine the economic and legal context in which the agreement was concluded (Case 22/71 *Béguelin Import* [1971] ECR 949, paragraph 13), its object, its effects, and whether it affects intra-community trade taking into account in particular the economic context in which the

241 V. Korah, Cases and Materials on EC Competition Law (Hart Publishing, 2006), 66.
242 Ezrachi, *EU COmpetion Law*, 109.
243 Whish and Bailey (n 56).

undertakings operate, the products or services covered by the agreement, and the structure of the market concerned and the actual conditions in which it functions (Case C-399/93 *Oude Littikhuis and Others*[1995] ECR I-4515, paragraph 10)."

Moreover, in a case such as this, where it is accepted that the agreement does not have as its object a restriction of competition, the effects of the agreement should be considered and for it to be caught by the prohibition if? it is necessary to find that those factors are present which show that competition has in fact been prevented or restricted or distorted to an appreciable extent. The competition in question must be understood within the actual context in which it would occur in the absence of the agreement in dispute; the interference with competition may in particular be doubted if the agreement seems really necessary for the penetration of a new area by an undertaking (*Société minière et technique* at 249–250).

Such a method of analysis, regarding particular the taking into account of the competition situation that would exist in the absence of the agreement, does not amount to carry out an assessment of the pro- and anti-competitive effects of the agreement and thus to apply a "Rule of Reason", which the Community judicature has not deemed to have its place under Article 81(1) EC (Case C-235/92 P *Montecatini* v *Commission* [1999] ECR I 4539, paragraph 133; *M6 and Others* v*Commission*, paragraphs 72 to 77; and Case T-65/98 *Van den Bergh Foods* v *Commission* [2002] ECR II-4653, paragraphs 106 and 107).

In this respect, to submit, as the applicant does, that the Commission failed to carry out a full analysis by not examining what the competitive situation would have been in the absence of the agreement does not mean that an assessment of the positive and negative effects of the agreement from the point of view of competition must be carried out at the stage of Article 81(1) EC. Contrary to the defendant's interpretation of the applicant's arguments, the applicant relies only on the method of analysis required by settled case-law (paras. 66–70).[244]

Fourth, Wouters v Algemene Raad van de Nederlandse Orde van Advocaten[245]. In this case, the primary concern is the possibility to rely upon non-economic policy considerations by the undertakings to jus-

244 Ezrachi, (n 239) 98–100.
245 ibid.113–15.

tify an otherwise anti-competitive agreement, namely a consumer welfare. The case concerned a dispute between Mr. Wouters and the Dutch Bar on the basis that the Bar's regulations prohibited its members form practicing in full partnership with accountants. Mr. Wouters argued that the prohibition was incompatible with the Union rules on competition and freedom of establishment. The Dutch court referred the case to the ECJ, asking, whether a regulation which, in order to guarantee the independence and loyalty to the client of members of the Bar who provide legal assistance in conjunction with the members of other liberal professions, adopts universally bindingrules governing the formation of multi-disciplinary partnerships, has the object or effect of retrciting competition within the internal market in the sense Article 81 (1) EC.[246]

The primary concern of the Court of Justice (ECJ) was the compatibility of Article 4 of the Regulation of the Dutch Bar Association, prohibiting partnerships of lawyers and accountants, with the Article 81 EC. The ECJ had decided in this case, as follows: First, the regulation abovementioned was defined as decision of association of undertakings pursuant to the Article 81 (1) EC. Second, the ECJ mentioned that this regulation restricted competition because its provision prevented multi-discplinary partnerships which were able to provide a wider scope of services. Third, the ECJ deemed that the Regulation affected trades between the Member States, due to its application national-wide in the Netherlands. Nevertheless, the ECJ finally decided that the regulation mentionedabove had not infringed the Article 81 (1) EC, because it is justifiable under the public-interests' consideration. Thus, the regulation aimed to legitimate goals, notably 'relating to organization, qualifications, professional ethics, supervision and liability, in order to ensure that the ultimate consumers of legal services and the sound administration of justice are provided with the necessary guarantees in relation to the integrity and experience.' Further, the Court of Justice argued that the regulation is necessary in order to ascertain that the lawyer's members to the Bar Association perform independently and responsible to the clients' interests. In contrast, according to the ECJ, the accountant professions have no similar professional require-

246 ibid.

ments as the lawyers do, that is to say, the accountants have merely a supervisory role.[247]

Accordingly, the ECJ arguably rendered the following conclusions:

"The prohibition at issue in the main proceedings prohibits all contractual arrangements between members of the Bar and accountants which provide in any way for shared decision-making, profit-sharing or for the use of a common name, and this makes any form of effective partnership difficult.
By contrast, the Luxembourg Government claimed at the hearing that a prohibition of multi-disciplinary partnerships such as that laid down in the 1993 Regulation had a positive effect on competition. It pointed out that, by forbidding members of the Bar to enter into partnership with accountants, the national rules in issue in the main proceedings made it possible to prevent the legal services offered by members of the Bar from being concentrated in the hands of a few large international firms and, consequently, to maintain a large number of operators on the market.
It appears to the Court that the national legislation in issue in the main proceedings has an adverse effect on competition and may affect trade between Member States.
As regards the adverse effect on competition, the areas of expertise of members of the Bar and of accountants may be complementary. Since legal services, especially in business law, more and more frequently require recourse to an accountant, a multi-disciplinary partnership of members of the Bar and accountants would make it possible to offer a wider range of services, and indeed to propose new ones. Clients would thus be able to turn to a single structure for a large part of the services necessary for the organisation, management and operation of their business (the 'one-stop shop' advantage).
Furthermore, a multi-disciplinary partnership of members of the Bar and accountants would be capable of satisfying the needs created by the increasing interpenetration of national markets and the consequent necessity for continuous adaptation to national and international legislation.
Nor, finally, is it inconceivable that the economies of scale resulting from such multi-disciplinary partnerships might have positive effects on the cost of services.
A prohibition of multi-disciplinary partnerships of members of the Bar and accountants, such as that laid down in the 1993 Regulation, is therefore liable to limit production and technical development within the meaning of Article 85(1)(b) of the Treaty."[248]

Fifth, Metropole Television (M6) and others v Commission.[249]

247 Ezrachi (n 239) 113–115.
248 Ezrachi (n 239) 113–115.
249 ibid. 104–107. Case T 112/99. Metropole Television (M6) and others v Commission [2001] ECR II 2459.

In this prominent case, the European Court (General Court) maintained the dissenting opinion as regards the acceptability of the US based "Rule of Reason" approach in implementing the competition rules of Article 101 (1) TFEU. The court argued that "the existence of such a rule has not, as such, been confirmed by the Community Courts. Quite to the contrary, in various judgements the Court of Justice and the General Court have been at pains to indicate that the existence of the "Rule of reason" in (EU) Competition law is doubtful."Furthermore, the General Court decided in favour of the European approach as to weighing the pro-competitive and anti-competitive effects under the Article 101(1) TFEU in conjunctions with Article 101 (3) TFEU. Thus, the General Court indicated that the analysis of Article 101 (1) TFEU shall be divided into five phases. Firstly, the Commission (or other persons seeking to demonstrate the same) must establish that the agreement restricts competition (identifying anti-competitive aspects). Secondly, whenever this has been proved, the parties (or undertakings claiming the legal exemptions of Article 101 (3) TFEU) must prove that the agreement will achieve pro-competitive effect. Third, that the agreement will give consumers a fair share of benefits. Fifth, the agreement is indispensable to the attainment of benefits pursued. Fourth, there is no possibilitie as the elimination of competition due to the agreement.[250]

According to *Kaczorowska*, the European "Rule of Reason" approach entails two aspects. Firstly, the Commission shall determine at least what would be the state of competition, both of actuall and poetential competitions, in the relevant market if the agreement, with the alleged restrictions, is absent. This is known as "counterfactual standard" or "but for" analytical method. This analytical method requires a three-step analysis, which looks like this: Firstly, the Commission must establish a hypothetical degree of competition in the relevant market if the agreement was absent. Secondly, the Commission shall be able to show a degree of competition caused by the agreement. Thirdly, the Commission shall compare these two competition scenarios. If the degree of competition has been reduced thus an infringement of Article 101 (1) takes place. Put differently, the "counterfactual standard" re-

250 *Jones and Surfin, (n 46)* 218.

quires analysis of both the actual and potential competitions on the market. Further, this analytical method prerequisites "the specific factors or conditions that differ between the two must be identified and how these factors or conditions lead (or potentially will lead) to consumers' losses shall be explained by means of elaborative analysis. Secondly, the European approach, the Court is able to take into account non-economic considerations in assessing the agreement in question under the provision of Article 101 (1) TFEU, whereas this had been exemplified in the Wouters case.[251] Television Par Stellite (TPS) was set up as a partnership by 6 major active companies in the television sector. Its aim was to devise, develop and broadcast a range of television programmes, to French speaking television viewers in Europe against payment. The agreement forming the TPS partnership were not notified to the Commission in order to obtain negative clearance and/or exemption. In its decision, the Commission did not object to the creation of TPS. However, the Commission raised concerns with respect to the impact of non-competition, exclusivity and other clauses in the agreement and subsequently granted limited negative clearance and exemption.

With reference to the non-competition clause the Commission held that there were no grounds for action in respect of that clause for a period of three years. With regard to an exclusivity clause and the clause relating to special interest channels the Commission held that those provisions could benefit from an exemption under Article 101 (3) TFEU for a period of three years. Furthermore, the applicant challenged the Commission decision and the limited period for which the negative clearance and exemption were granted. Among other things, the applicants argued that the Commsiison failed to apply the "Rule of Reason" when considering the agreement under Article 101 (1) TFEU.

Afterwards, the GC issued the decisions as follows:

> *"Article 85 of the Treaty expressly provides, in its third paragraph, for the possibility of exempting agreements that restrict competition where they satisfy a number of conditions, in particular where they are indispensable to the attainment of certain objectives and do not afford undertakings the possibility of eliminating competition in respect of a substantial part of the products in question. It is only in the precise framework of that provision*

251 Ezrachi (n 239) 104–111.

that the pro and anti-competitive aspects of a restriction may be weighed (see, to that effect, Case 161/84 Pronuptia [1986] ECR 353, paragraph 24, and Case T-17/93 Matra Hachette v Commission[1994] ECR II-595, paragraph 48, and European Night Services and Others v Commission, cited in paragraph 34 above, paragraph 136). Article 85(3) of the Treaty would lose much of its effectiveness if such an examination had to be carried out already under Article 85(1) of the Treaty.

It is true that in a number of judgments the Court of Justice and the Court of First Instance have favoured a more flexible interpretation of the prohibition laid down in Article 85(1) of the Treaty (see, in particular, Société technique minière and Oude Luttikhuis and Others, cited in paragraph 70 above, Nungesser and Eisele vCommission and Coditel and Others, cited in paragraph 68 above, Pronuptia, cited in paragraph 74 above, and European Night Services and Others v Commission, cited in paragraph 34 above, as well as the judgment in Case C-250/92 DLG [1994] ECR I-5641, paragraphs 31 to 35).

Those judgments cannot, however, be interpreted as establishing the existence of a rule of reason in Community competition law. They are, rather, part of a broader trend in the case-law acording to which it is not necessary to hold, wholly abstractly and without drawing any distinction, that any agreement restricting the freedom of action of one or more of the parties is necessarily caught by the prohibition laid down in Article 85(1) of the Treaty. In assessing the applicability of Article 85(1) to an agreement, account should be taken of the actual conditions in which it functions, in particular the economic context in which the undertakings operate, the products or services covered by the agreement and the actual structure of the market concerned (see, in particular, European Night Services and Others v Commission, cited in paragraph 34 above, paragraph 136, Oude Luttikhuis, cited in paragraph 70 above, paragraph 10, and VGB and Others v Commission, cited in paragraph 70 above, paragraph 140, as well as the judgment in Case C-234/89 Delimitis [1991] ECR I-935, paragraph 31).

That interpretation, while observing the substantive scheme of Article 85 of the Treaty and, in particular, preserving the effectiveness of Article 85(3), makes it possible to prevent the prohibition in Article 85(1) from extending wholly abstractly and without distinction to all agreements whose effect is to restrict the freedom of action of one or more of the parties. It must, however, be emphasised that such an approach does not mean that it is necessary to weigh the pro- and anti-competitive effects of an agreement when determining whether the prohibition laid down in Article 85(1) of the Treaty applies.

In the light of the foregoing, it must be held that, contrary to the applicants' submission, in the contested decision the Commission correctly applied Article 85(1) of the Treaty to the exclusivity clause and the clause relating to the special-interest channels inasmuch as it was not obliged to weigh the pro- and anti-competitive aspects of those agreements outside the specific framework of Article 85(3) of the Treaty.

It did, however, assess the restrictive nature of those clauses in their economic and legal context in accordance with the case-law. Thus, it rightly found that the general-interest channels presented programmes that were attractive for subscribers to a pay-TV company and that the effect of the exclusivity clause was to deny TPS competitors' access to such programmes (points 102 to 107 of the contested decision). As regards the clause relating to the special-interest channels, the Commission found that it resulted in a limitation of the supply of such channels on that market for a period of 10 years (point 101 of the contested decision). (paras. 74–79)."[252]

2.2.2.3.1 Inter-States Clause

Article 101 (1) TFEU requires that the agreement between undertakings may affect the trade between the EU Member States, whereas this provision is applied also by Article 102 TFEU and thus serves to achieve a single market objective. This objective has been confirmed by the Court of Justice in the Hugin case, as follows:

> "*The interpretation and application of the condition relating to effects on trade between Member States contained in Article [101 and 102] of the Treaty must be based on the purpose of that condition which is to define, in the context of the laws governing competition, the boundary between the areas respectively covered by the Community law and the law of the Member States. Thus, Community law covers any agreement or any practice which is capable of constituting a threat to freedom of trade between Member States, in particular by partitioning the national markets or by affecting the structure of competition within the common market. On the other hand, conduct, the effects of which are confined to the territory of a single Member State, is governed by the national legal order.*"

Furthermore, in accordance with the subsidiary principle in the EU this provision requires a proportional division of responsibilities in the enforcement of the competition regime between the National Competition Authorities ("NCAs") of the EU Member States and the European Competition Network ("ECN") of the Commission together with the courts to ensure that the Competition Law Enforcement mechanism prescribed by Regulation 1/2003 is reliable and efficient. Furthermore, the national competition laws and NCAs play an active role, whenever there is an agreement which at first sight deemed to be pure-

252 Ezrachi, EU Competition Law (n 239) 104–111.

ly domestic but can affect the structure of competition within the EU internal market.[253]

Equally important, according to Säcker and Wolf as to inter-State clause:

> "Article 101 (1) TFEU still requires an objective predictable suitability for appreciable effect on trade between Member States. Suffice it if the measures in question due to the overall objective (legal and factual) is circumstances capable of directly or indirectly, actually or potentially affects trade between Member States in a manner which may be the attainment of a single market between States adversely. With this feature, the scope of EU competition law is set to extraterritorial operations simultaneously."[254]

2.3 Cartel Prohibition pursuant to the German Act against Restraints of Competition (Gesetz gegen Wettbewerbsbeschränkungen-GWB)

2.3.1 Objective, Systematic and Juridical Source

In a general sphere, the GWB 7th Amendment which tooknto force as of 7th July 2005 and thus be amended by the GWB 8th Amendment, and lately be amended by the 9th GWB in the year of 2017, aims to pursue the following principal objectives:[255] First, to protect the competition in the market, both the institution and the process. On the one hand, the internal competition, the economic freedom of business actors in the market shall be preserved by the competition law. On the other hand, the social welfare of the consumers and the public in general as well as a comprehensive equal consumer protection shall be attained by the functional competition law. Second, to ensure an undistorted competition within the EU internal market. In line with the goals of the Treaty on the Functioning of the European Union (TFEU), the provisions of GWB are devised to achieve not only the protection

253 Geradin, Farrar, Petit, EU Competition (n 33), 25–27. See also N. Khan and C. Kerse, EU Antitrust Procedure (Sweet and Maxwell, 2012) 17–21.

254 Säcker and Wolf (n 95) 297.

255 R. Bechtold, O. Otting, W. Bosch, *Kartellgesetz: Gesetz gegen Wettbewerbsbeschränkungen; Kommentar*
(6 Aufl., CH. Beck, 2010), 31-et.seq. cf. Klees 'Grundlagen' in W. Killian and B. Heussen, *Computerrechts-Handbuch (34. Ergz. CH Beck, 2018) R 20–21.*

of competition but also the integration of the domestic market into the internal market of the EU by eliminating the distortions to the competition gradually. Since the Treaty of Lisabon, this purpose was stipulated in the Protocol 27 of the TFEU.[256]

In order to effectively attain the abovementioned purposes, the German cartel law prescribed in the GWB employs three main legislative instruments:

Firstly, the cartel prohibition, whereas this provision aims to suppress or at least to regulate any illegal agreement between the undertakings to reduce or even to eliminate the internal competition in the relevant market through price cartel, quota cartel and market zoning cartel.[257]

Secondly, the prohibition against abuse of the dominant position by an undertaking in the market. This provision is indeed not to prohibit an undertaking with a dominant position in the market to utilise its economic advantages in the market, provided this measure is in accordance with competition law. However, this provision applies in the event the undertaking misuses the dominant position to discriminate other competitors in the relevant market.[258]

Thirdly, regulation over merger and acquisitions of the undertakings. This provision aims to examine whether a corporate action of two or more undertakings to perform merger and acquisition plan can reasonable cause the restriction of competition in the relevant market. Thus, in applying this provision the structural aspects of the market prior to the merger plan (*ex-ante*) and after the merger plan (*ex-post*), for instance the concentration degree of a certain relevant market shall be taken into account.[259]

However, according to *Schmidt*, the German cartel law stipulated in the GWB has been principally envisaged to approach three anti-competitive practices, which are: Firstly, the negotiation strategy (*Verhandlungsstrategie*), which means restraint of negotiation or resolution liberty related to one or several action parameter due to agreements,

256 Säcker, ‚Materialien zum deutschen und europäischen Wettbewerbsrecht' (Fachbereich Rechtswissenschaft, Freie Universität Berlin, Berlin, 2012) 20–23.

257 Lober (n 118) 7–12.

258 ibid 27–28.

259 ibid. 5–7.

decisions and/or concerted practices between independent undertakings, either through horizontal or vertical strategies.[260] Secondly, the impediment strategy (*Behinderungsstrategie*), which refers to *de facto* and written restraint of negotiation or resolution liberty related to one or several action parameters due to obstruction of competitors, by means of agreements or factual market behaviours.[261] Thirdly, the concentration strategy (*Konzentrationsstrategie*), which means a factual restraint of negotiation or resolution liberty related to one or several action parameters due to quantity diminution of competition policy makers either through external or an overly proportional internal undertakings.[262]

Accordingly, the German cartel law provisions embodied in the GWB could be outlined into six main parts, whereas each sections stipulates elaborative provisions systematically, as follows: First part, which prescribes the intrinsic substances of the cartel law and sets out in Section 1 until Section 47 GWB.[263] Second part, which contains the provisions as to the governmental bodies (*Kartellbehörden*) and the competition cooperation network with other respective institutions particularly the European competition law enforcement institutions (Section 48 until Section 53 GWB).[264] Third part, which regulates the proceedings of the cartel law enforcement and which encompasses administrative matters, punitive damages, penalty payment and the civil litigation. This Part has been stipulated in conjunction with the general provisions (Section 90 until Section 95 GWB).[265] Fourth part, which stipulates provisions on the public procurement law and which deals with the contracts of public procurement in the public domain (Section 97 until Section 129b GWB).[266] Fifth part, which stipulates the legislative scope of application of GWB.[267] Sixth part, which prescribes

260 I. Schmidt and J.Haucap, Wettbewerbspolitik und Kartellrecht: Eine interdisziplinäre Einführung Taschenbuch (*8.Auflage*, Lucius &Lucius, 2005) 120–122.
261 ibid.
262 ibid.
263 Lober in (n 103) 28–30.
264 ibid.
265 Krauß in *Langen and Bunte* (n 99) 61–63.
266 ibid.
267 ibid.

the transitional provisions and the final provisions of GWB.[268] Whereas as regards to the Unfair business competition, the German Act against Unfair Practies ("UWG") instead of GWB shall be competent to regulate the existence of fair practices within the competition in the market.[269]

Furthermore, according to *Loeweinheim et.al*, the provisions of German Cartel Law is an ordinary statutory law in the German legal system. This means, that the German Cartel Law is subject to the provisions of Article 74 para.1 (16) of *the Grundgesetz* concerning the Matters under concurrent legislative power.[270] Thereby, the local Competition Authority has limited legislative competencies in the cartel law sphere. Moreover, the procedural provisions according to the German Administrative Proceeding Law (*Verwaltungsverfahrensgesetz* – VwVfG), the Act on Regulatory Offences (*Ordnungswidrigkeitengesetz* – OWiG) and the Civil Proceedings Law (*Zivilprozessordnung-ZPO*) purport to serve the complementation of the German Cartel Law. In this respect, the intersections of the Cartel Law's provision with the German Energy and Telecommunication Acts exist. As regards to the German Public Procurement Law (*Vergaberecht*) the provisions of 127 of GWB are of essentially important.[271]

268 ibid.

269 *Thorsten et.al*, Einführung in das europäische und deutsche Kartellrecht. 22.

270 The provision of Article 74 para. 1 (16) of the German Basic Law (*Grundgesetz*) concerning mattes under concurrent legislative powers, reads as follows: "Concurrent legislative power shall extend to the following matters: "[…] prevention of the abuse of economic power."

271 The provision of § 127 (1)–(3) GWB prescribes.
"The Federal Government may, by an ordinance requiring the approval of the *Bundesrat*, issue rules:
1. to implement the thresholds of the public procurement directives of the European Union as applicable at that time;
2. to define award procedures to be observed by contracting entities engaged in the fields of drinking water, energy supply or transport, including the selection and examination of the undertakings and the tenders, the conclusion of the contract, as well as other provisions relating to the award procedure;
3. regarding the procedure to be observed in awarding public contracts that are relevant in terms of defence and security, regarding the selection and examination of the undertakings and the tenders, the exclusion from the award procedure, the conclusion of the contract, the discontinuation of the award procedure and other provisions relating to the award procedure, including any defence and security-

2.3.2 Cartel Prohibition Provisions

2.3.2.1 Introduction

The normative legal basis for the Cartel prohibitions is the German Act against Restriction of Competition (*Gesetz gegen Wettbewerbsbeschränkungen – GWB*), as amended by the 9th Amendment to the GWB entering into force in March 2017. The provisions of § (Sec.) 1 of GWB corresponds to the Article 101 (1) TFEU, which principally prohibits agreements or concerted practices between undertakings that have as their object or effect the prevention, restriction or distortion of the competition. These substantive cartel laws apply both to companies and individuals. Equally important, the provisions of Sec. 1 of GWB stipulate cartel prohibitions, that encompass, not only the horizontal agreements, such as fixing prices or trade terms and conditions; but also, the vertical agreements, like resale price maintenance (RPM). Eventually, the provisions of Sec. 1 GWB will not apply to the competition restrictions in the agricultural or in the water supply sectors as well as to RPM in the magazines and newspaper sector. Hence, illegal cartel practices outside the German jurisdiction are subject to the prohibition rules of the GWB, if they had appreciable anticompetitive effects in Germany.[272]

Originally, the provision of Sec. 1 GWB prohibits mainly the horizontal agreement. However, since the 7th Amendment of the GWB in 2005 the prohibition rule of Sec. 1 GWB applies to the vertical agreement as well.[273] Accordingly, the provisions of Sec. 2 para. 2 GWB in conjunctions to the Vertical Block Exemption Regulation will apply in the pro-

related requirements as regards secrecy, general rules on the protection of confidentiality, the security of supply as well as specific rules on the award of sub-contracts;" Act against Restraints of Competition in the version published on 26 June 2013 (Bundesgesetzblatt (Federal Law Gazette) I, 2013, p. 1750, 3245), as last amended by Article 1 of the law of 1 June 2017 (Federal Law Gazette I, p. 1416) ‹http://www.gesetze-im-internet.de/englisch_gwb/englisch_gwb.html#p1118› accessed on 31th October 2018.

272 Bechtold and Siebert, '*Germany-Cartels and Leniency 2015* in the International Comparative Legal Guides, 2015' ‹. http://www.iclg.co.uk,› accessed on 8 October 2015.

273 Säcker in F.J. Säcker, et.al. (eds.), Deutsches *Wettbewerbsrecht* (Band 2). Münchener Kommentar europäisches und deutsches Wettbewerbsrecht (Kartellrecht): Kartellrecht, Missbrauchs- und Fusionskontrolle (CH Beck, 2015), 720–734

and anti-competitive weighing analysis of the vertical agreement. *Per definitionem,* the horizontal agreements 'are those concluded between undertakings operating at the same level of production or distribution. These agreements may reduce competition when they involve price fixing, sharing of markets or other restrictions on business operations. They may also reduce competition when they involve softer forms of cooperation which increase the transparency in the market and thus reduce uncertainty concerning the competitors' conduct. Accordingly, they may at times yield substantial efficiencies and economic benefits, allowing companies to cope better with changing market realities, when they deal, for example, with research and development, production, purchasing, commercialisation, standardisation and environmental matters'.[274] Under the German Cartel laws, the horizontal agreements can manifest in following agreements: (1) price cartel, (2) allocation of customers and territory, (3) agreements on distribution and production and (4) exchange of commercially sensitive information.[275]

With regard to the horizontal agreement, the prohibition rule of Sec. 1 GWB applies both to formal agreements between undertakings and to decisions of undertakings including concerted practices that have the object or effect of preventing, restraining or distorting competitions. Consequently, the agreements which infringed the prohibition of Sec. 1 GWB are null and void under the German Civil Code under the provision of Sec. 134 BGB.[276] However, the other provisions of the GWB provide further certain exemptions towards the cartel prohibition of Sec.1 GWB. In contrast to the legal exemptions of the 7th Amendment of GWB, the 8th Amendment of GWB regulates merely two categories of legal exemptions as stipulated in the provisions of Sec.Sec. 2 and 3 GWB, notably concerning the exempted cartel agreements and small or medium sized enterprises cartels.[277]

274 Ezrachi, EU Competition (n 239) 137–40.

275 Säcker (n 273) 14–17.

276 Article 134 BGB concerning Statutory prohibition reads:
"A legal transaction that violates a statutory prohibition is void, unless the statute leads to a different conclusion."
The German Civil Code (Bürgerliches Gesetzbuch) ‹https://www.gesetze-im-internet.de/englisch_bgb/index.html› accessed on 19 October 2018.

277 *Bundesministerium der Justiz und für Verbraucherschutz* (n 271), the provisions of § 2 and § 3 GWB.

As regards the horizontal agreements, according to the *Bundeskartellamt*, the effective enforcement of cartel prohibition pursuant to the provision of Sec. 1 GWB is of significantly importance because cartel agreements cause significant economic losses. For example, average cartel agreements lead to prices which are 25 per cent higher than the normal market prices. This experience could be shown in the cement cartel case before the Düsseldorf Higher Regional Court (OLG-Düsseldorf), which was successfully uncovered and thus prosecuted by the *Bundeskartellamt*. In this cartel infringement case, the *Bundeskartellamt* and the court used the economic evidences by appointing an economic expert to determine the price effect of long-standing illegal cartels in the cement market in Germany.[278]

Furthermore, in the enforcement framework of German Cartel law towards the horizontal and vertical agreements in accordance with the EU Competition Law, according to Säcker, have caused the abolishment of specific and elaborated exemptions under the previous provisions of GWB.[279] However, these abolishments reduced the legal certainties for the undertakings. Thereby, the prevailing legal exemptions according to the provision of Sec. 2 para.1 GWB have been complemented by the EU Block Exemptions Regulations, which are: First, the Regulation Number 1217/2010 on Research and Development Cooperation.[280] Second, the Regulation Number 1218/2010 on Specialization Agreement.[281] Third, the Regulation Number 316/2014 concerning the application of Article

278 The Federal Cartel Office (*Bundeskartellamt*) 'Effective Cartel Prosecution, Benefits for Economy and Consumers' http://www.bundeskartellamt.de/SharedDocs/Publikation/EN/Brosch%C3%BCren/Brochure%20-%20Effective%20cartel%20prosecution.pdf, accessed 19th October 2015, 13.

279 Säcker in F. J. Säcker et.al (n 273) 31–34.

280 Commission, The Regulation (EU) No. 1217/2010 on the application of Article 101(3) of the Treaty on the Functioning of the European Union to certain categories of research and development agreements (14 December 2010). ‹http://eur-lex.europa.eu/legal-content/EN/TXT/?uri=CELEX%3A32010R1217,› accessed on 19th October 2015.

281 Commission, The Regulation (EU) No 1218/2010 of 14th December 2010 on the application of Article 101(3) of the Treaty on the Functioning of the European Union to certain categories of specialisation agreements, OJ L 335, 18.12.2010. ‹http://eur-lex.europa.eu/legal-content/EN/TXT/?uri=URISERV:cc0013›, accessed on 19th October 2015.

101 (3) TFEU Technology Transfer Agreements (TTBER).[282] Fourth, the specific regulations for transportation and insurances sectors.[283] By virtue of the Sec. 2 para. 2 of GWB, the EU Block Exemptions rules are applicable to analysis of the vertical agreements in Germany. Moreover, the legal exemptions pursuant to the Sec. 2 para. 1 of GWB have limited scope of application, because of the prior implementation of exemptionary rules under the Horizontal Block Exemption Regulations.[284]

Previously, the provision of German Cartel Law recognized certain legal exemptions, to compensate small-medium companies for structural disadvantages towards large corporations. These statutory exemptions encompass agreements stipulating:[285] First, standards and types cartels; whereas the agreements and decisions in question regulating the uniform application of standard of types only.[286] Second, condition cartels; whereas the agreements and decisions whose subject matter is the uniform application of business and trade's terms and conditions, such as delivery, payments, cash discounts as long as these agreements correlate not to prices or prices'elements.[287] Third, specialisation cartels; whereby the substances of agreements or decisions concern mainly to the rationalisation of economic activities through specialisation, provided the restraints of competition do not lead to the creation or strengthening of a dominant position.[288] Fourth, rationalisation cartels, in which the agreements and decisions serving to rationalise economic activities have no specialisation elements. Further, these agreements/decisions should be suitable means to increase efficiencies or productivities of the undertakings substantially as well as to increase the consumers' satisfaction.[289] Fifth, structural crisis cartels. In the event sales volumes significantly

282 Commission, The Regulation (EU) No 316/2014 of 21 March 2014 on the application of Article 101(3) of the Treaty on the Functioning of the European Union to categories of technology transfer agreements Text with EEA relevance OJ L 93, 28.3.201.

283 Säcker in F.J. Säcker (n 273) 31–32.

284 ibid.

285 Harris, 'Competition Law outside the US' (ABA Section of Antitrust Law, Washington DC, 2001) 24–5.

286 ibid. 24–27.

287 ibid.

288 ibid.

289 ibid.

reduce due to structural changes of demands, the agreement and decisions in question may adopt structural cartels comprising production, manufacturing and processing. However, these agreements/decisions must take into account competition circumstances in the related sector.[290] Sixth, cartels of small-medium sized enterprise; whereas the agreements or decisions have the subject matter to rationalise economic activities by means of cooperation forms between the small-medium enterprises without jeopardising competitions in the relevant market. Further, these agreements/decisions must aim to improve the competitiveness of the small-medium enterprises.[291] Seventh, joint purchase agreements; whereby the agreements/decisions have purpose to improve the competitiveness of small-medium sized enterprises as well as they do not substantially restrict competitions on the market.[292]

Nowadays, according to *Loewenheim et.al*, the elaborative legal exemptions abovementioned have been abolished and thus replaced by the provision of Sec. 3 GWB concerning cartels of small or medium-sized enterprises (SMEs). Regardless the legal uncertainties due to application of the legal exemptions, the administrative and judicial practices of the German Cartel law have been consistently taking into considerations the abovementioned legal exemptions in their benefit-risk asssements processes in accordance with the provision of Sec. 2 para.1 GWB.[293]

Furthermore, as regards to the vertical agreements, the Commission provides that vertical agreements are "agreements or concerted practices entered into between two or more undertakings each of which operates, for the purposes of the agreement or the concerted practice, at a different level of the production or distribution chain, and relating to the conditions under which the parties may purchase, sell or resell certain goods or services". Accordingly, as regards to the enforcement framework of vertical agreements, the provision of Sec. 2 para.2 in conjunctions with Sec. 1 GWB shall dominantly apply, instead of the provision of Sec. 1

290 ibid.
291 ibid.
292 ibid.
293 U. Loewenheim, K. M. Meessen A. Riesenkampff, *Kartellrecht: Kommentar* (C. H. Beck München, 2009), R. 44–45.

para. 1 GWB.[294] Logically, this is because of the prior implementation of the safe-harbour rule as well as the existence of hard-core restriction analysis under the EU Vertical Block Exemption Regulation. Thereby, the individual legal exemptions stipulated in the provision of Sec. 2 para. 1 GWB will apply, provided the vertical agreement does not fulfill the rules abovementioned. Consequently, the parties to vertical agreements must prove the four cumulative requirements: First, the contribution to improve the production or distribution of goods or contribute to promoting technical or economic progress. Second, the consumers must receive a fair share of the resulting benefits. Third, vertical restrictions must be indispensable to the attainment of these objectives. Fourth, the vertical agreement must not afford the parties the possibility of eliminating competition in respect of a substantial part of the products in question. In the case an examination of individual exemptions, the undertakings claiming the benefit of Article 101(3) TFEU shall bear the burden of proving that the necessary conditions are fulfilled.[295]

Equally important as regards to the provisions of German Cartel law, according to Bechtold et.al, the German Government has decided a so-called "far-reaching legislative harmonisation with the cartel prohibitions and the legal exemptions with the European Competition Law", even for cases which do not affect trades between the Member States. Thereby, the sentences of Sec. 1 and Sec. 2 para.1 GWB have been mirroring the provisions of Articles 101 (1) and 101 (3) TFEU. Further, the provision of Sec. 2 para. 2 GWB renders that both of the Council and Commission Regulations concerning the application of Article 101 (3) to certain agreements, decisions of association of undertakings, and con-

294 According to Ezrachi:
„Vertical agreements are agreements entered into between undertakings operating at different levels of production or distribution chains. These agreements differ in their potential anticompetitive effects form horizontal ones. Whereas the latter (the horizontal agreement) may eliminate competition between competing undertakings, the former ones (the vertical agreement) concerns the relationships between upstream operators and downstream distributor or dealers. As a result, vertical agreements often generate positive effects and would raise concerns predominantly when there is some degree of market power at the upstream and/or downstream levels.", Ezrachi, EU Comeptition Law, 137.

295 Commission, The Regulation (EU) No 330/2010 of 20 April 2010 on the application of Article 101(3) of the Treaty on the Functioning of the European Union to categories of vertical agreements and concerted practices OJ L 102, 23.4.2010.

certed practices (Block Exemption Regulations) are applicable mutatis mutandis to the Sec. 2 para. 2 GWB. Moreover, these Block Exemption Regulations will apply to the agreements, decisions of associations of undertakings and concerted practices which have no appreciable effects to trades between the Member States.[296]

With regard to the statutory interpretation, according to *Berg and Mudrony*[297], the Legislations Backgrounds of the GWB, the German Cartel laws are oriented towards the provisions of EU Competition laws.[298] Accordingly, the *Bundesgerichtshof* stated that the interpretation and application of the cartel prohibition provisions in the GWB shall refer to the EU Competition laws, such as the European Court case-laws and the Commission legislations.[299]

2.3.2.2 Statutory Elements of the Cartel Prohibition

Pursuant to the provision of Sec. 1 GWB concerning Prohibition of Agreements Restricting Competition:

> *"Agreements between undertakings, decisions by associations of undertakings and concerted practices, which have as their object or effect the prevention, restriction or distortion of competition, shall be prohibited."*

Accordingly, this cartel prohibition provision envisages the elements of the statutory act, which are as follows:

2.3.2.2.1 Undertakings

With regard to the concept of undertakings, the GWB embraces the functional approach in correspondence to the cartels prohibition of Article 101 (1) TFEU, whereas they include "every entity engaged in an economic activity, regardless of the legal status of the entity or the way in

296 Nordemann, GWB § 2 Freigestellte Vereinbarungen' in U. Loewenheim et.al, *Kartellrecht* (3. Aufl. CH Beck 2016) 22–27.

297 Berg and Mäsch (eds.) Deutsches und Europäisches Kartellrecht: Kommentar (2. Auflage 2018, *Luctherhand 2015)24–27.*

298 ibid.

299 ibid.

which it is financed".[300] Hence, the term undertakings encompasses not only private individual business persons, but also freelancers, craftsmen and small-scale traders. However, as regards to private households have been dilemmatic, whether they are subject to the meaning of undertakings, for example whenever they act both as consumer and purchaser of products consecutively. However, the *Bundesgerichtshof* (BGH) had cleared that private households are undertakings, whenever they are continuously and methodically seeking to reap financially or economically profits.[301] In the German cartel law, as regards to the concept of undertaking, two main principles prevail, which are: the *Selbständigkeitpostulat* and undertaking with public interest trait pursuant to Sec. 130 para.1 GWB. Under the first principle, the ability of an entity to act independently and autonomically in the market becomes the main parameter to determine whether an entity is an undertaking under prohibition of Sec.1 GWB.[302] Accordingly, as to the public service interest entity, the provision of Sec. 130 GWB reads:[303]

> ***Sec. 130***
> ***Public Undertakings, Scope of application***
>
> *This Act shall apply also to undertakings which are entirely or partly in public ownership or are managed or operated by public authorities. The provisions of the Parts I to III of this Act shall not be applicable to the German Central Bank [Deutsche Bundesbank] and to the Reconstruction Loan Corporation [Kreditanstalt für Wiederaufbau].*

300 The European Court of Justice in the case of Höfner and Elser v. Macrotron (1991) "An economic activity means undertakings perform as follows:
1) it provides for the supply of goods or services on the market;
2) it could – in principle – be carried on by a private undertaking to make profit;
3) no matter if the body is not in fact profit making/is not set up for an economic purpose."
cf. Herrmann, in Säcker, et.al, Europäisches Wettbewerbsrecht (n 13), 324–327.

301 Lange and Pries (n 40) 77–78.

302 Säcker in Säcker (n 273), 17.

303 Lange and Pries (n 40) 78.

2.3.2.2.2 Agreements, Decision of Association of Undertakings, and Concerted Practice

2.3.2.2.2.1 Agreements

2.3.2.2.2.2 General Meaning

The term 'agreements' pursuant to the German cartel law had been defined as 'every concurrence of wills between undertakings regarding their occurrence or market behaviour on the relevant market'. Accordingly, the forms, subject matter and intention of agreements are irrelevant. However, the term 'agreements' would not cover a unilateral measure by undertakings.[304] Furthermore, as regards to the prime characteristic of the 'agreements', the German Court in the case of *Kontaktlinsen* has stipulated that 'an existence of subjective element of concurrence of wills between the participating parties'. Accordingly, whenever 'agreements' prohibited by the GWB took place, even though the participating undertakings carry out or not implement the 'agreements', they are still subject to sanctions stipulated by the GWB.[305]With regard to the unilateral conduct of undertakings, they could be subject to prohibited 'agreements' in the German cartel law, provided the unilateral conduct had been subsequently followed by other undertakings either through explicit or implicit (tacit) approvals in the relevant market.[306] Nevertheless, in the case of *Kontaktlinsen* these implicit or tacit approvals must be successfully proved before the Courts.[307] Furthermore, in the German cartel law, as regards to term 'agreements', several types could be identified, as follows: First, the legally, enforceable contractual agreement under the law of obligations pursuant to Sec. 145.ff of the Civil Code (*Burgerliches Gesetzbuch* – BGB)[308] Second, the contractual agreement in which actionability for legal action is being exceptionally excluded by the parties.[309] Third, a so-called 'gentlemens' agreement', in which there was none of legally

304 Krauß, in *Langen and Bunte* (n 99) 84–87.
305 Berg and Mudrony, in Berg and Mäsch (n 297) 33–35.
306 ibid.
307 ibid.
308 Schmidt and Haucap (n 260) 268–269.
309 Compare with the *Naturalobligation* agreement pursuant to Sec. 762 of the BGB. ibid.

binding obligation, but there are socially-morally obligations or business ones between parties to perform consensus therein.[310]

2.3.2.2.2.3 Model contract

A model contract, drafted unilaterally could be subject to prohibited 'agreements' provided there were subsequent individual agreements which precipitate the realisation or performance of a contract between undertakings.[311]

2.3.2.2.2.4 General Terms and Conditions

The term 'agreements' encompasses also a so-called 'standard or general terms and conditions', which had been previously formulated by an undertaking. Arguably, it could be largely possible that in a conclusion of contracts, the parties come to agreements, which were deviating from these terms and conditions.[312]

Additionally, whenever the stronger party, in terms of economic or business power, unilaterally force other parties to come to agreements and thus were not able to resist due to economic or business dependency, these could be subject to the prohibited agreements.[313]

2.3.2.2.2.5 Circular Letter

Initially a circular letter is not subject to concept of business 'agreements'due to its unilateral formulated characteristic. However, circular letters could be shifted to the prohibited agreements whenever there were mandates to subsequently concretise the performance of continuous agreements between undertaings. Accordingly, a circular letter could be considered as an integral and initial part of sequences toward the prohibited 'agreements'.[314]

310 ibid.
311 Krauß, in *Langen and Bunte (n 99)* 84–87.
312 ibid.
313 ibid.
314 ibid.

2.3.2.2.2.6 Hub and Spoke Cartels ("Sternvertrag")

Nowadays, according to *Odudu*, the hub and spoke agreements constitute one of the most interesting and challenging competition law questions, whereas undertakings could receive information about their competitors, not directly from their competing undertakings but via the common trading partner. In general, according to Krebs and Becker, the hub and spoke (cartels) agreement refers to practices which have the object or effect to collude on prices and other competition parameters which involves triangle relationships between suppliers, wholesale traders and retail traders. Thereby, there is no collusion on the horizontal level, however the collusive agreement between the undertakings take place indirectly through suppliers. A primary trait of the huband spoke cartels is the disclosure of terms of trade or contracts through suppliers for the other traders, for example the Most Favoured Customer (MFC) clause, information exchanges on prices and advertising strategy. However, there is a difficulty to prove this cartels scenario because this involves a lawfully independent vertical agreement. Under the EU Competition law framework, the hub and spoke cartels are prohibited by the provisions of Article 101 (1) TFEU and Sec. 1 GWB.[315]

Moreover, according to *Sahuguet and Walckiers*, in the practice of EU competition law, the Competition Authorities have primarily acknowledged and thus regulated the horizontal and vertical agreements. However, de facto, there has been an increase of cartels agreement involving combination of horizontal and vertical concerted practices, that is to say, the agreements are horizontal in nature, but involve competitors and their suppliers (or retailers), which are known as the hub and spoke (or A-B-C) agreements. In this type of agreement, the spokes are undertaking operating in the same horizontal level, whereas these undertakings exchange information indirectly through the hub, operating at the different level of business activities.[316]

315 P Krebs, M. Lexikon des Wettbewerbsrechts: Kartellrecht und Lauterkeitsrecht (1. Auflage, CH Beck, 2015) 139.

316 Sahuguet and Walckiers, 'Hub-and-Spoke Conspiracies: The Vertical Expression of a Horizontal Desire?' (Journal of European Competition Law & Practice, 2014), ‹http://papers.ssrn.com/sol3/papers.cfm?abstract_id=2502147, accessed on 19 October.2015, 15.

On the one hand, as regards to backgrounds of the hub and spoke collusion, Odudu assumes that three factors play a key role. First, achieving market coordination between undertakings in order to: (a) identify a mutually beneficial strategy, (b) detect deviation from that strategy, (c) apply pressure to prevent deviation from the mutually beneficial strategy.[317] Second, achieving market related information disclosure enabling the undertakings to achieve a first element of a coordinated market response-identifying a mutually beneficial strategy.[318] Third, achieving a second element of a coordinated market response by means of detecting deviation from the mutually beneficial strategy between undertakings.[319]

On the other hand, the European Court has a different opinion in viewing the hub and spoke agreements, whereas in the *Suiker Unie* case, the court argued that information exchange abovementioned could lead to a breach of competition law:

> "the concept inherent in the provisions of the Treaty relating to competition [requires] that each economic operator must determine independently the policy, which it intends to adopt on the common market including the choice of persons and undertakings to which he makes offers or sells."[320]

Accordingly, the Court of Justice further explained that:

> "*any direct or indirect contact between such operators*, the object or effect whereof is either to influence the conduct on the market of an actual or potential competitor or to disclose to such a competitor the course of conduct which they themselves have decided to adopt or to contemplate adopting on the market."[321]

Whereas the hub and spoke agreements have been the EU and National Competition Authorities' concern, there has been obscure explanation as to under which conditions this primarily vertical construct modifies to a horizontal collusive agreement.[322] Equally important, a

317 Odudu, 'Hub and Spoke Collusion', in Lianos and Geradin, "*Handbook on European Competition Law: Substantive Aspects*", (Edward Elgar Publishing: 2015) 242.

318 ibid. 242–243.

319 ibid., 242–245.

320 ibid. 242–243.

321 ibid., 242–245.

322 Hainz and Benditz, Indirekter Informationsaustausch in Hub and Spoke-Konstellationen – Der Teufel steckt im Detail' EuZW 2012, 686.

main problematical matter for the Competition Authorities is how they are able to reveal the existing horizontal agreement, colluded through a vertical agreement, as well as to disclose collusive surrounding circles of the Spokes.[323]

Furthermore, from an analytical framework of the Commission Guidelines on Horizontal cooperation agreement concerning the hub and spoke agreement:

> "data (market information) can be shared indirectly through a common agency (for example, a trade association) or a third party such as a market research organization or through the companies' suppliers or retailers."[324]

However, the indirect information exchanges could lead to the restrictions of competition and thus infringing the cartels prohibition, whereas the Commission is of the opinion:

> "However, the exchange of market information may also lead to restrictions of competition in particular situations where it is liable to enable undertakings to be aware of market strategies of their competitors. The competitive outcome of information exchange depends on the characteristics of the market in which it takes place (such as concentration, transparency, stability, symmetry, complexity etc.) as well as on the type of information that is exchanged, which may modify the relevant market environment towards one liable to coordination."[325]

> "Moreover, communication of information among competitors may constitute an agreement, a concerted practice, or a decision by an association of undertakings with the object of fixing, in particular, prices or quantities. Those types of information exchanges will normally be considered and fined as cartels. Information exchange may also facilitate the implementation of a cartel by enabling companies to monitor whether the participants comply with the agreed terms. Those types of exchanges of information will be assessed as part of the cartel."[326]

Besides, the Commission indicates in the Guidelines on Vertical restraints that the hub and spoke agreement could constitute an infringement against the Competition law:

> "[…] agreements may facilitate collusion between distributors when the same supplier serves as a category captain for all or most of the compet-

---

323 ibid.
324 the Commission, the Horizontal Agreement Guidelines, para 53.
325 The Commission, the Horizontal Agreement Guidelines, para 53.
326 The Commission, the Horizontal Agreement Guidelines, para 59.

> ing distributors on a market and provides these distributors with a common point of reference for their marketing decisions."[327]

Accordingly, the Commission outlines as follows:

> "[...] may also facilitate collusion between suppliers through increased opportunities to exchange via retailers sensitive market information, such as for instance information related to future pricing, promotional plans or advertising campaigns."[328]

Noteworthy to discuss, that as regards to the hub and spoke agreement, in the US Antitrust law judicatures in the early case of *Interstate Circuit, Inc. v United States (1939)*, the US Supreme Court held:

> "[...] that owners of two theatre chains in which copyrighted films were first exhibited engaged into illegal agreements in several US cities through identical contracts with eight copyright owners. The contracts for the first run of a movie imposed that distributors would license subsequent runs of films under a number of restrictive conditions, including a minimum admission price. The Court held that theatre chains and distributors entered into anticompetitive agreements, which implied that the costs of Interstate's rivals were raised."[329]

Subsequently, the US Court of Appeals 7th Circuit, in the case of *Toys 'R Us, Inc. v FTC* (2000), in its decision as to the hub and spoke collusion committed by a dominant seller of toy and its suppliers argued:

> "that Toys 'R Us entered into a series of illegal agreements with its suppliers, to acquire exclusivity on the products from manufacturers in order to limit supply to its competitors. Although the infringement was based on vertical agreements, the conspiracy was essentially a horizontal conspiracy, where suppliers made their participation contingent upon the agreement of their competitors to the same terms."[330]

Most importantly, with regard to the concept of hub and spoke agreement, the Decision of the British Court of Appeal provided a guiding principle:

> "The proposition which, in our view, falls squarely within the *Bayer* judgment in the ECJ and which is sufficient to dispose of the point in the present appeal can be stated in more restricted terms: *if (i) retailer A dis-*

327 The Commission, the Horizontal Agreement Guidelines, para 211.

328 The Commission, the Horizontal Agreement Guidelines, para 212.

329 Odudu in Lianos and Gerardine (n 317), 242–243. See *United States Supreme Court, Interstate Circuit, Inc. v United States, 306 US 208 (1939) [Interstate Circuit].*

330 ibid. 242–243. See United States Court of Appeals, Toys 'R Us, Inc. v Federal Trade Commission, No. 98–4107 (2000) [Toys' R Us].

> *closes to supplier B its future pricing intentions in circumstances where A may be taken to intend that B will make use of that information to influence market conditions by passing that information to other retailers (of whom C is or may be one), (ii) B does, in fact, pass that information to C in circumstances where C may be taken to know the circumstances in which the information was disclosed by A to B and (iii) C does, in fact, use the information in determining its own future pricing intentions,* then A, B and C are all to be regarded as parties to a concerted practice having as its object the restriction or distortion of competition. The case is all the stronger where there is reciprocity: in the sense that C discloses to supplier B its future pricing intentions in circumstances where C may be taken to intend that B will make use of that information to influence market conditions by passing that information to (among others) A, and B does so."[331]

In the judiciary practice in Germany as regards to the hub and spoke agreement, the *Bundesgerichtshof* (BGH) in the Ruling of 19th June 1975 argued that, as long as the horizontal corporate relationship exists between undertakings, which s a dominant joint venture company, thus a concerted practice or collusion exists.[332] However, in other cases the case-laws and the administrative practices indicate a high importance of the indirect evidences to prove cartels violation. Meanwhile, the *Oberlandsgerichtshof* (OLG) Düsseldorf in the Decision concerning hub and spoke agreement dated 12th June 1990 asserted that to be qualified as hub and spoke agreements, the main purpose of vertical agreement in question rests not in the horizontal agreement. Put differently, the objectives stipulated in the vertical agreements could not be achieved without the horizontal concerted practice existed in advance.[333]

Also, the *Bundeskartellamt* (German Federal Cartel Office-FCO) indicates in the Guidance Letter year of 2010 on approach to distinguish legal RRP (recommended resale price) and illegal RPM (Resale Price Maintenance) stipulates that the following practices by undertakings, considered independently, do not restrain competition but may trigger risks, in particular if they accompany generally-prohibited measures, which are: (a) (re-)addressing resale prices during follow-up

331 Odudu in Lianos and Gerardine (n 317), 242–245. See also *Argos Ltd. and Littlewoods Ltd. v Office of Fair Trading (OFT); JJB Sports Plc v OFT [2006] EWCA Civ. 1318, para. 141.*

332 Hainz and Benditz (n 322) 686.

333 ibid.

contacts, to the extent that the indications given to distributors or retailers go beyond explanations for the original resale price and product positioning strategy; (b) *systematic price monitoring in cooperation with distributors or retailers*; (c) compilation of price comparison lists or related sensible information in order to disclose them to other retailers; (d) providing calculation or pricing manuals or guidelines to distributors or retailers, and (e) exchanging information on, or complaining about, resale prices observed in the market or involving retailers in monitoring resale prices. Likewise, the *Bundeskartellamt* emphasises that those practices, in addition to vertical price fixing, have indirect horizontal effects as well, as they may lead to a "hubandspoke" collusion between undertakings, notably retailers and distributors. Accordingly, the *Bundeskartellamt* explains that the following practices are generally illegal: (a) disclosure by producers to distributors or retailers of conditions or agreements with, or sensible pricing information from competing distributors or retailers; (b) most-favoured treatment clauses aiming at a coordinated retail price level; (c) coordinating assortments, marketing strategies, or sales campaigns, whenever these have the object or indirect effects to prices coordination and other conditions.[334]

As has been noted, the proper analysis of hub and spoke agreements requires a two-tier legal analysis. Firstly, the relationships between the undertaking generating information (undertaking A) and third-party agent (undertaking B). Secondly, the relationships between the undertaking receiving information (undertaking C) and third-party agent (undertaking B).

Accordingly, pertaining the first relationships, namely between spoke A and hub B, there are three constitutive elements to be considered. First, subjective element of infringement of undertaking A. This means undertaking A must know or is supposed to know about the information dissemination which purport to or could lead to a collusive agreement. According to the Court of Justice, as regards to this subjective element in the *Commission v Anic Partecipazioni*:

334 Odudu, Hub and Spoke Collusion (n 317) 242–49. See also Costin, 'Information Exchange among Undertakings in EU Competition Law' (MBL Thesis, Geneva, July 2011) 17.

> "On this question the Court must observe, first of all, that, given the nature of the infringements in question and the nature and degree of severity of the ensuing penalties, responsibility for committing those infringements is personal in nature."[335]

Further, the Court of Justice asserted:

> "[...] In doing this, the Commission must establish in particular all the facts enabling the conclusion to be drawn that an *undertaking participated in such an infringement and that it was responsible for the various aspects of it.*"[336]

> "When, as in the present case, the infringement involves anti-competitive agreements and concerted practices, the Commission must, in particular, *show that the undertaking intended to contribute by its own conduct to the common objectives pursued by all the participants and that it was aware of the actual conduct planned or put into effect by other undertakings in pursuit of the same objectives or that it could reasonably have foreseen it and that it was prepared to take the risk.*"[337]

Second, indications or circumstantial evidence. Whereas it has been undeniably difficult to prove the hub and spoke collusion, the Court of Justice explained:

> "[...] within the prohibition of that article [Article 101 (1) TFEU] a form of coordination between undertakings which, without having reached the stage where an agreement properly so-called has been concluded, knowingly substitutes practical cooperation between them for the risks of competition."[338]

Accordingly, one could observe the indications of hub and spoke collusion whenever the supplying undertakings exchange the information to the retailers with a view to influence the resale prices of products. For example, whenever the retailing undertaking receives any market information, without previously being asked from the supplier; whereas the supplier aims to unilaterally influence market behaviours of the retailing undertakings. Furthermore, from the circumstance's aspect, private meetings and partially private meetings of the undertakings'

335 Case C-49/92 P. Commission of the European Communities v Anic Partecipazioni SpA. Judgment of the Court (Sixth Chamber) (n 113).

336 Odudu, Hub and Spoke Collusion (n 317) 242–249. See Anic Partecipazioni (n 113) para. 86.

337 Odudu, Hub and Spoke Collusio (n 317) 242–249

338 ibid.242–249?

representatives, such as managers or directors, constitute valuable indications of hub and spoke collusion.

Third, the undertaking A's legitimate interest to remit information. As regards to the legitimate interest, the Court of Appeal in the JJB Sports PLC v OFT case, stipulated:

> "As regards A, the position might in our view be different only if it could be shown that retailer A revealed its future pricing intentions to its supplier B for some legitimate purpose not related in any way to competition, and could not reasonably have foreseen that such information would be used by B in a way capable of affecting market conditions. It seems to us that such disclosure by a retailer to a supplier will rarely be legitimate, otherwise resale price maintenance could be reintroduced by the back door."

Equally important, concerning the relationships between the undertaking receiving information (undertaking C) and third-party agent (undertaking B), there are two factors deserving legal considerations. Firstly, the tacit consent between the undertakings. This refers to the existence of a collusive agreement between the undertakings, whereas the Court of Justice in the *T-Mobile Netherlands BV and Others* argued thereof:

> "As a preliminary point, the definitions of 'agreement', 'decisions by associations of undertakings' and 'concerted practice' are intended, from a subjective point of view, to catch forms of collusion having the same nature which are distinguishable from each other only by their intensity and the forms in which they manifest themselves."[339]

Further, the Court of Justice asserted as to the existence of collusive agreement.

> "For one thing, subject to proof to the contrary, which it is for the economic operators concerned to adduce, there must be a presumption that the undertakings participating in concerting arrangements and remaining active on the market take account of the information exchanged with their competitors when determining their conduct on that market, particularly when they concert together on a regular basis over a long period, as was the case here, according to the findings of the Court of First Instance."[340]

---

339 Odudu, Hub and Spoke Collusion (n 317) 242–249. Case C-8/08, T-Mobile Netherlands BV and Others v Raad van bestuur van de Nederlandse Mededingingsautoriteit, para. 23 [T-Mobile].

340 Odudu, Hub and Spoke Collusion (n 317) 242–249.

Nonetheless, in the hub and spoke relationship, the undertakings receiving the market information would have not known the sources of information and thus could not rely upon the validity and accuracy of market information received. Accordingly, the exchanged information would have insignificant effects and thus could not direct or influence themarket behaviours. Moreover, as regards to vagueness of existence of collusive agreement in such relationship, the Court of Appeal commented:

> "We have set out the relevant passages in the judgments of the CFI and the ECJ in *Bayer v Commission* (Joined Cases C-2/01 and C-3/01) [2000] ECR II-3383 earlier in this judgment, at paragraphs [23] to [26]. We draw attention, in the present context, to the observation, at paragraph 102 in the judgment of the Court of Justice, that "it is necessary that the manifestation of the wish of one of the contracting parties to achieve an anti-competitive goal constitute an invitation to the other party, whether express or implied, to fulfil that goal jointly". We have expressed our view, in paragraph [91], when discussing the Tribunal' s judgment on liability in the Football Shirts. Appeal, that the Tribunal may have gone too far in paragraph 659 of that judgment, with its suggestion that if a retailer (A) privately discloses to a supplier (B) its future pricing intentions "in circumstance s where it is reasonably foreseeable that B might make use of that information to influence market conditions" and B then passes that pricing information on to a competing retailer (C), that is sufficient basis for concluding, even if A did not in fact foresee what was reasonably foreseeable or C did not appreciate the basis on which A had provided the information, that A, B and C are all to be regarded as parties to a concerted practice having as its object or effect the prevention, restriction or distortion of competition. But it is not necessary to decide whether a proposition in such wide terms could be supported in order to determine the appeal in Toys and Games any more than it is for the other appeal."[341]

Secondly, the causality of market behavior. Whereas to establish a causal link between the exchanged information and the undertakings' market conducts, the Court of Justice in the Anic Partecipazioni SpA v Commission of the European Communities explained that:

> *"For one thing, subject to proof to the contrary, which it is for the economic operators concerned to adduce, there must be a presumption that the undertakings participating in concerting arrangements and remaining active on the market take account of the information exchanged with their competitors when determining their conduct on that market, particularly when they*

341 ibid.

concert together on a regular basis over a long period, as was the case here, according to the findings of the Court of First Instance."

"*[...] although the concept of a concerted practice presupposes conduct of the participating undertakings on the market, it does not necessarily imply that conduct should produce the concrete effect of restricting, preventing or distorting competition.*"

Arguably, the causality element would not exist, if the undertakings receiving the information believed its reliability and accuracy. Additionally, the content of information is irrelevant, thus the undertakings would not also alter or follow its market conducts due to the information.[342]

Equally important, with respect to the legal remedy, it is argued that the employment of provisions of Sec. 1 GWB and Article 101 (1) TFEU in conjunction with Sec. 21 (2) GWB could serve as an appropriate legal remedy to catch and thus to eradicate the hub and spoke collusion. Certainly, provisions of Sec. 21 (2) GWB do not prerequisite the tacit consent of the undertakings or transmission or dissemination of market information (indirect information exchange) between the undertakings.

Accordingly, provisions of Sec. 21 (2) GWB concerning Prohibition of Boycott and Other Restrictive Practices stipulate:

"Undertakings and associations of undertakings shall not threaten or cause disadvantages, or promise or grant advantages, to other undertakings to induce them to engage in conduct which, under this Act or according to a decision issued by the cartel authority pursuant to this Act, shall not be made the subject matter of a contractual commitment."[343]

2.3.2.2.2.7 Decision of Association of Undertakings

In the German cartel law, the inclusion of the decisions of association of undertakings, principally to counter the collusive practices which took place not between undertakings, but through third parties and thus are not subject to the prohibition of 'agreements' aforementioned. Furthermore, according to the *Bundesgerichtshof* (BGH), the decisions of association of undertakings are to be existent whenever the associa-

342 Hainz and Benditz, „Indirekter Informationsaustausch (n 322) 686–688.

343 Odudu, Hub and Spoke (n 317) 242–49. cf. Hainz and Benditz, „Indirekter Informationsaustausch (n 322) 686–690.

tion of undertakings consciously express their will to coordinate the conducts or business behaviours of their members into a specific and targeted market collectively.[344] Subsequently, according to the German courts, the recommendation of the association of undertakings is subject to the prohibition of Sec. 1 GWB, provided the recommendation either had been legally bound to the articles of association (*Satzung*) or had been collectively accepted and thus followed by all members of the association.[345]

In a further analysis, the decisions of association of undertakings subject to the prohibition of Sec.1 of the GWB, could also be a result of decision of another organ of the association, for example a managing committee. According to the *Bundesgerichtshof* (BGH), whether the decisions had been composed either based on internal rules of association or prevailing commercial national rules, is irrelevant.[346] Moreover, the association of undertakings must be responsible for every action or conduct of its organs, regardless, either the decisions had been made in accordance or in contrary to decision-making procedures of the association. In the following precedent, the *Bundesgerichtshof* has decided that a public service entity could generate the prohibited decisions through other representative organs.[347]

2.3.2.2.2.8 Concerted Practices

In accordance with the principle ofthe European competition law, the concept of concerted practices of the German Cartel law been interpreted parallel with the term concerted practice stipulated in Article 101 (1) TFEU. However, in the jurisprudence of German cartel law, concerted practices take place whenever the actual or potential competing undertakings establish indirect or direct mutual contacts in order to influence the market behaviour of competitors or to bring other undertakings' market considerations into parallel action on the relevant market.[348] Indeed, the concerted practice could occur indirectly

344 Berg and Mudrony, in Berg and Mäsch (n 297) 34.
345 Krauß, in *Langen and Bunte*, Kommentar (n 99) 92–95.
346 ibid.
347 ibid.
348 Berg and Mudrony in (n 297).

through a third party.[349] Moreover, according to the *Bundesgerichtshof* (BGH), concerted practices exist whenever undertakings adjust their market behaviours and thus dependent on other undertakings without exercising obligatory measures to other competing undertakings in the relevant market.[350]

Furthermore, the German Court requires, as regards to concerted practices, an existence of the 'causal impacts or effects of the practices to the relevant market'.[351] However, whenever the undertakings' parallel behaviours had been a result of an oligopolistic interdependence on the relevant market, thus they could not be considered as concerted practices.[352]

Accordingly, concerted practices could largely result of initial exchanges of information between undertakings through formal or informal meetings. Although the undertakings only participate in the meetings, they could be subject to cartel law sanctions, provided they accept transmission of the sensitive information concerning future market behaviours.[353]

2.3.2.2 Restriction of Competition

According to *Lange and Pries*, 'the agreements, decisions of association of undertakings and concerted practices have to as their effects and/or objects to distort, restrict and to circumvent competitions on the market'.[354] Indeed, this statutory element corresponds to the provisions of Article 101 (1) TFEU.

Further, as regards to the restriction of competition concept, the jurisprudence of *Bundesgerichtshof* provided that whenever an undertaking has an economic freedom *de jure*, the undertaking could not ex-

349 ibid.

350 Thus, through the exogenous indications the jurisprudence of BGH distinguishes between the conscious parallelism and the concerted practice, whereby in the concerted practice not only the exchanges of future market information but also the concrete efforts for collusion take place between the undertakings. Krauß, in *Langen and Bunte*, Kommentar (n 99) 74–77.

351 ibid.

352 ibid.

353 Lober in Schulte and Just, *Kartellrecht (n 103)*.29–31.

354 Lange and Pries, Einführung (n 40) 79–81.

ercise the economic freedom because its connection with several business disadvantages *de facto* (BGH Decision 22.4.1980). Moreover, *Bundeskartellamt* and *Bundesgerichtshof* are to apply both of economic and legal examinations to determine the existence of restriction of competition. In addition, the methods of interpretation of Article 101 (1) TFEU particularly regarding the hardcore practices catalogue, such as price agreement, discount cartel, quota cartel, zoning cartel, and bundling deal practice must be abided in the application of Sec. 1 GWB.[355]

Consequently, in the German cartel law enforcement, the Bundeskartellamt and German courts have to provide profoundly convincing evidences, notably indirect evidences, which are able to establish the conclusion that the parallel behaviours are the result of concerted practices, not the other factors in the relevant market.[356]

2.3.2.3 Appreciability (Substantial Effect)

With regard to appreciability (substantial effect), *Lange and Pries* are of the opinion that 'as the unwritten elements of offence, the German cartels prohibition of the GWB prerequisite that the competition restrictions' impacts to the market conditions are appreciable or rigorous.' Accordingly, the appreciable or rigorous impacts to the market conditions are to be existent, whenever the restrictions to competitions have minimally 'a measurable and predictable implications or effects to the relevant market. Conversely, there would be none of appreciable or rigorous impacts, whenever there were only unessential or insignificant encroachments to the business actors or participants within the relevant market.[357]

Furthermore, with regard to the 'appreciability' or 'substantial effects' the *Bundeskartellamt* possesses discretionary capacity as to *De Minimis* rule, whereas the *Bundeskartellamt Notice No.18/2007 on the Non-Prosecution of Cooperation Agreements of Minor Importance* ("De Minimis Notice"), notably Sec.1 stipulates, as follows:[358]

---

355 Lange and Pries, Einführung (n 40) 79–81.

356 Lober in Schulte and Just, Kartellrecht (n 103) 29–31.

357 Lange and Pries (n 40) 79–81.

358 The Federal Cartel Office *(Bundeskartellamt)* Bekanntmachung Nr. 18/2007 des Bundeskartellamtes über die Nichtverfolgung von Kooperationsabreden mit

"The Bundeskartellamt can oblige undertakings or associations of undertakings to put an end to agreements, decisions and concerted practices which have as their object or effect the prevention, restriction or distortion of competition. It is within the Bundeskartellamt's discretion to initiate proceedings on the suspicion of such an infringement. The de minimis Notice lays down the discretionary principles establishing when proceedings are generally not initiated (on the grounds of insignificance)."

2.3.3 Restriction to the Cartel Prohibition

2.3.3.1 Immanence Theory (*Immanenztheorie*)

In the German Cartel law, the immanence thought (*Immanenztheorie*) has been applied to confine the application of cartel prohibition provision under Sec. 1 GWB. According to *Emmerich*, the immanence doctrine refers to the assumption that certain restrictive agreements or clauses may fall outside the cartel prohibition rule if the agrements or clauses in question are deemed inherent or inevitably essential for the operation of a larger agreement, which is neutral and pro-competitive in nature. A primary example are the non-competition clauses in corporate divestiture and partnership agreements. (*Unternehmensveraußerung und Gesellschaftsvertrag*).[359] According to *Säcker*, the immanence thought refers principally to a concept that in certain qualified agreements or contracts immanent restrictions are permissioned and could be justified.[360]Although different in concepts, this doctrine, closely corresponds to the "Rule of Reason" approach, that has been embodied in the German Cartel Law.[361]

Equally important, the previous provisions of GWB had incorporated this immanence theory in the provions of Sec. 2 and Sec. 3 as well as the provisions of Sec. 28, Sec. 30 and Sec. 31. Likewise, in the regional sphere, the provisions of the EU Merger Regulation Number 139/2004 as well as the Commission Notice on restrictions are directly related and

geringer wettbewerbsbeschränken der Bedeutung („Bagatellbekanntmachung"), 13. März 2007. cf. Lange and Pries (n 40) 79–81.

359 Emmerich in Immenga and Mestäcker, Kartellrecht (n 44) 260–268.

360 Säcker in Säcker,et.al, (n 273) 20–21.

361 ibid. 18–20.

necessary to concentrations (the Notice on Ancillary Restraint).[362] Moreover, the cartel prohibition rule of Sec. 1 GWB does not apply to: First, joint ventures for a limited period and limited purpose (Arbeitsgemeinschaften).[363] Second, non-competition clauses between general partners of a partnership, managing directors of close corporations, controlling shareholders of a close corporation, the sellers and buyers of a business (usually for a limited period of time upon to five years), parties to lease agreements whereas the landlord promise not to lease space in same area to competing enterprises, and settlementto resolve dispute between copetitiors.[364] Third, intragroup restrictions of competition, such as restrictive agreement between a parent company and its controlled subsidaray office.[365] Forth, the arbitration awards.[366] Fifth, the environmental protection measures.[367]

2.3.3.2 Exempted Sectors of the Application of Sec. 1 GWB

The cartel prohibitions in the Sec. 1 GWB is principally applied to whole economic sectors. However, in Germany, there are several economic sectors which are not subject to this principle.[368] First, the agriculture sector. According to the Sec. 28 para. 2 GWB the cartels prohibition of Sec. 1 GWB is not applicable to agricultural cultivators and producers, for example for the collective use of institutions for storehouse. However, there are prohibitions on horizontal price fixing and boycott of products in terms of the Sec. 21 (1) GWB. Further, the provision of Sec. 28 GWB relates to this sector exemption. Additionally, the Sec. 40 Forestry Act (*Bundeswaldgesetz*) regulates on the forestry-sector. Second, the price fixing in newspaper, magazines and books pursuant to the Sec. 30 GWB. Third, the press-sector (*Presse Grosso*), whereas according to the GWB the pure press wholesaler's agreements are exempted from the cartels prohibition. This provision correlates to

362 ibid.
363 ibid. 18–19.
364 ibid.
365 ibid.
366 ibid.
367 ibid.
368 Von Dietze and Janssen, *Kartellrecht in der Anwaltlichen Praxis*, 5. Auflage, (CH Beck, München, 2015), p. 23–5.

the Article 106 (2) TFEU. Fourth, the telecommunication and postal services. According to *the Telekommunikationsgesetz (TKG)* and *the Postgesetz* specific rules apply to these two vital sectors. Due to the amendment of10th February 2012, *the Bundesnetzagentur*, which is responsible for regulating these two sectors, is obliged to cooperate with the *Bundeskartellamt*. Fifth, the transportation. This sector subject to particular rules is stipulated in the para. 3b. of the P*ersonenbeförderungsgesetz* and Sec. 12 para. 7 and Sec. 14 of the *Allgemeines Eisenbahngesetz* (AEG). Sixth, the energy. The provisions of the *Energiewirtschaftsgesetz* (EnWG) shall particulary apply in this sector. For the regulatory over this sector, the Bundesnetzagentur, shall be responsible for the unbundling of concentrations and ensuring fair access to electricity and gas networks. Furthermore, the Bundeskartellamt is responsible for the application of the Article 101 and 102 TFEU concerning electricity trade, supplies and acquisition of electricity and conglomerations in this sector. Seventh, the water supplies sector. Prior to the 8th Amendement of GWB, the provisions of Sec. 131 (6) GWB and Sec.Sec. 103, 103a, 105 GWB. Furthermore, the cartels exemptions are enumerated and regulated in the provisions of Sec. 31 (1) until (3) of GWB. Eighth, state insurance (*Gesetzliche Krankenversicherung*). Whereas the state insurance companies operate under the principle of solidarity (Solidaritätsprinzip), thus their conducts are not subject to cartels prohibition of Sec. 1 GWB. However, the Bundeskartellamt initiated a procedure against the new legal health insurance company, which had announced to charge a single monthly additional amount. In September 2011, the *Hessian Social Court* (*Hessisches Sozialgericht*) ruled that statutory health insurance companies do not constitute a company within the meaning of German and EU antitrust law. Further, Sec. 69 SGB V also regulates on the relations of health insurance to the performance achievement.[369]

369 P. von Dietze and H. Janssen, *Kartellrecht in der anwaltlichen Praxis* (5. Aufl. CH. Beck, 2015), 23–25.

2.3.4 Legal Exemptions Provisions pursuant to the provision of Sec. 1 GWB

First, the legal exemption principle, whose provisions designed similar to the Article 101 para 3 TFEU and which stipulates as follows:[370]

> ***Section 2***
> ***Exempted Agreements***
>
> *a. Agreements between undertakings, decisions by associations of undetakings or concerted practices, which allowing consumers a fair share of the resulting benefits contribute to improving the production or distribution of goods or to promoting technical or economic progress, which do not:*
> *1. impose on the undertakings concerned restrictions which are not indispensable to the attainment of these objectives, or*
> *2. afford such undertakings the possibility of eliminating competition in respect of a substantial part of the products in question shall be exempted from the prohibition of Section 1.*
> *(2) For the application of para.1, Regulation of the Council or the Commission of the European Community on the application of Article 81 (3) of the Treaty Establishing the European Community (today Article 101 (3) of the TFEU) to certain categories of agreements, decisions by associations of undertakings and concerted practices (block exemption regulations), shall apply mutatis mutandis. This shall also apply where the agreements, decisions and practices mentioned therein are inappropriate to affect trade between Member States of the European Community.*

According to Säcker, the legal exemptions in the Sec. 2 GWB reflect the provisions of Article 101 (3) and its derivate regulations concerning exception from the cartel prohibitions in Article 101 (1) in conjucitons with the Sec. 1 GWB. The previous exemptions stipulated in the provisions of Sec. 2 until Sec. 7 GWB (7th Novelle) are deemed merely as the "numerous clausus". Moreover, the application of exemptions is subject either through application or through registration to the *Kartellbehörde*. Furthermore, the analytical approach of the legal exemptions follows the EU Competition Law, whereas the agreements in question are, analysed under the Block Exemption Regulations, which provides the Safe Harbor thereof. Subsequently, if the agreements in question do not fall under the EU Block Exemptions Regualitons, thus the agreements in question are subject to individual exemption analy-

370 Säcker, in Säcker, et.al (n 273) 31–39.

sis under the cumulative requrirements of Article 101 (3) TFEU. Equally important, the provision of Sec. 2 para. 2 GWB stipulates that the EU Block Exemption Regulations shall apply mutatis mutandis to the application of the Sec. 1 GWB. This includes as well the agreements in question, which have no appreciable effect on trades between the Member States. Accordingly, the Block Exemptions Reuglautis aim to provide legal certanties to the parties in doing the self-assemetn of the legal exemptions under the Articlc 101 (3) TFEU in conjuctions to the Sec. 2 (1) GWB. According to Säcker, the provisions stipulated in the Block Exemptoins Regulations do not have only a declarative character, but also a constitutive one.[371]

Equally important, in the German Cartel law framework, the following Block Exemption Regulations shall apply. With regard to the horizontal agreements: First, the Regulation Number 1217/2010 on the Application of Article 101 (3) TFEU to the Research and Development Agrements. Second, the Regulation Number 1218/2010 on the Application of Article 101 (3) TFEU to the Spezialization Agreements.[372] Furthermore, as regards to the vertical agreements:

First, the Regulation Number 330/2010 on the Application of Article 101 (3) TFEU to the Group of Agremeents and Concerted Practices. Second, the Regulation Number 461/2010 on the Application of Article 101 (3) TFEU to the Group of Agreements and concerted practices in the transportation sector (*Kraftsfahrzeugsektor-Kfz*). Third, the Regulation Number 267/2010 on the Application of Article 101 (3) TFEU to the Group of Agreement and concerted practices in the insurances sector. Fourth, the Regulation Number 246/2009 in conjunctions with the Regulation Number 906/2009 on the application of Article 101 (3) TFEU to the Group of Agreements and Concerted Practices in the sea-transportation sector. Fifth, the Regulation Number 169/2009 on the application of Article 101 (3) TFEU to the Group of Agreements and Concerted Practices in Railway, Roads and Domestic transportation sectors.

Sixth, the Regulation Number 1184/2006 in conjunctions with the Regulation Number 1234/2007 on the application of Article 101 (3)

371 ibid.

372 ibid.9.–10.

TFEU to the Group of Agreements and Concerted Practices in Agricultural Production sectors.[373]

Furthermore, if the Block Exemption Regulations abovementioned did not apply to the agreements in question, accordingly the individual legal exemptions which are regulated in the Article 101 (3) TFEU shall apply. Principally there are four cumulative requirements of the legal exemptions. First, the achievement of benefits, which means achieving an improvement in the production or distribution of goods or the promotion of technical or economic progress. Second, through the agreement, consumers must receive a fair share of the resulting benefits. Third, the restrictions in the agreement must be indispensable to the attainment of these objectives. Fourth, the agreement in question must not afford the parties the possibility of eliminating competition in respect of a substantial part of the products in question.[374]

Second, the cartel exemption for the Small and Medium Companies Enterprises (SMCs) which is the distinct characteristic to the EU Competition laws, whereas Sec.3 GWB stipulates as follows:

> ***Cartels of Small or Medium-Sized Enterprises***
> *Agreements between competing undertakings and decision by associations of undertakings, whose subject matter is the rationalization of economic activities through cooperation among enterprises, fulfill the conditions of Sec.2(1) if:*
> *competition on the market is not significant affected thereby, and*
> *2. the agreement or the decision serves to improve the competitiveness of small or medium-sized enterprises.*[375]

373 Säcker, in Säcker, *et.al* (n 273) 31–39.

374 ibid.

375 *Gesetz gegen Wettbewerbsbeschränkungen*, http://www.gesetze-im-internet.de/gwb/, accessed on 2nd January 2019

2.4 Cartels Prohibition pursuant to the Indonesia Competition Law Number 5/1999

2.4.1 Historical Background[376]

According to *Maarif*, a former KPPU's Commissioner, two factors had prompted the adoption of the Law Number 5/1999: First, the massive economic crises took place in the Asian region in 1998, which led to

376 Pursuant to Article 33 of the 1945 Indonesian Constitution, the economic democracy serves as founding principle of the Indonesian free market-economy. This principle refers to the notion that every participant within economic life refuses to impair its competitors and other economic or business actors through detrimental practices. Further, every participant within the economic life must behave fairly, that is to say, that every participant is prohibited from obtaining profits through anti-competitive practices and jeopardising other competitors through abusive practices on the market. Embarking from German competition scholars' school of thoughts, the Indonesia Competition Law Number 5/1999 serves four main functions: First, Economic Freedom Function. The term 'economic freedom' is not definitively stipulated in the Indonesia 1945 Constitution. However, Article 27 (2) of the Indonesia 1945 Constitution stipulates "Every citizen shall have the right to work and to earn a humane livelihood." On the other hand, Article 2 (1) of the German Grundgesetz provides that "Jeder hat das Recht auf die freie Entfaltung seiner Persönlichkeit, soweit er nicht die Rechte anderer verletzt und nicht gegen die verfassungsmäßige Ordnung oder das Sittengesetz verstößt." In general sense, economic freedom refers to conditions, whereby every participant in the economic life is able to effectively generate and to market their goods and/or service products as well as to determine prices of the products on the market. Conceptually, economic freedom can be distinguished into material freedom and a formal one. Moreover, Hoppman differentiates between economic freedom in the exchange process and economic freedom in the parallel process. Second, the supervising function. Through supervising function, the state is responsible to ensure compliances with the juridical framework requirements, that is to say, the state supervises inbuilt institutions and behavioural instruments of all economic participants. In this process, the state regulates conflicts of interests between suppliers and consumers, whereas in the supervision of exchange processes, whereas the state supervises. Third, the navigating function, which consists of (1) coordination and conformation functions "The coordination function of competition is that the demand is coordinated with the production, so that goods and services are offered in the type, quality and quantity that meet the demand." "The adjustment function of competition then ensures that production adjusts to the changing needs over time." "An optimal coordination is made possible by a functioning price system, which in effective competition with important information about the scarcity level of the respective goods supplies." "The coordination and adjustment function of competi-

massive reforms in Indonesia. Second, the public summons concerning reforms of public election, anti-corruption and fair competitions.

---

tion therefore ensures that providers seek to demand what meets their expectations, to cease production as possible to the needs of customers and adapt them so that production is demand compliant. Products that do not attract the interest of users, cannot be sold, further ensures the competition for an acceleration of the coordination process." (2) The allocation function. "The allocation function is connected to the co-ordination and adjustment function, but also has constant effects. Under the pressure of competition entrepreneurs are always looking for the minimum cost combination of factors and services used by relatively inexpensive substitutieren relatively expensive factor services if this is technically possible." "But the competition can bring the things to be constantly to strive for the economic use of its factors of production in order to reduce their costs (so-called optimal factor allocation)." "But also the adjustment process ensures the competition for optimal allokaton factors of production, by deducting from a shrinking by a change in the structure of demand market production factors and puts them in the production of goods of the growing market." (3) The stimulus and selecting functions. "Competition keeps the rival at a market side market participants to constantly ask their worth, because generally preferred are those with the higher performance of the other side of the market. Efficiency on the supply side means: Production requires compliant products, minimum production cost, adequate adjustment flexibility and enforcement of the technical developments ride through an appropriate innovation and imitation ability and willingness to." "With the incentive function, the selection function of competition is directly linked. The selection in the competitive process based on the criterion of economic performance." "The incentive and download function supports the one hand effectively the economic policy the primary objective of "increasing the Wohlfahrt" and the socio-political primary objective "social market economy" and the socio-political overall objective "justice" because always the weaker supply and demand are out of the market, thereby creating social problems." There is something wrong in this quote. Fourth, the apportionment function. "The distribution function of competition is closely related to the allocation function. In the economical production process, the performance of the production factors labor, environment and productive capital are transformed to use acquis." The ideas that the functional distribution of income is fair, is characterised by different, even divergent principles. A distinction, the principle of the power of justice: (a) The income to the market value of the performance requirements for which they are paid; (b.) the principle of equality: for the same services and the same income is to be paid; (c.) the principle of responsiveness: Who because of its social and economic situation has an objectively higher demand (eg a large family), should also receive a higher income; (d.) the principle of sacrifice justice: Who needs to bring in a higher power among victims than others (eg because of a physical disability), must not be disadvantaged." cf. Silalahi. Fusionskontrolle in Indonesien gemäß Regierungsverordnung Nr. 27/1998 (n 1), 33–55. See also S.Y. Wahyuningtyas, *Unilateral Restraints in the Retail Business: A Comparative Study on Competition Law in Germany and Indonesia* (Stämpfli Publisher Bern 2011) 74–77.

During this period, there were widespread public concerns as to pervasive monopolistic and cartel practices mixed with corruptions in Indonesia.[377]

Moreover, *Sirait* explains that the Indonesian Competition Law Number 5/1999 is part of the structural adjustment programme, which was prescribed by the Letter of Intent (LoI), signed between the International Monetary Fund (IMF) and the Government of Indonesia (GoI), on 15th January 1998.[378] In a further analysis, according to *Säcker and Lohse,* the LoI prescribed not only the urgency of a competition legislation, but also economic reforms in Indonesia. With regard to the term 'economic reforms', the United Nations Conference on Trade and Development (UNCTAD) provides the following explanations:

> "A common aspiration underlying economic reforms efforts has been that the reduction of governments' direct involvement or intervention in economic activity would, by providing enterprises with more freedom and stronger incentives, stimulate entrepreneurial activity, business efficiency, productive investment and economic growth as well as enhancing consumer welfare through increased quantitiy and quality of goods at lower prices. Throughout the economy, therefore, productive resources would be allocated in an efficient and flexible manner through thorough the decentralized decisions of market operators rather than by government direction or thorogh rent-seeking activity, and economic growth could improve. However, such aspirations are likely to be fully realized only if enterprises are acting under the spur of competition, so that the consumer dissatisfaction is able to provide a market sanction against poor performance. Thus, the strengthening of competition (in conjunction with measures to stimulate consumer awareness) is a key element in ensuring the success of economics reforms."[379]

Prior to the promulgation of the Law Number 5/1999, provisions prohibiting anti competitive and unfair business practices had been frag-

377 United Nations Conference on Trade and Development (UNCTAD), 'Voluntary Peer Review on Competition Law: Indonesia' (UNCTAD Secretariat, 2009) 2.

378 N. N. Sirait, 'Overview of the Indonesia Competition Law Law Number 5/1999 concerning Prohibition of Monopolistic Practices and Unfair Business Competition' (Presentation Paper, Law School University Sumatra Utara, 2015) ‹http://www.jftc.go.jp/eacpf/05/AOTS/indonesia_ningrum.pdf›, accessed 12th May 2015.

379 *Säcker and Lohse* in in F.J. Säcker, et.al (eds.), *Law Concerning Prohibition of Monopolistic Practices and Unfair Business Competition (n 3)* 118–119.

mentarily stipulated in the Indonesia Civil Code (KUH Perdata or *Burgerlijk Wetboek-BW*) and Indonesia Criminal Code (KUHP).[380]

2.4.2 Key Provisions of the Law Number 5/1999

2.4.3 Objective of the Law Number 5/1999

Pursuant to Article 3 of the Law Number 5/1999, the Law seeks to attain the following objectives:

1. to guard the public interest and increase national economic efficiency as one method to increase the people's welfare;
2. to realise a conducive business environment by regulating fair competition so that equal opportunity to do business between small scale, medium scale and large scale;
3. businesses can be guaranteed;
4. to prevent monopolistic practices and unfair competition caused by business actors, and
5. to achieve effectiveness and efficiency in doing business.[381]

Based upon Article 2 in conjunction with Article 3 of the Law Number 5/1999, the Law Number 5/1999 aims to achieve the following objectives: First, the economic democracy inspired by Article 33 of the 1945 Indonesia Constitution. Thus, this constitutional notion is opposite to the: (1) free fight liberalism; (2) etatism system; (3) system of economic concentration by centralised monopolisation and conglomerates. Second,the achievement and maintenance of following targets: (1) a system of free, fair competition characterised by equal opportunities

380 Article 52 (1) of the Indonesia Competition Law Number 5/1999 explains that the relevant provisions in the Indonesia Civil Code and Indonesia Criminal Code remain prevail, provided these provisions are in line with the Indonesia Competition Law Number 5/1999. See the Law Number 5 Year 1999 concerning the Prohibition of Monopolistic Practices and Unfair Business Competition. ‹http://eng.kppu.go.id/newkppu/wp-content/uploads/2016/11/law_5_year_1999_.pdf› accessed 28 December 2018.

381 Article 3 of the Law Number 5 Year 1999 concerning the Prohibition of Monopolistic Practices and Unfair Business Competition. ‹http://eng.kppu.go.id/newkppu/wp-content/uploads/2016/11/law_5_year_1999_.pdf› accessed 28 September 2019.

for all business actors; (2) a maximum economic freedoms of movement for all business actors; (3) the prosperity for the people and an efficient economic system; (4) optimal providences of goods and services for consumers leading to consumers welfare; (5) driving technological progress leading to the competitiveness of business actors. Third, the attainment of the free and fair competition, whereas UNCTAD defines this goal, as follows:

> "Exposure to competition is both the most effective way of promoting the ability of firms and industries to perform effectively on national and international markets (including by lowering the costs of intermediate inputs for final producers) and of ensuring that enterprises pass on to the consumer at least some of the benefits obtained from efficiency improvements."[382]

2.4.4 Main Concepts in the Law Number 5/1999

2.4.4.1 Per-se Illegal and Rule of Reason Approach

According to Sirait, as regards to Rule of Reason approach:

> "The rule of reason is a legal approach by competition authorities or courts under which an attempt is made to evaluate the procompetitive features of a restrictive business practice versus its potential anticompetitive effects in order to decide whether or not the practice should be prohibited. Some market restrictions, which prima facie give rise to competition issues, may on further examination be found to have valid efficiency-enhancing benefits."[383]

---

382 *Säcker and Lohse* in F.J. Säcker et.al (eds) Law Concerning (n 3) 118–119.

383 Further, according to Sirait as to the Rule of Reason approach:
"The best illustration of how the Commission interpreted broadly the rule of reason approach can be seen in the Temasek case, Decision No: 07/KPPU-L/2007, when the Commission invented and applied a minimalist and maximal approach in interpreting the rule of reason and the *Per-se Illegal* conduct. The Commission determined that the minimalist approach must fulfill two elements: a business actor controlling relevant market and such control affecting more than 50% of the relevant market. The maximal approach added one more element, that is, the conduct has had a negative impact on the market competition."
Sirait, '*The Development and Progress of Competition Law in Indonesia*' (The Antitrust Bulletin: *Vol. 54, No. 1/Spring 2009)* 27.

In contrast, as regards to *Per-se Illegal* approach, *Khemani and Shapiro* from the Organisation for Economic Co-operation and Development (OECD) provide, as follows:

> "Per se Illegal approach declares that every contractual agreement or business conduct is illegal, without further necessity to prove as to the subsequent impacts of the contractual agreement and/or business conducts. Business conducts which are deemed as illegal encompass among others a collusive price fixing and resale price maintenance.[384]"

According to *Wahyuningtyas*, both the per se prohibitions and Rule of Reason approaches in the Law Number 5/1999 can be known from the clause "[...] could result in monopolistic practices or the occurrence of unfair business competition." Hence, two statutory elements are important, notably: First, "a requirement to assess the effect of a particular agreement or conduct in the relevant market, which is shown in the term "could result in" or in some provisions "could be suspected to result in". Second, the benchmark for the harmful effect to the relevant market, which is described as "monopolistic practices" and "the occurrence of unfair (business) competition".[385] Furthermore, the effect assessment requirement refers to the three significant consequences. First, the respective agreement or conduct as such (per se) is not prohibited and becomes prohibited, provided the second part of the clause is fulfilled. Second, even though an effect assessment is required, this approach does not require an actual effect. Thus, a potential effect is sufficient for the prohibition. Put differently, the Competition Authorithy (CA) must necessarily substantiate that a concrete detrimental effect resulted from the agreement or conduct in question.[386]

2.4.4.2 Product and Geographical Relevant Market

The definition of market and relevant market is of principally importance for analysis in competition law, notably to assess market structure and anti-competitive conduct of an undertaking. According to Article 1 No. 10 of the Law Number 5/1999 a market is defined as follows:

384 Khemani and Shapiro, OECD Glossary (n 39) 51.
385 Wahyuningtyas, *Unilateral Restraints* (n 376) 96–98.
386 ibid.

> "[...] An economic institution in which sellers and buyers, either directly or indirectly, can conduct trading transactions of goods and or services."[387]

Furthermore, Article 1 Number 11 of the Law Number 5/1999 provides definition of relevant market, which is as follows:

> "The relevant market shall be the market related to a certain marketing scope or area by business actors for goods and or services of the same or similar type or substitutes for such goods and or services."[388]

Accordingly, from the wordings of Article 1 No.11 of the Law Number 5/1999, there are two categories of relevant markets: product markets and geographical markets. In this respect, the KPPU Regulation No.03/2009 concerning the Implementing Guideline of Article 1 No.10 Law Number 5/1999 provides explanations for product and for geographical markets.

A product market is defined as products, which compete with a product at hand as well as with products that can substitute a product at hand.[389] Thus, analysis of product markets involves two steps, which are: (1) an analysis of characteristic similarities of a product at hand, and (2) an analysis of an interchangeability of a product at hand. Moreover, a product market can be identified from the supply and demand sides. Referring to the demand side: product A has, for example, three similar products: B, C, D. If product A's price increase impact demand quantities of B and C, but not D; thus B and C deemed as the product market of A. From a supply side: there are the products A, B and C, which are offered on the market and there are X and Y as potential products. If products A, B and C price increases impact under-

387 See Article 1 (10) of the Law Number 5 Year 1999 concerning the Prohibition of Monopolistic Practices and Unfair Business Competition. ‹http://eng.kppu.go.id/newkppu/wp-content/uploads/2016/11/law_5_year_1999_.pdf› accessed 28th December 2017.

388 Article 1 (11) of the Law Number 5 year 1999 concerning the Prohibition of Monopolistic Practices and Unfair Business Competition‹http://eng.kppu.go.id/newkppu/wp-content/uploads/2016/11/law_5_year_1999_.pdf› accessed 28th December 2017.

389 Products can substitute a product at hand if products are able to restrict or limit the price increases of a product at hand. See Lubis and Sirait (eds), *Hukum Persaingan Usaha* (n 225) 23–25.

taking to produce X to substitute A, B and C and thus to access a market.[390]

Based upon the Article 1 No. 11 of the Law Number 5/1999, the term geographical market refers to "a market related marketing range or area. Marketing area describes the area where competition takes place, which covers local, regional, nationwide or international spheres.[391] According to *Säcker and Fuller*, referring to the UNCTAD Model Law, the criteria for defining a geographical market contains following indicators: "transportation costs, degree of inconvenience in obtaining goods or services, choice available to consumers and the functional level at which undertakings operate."[392]

2.4.4.3 Oligopoly

Oligopoly is categorised by the Law Number 5/1999 as the prohibited agreement, whereas Article 4 of the Law Number 5/1999 stipulates, as follows:

> "Business actors shall be prohibited from entering into agreements with other business actors for jointly controlling the production and/or marketing of goods and or services *which may potentially cause* the occurrence of monopolistic practices and or unfair business competition."

Accordingly, from the wording "[…] which may potentially cause […]" it can be inferred that Oligopoly is subject to the *rule of reason* approach, instead of the *per se* illegal one.[393]

---

390 ibid.

391 ibid.

392 *Säcker and Lohse* in in F.J. Säcker, et.al (eds.), *Law Concerning Prohibition of Monopolistic Practices and Unfair Business Competition (n 3)* 118–122.

393 Article 4 of the Law Number 5/1999 has five core elements:
i. the existence of an agreement
ii. an agreement between undertakings
iii. the goal of an agreement is to jointly control the production and/or marketing of goods and/or services;
iv. the possibility to potentially cause the occurrence of monopolistic practices and or unfair business competition
v. oligopoly presumption prevails if 2 or 3 business actors or a group of business actors control over 75% of the market segment of a certain type of goods or services.

Based upon the provision of Article 4 (1) the Law Number 5/1999, agreements to take control over the production and/or marketing of goods and/or services jointly among or an agreement to establish an oligopoly, if theycan result in monopolistic practices or unfair competition they are prohibited. Thus, according to Article 4(2) the Law Number 5/1999, an oligopoly is presumed whenever two or three undertakings or groups of undertakings control more than 75% of the market share of a certain type of goods or services. Accordingly, Article 13 the Law Number 5/1999 explains market share, as follows: "the percentage of sales or purchase value of certain goods or services controlled by an undertaking in the relevant market in a certain calendar year."[394]

2.4.5 Legislative Exemptions in the Law Number 5/1999

Normatively, the Law Number 5/1999 provides the legislative exemptions, which are elaboratively stipulated in the provisions of Article 50 and 51. Hence, these exemptionary provisions are structured into four categories: First, the regulation of natural monopoly subject to the state administration.[395]

394 Wahyuningtyas, *Unilateral Restraints* (n 376) 109.

395 Sirait openly criticised this exemption, which is stipulated in Article 51 of the Law Number 5/1999, as follows: Criticism has focused on Article 51, which grants exemptions to enterprises operating in strategic areas reserved exclusively for the State-Owned Companies (Badan Usaha Milik Negara or BUMN). Based on a literal reading of the law, it is still unclear whether the exemption of government monopolies must be stipulated by the law,53 or whether these agencies or companies shall be subject to Law No. 5 do you want to write the law numbers in the same way? of1999. Some business groups such as small- and medium-scale businesses or cooperatives are regulated under other existing laws and so may be exempted. 54 state oned companies have invoked Article 33 of the 1945 Indonesian Constitution: (1) The economy shall be organised as a common endeavour based upon the principles of the family system. (2) Sectors of production, which are important for the country and affect the people's life shall be under the power of the State. (3) The land, waters and the natural resources shall be controlled by the State and shall be used to the greatest benefit of the people. (4) The organisation of the national economy shall be conducted on the basis of economic democracy upholding the principles of togetherness, efficiency with justice, continuity, safeguarding the environment, self-sufficiency, and keeping a balance in the progress and unity of the national economy.

Second, the exemption for certain activities or actions. Third, the exemption for certain agreements. Fourth, the exemption for particular undertakings.[396]

Furthermore, Article 50 of the Law Number 5/1999 stipulates that the following agreements or activities, are excluded from the Law Number 5/1999's application, which are:

This article in the Constitution has been broadly translated into discretionary powers granted to the State-Owned Companies under Law No. 19/2003, which determines the structure of the state-owned companies. Article 66 of Law No.19/2003 states that the government grants privileges to State Owned Companies when implementing public utility services. This has been implemented by granting a monopoly to the state-owned companies in operating their businesses. Additionally, Law No. 5 of 1999 states that all state-owned companies are fully exempted. However, critics disagree and argue Competition Law In Indonesia: 31 53 Article 51 states that monopoly or concentration of activities related to the production or marketing of goods or services affecting the livelihood of society at large and branches of production of a strategic nature for the state shall be stipulated in a law and shall be implemented by state-owned companies or institutions formed or appointed by government. Very long sentence!

See Sirait, "The Development and Progress of Competition Law in Indonesia", 42.

396 See the Law No. 5 of 1992 concering Cooperative and Small Medium Businesses: Examples of specific statutory exemptions where monopoly is granted can be found in article 52(1), Law No. 40/2004, on the National Social Security System (Sistem Jaminan Sosial Nasional (SJSN). This article states that the operation of the systems is granted to Perusahaan Perseroan (Persero) Jaminan Sosial Tenaga Kerja (Jamsostek)— the worker's social security company; Perusahaan Perseroan (Persero) Dana Tabungan dan Asuransi Pegawai Negeri (Taspen)—the civil servant retirement and insurance company; Perusahaan Perseroan (Persero) Asuransi Sosial Angkatan Bersenjata Republik Indonesia (ASABRI)—the social insurance company for military personnel; and Perusahaan Perseroan (Persero) Asuransi Kesehatan Indonesia (ASKES)—the health insurance company, all of which are entirely owned by the government. These companies, however, have been heavily criticised for unsatisfactory performance in providing public services and for competing with other providers and private insurance companies. Presumably, article 51 of Law No. 5 of 1999 will be used as the shield to protect the state monopoly and could discourage more efficient performance of State Owned Companies. 55??? Therefore, the demand for better services has put pressure on the government to privatise these companies as well as to open the relevant markets to competition. The best example of the Commission's functions to deregulate a sector was its decision to require the Ministry of Transportation to revoke a decree and allow new competitors to enter the airline business. This certainly has provided a benefit to consumers through cheaper prices, better service, and more choice." where is the beginning of the quote, no quotation marks.

a. actions and/or agreements intended to implement applicable laws and regulations
b. agreements related to intellectual property rights, such as licenses, patents,
c. trademarks, copyright, industrial product design, integrated electronic circuits, and trade secrets as well as agreements related to franchise; agreements for the stipulation of technical standards of goods and or services which do not inhibit, and or impede competition
d. agency agreements which do not stipulate the resupply of goods and or services at a price level lower than the contracted price
e. cooperation agreements in the field of research for the upgrading or improvement of the living standard of society at large
f. international agreements ratified by the Government of the Republic of Indonesia
g. export-oriented agreements and/or actions not disrupting domestic needs and/or supplies
h. business actors of the small-scale group
i. activities of cooperatives aimed specifically at serving their members.

Equally important, as regards the monopolies administered by the State, Article 51 the Law Number 5/1999 provides:

> "Monopoly and or concentration of activities related to the production and or marketing of goods and or services affecting the livelihood of society at large and branches of production of a strategic nature for the state shall be stipulated in a law and shall be implemented by State-Owned Enterprises and or institutions formed or appointed by the government."[397]

397 Article 51 of the Law Number 5 Year 1999 concerning the Prohibition of Monopolistic Practices and Unfair Business Competition. ‹http://eng.kppu.go.id/newkppu/wp-content/uploads/2016/11/law_5_year_1999_.pdf› accessed on 28th December 2018.

2.4.6 Cartel Prohibition Provisions in the Law Number 5/1999

Whilst the Law Number 5/1999 does not provide a definition concerning cartels, the KPPU Regulation No.4/2010 defines cartels practice, as follows:

> "Cooperation between several competing undertakings to coordinate their activities resulting the control of production and prices of certain goods and/or services which leads to an excessive profit."[398]

Specifically, Article 11 the Law Number 5/1999 stipulates cartel prohibition provision, as follows:

> "An undertaking shall be prohibited to make agreements with their business competitors, with the intention of influencing prices by arranging production and/or marketing of a good and/or service, *which could result* in the occurrence of monopolistic practice and/or unfair business competition."[399]

Arguably, in the analysis of the Law Number 5/1999, it is important to distinguish between the 'restrictive' and 'broad' definitions of cartels prohibition.[400] Broad definition of cartels prohibition means that cartels prohibition in the Law Number 5/1999 refers not only to Article Article 11, but also to Article 5 concerning price fixing and Article 9 regarding territorial division.[401] Nevertheless, based upon the KPPU Regulation concerning Guideline for Implementation of Article 11 of the Law Number 5/1999, Article 11 does not include other types of cartels, which have been regulated in Article 5 and Article 9. Article 11

398 Article 5 of the Law Number 5 Year 1999 concerning the Prohibition of Monopolistic Practices and Unfair Business Competition. ‹http://eng.kppu.go.id/newkppu/wp-content/uploads/2016/11/law_5_year_1999_.pdf› accessed on 28th December 2018.

399 Article 11 of the Law Number 5 Year 1999 concerning the Prohibition of Monopolistic Practices and Unfair Business Competition. ‹http://eng.kppu.go.id/newkppu/wp-content/uploads/2016/11/law_5_year_1999_.pdf› accessed on 28th December 2018.

400 According to the broad definition of a cartel, a cartel comprises agreement on prices, market shares, allocation of customers and allocation of territories. While according to the restrictive one, a cartel is an agreement by a group of undertakings, which compete in a same market, to fix prices for obtaining monopolistic profits.
cf. A.M.T. Anggraini, '*Penggunaan Bukti Ekonomi dalam Kartel (n 33)* 4.

401 *Silalahi,*'Circumstantial Evidence' *(n 14)* 5–7.

of the Law Number 5/1999 comprises only a cartel with intention of influencing prices by arranging production and/or marketing of a good and/or service.[402] Hence, by referring to the provisions of Article 11 the Law Number 5/1999, a cartel must fulfil the following statutory elements, notably: Fist, the existence of an agreement between undertakings. Second, having intention to influence prices on the market. Third, arranging production and/or marketing of goods and/or services. Fourth, it could resulting in the occurrence of monopolistic practices and/or unfair business competition.[403]

2.4.6.1 The existence of an agreement between undertakings

By virtue of Article 1 No. 7 the Law Number 5/1999, the term 'agreement' refers to " an action of one or more business actors for binding themselves to one or more other business actors under whatever name, either in writing or not."

Indeed, *Säcker and Füller* argue that agreements are "the joint market strategies of several business actors, whereby the competing business actors agree with one another about the whole market behaviour or even single portions from the whole market behaviour, which cause the business actors act in an un-isolated manner and unindependly in the market. Hence, the term "agreement" has a particular definition in the competition law and thus does not interlink with the term agreement under the civil law concept.[404]

Equally important, *Säcker and Füller* emphasise that the term 'agreement' in the provisions of Article 1 No.7 the Law Number 5/1999 implies the following concepts: *First*, concurrence of wills and forming a collective intention, whereas there are at least two parties agreeing on a joint market strategy chiefly through the mutual flows of information, be it ever so rudimentary, irrespective of the causa of the agreement as well as the voluntary or non-voluntary nature of an agreement.[405] *Second*, binding effect, whereas the binding effects of an

402 ibid.

403 ibid.

404 *Säcker and Lohse* in F.J. Säcker, et.al (eds.), *Law Concerning Prohibition of Monopolistic Practices and Unfair Business Competition (n 3)*.79–83.

405 ibid.79–84.

agreement comprise not only the legal binding effect but also economic, moral and social binding effects. Had an agreement anti-competitive effects, thus this agreement can be rescinded and declared *null and void* by KPPU pursuant to Article 47 (2) the Law Number 5/1999. Moreover, the economic, moral and social binding effects of an agreement in this context are, among others, a below cost pricing policy agreement whereby the participants in such agreements will demand a low price in order not to suffer from competition. Thus, with these economic advantages and disadvantages the business actors shall be indirectly compelled to abide by the agreement's terms and condition.[406] *Third*, a distinction against "conspiracy", whereas the term "agreement" under Article 1 No.7 of the Law No.5/1999 has a broad interpretation and comprises also "a gentleman's agreement". However, the Law No.5/1999 does not follow the UNCTAD Model Law, whereby the Law Number 5/1999 distinguishes between the terms "agreement" and "concerted practice or actions". The term "concerted practices", similar to the competition law legislations in developed countries, has been stipulated in a specific provision, namely in Article 1 No.8 of the Law Number 5/1999.[407] *Fourth*, the written or oral forms of an agreement, whereas an agreed restraint of competition to be in written or not, is irrelevant. This provision is in accordance with the competition law practices in many countries. However, the non-written form of an agreement, for example gentlemen's agreements expose another profound problem to the Competition authority and to the Court, particularly the evidentiary problem that largely correspond to a similar problem in the concerted action.[408] In the analysis of the term agreement in Article 1 No.7 of the Law Number 5/1999 it is important to make differentiation as regards to: First, mere agreement. Second, related or ancillary agreement and third, joint venture agreement.[409]

---

406 ibid.

407 ibid.

408 ibid.

409 According to Säcker and Lohse, mere agreements are carried out where the content of an agreement amounts to nothing more than agreeing to arrange production and/or marketing. The most important group of these are quota cartel, identifying market information procedures, pure customer division and market entry barriers, and standard or type cartels. Related agreement, which arises from a collateral clause of complex contract whose main purpose, is neutral in terms of a

As regards the term 'undertaking' or 'business actors', Article 1 No. 5 the Law Number 5/1999 defines as follows:

> *"Business actor shall be any individual or business entity, incorporated or not incorporated as legal entity, established and domiciled in or conducting activities in the jurisdiction of the Republic of Indonesia, either individually or jointly based on an agreement, conducting various business activities in the economic sector."*[410]

According to *Säcker and Füller*, this provision mirrors the international approach of a functional definition, regardless of its natural person or legal entity and which stipulated further by the UNCTAD Model Law Article 2 I (a):

> *"Enterprises mean firms, partnerships, corporations, companies, associations and other juridical persons, irrespective of whether created or controlled by private persons or by the State, which engange in commercial activities, and include the branches, subsidiaries, affiliates or other entities directly or indirectly controlled by them."*[411]

Hence, the international term of enterprises is similar to business actors in the Law No.5/1999, which encompasses: First, enterprise groups. Second, association of business actors. Third, State Owned Enterprise (SOE). However, it does not include the entities for meeting private needs, for example the final consumer and the employment agreement.[412] The term public or state-owned business actor according to Article 16 Sec. 1 the UNCTAD 1994 International Antitrust Code, is defined as follows:

---

competition law. This includes accompanying customer division and accompanying barriers to market entry. Regarding a joint venture agreement, arranging production and marketing might have an effect of a joint venture agreement and arranging production and/or marketing can take place precisely based on a joint venture agreement. ibid. 211.

410 Pasal 5 Undang-undang Nomor 5 Tahun 1999 tentang Larangan Praktik Monopoli dan Persaingan Usaha Tidak Sehat (Law concerning Prohibition of Monopolistic Practices and Unfair Business Competition). cf. Heermann in F.J. Säcker, et.al (eds.), *Law Concerning Prohibition of Monopolistic Practices and Unfair Business Competition (n 3)* 48–52.

411 ibid.

412 ibid.

> "Public business actors, irrespective of their legal status, are subject to application of this Agreement as far as they enganged in economic activities that could be carried out by private business actors".[413]

Thus, the key word is the predominant influence by the State by any other means.[414] Furthermore, the tems enterprise groups, association of business actors, and meeting private needs and employment agreement are largely similar to the corresponding concepts in the EU and German Competition laws.[415] In fact, it is important to note that there are seven types of undertakings in the Indonesia business law system, notably: First, State-Owned Company ("BUMN/BUMD").[416] Second, cooperative ("Kooperasi").[417] Third, limited liability company ("Perseroan Terbatas-PT").[418] Fourth, partnership ("Maatschap").[419] Fifth, firm ("Firma").[420] Sixth, limited partnership ("Commanditaire Venootschap-CV"). Eigth, foundation ("Yayasan").[421]

2.4.6.2 Having intention to influence prices on the market

Säcker and Lohse explain that the element "with the intention of influencing price" has no significance alone, because the undertakings' conduct to arrange productions and/or marketings not only excludes competition between the undertakings participating in cartels, but also leads to price increases of the products of goods and/or services gener-

---

413 ibid.

414 ibid.

415 ibid.

416 The Indonesian Law Number 19/2003 concerning the state-owned company (Badan Usaha Milik Negara/Badan Usaha Milik Daerah)

417 The Indonesian Law Number 25/1992 concerning the cooperative (Kooperasi)

418 The Indonesian Law Number 40/2007 concerning the Limited Liability Company (Perseroan Terbatas-PT).

419 Codification of Civil Law (Kitab Undang-undang Hukum Perdata-Burgerlijk Wetboek), Article 1618. This provision still prevails based upon the Indonesia Constitution, Transition Provisions, Article II.

420 Codification of the Commercial Law (Kitab Undang-undang Hukum Dagang-Wetboek van Koophandel), Article 16 on Firma and Article 19 concerning *Commanditaire Venootschap* (CV).

421 The Indonesian Law Number 25/2000 on the Foundation (Yayasan).

ated and/or marketed by the undertakings because of the absence of competitive pressures on the market.[422]

2.4.6.3 Arranging production and/or marketing of goods and/or services

The notion of arranging production and/or marketings of goods and/or services refers to an effort to determine the amount of goods produced or marketed for a cartel as a whole and for all the members, that is to say, either greater or lesser than the undertaking's production capacity or the demand of goods or services in the market. Whereas to govern the market refers to the undertakings' effort to determine, for example, certain marketing areas in which the undertakings could sell their goods and/or services.[423]

2.4.6.4 Could resulting in the occurrence of monopolistic practice and/or unfair business competition

By virtue of Article 1 point 6 the Law Number 5/1999, unfair business practices refer to:

> "Competition shall be competition among business actors in conducting activities for the production and or marketing of goods and or services in an unfair or unlawful or anti-competition manner."

Even more, as regards the 'restriction to the competition' on the market, *Heermann* asserts that this concept reflects a fact that the existence of merely potential restraints of competition is sufficient to categorise a specific competitive conduct as a monopolistic practice. Hence, in application of the competition law prohibition provisions are expanded significantly, because the competition law authorities need not to wait until the restrainst of competition have actually taken into effect. Thus, the competition law authorities are able to intervene immediately as of the potential restrictions to competition emerge.[424]

---

422 *Säcker and Lohse* in Säcker, et.al (eds.), *Law Concerning Prohibition of Monopolistic Practices and Unfair Business Competition (n 3)* 208–209.

423 ibid.

424 *Heermann* in Säcker, et.al (eds.), *Law Concerning Prohibition of Monopolistic Practices and Unfair Business Competition (n 3)* 50–53.

According to *Säcker and Lohse*, KPPU is supposed to apply the rule of reason approach in implementing the provisions of Article 11 the Law Number 5/1999. This is particulary important to examine whether an agreement in question is necessary to achieve a main goal, which is neutral to the competition law (reasonably ancilliary agreements). Further, this approach is of significant important to value whether an agreement in question is necessary to attain the procompetitive benefits (reasonably necessary agreements). Nevertheless, it must be carefully noticed that the rule of reason approach is not applicable to the following 'red-light' cartels, for instance quota cartels, identifiying market information procedures, pure costumer divisions and pure barriers to market entry due to their serious detrimental effects to the competition. In contrast, the rule of reason approach is applicable to the following 'yellow-light' cartels, namely standard and type cartel, condition cartel, accompanying customer division, accompanying barriers to market entry and joint venture agreements. In the second place, in the implementation of Article 11 the Law Number 5/1999, KPPU must take into account the legislative exemptions in the provisions of Article 50 the Law Number 5/1999. In the event that KPPU can prove than an agreement in question had violated the provisions of Article 11 the Law Number 5/1999, consequently the agreement is to be null and void. Accordingly, KPPU is able to impose administrative and penal sanctions to the undertakings involved in cartels.[425]

Furthermore, in the implementation of Article 11 the Law Number 5/1999, KPPU must take into consideration the *de minimis rule*, whereas UNCTAD defines:

> "*De minimis* exemptions are those which are granted for transactions involving firms with turnover or market share below a certain threshold, which are not considered to affect competition significantly enough to make it necessary for the law to be made applicable to them or to be applied by them." In the EU, the *de minimis* bound is to be assumed by a joint market share of cartel members from 5–10 percent.[426]

425 *Säcker and Lohse* Säcker, et.al (eds.), *Law Concerning Prohibition of Monopolistic Practices and Unfair Business Competition (n 3)* 206–210.

426 ibid.

Principally, pursuant to the KPPU Regulation No. 04/2010, cartels on the market can be identified by observing the following characteristics: First, the existence of a conspiracy between undertakings. Second, the involvement of senior executive or official of alleged undertakings in making collusive agreements. Third, the misuse of trade or business association for camouflaging their illicit activities and/or collusions. Fourth, price fixing, which must be followed by allocation of consumers, territories and productions as well as an agreement to decrease quantities of production for effective implementation of price fixing. Fifth, the threat and internal punishment for participating undertakings for deterring deviating conduct from cartels agreement. Sixth, the distribution of information for all members of cartels agreement. Further, the undertakings would involve an internal auditor to verify given information concerning quantities of production and marketing of goods. Subsequently, the auditor distributes the information to all members of cartels agreement.[427]

427 The KPPU Regulation No. 04/2010 concerning the guidelines of Article 11 of the Law Number 5/1999 on cartels (dated 9th April 2010).

Chapter Three Procedural Law Pursuant to the EU Competition Law, the German Cartel Law and the Law Number 5/1999

3.1 Procedural Law pursuant to the European (EU) Competition Law

3.1.1 Introduction

Principally, the enforcement proceedings of the European Competition law, are administrative proceedings, instead judicial ones.[428] According to *Klees* the administrative nature thereof would manifest during the preliminary and investigation phases, where the evidences are collected.[429] According to *Schweitzer and Mestmäcker*, the European Commission (the Commission) enforcement proceedings as to the EU competition rules have been considered mainly as the administrative proceedings. This applies not only to the Commission decision on finding and terminating of infringement[430], the Decision on penalties in form of the fines[431], the Decision on periodic penalty payments.[432]

Traditionally, in contrast to the United States (US) Antitrust law enforcement proceeding, the European and German Competition laws, rely predominantly upon the public enforcement method. In terms of a difference between the private and public enforcement aforementioned,

---

428 A. Klees, *Europäisches Kartellverfahrensrecht: Mit Fusionskontrollverfahren* (2. Aufl. Heymanns Carl. Verlag, 2013) 79–82.

429 ibid. 82–84.

430 H. Schweitzer and E.J. Mestmäcker, Europäisches Wettbewerbsrecht (3 Aufl. CH Beck, 2014) 511–514.

431 ibid.

432 ibid.

the normative structure is a determinant factor.[433] This means, in the private enforcement method, the enforcement rules are to be written sophisticated enough, thus the Court could apply those rules correctly. In contrast, in the public enforcement method, those rules are subject to dissenting interpretations.[434] Further, in terms of the enforcement method aforementioned, the German Cartel law has been characterised by a dualism of the public enforcement and supervision as well as the private enforcement (litigations).[435]

Henceforth, according to Gerardine *et.al,* there are five rationales for the European Competition law's application of the public enforcement approach.[436] First, enforcement of the Competition Law requires complex and specialised analytical appraisal, whereas an ordinary Court is not capable to perform this task. Hence, an administrative enforcement body, equipped with law and economic experts, is a key necessity. Second, due to the secretive nature of cartels, an independent administrative enforcement authorithy is very important to carry out sector-inquiries and market monitorings in order to detect anti-competitive practices. Third, a Court frequently hesitates to issue a judicial order for concluding the investigations over cartels infringement. Fourth, in the event of all necessary evidences are collected, a Court is often not able to manage a large number of documents and electronic data thereof. Consequently, a Court could not process the evidence to accomplish cartels cases. Fifth, a Court can only adjudicate cartels cases submitted by third parties. However, a Court could not initiate sector inquiries aimed to specific economic sectors and anti-competitive practices, which are highly important in the sense of economic value.[437]

With respect to the private enforcement (litigations) the European Competition law recognises an action for nullity of a collusive agreement; civil claims for elimination and forberarance of collusive agree-

433 Schweitzer, ‚Vorlesung zum deutschen und europäischen Wettbewerbsrecht' (WS 15/16, Fachbereich Rechtswissenschaft Freie Universität Berlin) 2–3.

434 ibid.

435 M. Heße, *Wettbewerbsrecht: Schnell Erfasst* (Springer, 2006) 35–36.

436 Geradin, Farrar, Petit, *EU Competition Law (n 33) 47*.

437 ibid.

ments and a claim for set-off and indemnities thereof.[438] Whereas in the German Cartel law, the German Act against Restraint of Competition (GWB), in conjunctions with the German Civil Code (Burgerliches Gesetzbuch-BGB), recognises the civil claims similar to the EU aforementioned, but with an addition of the legal standing (power) of representative (class) action *(Verbandsklagebefugnis)*.[439]

Equally important, the European Competition as well as the German Cartel law have been equipped with the public enforcement by the Antitrust/Competition Authorities, notably the Commission and the *Bundeskartellkartellamt* (the Federal Cartel Office), though the administrative instruments, consisting of:[440] First, an order to bring the infringement to an end.[441] Second, the provisional (interim) measures.[442] Third, the commitments.[443] Fourth, the 'positive decision'.[444] Fifth, the fines and periodic penalty payment.[445] Sixth, the disgorgements (*Vorteilsabschöpfung*) by the Cartel Office (*Bundeskartellamt*), which is supported by the Association's disgorgement.[446]

In general, the procedural rules of European competition are embodied in the Council Regulation (EC) No. 1/2003 of 16 December 2002 on the Implementation of the Rules on competition laid down in Articles 81 and 82 of the Treaty ("the Regulation Number 1/2003), the Commis-

---

438 Article 102 (ex Article 82 TEC), Consolidated version of the Treaty on the Functioning of the European Union – Part Three: Union Policies And Internal Actions – Title Vii: Common Rules On Competition, Taxation And Approximation Of Laws – Chapter 1: Rules on competition – Section 1: Rules applying to undertakings OJ C 115, 9.5.2008, 89–89.

439 Schweitzer, ‚Vorlesung zum deutschen und europäischen Wettbewerbsrecht: Sitzung 6' (WS 15/16, Fachbereich Rechtswissenschaft Freie Universität Berlin) 2–3.

440 ibid.

441 Art. 7 Regulation Nr. 1/2003. cf. Sec. 32 para. 1 GWB. Schweitzer, „Vorlesung zum deutschen und europäischen Wettbewerbsrecht" (n 432) 5–8.

442 Art. 8 Regulation Nr. 1/2003. cf. Sec. 32 (a) GWB. Schweitzer, „Vorlesung zum deutschen und europäischen Wettbewerbsrecht" (n 432) 5–8.

443 Art. 9 Regulation Nr. 1/2003. cf. Sec. 32 (b) GWB. Schweitzer „Vorlesung zum deutschen und europäischen Wettbewerbsrecht", (n 432) 5–8.

444 Art. 10 Regulation Nr. 1/2003. cf. Sec. 32 (c) GWB. Schweitzer „Vorlesung zum deutschen und europäischen Wettbewerbsrecht" (n 432) 5–8.

445 Art. 23, 24 Regulation Nr. 1/2003. cf. Sec. 81–84 GWB. Schweitzer „Vorlesung zum deutschen und europäischen Wettbewerbsrecht" (n 432) 5–8.

446 cf. Sec. 34 and 34 (a) GWB. Schweitzer „Vorlesung zum deutschen und europäischen Wettbewerbsrecht" (n 432) 5–8.

sion Regulation (EC) No. 773/2004 of 7th April 2004 relating to the conduct of proceedings by the Commission pursuant to Articles 81 and 82 of the ECT as well as a series of the Commission's Guidelines, Notices, Directives, including the Commission notice on best practices for the conduct of proceedings concerning Articles 101 and 102 TFEU (2011/C 308/06).[447]

In terms of the law enforcement the European Competition laws, there are 5 principal institutions, therefor: First, the EU Commission ("the Commission"). Second, the National Competition Authorities (NCAs).[448] Third, the National Courts of EU Member States ("the EU National Courts"). Fourth, the European Competition Network ("ECN"). Fifth, the Courts of Justice of the EU.[449] However, it should be bore in mind, that the antitrust enforcement proceedings rely predominantly on the National Competition Authority, such as the *Bundeskartellamt,* which implements those proceedings according to the Domestic Procedural Rules, but with its implementation is subject to the principle of effectiveness.[450]

Initially, the Commission, as a central figure, has been bestowed with three key duties.[451] Firstly, the Commission 'shall ensure the application of the Treaties, and of measures adopted by the institutions pursuant to them' pursuant to Article 17 TFEU.[452] Secondly, the Commission pursues a general policy aimed to apply the principles enshrined in the EU

---

447 P. Behrens, *Europäisches Marktöffnungs- und Wettbewerbsrecht: Eine systematische Darstellung der Wirtschafts- und Wettbewerbsverfassung der EU* (CF Müller, XLIX, 2017) 917–918.

448 Geradin, Farrar, Petit, *EU Competition Law (n 33)* 325–327.

449 ibid. 321.

450 This procedural principle means that the norms and rules enshrined in the EU Treaties, in the National laws, must not be designed such as in the practice to make its implementation impossible or excessively difficult, such as to obtain judicial protection.
S. Kadelbach, *Allgemeines Verwaltungsrecht unter europäischem Einfluss, Jus Publicum Bd.36 (Mohr Siebeck: 1999)* 131. cf. Schweitzer, „Vorlesung zum deutschen und europäischen Wettbewerbsrecht" (n 432) 3–5.

451 Jones and Sufrin, *EU competition law. Text, cases, and materials.* (4.th Ed. OUP, 2011) 1147–1150.

452 Article 17 (1) of the TFEU reads:
"1. The Commission shall promote the general interest of the Union and take appropriate initiatives to that end. It shall ensure the application of the Treaties, and of measures adopted by the institutions pursuant to them. It shall oversee the

Treaty as well as guides the undertakings' conduct in implementing the principles thereof. As an illustration, the Commission issues Guidelines to implement the Article 101 (3) TFEU's provisions. Thirdly, by virtue of Article 103 (1) and (2) TFEU, the Commission is able to propose necessary legislations for implementing the Article 101 and 102 TFEU's provisions.[453]

In addition, as regards the National Competition Authorities (NCA)'s responsibilities, Article 35 of the Regulation Number 1/2003 stipulates, as follows:

> "1. The Member States shall designate the competition authority or authorities responsible for the application of Articles 81 and 82 of the Treaty in such a way that the provisions of this regulation are effectively complied with. The measures necessary to empower those authorities to apply those Articles shall be taken before 1st May 2004. [...]

---

application of Union law under the control of the Court of Justice of the European Union. It shall execute the budget and manage programmes. It shall exercise coordinating, executive and management functions, as laid down in the Treaties. With the exception of the common foreign and security policy, and other cases provided for in the Treaties, it shall ensure the Union's external representation. It shall initiate the Union's annual and multiannual programming with a view to achieving interinstitutional agreements." ibid.

453 The provisions of Article 103 TFEU (ex Article 83 TEC) stipulates.
1. The appropriate regulations or directives to give effect to the principles set out in Articles 101 and 102 shall be laid down by the Council, on a proposal from the Commission and after consulting the European Parliament.
2. The regulations or directives referred to in paragraph 1 shall be designed in particular:
(a) to ensure compliance with the prohibitions laid down in Article 101(1) and in Article 102 by making provision for fines and periodic penalty payments;
(b) to lay down detailed rules for the application of Article 101(3), taking into account the need to ensure effective supervision on the one hand, and to simplify administration to the greatest possible extent on the other hand;
(c) to define, if need be, in the various branches of the economy, the scope of the provisions of Articles 101 and 102;
(d) to define the respective functions of the Commission and of the Court of Justice of the European Union in applying the provisions laid down in this paragraph;
(e) to determine the relationship between national laws and the provisions contained in this section or adopted pursuant to this Article.
Article 103 (ex Article 83 TEC), Consolidated version of the Treaty on the Functioning of the European Union – Part Three: Union Policies And Internal Actions – Title Vii: Common Rules On Competition, Taxation And Approximation Of Laws – Chapter 1: Rules on competition – Section 1: Rules applying to undertakings OJ C 115, 9.5.2008.

2. When enforcement of Community competition law is entrusted to national administrative and judicial authorities, the Member States may allocate different powers and functions to those different national authorities, whether administrative or judicial."[454]

Even more, the EU National Courts function in three possible scenarios. First, they have jurisdictions as to civil litigation complaints between private undertakings, e.g. action for damages. Second, they act as a public enforcement actor of the Competition Law, for instance the Courts in Finland and Ireland.[455] Third, they function as the Reviewer Court over the National Competition Authorities' decisions.[456] Hence, Article 15 of the Regulation Number 1/2003 mandates the institutional cooperation of National Courts with the Commission.[457]

454 Furthermore, the subsequent provisions of Article 35 of the Regulation 1/2003:
"3. The effects of Article 11(6) apply to the authorities designated by the Member States including courts that exercise functions regarding the preparation and the adoption of the types of decisions foreseen in Article 5. The effects of Article 11(6) do not extend to courts insofar as they act as review courts in respect of the types of decisions foreseen in Article 5.
4. Notwithstanding paragraph 3, in the Member States where, for the adoption of certain types of decisions foreseen in Article 5, an authority brings an action before a judicial authority that is separate and different from the prosecuting authority and provided that the terms of this paragraph are complied with, the effects of Article 11(6) shall be limited to the authority prosecuting the case which shall withdraw its claim before the judicial authority when the Commission opens proceedings and this withdrawal shall bring the national proceedings effectively to an end."
EU Council, Regulation (EC) No 1/2003 of 16 December 2002 on the implementation of the rules on competition laid down in Articles 81 and 82 of the Treaty Official Journal L 001, 04/01/2003 P. 0001–0025.

455 The Commission, Cooperation with national courts (Antitrust). ‹http://ec.europa.eu/competition/court/antitrust.html› accessed on 19th October 2015, 2–5.

456 ibid.

457 "1. In proceedings for the application of Article 81 or Article 82 of the Treaty, Courts of the Member States may ask the Commission to transmit to them information in its possession or its opinion on questions concerning the application of the Community competition rules.
2. Member States shall forward to the Commission a copy of any written judgment of national courts deciding on the application of Article 81 or Article 82 of the Treaty. Such copy shall be forwarded without delay after the full written judgment is notified to the parties.
3. Competition authorities of the Member States, acting on their own initiative, may submit written observations to the national courts of their Member State on issues relating to the application of Article 81 or Article 82 of the Treaty. With the permission of the court in question, they may also submit oral observations to the

Nevertheless, Article 15 of the Regulation Number 1/2003 in conjunction with Article 267 TFEU enunciate that the EU National Courts' request of legal opinion to the Commission does not preclude their rights to file a preliminary ruling to the Court of Justice of the EU. For that reason, Article 267 TFEU prescribes:

> "The Court of Justice of the European Union shall have jurisdiction to give preliminary rulings concerning: (a) the interpretation of the Treaties; (b) the validity and interpretation of acts of the institutions, bodies, offices or agencies of the Union;
> Where such a question is raised before any court or tribunal of a Member State, that court or tribunal may, if it considers that a decision on the question is necessary to enable it to give judgment, request the Court to give a ruling thereon. Where any such question is raised in a case pending before a court or tribunal of a Member State against whose decisions there is no judicial remedy under national law, that court or tribunal shall bring the matter before the Court.
> If such a question is raised in a case pending before a court or tribunal of a Member State with regard to a person in custody, the Court of Justice of the European Union shall act with the minimum of delay."[458]

In addition, as regards the European Competition Network (ECN)'s duties, the Recitals 15 of the Regulation Number 1/2003 prerequisites, as follows:

> "The Commission and the competition authorities of the Member States should form together a network of public authorities applying the Community competition rules in close cooperation. For that purpose, it is necessary to set up arrangements for information and consultation. Further modalities for the cooperation within the network will be laid down and revised by the Commission, in close cooperation with the Member States."[459]

---

national courts of their Member State. Where the coherent application of Article 81 or Article 82 of the Treaty so requires, the Commission, acting on its own initiative, may submit written observations to courts of the Member States. With the permission of the court in question, it may also make oral observations. For the purpose of the preparation of their observations only, the competition authorities of the Member States and the Commission may request the relevant court of the Member State to transmit or ensure the transmission to them of any documents necessary for the assessment of the case."
The Regulation (EC) No 1/2003 (n 453) Article 15.

458 Geradin, Farrar, Petit, *EU Competition Law* (n 33) 321–325.

459 The Regulation Number 1/2003 (n 453), Recitals 15.

Equally important, the Courts of Justice of the EU play a very important role in the EU Competition Law's enforcement. Whereas the Court of Justice of the EU consists of the General Court (GC) and the Court of Justice (ECJ), they have 3 chief duties. First, the annulment proceeding under Article 263 TFEU. Second, the revision of administrative fines according to Article 261 TFEU. Third, the adjudication of indemnity actions regulated by Article 268 TFEU.[460] In like manner, Kokkoris outlines three duties of the Court of Justice of the EU. Firstly, pursuant to Article 267 TFEU the General Court and the Court of Justice ("ECJ") have the principal juridical competences to adjudicate the competition law matters based upon the preliminary rulings by the Courts of Member States. Secondly, based on the appeal upon the Decision of the Commission the General Court in the first instance is able to adjudicate the competition laws dispute either by ordering a new investigation of the case or confirm the prior Decision of the Commission. Thirdly, the Court of Justice (ECJ), as the final instace court, can re-adjudicate the Decision of General Court. Thus, the ECJ can annul the previous decision based upon the parties' further appeal. Moreover, the Court of Justice of the EU's decisions serve as the subsequent jurisprudence of the EU Competition Law, whereby these decisions have a supremacy effect *vis-à-vis* the national Competition Laws of the Member States.[461]

As a matter of fact, hitherto, there have been critics as to the balancing of powers of the Commission in the enforcement European competition law. Whereby the Commission performs whole three functions in the enforcement proceedings, namely: investigations, prosecution, and decisions making as well as a 'quasi legislative' function, the public question as to the judicial protection guarantee mandated by Article 6 para 1 European Convention for the Protection of Human Rights and Fundamental Freedoms and Article 47 Charter of Fundamental Rights of the European Union would not be jeopardised. Nevertheless, after the Court of Human Rights of EU Decision in the *Menarini case*, the judicial supervision of the Court of Justice of EU over the Commission's decisions has reflected the proper allocation of judicial

460 Jones and Sufrin, *EU Competition law* (n 450) 1147–1150.

461 I. Kokkoris, *Competition cases from the European Union: the ultimate guide to leading cases from the EU, Member States and EFTA*. (2nd edition. Sweet and Maxwell, 2010) 1–12.

powers; thus it would enable the guarantee and the maintenance of judicial protection as well as the guarantee of fair, impartial and objective trials.[462]

3.1.2 Fundamental Guiding Principles

Within the European Competition law, particulary in the enforcement proceedings, theses guiding principles are utmost important and would serve as the common of the EU Law. In fact, the guiding principles have been developed by the Court of Justice of the EU in order to guarantee that 'the law is observed' in accordance with Article 19 (1) Treaty on European Union (TEU) as well as the compliance of the other EU insitutions, for instance, in their legislations.[463] Indeed, Article 2 TEU [Article 6(1) EU] states clearly:

> "The Union is founded on the values of respect for human dignity, freedom, democracy, equality, the rule of law and respect for human rights, including the rights of persons belonging to minorities. These values are common to the Member States in a society in which pluralism, non-discrimination, tolerance, justice, solidarity and equality between women and men prevail".[464]

Arguably, the guiding principles are profoundly important in the EU Competition Law's enforcement owing to three reasons. First, the principles provide a platform for a fair and efficient administrative decision-making process. In other words, these principles ensure that officials

---

462 EU Courts of Human Rights, Decision 27.9.2011, Menarini: «*Le respect de l'article 6 de la Convention n'exclut donc pas que dans une procédure de nature administrative, une «peine» soit imposée d'abord par une autorité administrative. Il suppose cependant que la décision d'une autorité administrative ne remplissant pas ellemême les conditions de l'article 6 Sec. 1 subisse le contrôle ultérieur d'un organe judiciaire de pleine juridiction […]. Parmi les caractéristiques d'un organe judiciaire de pleine juridiction figure le pouvoir de réformer en tous points, en fait comme en droit, la décision entreprise, rendue par l'organe inférieur. Il doit notamment avoir compétence pour se pencher sur toutes les questions de fait et de droit pertinentes pour le litige dont il se trouve saisi.*"
Behrens, Europäisches Marktöffnungs- und Wettbewerbsrecht (n 446) 918–919.

463 H. Hofmann, G.C. Rowe, A. Türk, *Administrative Law (n 24)* 57–59.

464 ‹http://eur-lex.europa.eu/LexUriServ/LexUriServ.do?uri=OJ:C:2008:115:0013:0045:en:PDF› accessed on 14th October 2015.

perform their duties impartially and make decisions rationally and proportionally. Second, the principles guarantee individuals and affected parties against arbitrary administrative decisions, to illustrate, duty to provide reason and protection of human (fundamental) rights. Third, the principles promote the accountability of administrative acts vis-*à-vis the* publics, for instance accessibility and openness rule.[465]

These guiding principles are internalised and manifest in three main aspects of the EU Competition law's enforcement proceedings, notably: First, the efficient and effective implementation of the Commission's investigatory powers. Second, the rights of defence of the Parties, affected by the onerous investigative measures of the Commission.[466] Third, the judiciary control or supervision by the Court of Justice of EU over the Commission's measures and decisions abovementioned.[467]

3.1.2.1 Principle of Legality

Normatively, during the administrative proceedings, the Commission must act pursuant to the EU Laws, whether they stipulated in the primary or secondary legislations or in the jurisprudence of the Courts of Justice of the EU. Accordingly, these principles mandate several interlinked requirements, as follows: First, the administrative officials must act within power and doctrine of *ultra vires* acts. Second, the proper exercise of discretions. Third, the administrative officials must act in good faith (*bona-fide*) and to avoid an improper goal. Fourth, they must act in accordance with the prescribed legal procedures, such as conduct enquiries, right of defense, public participation and duty to state reasons. Fifth, they must respond to justified individual claims, such as comprehensive and necessary inquiries, provision of information and punctual consideration of application.[468]

Equally important, according to the Article 263 (1) and (2) of TFEU concerning the judicial review competences of the Court of Justice of EU, the compliance with the legality principle is the main guiding principle

465 H. Hofmann, G.C. Rowe, A. Türk, *Administrative Law (n 24)* 57–59.
466 Schweitzer, ‚Vorlesung zum Wettbewerbsrecht' (n 432)
467 Behrens, *Europäisches Marktöffnungs- und Wettbewerbsrecht (n 446)* 917–921.
468 H. Hofmann, G.C. Rowe, A. Türk, *Administrative Law (n 24)* 57–60.

for the European Courts.[469] Accordingly, the provisions of Article 263 (1) and (2) TFEU provides:

> "The Court of Justice of the European Union shall review the legality of legislative acts, of acts of the Council, of the Commission and of the European Central Bank, other than recommendations and opinions, and of acts of the European Parliament and of the European Council intended to produce legal effects vis-à-vis third parties. It shall also review the legality of acts of bodies, offices or agencies of the Union intended to produce legal effects vis-à-vis third parties."
>
> *"It shall for this purpose have jurisdiction in actions brought by a Member State, the European Parliament, the Council or the Commission on grounds of lack of competence, infringement of an essential procedural requirement, infringement of the Treaties or of any rule of law relating to their application, or misuse of powers".*[470]

3.1.2.2 Officiality Principle

Within the administrative proceedings, the Commission is principally subject to the principle of ex-officio Discretion (*Opportunitätsprinzip*), which means that the initiation of investigation or inquiries against the Competition law's infringement depends on the Commission. Further, the Commission has also discretionary power over indictments against the alleged undertakings.[471]

In addition, during the administrative proceedings, the Inquisitorial principle applies (*Untersuchungsmaxime*). Generally, this principle refers to the following duties: Firstly, the Commission shall examine all the facts *ex-officio*. Thus, the Commission determines the natures and scope of investigatory measures. Secondly, the Commission shall take into account all significant facts individually as well as the circumstances in favour of the alleged undertakings. Thirdly, the Commission could not refuse applications and thus give none of reasonable grounds. Further, according to Immenga and Mestmäcker, this principle implies the obligation to find the substantive truth (*materiellen Wahrheit*) as well the respect of legality of an administrative act (*Rechtmäßgikeit)*.[472]

469 ibid.

470 ibid.

471 Klees, *Europäisches Kartellverfahrensrecht (n 427) 80.*

472 Immenga and Mestmäcker, *Wettbewerbsrecht: Kommentar* (n 44) 2212–2215.

Whereas the provision of Article 296 (2) TFEU provides:

> "Legal acts shall state the reasons on which they are based and shall refer to any proposals, initiatives, recommendations, requests or opinions required by the Treaties."

Accordingly, the violation of this principle constitutes a breach against the important formal requirements of administrative act under the provision of Article 263 (2) TFEU.[473] Accordingly this Article stipulates:

> "It shall for this purpose have jurisdiction in actions brought by a Member State, the European Parliament, the Council or the Commission on grounds of lack of competence, infringement of an essential procedural requirement, infringement of the Treaties or of any rule of law relating to their application, or misuse of powers."[474]

3.1.2.3 Protection of the Fundamental Rights Principle

Beumer maintains that protection of the fundamental rights principle is a cornerstone of fair administrative proccedings and of a fair trial in the EU Competition Law.[475] In fact, since the entry into force of the Lisbon Treaty, the fundamental rights protection principle, e.g. right to be heard has a legally binding effect in the EU legal system.[476] Specifically, Article 6 ECHR constitutes the fundamental rights protection principle in the EU procedural laws. Hence Article 6 ECHR covers two kinds of the EU procedures: First, the procedure concerning dispute on civil rights and obligations. Second, protection to procedures on criminal charges.[477] As an illustration, in the *Jussila v Finland* case, the European Court of Human Rights (ECtHR) invoked the provisions of Article 6 ECHR in competition law matters.[478] Furthermore, *in the Menarini case,* the ECtHR maintained that 'the EU Competition Law proceedings are fully

473 Schweitzer and Mestmäcker, *Europäisches Wettbewerbsrecht* (n 429) 511–514.

474 Consolidated version of the Treaty on the Functioning of the European Union, Section 5: The Court of Justice of the European Union. ‹https://eur-lex.europa.eu/legal-content/EN/TXT/?uri=celex%3A12012E%2FTXT› accessed on 05th October 2019.

475 E. Beumer, 'The Interaction between EU Competition Law Procedures and Fundamental Rights Protection: The Case of the Right to Be Heard' *(Yearbook of Antitrust and Regulatory Studies, Vol. 2014 7 (10)) 11–12.*

476 ibid.

477 ibid.

478 ibid.

subject to Article 6 ECHR's protection'. Put differently, in the EU Competition Law's proceedings, the fundamental rights protection starts when the Commission informs the undertaking in writing objection statements against the undertaking.[479]

Accordingly, the provisions of Article 6(1) and (3) of the Lisbon Treaty stipulate:

> "1. The Union recognises the rights, freedoms and principles set out in the Charter of Fundamental Rights of the European Union of 7 December 2000, as adapted at Strasbourg, on 12 December 2007, which shall have the same legal value as the Treaties. The provisions of the Charter shall not extend in any way the competences of the Union as defined in the Treaties.
> The rights, freedoms and principles in the Charter shall be interpreted in accordance with the general provisions in Title VII of the Charter governing its interpretation and application and with due regard to the explanations referred to in the Charter, that set out the sources of those provisions.
> 3. Fundamental rights, as guaranteed by the European Convention for the Protection of Human Rights and Fundamental Freedoms and as they result from the constitutional traditions common to the Member States, shall constitute general principles of the Union's law."[480]

Furthermore, Recitals 37 of the Regulation Number 1/2003 provides:

> "This Regulation respects the fundamental rights and observes the principles recognised in particular by the Charter of Fundamental Rights of the European Union. Accordingly, this Regulation should be interpreted and applied with respect to those rights and principles."[481]

In general, the fundamental rights protection principle in the EU Competition Law's proceedings manifest in five aspects. First, the fair trial right. Second, the right to an oral hearing. Third, the right to access documents. Fourth, the professional secrecy right. Fifth, the limited right against self-incrimination.[482]

Also, as regards the fair trial's right, Article 6 ECHR in conjunctions with Article 47 of the Charter of Fundamental Rights of the EU (CHFR-EU) possess "an open-ended, residual quality", that is to say, several

479 ibid.
480 Khan and Kerse, EU Antitrust Procedure (n 253) 17–21.
481 The Regulation Number 1/2003, Recitals 37 (n 453).
482 Beumer, '*the Interaction*' (n 474) 11–14, See Ezrachi, *EU Competition Law, An Analytical Guide (n 239)* 478–481.

fundamental rights have been added into Article 6 ECHR, for instance right to oral hearing in one's presence and protection against arbitraty decisions.[483] Accordingly, Article 6 ECHR provides:

> "In the determination of his civil rights and obligations or of any criminal charge against him, everyone is entitled to a fair and public hearing within a reasonable time by an independent and impartial tribunal established by law. Judgment shall be pronounced publicly but the press and public may be excluded from all or part of the trial in the interests of morals, public order or national security in a democratic society, where the interests of juveniles or the protection of the private life of the parties so require, or to the extent strictly necessary in the opinion of the court in special circumstances where publicity would prejudice the interests of justice."

Further, the provisions of Article 47 (CHFR-EU) states:

> "Everyone is entitled to a fair and public hearing within a reasonable time by an independent and impartial tribunal previously established by law. Everyone shall have the possibility of being advised, defended and represented."

Equally important, Article 27 of the Regulation Number 1/2003 in conjuctions with Article 10–14 of the Commission Regulation Nr. 773/2004 elaborate procedural rights of the parties in competition law proceedings, e.g. right to be heard.[484] Thus, the provisions of Article 27 of the Regulation Number 1/2003 read:

> „1. Before taking decisions as provided for in Articles 7, 8, 23 and Article 24 (2), the Commission shall give the undertakings or associations of un-

483 Beumer (n 474) 12–17.

484 The provisions of Article 10 until 14 of the Commission Regulation No. 773/2004 concerning the Right to be heard stipulates as follows:
Article 10 concerning the Statement of objections and reply:
"1. The Commission shall inform the parties concerned in writing of the objections raised against them. The statement of objections shall be notified to each of them. 2. The Commission shall, when notifying the statement of objections to the parties concerned, set a time-limit within which these parties may inform it in writing of their views. The Commission shall not be obliged to take into account written submissions received after the expiry of that time-limit. 3. The parties may, in their written submissions, set out all facts known to them which are relevant to their defence against the objections raised by the Commission. They shall attach any relevant documents as proof of the facts set out. They shall provide a paper original as well as an electronic copy or, where they do not provide an electronic copy, 28 paper copies of their submission and of the documents attached to it. They may propose that the Commission hear persons who may corroborate the facts set out in their submission."

dertakings which are the subject of the proceedings conducted by the Commission the opportunity of being heard on the matters to which the Commission has taken objection. The Commission shall base its decisions only on objections on which the parties concerned have been able to comment. Complainants shall be associated closely with the proceedings. [...]
3. If the Commission considers it necessary, it may also hear other natural or legal persons. Applications to be heard on the part of such persons shall, where they show a sufficient interest, be granted. The competition

Article 11 concerning the Right to be heard:
"1. The Commission shall give the parties to whom it has addressed a statement of objections the opportunity to be
heard before consulting the Advisory Committee referred to in Article 14(1) of Regulation (EC) No 1/2003.
2. The Commission shall, in its decisions, deal only with objections in respect of which the parties referred to in paragraph 1 have been able to comment." See the European Commission Regulation (EC) No 773/2004 of 7 April 2004 relating to the conduct of proceedings by the Commission pursuant to Articles 81 and 82 of the EC Treaty (OJ L 123, 27.4.2004, p. 18–24).
Article 14 concerning the conduct of oral hearings:
"1. Hearings shall be conducted by a Hearing Officer in full independence.
2. The Commission shall invite the persons to be heard to attend the oral hearing on such date as it shall determine.
3. The Commission shall invite the competition authorities of the Member States to take part in the oral hearing. It may likewise invite officials and civil servants of other authorities of the Member States.
4. Persons invited to attend shall either appear in person or be represented by legal representatives or by representatives authorised by their constitution as appropriate. Undertakings and associations of undertakings may also be represented by a duly authorised agent appointed from among their permanent staff.
5. Persons heard by the Commission may be assisted by their lawyers or other qualified persons admitted by the hearing officer.
6. Oral hearings shall not be public. Each person may be heard separately or in the presence of other persons invited to attend, having regard to the legitimate interest of the undertakings in the protection of their business secrets and other confidential information.
7. The hearing officer may allow the parties to whom a statement of objections has been addressed, the complainants, other persons invited to the hearing, the Commission services and the authorities of the Member States to ask questions during the hearing.
8. The statements made by each person heard shall be recorded. Upon request, the recording of the hearing shall be made available to the persons who attended the hearing. Regard shall be had to the legitimate interest of the parties in the protection of their business secrets and other confidential information." *ibid.*

> authorities of the Member States may also ask the Commission to hear other natural or legal persons."

Even more, according to Beumer, Article 6 ECHR provides the fair hearing guarantee, notably the right to an oral hearing. In fact, the right to an oral hearing in one's presence serves as a safeguard against the Commission's arbitrary decisions. Albers and William pointed out the high importance of an oral hearing right in order to ensure checks and balances in the administrative proceedings, mainly due to: First, the complexity of competition cases and second, the discretionary competences of the Commission as a law enforcement institution.[485] Moreover, the Commission Regulation No. 773/2004 explicitly mandate the right to an oral hearing, whereas Article 12 of the Commission Regulation No. 773/2004 reads, as follows:

> "The Commission shall give the parties to whom it has addressed a statement of objections the opportunity to develop their arguments at an oral hearing, if they so request in their written submissions."

Further, as regards to hearing of other persons, Article 13 stipulates:

> "1. If natural or legal persons other than those referred to in Articles 5 and 11 apply to be heard and show a sufficient interest, the Commission shall inform them in writing of the nature and subject matter of the procedure and shall set a timelimit within which they may make known their views in writing.
> 2. The Commission may, where appropriate, invite persons referred to in paragraph 1 to develop their arguments at the oral hearing of the parties to whom a statement of objections have been addressed, if the persons referred to in paragraph 1 so request in their written comments.
> 3. The Commission may invite any other person to express her or his views in writing and to attend the oral hearing of the parties to whom a statement of objections has been addressed. The Commission may also invite such persons to express their views at that oral hearing."

Equally important, Article 28 of the Regulation Number 1/2003 in conjunctions with Article 16 until 17 of the Commission Regulation No. 773/2004 explicitly regulates the protection of professional secrecies and confidential information. Accordingly, these stipulated rights refer as well to the right to refuse to give evidence (*Zeugnisverweigerungsrecht)*

485 M Albers and K Williams 'Oral Hearings – Neither a Trial Nor a State of Play Meeting' (Working Paper, 2010) ‹http://ec.europa.eu/competition/hearing_officers/albers_williams_article.pdf› accessed on 31th December 2018.

which is subject to the Courts' discretion (*nemo tenetur se ipsum accusare).*

Interlinked with the right abovementioned, Article 27 (2) of the Regulation Number 1/2003 in conjunctions to Article 15 until 16 of the Commission Regulation No.773/2004 stipulates the right to access files during the administrative proceedings, as follows:

> "The rights of defence of the parties concerned shall be fully respected in the proceedings. They shall be entitled to have access to the Commission's file, subject to the legitimate interest of undertakings in the protection of their business secrets. The right of access to the file shall not extend to confidential information and internal documents of the Commission or the competition authorities of the Member States. In particular, the right of access shall not extend to correspondence between the Commission and the competition authorities of the Member States, or between the latter, including documents drawn up pursuant to Articles 11 and 14. Nothing in this paragraph shall prevent the Commission from disclosing and using information necessary to prove an infringement."[486]

In the second place, *Ezrachi* explains, the Courts of Justice of the EU, in the Orkem v. Commission and Mannesmannröhren-Werke AG v. Commission cases, has introduced the limited right against self-incrimination in the competition law enforcement proceedings.[487] By virtue of Recitals 23 of the Regulation Number 1/2003, Ezrachi outlines that the limited right against self incrimination refers to the following notions:

> "The Commission is empowered to take statements and interview natural and legal persons who consent to be interviewed for the purpose of collecting information relating to the subject-matter of an investigation. When complying with a decision of the Commission, undertakings have a right of silence only to the extent that they would be compelled to provide answers which might involve an admission on their part of the existence of an agreement which it is incumbent upon the Commission to prove. However, undertakings are obliged to answer factual questions and to provide documents, even if this information may be used to establish against them, or against another undertaking, the existence of an infringement."[488]

Indeed, the implementation of the limited right against self-incrimination is stipulated in the provisions of Article 3 and 4 of the Regulation

486 The Regulation Number 1/2003 (n 453) Article 27 (2
487 Ezrachi, *EU Competition Law (n 239)* 478–80.
488 ibid. 478–482.

773/2004 concerning the Commission's competences to take statements and inquire information from the undertakings during the administrative proceedings.[489]

3.1.2.4 *In dubio pro reo*Principle

According to *Holtappels,* historically the *in dubio pro reo* principle originates from the Roman civil and subsequently penal laws.[490] By virtue of the Reception process in the German legal system, initially in the penal proceedings during the Frankish Kings in the 5th until 6th centuries, continued by the medieval period's criminal law, this principle has evoluted progressively.[491]

Within the European procedural law, the principle of *in dubio pro reo* (presumption of innocence or doubt benefits to the accused) means, whenever the Court demands the conviction, that the accused had indeed unlawfully substantiated or violated whole statutory elements of the provision.[492] In particular, within the European Competition law, especially in the review or verification proceedings, this principle is of crucially importance.[493] According to Ott, the *in dubio pro reo* principle would be the decision rule, instead of an evidentiary one, within the

489 ibid.

490 P Holtappels, *Die Entwicklungsgeschichte des Grundsatzes "in dubio pro reo"* (de Gruyter Verlag, 1965) 2–5. The manuscripts (Edict) of Roman laws stipulated accordingly:
Inter pares numero iudices si dissonae sententiae proferantur, in liberalibus quidem causis, secundum quod a divo Pio constitutum est, pro liberiate statutum optinet, in aliis autem causis pro reo. Quod et in iudiciis publicis optinere oportet, 14).

491 In the *Constitutio Criminalis Carolina, notably the Halsgerichtsordnung Karls V.,* stipulated *„und daß […] an viel orten offter mais wider recht und gute vernunfft gehandelt und entweder die unschuldigen gepeinigt und getötet werden. Im Artikel 150 heißt es dann, die Richter sollten ja nicht eigene unvernünfftige Regel oder Gewohnheit. […] sprechen machen, die den Rechten widerwärtig seynd als je Zeiten an den peinlichen Gerichten hißhero geschehen" ibid.*19–25.

492 J.G. Fischer et.al (eds.) *Karlsruher Kommentar zur Strafprozessordnung* (7. Auflage CH Beck 2013), R. 62

493 Loewenheim et. al (eds) *Kartellrecht: Europäisches und Deutsches Kartellrecht, Kommentar* (3 Aufl, CH Beck, München: 2016), R 43.

judiciary process, that the Judge must follow in evaluating the whole evidence and circumstances.[494]

Whereas the *in dubio pro reo principle* serves as a corner stone principle in the European Competition procedural laws, it requires mandates that, whenever the Commission and the Court of Justice of EU remain doubt as to the violation of an accused during the Antitrust enforcement proceedings, having assessed whole facts as well as direct and indirect evidences emerged; thus, the accussed undertaking must enjoy judicial benefits and cannot be deemed guilty by the Commission or by the Court.[495] Altough the principle of *in dubio pro reo* has not been explicitly stipulated in the European Competition legislations, the provisions of Article 6 para. 2 of the European Convention of Human Rights (ECHR) and Sec. 261 of the German Code of Criminal Procedure (StPO) enunciate this principle.[496] *Lianos and Genakos* emphasise that the

494 According to Ott: „This, in the StPO nowhere explicitly pronounced, the evidence evaluation dominating "rule of law fundamental principle" with constitutional rank whose violation already observed the review court on the Sachricht, means that everyone, despite having exhausted all the evidence, must object to unrecoverable doubts as to the fact that the defendant has significant grounds for the decision. The principle "in dubio pro reo" is a decision rule and not a rule of proof, which the trial judge only has to obey if he has not fully convinced himself of the existence of a fact that is directly relevant to the decision after the evidence has been completed. Only if there are still doubts after the conclusion of the evaluation of the evidence which the trial judge can not overcome will he have to decide in favor of the defendant by always choosing the most favorable of the defendants from several possible conclusions. For individual elements of the evaluation of evidence, the principle of doubt (with regard to the main fact) is in principle not applicable not just as little isolated from the existence of a concrete indices of relief or exoneration. The doubts do not say anything about how the trial judge has to appreciate the evidence, nor about the standard by which the judge may consider a fact certain. The principle is therefore not violated if the judge should have doubted, but only if he is convicted, although he doubts, which in turn is reversible only if it also results from the grounds of the judgment. On the other hand, the application of the "doubts" does not need it if the doubts which Richter still has after concluding the evaluation of the evidence are based only on the assumption of a purely intellectual, abstract-theoretical possibility, which lack real points of contact; In this case, the judge already spans the requirements of the judicial conviction formation, if he gives in to the not "reasonable" doubt and not convicted." (unofficial translation). Ott in *Karlsruher Kommentar zur Strafprozessordnung* (n 491) 56.

495 ibid.

496 Nigel Foster and Satish Sule, German Legal System and Laws (4th Ed OUP,2014) 139–140.

principle of 'in dubio pro reo' has been embodied in Article 48 (1) of the Charter of Fundamental Rights of the EU (CHFR-EU), which prescribes that 'any doubt in the mind of the Court must operate to the advantage of the undertaking to which the decision finding an infringement was addressed'.[497]

Nehl argues, taking into account the 'quasi-penal character of the imposition of fines of EU Competition procedural law, the European Competition law recognizes" the principle *in dubio pro reo* and the applicable evidentiary requirement rules, for instance the burden of proof, were general principles of law, whose non-observance amounted to an error of law.[498] Accordingly, the *ECJ in the Hülls* case explained, as follows:

> "[...] the presumption of innocence resulting in particular from Article 6(2) ECHR is one of the fundamental rigthts which [...] reaffirmed in the Preamble of the Single European Act and in Article F(2) of the Treaty on European Union, are protected in the (Union) legal order."[499]

Further, the ECJ asserted:

> "[...] given the nature of the Competition Law infringements [...] and the nature and degree of severity of the ensuing penalties, the principle of the presumption of innocence applies to the procedures relating to infringements of the competition rules applicable to undertakings that may result in the imposition of fines or periodic penalty payments."[500]

Equally important, as to the scope of application of the *in dubio pro reo*, the Court of Justice of EU in the joined case of *Sumitomo Chemical and Sumika Fine Chemical v. Commission* argued, as follows:

> "[...] *the presumption of innocence implies that every person accused is presumed to be innocent until his guilt has been established according to law. It thus precludes any formal finding and even any illusion to the liability of an accused person for a particular infringement is a final decision,* unless that person has enjoyed all the usual guarantees accorded for the exercise of

497 ibid. 140–142.

498 Nehl, 'Commentary Article 48 (1) – Presumption of Innocence' in Peers, et.al, *The EU Charter of Fundamental Rights: A Commentary* (Bloomsbury,2014) 1278–1280.

499 Case C-199/92 P Hüls AG v Commission of the European Communities 1999 I-04287, paras. 141–55. cf. Ezrachi, *EU Competition Law* (n 239) 71.

500 Case C-199/92 P Hüls para. 150.

> the rights of the defence in the normal course of proceedings resulting in a decision on the merits of the case."[501]

Accordingly, *Nehl* hypothesizes that implementation of the *in dubio pro reo* principle encompasses three application scopes. First, the personal scope of application, which means the principle *in dubio pro reo* "covers any natural or legal person charged with and liable to be held responsible for an infringement of the EU Competition Law, that may give rise to a decision stating the infringement and imposing a pecuniary sanction." This scope of application correlates mainly to imposition of fines (periodic penalties). Second, the *in dubio pro reo principle* applies mainly to whole competition law proceedings, both in the administrative and judicial phases, aiming at finding or confirming any competition law infringement and at imposing a pecuniary sanction. Nevertheless, this principle applies outside the formal proceedings, for example the premature/undue public statements by the Commission. Also, in the administrative and judicial proceedings as to competition law infringements, the presumption of innocence principle prerequisites mainly the governing rules on the administration of evidence, namely by the Commission. Put differently, whenever the Commission either commits an improper reversal burden of proof, jeopardising the alleged undertakings or the Commission has failed to meet the standard of proof in its final decisions; these will result in the breach of *in dubio pro reo* principle, that is to say, an error of law. Third, the temporal scope of application, whereas the *in dubio pro reo* principle's application reaches beyond merely the investigation of an infringement and imposition of pecuniary sanctions (fines) proceedings, notably the Commission's final decision at the end of administrative proceedings.[502]

In fact, the GC has emphasised in the Pergan Hilfsstoffe case, as follows:

> "the guilt of a person accused of an infringement is established, definitively only where the decision finding that infringement has acquired the force of *Res judicata*, which implies either the absence of an appeal against

501 See General Court, Joined Cases T-22/02 and T-23/02, Sumitomo Chemical and Sumika Fine Chemicals v Commission (6 October 2005) [Sumitomo Chemicals], http://curia.europa.eu/juris/liste.jsf?language=en&num=T-22/02, accessed on 19th October 2018.

502 Nehl, Commentary Article 48 (n 497) 283.

> that decision by the person concerned within the time limits provided in the sixth paragraph of Article 263 TFEU or after such appeal, the definitive closure of the contentious proceedings, in particular by a judicial decision confirming the lawfulness of that decisions."[503]

As a matter of fact, in the Rhône-Poulenc case, the Advocate General Vesterdorf strongly advocated the application of '*in dubio pro reo*' principle, as follows:

> "Considerable importance must be attached to the fact that the competition cases of this kind (cartels) are in realtiy of a penal nature, which naturally suggests that a high standard of proof is required (…). There must be a sufficient basis for the decision and any reasonable doubt must be for the benefit of the applicants according to the principle of *in dubio pro reo*."[504]

Further, the *Advocate General Vesterdorf* emphasised:

> "This principle is of essentially importance in the competition case presenting indirect (circumstantial) evidences of a concerted practice, such as parallel conducts of alleged undertakings. The European Courts have been reluctant to simply conclude the existence of concerted practices based upon merely price parallelism. Thus, the European Court demands a realtively higher standard of proof in order to prevent the false-positive error, notably by judging the oligopolistic interdependence as a cartel infringement against the Article 101 (1) TFEU."[505]

Consequently, *Thanos* describes that in the EU Competition Law's proceedings, *the in dubio pro reo principle* has three juridical effects, as follows:[506] First, in the evidentiary requirements rule. Altough the *in dubio pro reo principle* has been implicit in the competition laws of the EU and Member States, this principle has been indeed the cornerstone for the EU Competition Law's rules of evidence. Second, in the Commission's professional activities and discretionary competences to issue decisions. Thus, the Commission is subject to the *in dubio pro reo principle*, that is to say, the Commission must be prudently careful in issuing the decisions and holding press-release related to the alleged undertakings in cartel cases.

---

503 Nehl, Commentary Article 48 (n 297) 1282–1283.

504 Lianos and Genekos, *Econometric Evidence* (n 26) 86–87.

505 ibid.

506 I. Thanos, *Die Reichweite der Grundrechte im EU-Kartellverfahrensrecht Schriften zum Europäischen Recht (EUR)*, Band 172 (Duncker & Humblot, 2015) 352–354.

Third, in the Leniency programme's application. This means the Leniency programme must comply with the legality principle (*Rechtsmäßigkeit*) in the implementation and arrangement thereof.

Consequently, by virtue of Article 101(1) and (3) TFEU as well as Article 2 of the Regulation Number 1/2003, Thanos concludes that the *in dubio pro reo* principle will require the Competition Authorithy to bear: First, the subjective burden of proof (*formelle Beweislast*), which means who must present the evidence to substantiate the allegation (assertion) before the Court. Second, the objective burden of proof (*materielle Beweislast*), meaning who must burden a risk of an unprovability resulted from the allegation (*assertation*).[507]

3.1.3 The Administrative Proceeding's Phase and Principle

By virtue of the Regulation Number 1/2003, the EU Competition Law's proceeding recognises the following possibilities for the Commission to initiate inquiry or investigation measures. First, by means of market monitoring.[508] Second, obtaining information from other authorities.[509] Third, receiving information from the complainants.[510] Fourth, acquiring information from consumers.[511] Fifth, secure information through the Leniency programme and sector inquiry.[512]

507 ibid.
508 ibid.
509 ibid.
510 ibid.
511 ibid.
512 According to Geradine, et.al as regards to the initiation of administrative proceedings verb is missing, as follows:
a. Market monitoring
"The Commission is not a repressive Authority. It does not hide and spy on the market players in an obsessive quest for evidence for unlawful conduct. Yet and contrary to what is often written, the Commission constantly monitors the evolution of markets. The Commission pays close attention to market facts and data, through the monitoring of business journals, academic papers, economic reports, radio and television information"
b. Information receive through other institutional channels
"Information that circulates within DG COMP. As explained previously, within sectoral Directorate, several units generally work on distinct antitrust matters (in general antitrust, mergers and State aid). Those units are not supposed to act as silos. Rather,

Subsequently, according *to Klees*, the Commission attempts to obtain necessary knowledge of facts, enabling the Commission to prove

---

information retrieved by the merger and State aid units should be shared with the antitrust unit and vice versa. This may thus lead to the opening of Articles 101 and 102 TFEU cases."
c. Information received from complainants
"Pursuant to Article 7 (3) of the Regulation 1/2003, a 'natural or legal person can show al legitimate interest and Member States' can lodge complaints alleging breaches of Article 101 and 102 TFEU. The Commission adopted a Notice on the handling of complaints, which sets out the conditions of admissibility of complaints, the rights of complainants, and their involvement in the procedure.
Informal vs Formal complaints. There are two possible ways to complain before the Commission. First, natural or legal persons can complain informally. The complainant is then a mere informant. He or she brings information on potentially anti-competitive practices to the attention of the Commission, through unofficial contacts. Should the Commission open proceedings subsequently, it will be deemed to have acted ex officio. Informal complainants enjoy no specific rights to participate in the subsequent proceedings (through for example the submission of observations). Second, natural or legal persons can formally complain to the Commission pursuant to Article 7 (2) of the Regulation 1/2003. Those complaints must comply with the requirements set out in the Regulation 773/2004 relating to the conduct of the proceedings. In contrast to informal complainants, formal complainants benefit from specific rights. First, the formal complainants have a right to a reasoned reply from the Commission. Second, formal complainants can participate in the subsequent proceedings. This, however, comes at certain prices: drafting a formal complaint consumes time, effort and money. Moreover, formal complainants, whose identity is disclosed to the firm(s) accused of anti-competitive conducts – may be subject to retaliation.
4. Information received from consumers
"Whilst the consumers are often said to be the true addressees of competition policy, their role in competition proceedings, and in particular in the detection of competition infringements, has remained embryonic.
Consumer Liaison Office. In a bid to foster consumer participation in competition proceedings, in 2003 the Commission created a Consumer Liaison Office (CLO) within the DG Competition. The CLO is primarily responsible for receiving information and request concerning competition problems faced by the end users, namely the consumers. A team of Consumer Liaison Correspondent responsible for each economic sector gives advice to consumers within a month of receiving queries."
5. Information received through specific legal instruments
"The EU competition framework also provides for two Ad-hoc insturments that purport to improve the Commission's ability to detect infringements, that is, Sector inquries and the Leniency Programme" cf. Geradine, Farrar, Petit *EU Competition Law* (n 44) 391–405.

cartels infringement under Article 101 TFEU.[513] According to the Regulation Number 1/2003, the Commission is vested with investigatory competences in order to collect necessary information from the affected parties. *Kerse and Khan* point out that the Commission's investigatory competences are twofold. First, for requesting necessary information to establish a case's facts. Second, for inspecting the undertaking's premise. In addition, the Commission can opt either to ask necessary information by request or by issuing an order.[514] Accordingly, the Commission can request necessary information, which encompasses: First, contemporary documentary evidence of the alleged undertaking. Second, the parties's ex-post facto statement during the investigation proceeding.[515]

Altough the Commission has the considerably wide investigatory competences in the administrative proceedings, Article 18 until Article 21 of the Regulation Number 1/2003 confine the Commission's competences. In fact, the Regulation Number 1/2003's limitation applies to the Commission investigatory competences, as follows: First, the inquiries into certain economy sectors and into certain types of agreement.[516] Second, the competence to investigate allegations of violation against the provisions of Article 101 and 102 and the Merger Regulations of the EU.

513 Klees, *Europäisches Kartellverfahrensrecht (n 427)* 83–87.

514 Kerse and Khan, *EU Antitrust Procedure (n 253)*103–105.

515 ibid. 125.

516 The provisions of Article 17(1) of the Regulation Number 1/2003 read:
"1. Where the trend of trade between Member States, the rigidity of prices or other circumstances suggest that competition may be restricted or distorted within the common market, the Commission may conduct its inquiry into a particular sector of the economy or into a particular type of agreements across various sectors. In the course of that inquiry, the Commission may request the undertakings or associations of undertakings concerned to supply the information necessary for giving effect to Articles 81 and 82 of the Treaty and may carry out any inspections necessary for that purpose. The Commission may in particular request the undertakings or associations of undertakings concerned to communicate to it all agreements, decisions and concerted practices. The Commission may publish a report on the results of its inquiry into particular sectors of the economy or particular types of agreements across various sectors and invite comments from interested parties."

3.1.4 Judiciary Review by the Court of Justice of the EU

With respect to the EU Competition Law proceedings, Schweitzer explains that the judiciary review (judicial supervision) by the Court of Justice of the EU has been a fundamental element of the EU's commitment to the rule of law principle.[517] Principally, the judicial review by the Court of Justice of the EU serves the following functions: First, to protect the institutional balance under the EU Treaties as well as to ensure the Commission does not commit *ultra-vires*[518] Second, to ensure consistent judicial interpretation of the competition legislations by means of observing their systematic function and defined goals. Ultimately, this leads to equal treatment and legal certainty. Third, to protect the affected undertakings or parties, that is to say, their procedural and substantive rights.[519]

Also, *Schweitzer* asserts the importance of the EU judicial review in the competition law cases, particulary to minimise the Commission's prosecutorial biases, as follows:

> "A principled and well-functioning regime of judicial review is a fundamental part of the European Union's commitment to the rule of law, and of particular relevance in the field of EU competition law: Over the last 50 years, the EU Commission has become one of the most powerful competition authorities worldwide. Efforts to strengthen private enforcement notwithstanding, the EU heavily relies on public enforcement to implement its competition rules. The EU Commission is at the center of this public enforcement regime. It is a specific feature of the EU Commission's enforcement powers that it combines investigative, prosecutorial and decision-making powers. The risk of a prosecutorial bias is an obvious corollary of such an institutional design. Apart from procedural guarantees during the administrative proceedings and internal checks and bal-

517 Schweitzer, '*Judicial Review in EU Competition Law*' in Lianos and Geradin (eds.). *Handbook on European competition law: Enforcement and procedure* (Edward Elgar Publishing, 2013) 491.

518 Etimology, *ultra-vires* means ‚beyond the powers or, an act in excess of their existing powers'. Historically, "The ultra vires doctrine originated in the Anglo -American legal system, but is now recognised also with us. After the ultra vires doctrine are transactions which enter a legal entity under public law by her outside the specified by law or the articles purview said legal person, legally invalid." ‹http://www.proverbia-iuris.de/ultra-vires› accessed on 17th March 2017.

519 Schweitzer, *Judicial Review (n 516) 491.*

> ances, it must be countered by a strong and efficient regime of judicial review."[520]

Equally important, *Mestmäcker and Schweitzer* assert that in the EU Competition Law's system, whereby the administrative authorithy (*Verwaltungsbehörde)* can both investigate and make decision over competition law cases, an effective judicial review is profoundly important. In fact, the effective judiciary review principle has been integrated in the EU legal system by virtue of Article 6 (2) ECHR and Article 47 of the CHFR-EU. Even more, in the Menarini case the European Court of Human Rights (ECtHR) emphasised the judicial review of an imposition of fines decision (Bußgeldbeschluss), that is to say, to rectify the administrative body's decision in terms *of de jure and de facto* revisions. If necessary, the Courts of Justice of the EU can replace the administrative body's decision with their rectified decisions.[521]

On the one hand, *Mestmäcker and Schweitzer* outline that Article 263 TFEU enables the Courts of Justice of the EU to perform the judicial review, namely the legality of Commission's decision. Nonetheless, the Courts's judicial review competences are limited by the EU Competition Law's jurisprudences, whereby the Commission has discretionary competences in the judgements involving appraisal of complex economic circumstances. For example, the relevant market analysis and the working effects of anticompetitive practices. On the other hand, the EU Competition Law's jurisprudences have been advocating the intensive judicial reviews over the Commission's decisions regardless the Commission's discretionary competences. Accordingly, by virtue of the EU Competition Law's jurisprudences, the Courts of Justice of the EU are obligated to:

> "examine not only the objective truth of the evidence presented, namely the reliability and consistency, but also to inspect whether the evidence contains all relevant data for assessing complex circumstances and thus the evidence can substantiate the conclusions, inferred from the evidence."[522]

In the EU Competition Law's proceedings, the Courts of Justice of the EU can perform three different functions: First, as the administrative

520 ibid.

521 Schweitzer and Mestmäcker, *Europäisches Wettbewerbsrecht* (n 429) 530–531.

522 ibid.

court, for example reviewing the legality of the Commission's decision. Second, as the civil court, that is to say, to give material compensations for damages due to the EU organs' action. Third, as the constitutional court, notably, to adjudicate cases pertaining the legal interpretations of the EU Treaties.[523]

Principally, the provisions of Article 263 TFEU serve as the juridical platform for the judicial review of competition law cases. Hence Article 263 TFEU prescribes, as follows:

> "The Court of Justice of the European Union shall review the legality of legislative acts, of acts of the Council, of the Commission and of the European Central Bank, other than recommendations and opinions, and of acts of the European Parliament and of the European Council intended to produce legal effects vis-à-vis third parties. It shall also review the legality of acts of bodies, offices or agencies of the Union intended to produce legal effects vis-à-vis third parties.
> It shall for this purpose have jurisdiction in actions brought by a Member State, the European Parliament, the Council or the Commission on grounds of lack of competence, infringement of an essential procedural requirement, infringement of the Treaties or of any rule of law relating to their application, or misuse of powers."

According to *Schweitzer*, under the provisions of Article 263 TFEU concerning the legality supervision mechanism, the judiciary review of the Courts of Justice of the EU encompasses: First, review over the infringement of an essential procedural requirement (procedural propriety review). Second, review over the infringement of the EU Law.[524]

With regard to the procedural propriety review, the Courts of Justice of the EU will examine the Commission's investigation competence application, that is to say, whether the Commission obeys the EU procedural laws. Further, *Schweitzer* asserts, as follows:

> "[...] with the burden of proof being on the Commission, the Court will, inter alia, inquire whether the Commission has complied with its duty 'to examine carefully and impartially all the relevant aspects in the individual case, whether it has fully respected the right to be heard and the duty to provide a statement of reason (Article 296(2) TFEU)."

523 Kerse and Khan, *EU Antitrust Procedure*, 521–522.
524 Schweitzer, *Judicial Review (n 516)* 495–500.

The ECJ explains as to the statement of reason, as follows:

> "show clearly and unequivocally the reasoning of the Community authority which adopted the measure so as to inform the persons concerned of the justification for the measure adopted and to enable the Court to exercise its powers of review"[525]

In the second place, as regards to the review of the EU Law's infringement, the Court of Justice of the EU must guarantee the institutional balances, that is to say, to ensure that the Commission complies with the EU substantive laws. Further, the Courts of Justice of EU shall ensure a consistent interpretation and application of EU laws in order to protect the legal certainty. Eventually, the Court of Justice of EU must protect the fundamental and human rights as mandated by the EU treaties and international laws. Put differently, the Court of Justice of EU as '*recours pours excess de pouvoir*', in terms of administrative court, shall examine the administrative acts of Commission under the principle of legality, for example reviewing the Commission 'margin of discretion'.[526]

According to *Schweitzer*, in the judicial practice of EU Competition Law, the European Courts of Justice of the EU distinguish three types of judicial review over competition law cases.[527] First, the review of law. Second, the review of facts. Third, the review of application of laws to facts.[528] Also, the first type of review is subject to 'full and comprehensive judicial review'. Whereas, the second and third type of review are subject to 'full judicial review'. Accordingly, as regards the first type of review, pursuant to the Article 19 (1) TFEU the European Courts will "ensure that in the interpretation and application of the Treaties the law is observed". On the one hand, the Court of Justice of EU will perform judicial review as to substantial aspect of the EU Competition rules, for example whether the terms 'agreements', 'concerted practices' and 'restriction of competition' have been correctly applied. On the other hand, in the second and third types of review, the Court of Justice of EU shall merely examine the correctness and comprehensiveness of facts used by the Commission. Besides, pur-

525 Schweitzer, *Judicial Review (n 516)* 495–499.
526 Schweitzer, *Judicial Review (n 516)* 494–499.
527 ibid.
528 ibid.

suant to the Article 32 of Protocol on the "Statute of the Court of Justice of the European Union" the European Courts can ask expert evidences to find the material truth in the judicial proceedings. However, the presentation of economic expert evidences in the competition law cases is difficult to implement.[529] Moreover, the European Courts of Justice of the EU will perform the judicial review to facts as well as to the application of the law to the facts involving complex assesments.

3.1.5 Principle and Rule concerning Evidence

3.1.5.1 Burden and Standard of Proof

In the European Competition law's enforcement proceedings, Article 2 of the Regulation Number 1/2003 stipulates, as follows:

> "Burden of proof
> In any national or Community proceedings for the application of Articles 81 and 82 of the Treaty, the burden of proving an infringement of Article 81(1) or of Article 82 of the Treaty shall rest on the party or the authority alleging the infringement. The undertaking or association of undertakings claiming the benefit of Article 81(3) of the Treaty shall bear the burden of proving that the conditions of that paragraph are fulfilled."[530]

Historically, the evidentiary provisions of Article 2 of the Regulation Number 1/2003 derogated from the procedural rules contained in the previous Regulation Number 17/62, whose objectives are to solidify the 'direct enforcement' system as well as the legal exemptions of Article 101 (3) TFEU, which subsequently would reduce the judicial uncertainties over the facts'conclusion.[531]

Systematically, the evidentiary rules in Article 2 of the Regulation Number 1/2003 have been manisfested in three kinds of proceedings of the European Competition law, notably: Initially, the administrative

---

529 ibid.

530 G.K de Bronett, Europäisches Kartellverfahrensrecht: Kommentar zur VO 1/2003 (2. *Auflage* Carl Heymanns, 2012) 56–59.

531 These provisions of Article 2 are to be read in conjuctions with Article 103 paragraph 2 TFEU, notably alphabet b:
1. The appropriate regulations or directives to give effect to the principles set out in Articles 101 and 102 shall be laid down by the Council, on a proposal from the Commission and after consulting the European Parliament.

proceeding.[532] Secondly, the imposition of administrative fines proceeding.[533] Thirdly, the civil litigation proceeding.[534] For an example in the administrative proceedings, the Commission shall corroborate or present convincing (firm) evidences, that solidify the conviction, that a cartel infringement had indeed took place.[535] Subsequently, for example, in the imposition of administrative fine proceedings, the *in dubio pro reo principle* has a precedence (primacy) before the evidentiary provisions of Article 2 thereof. This rule applies both to the imposition of administrative fines under Article 23 of the Regulation in conjunctions to Sec. 81 of the German Cartel Act. Respectively, this rule must be read in conjunctions with the German's Declarative Protocol concerning the precedence of the presumption of innocence.[536]

Chronologically, prior to Article 2 of the Regulation Number 1/2003 the ECJ the *Anic case*, had envisaged the meaning of burden of proof, namely:

> "[...] it is incumbent on the Commission to prove the infringements which it has found and to adduce evidence capable of demonstrating to the requisite legal standard the existence of circumstances constituting the infringement. [...] In doing this, the Commission must establish in particular all the facts enabling the conclusion to be drawn that an undertaking participated in such an infringement and that it was responsible for the various aspects of it."[537]

Furthermore, Recitals 5 of the Regulation Number 1/2003 prerequisites:

> "It should be for the party or the authority alleging an infringement of Article 81(1) and Article 82 of the Treaty to prove the existence thereof to the required legal standard."[538]

---

2. The regulations or directives referred to in paragraph 1 shall be designed in particular:
(b) to lay down detailed rules for the application of Article 101(3), taking into account the need to ensure effective supervision on the one hand, and to simplify administration to the greatest possible extent on the other.

532 Schmidt in Immenga and Mestmäcker, *Wettbewerbsrecht (n 44) R. 35–37.*
533 ibid., R 38–39.
534 ibid., R 35–37.
535 Schmidt in Immenga and Mestmäcker, *Wettbewerbsrecht (n 44) R. 38–39.*
536 ibid.
537 ibid., R. 1–15.
538 de Bronett, *Europäisches Kartellverfahrensrecht* (n 529) 56–58.

Hence the burden of proof rests primarily upon parties or authorities alleging an infringement against Article 101 (1) TFEU. Once this could be established, the burden of proof shifts to alleged undertakings in order to counter allegations. Thus, alleged undertakings could argue that the concurrence of wills is subject to beneficial exemptions of Article 101 (3) TFEU.[539] Accordingly, the European Competition law embraces the principle *incumbit, probatio, qui dicit, non qui negat*.[540]

With regard to the burden of proof, it should be bore in mind that the Courts of Justice of the EU embrace the principle of *in dubio pro reo*, pursuant to Article 6 (2) European Court of Human Rights (ECHR) Convention. Consequently, an imposition of fines or penaltic payments upon undertakings due to competition law violation should be subject to this principle. This presumption of innocence principle refers to the notion, as follows:

> "[...it] implies that every person accused is presumed to be innocent until his guilt has been established according to law. It thus precludes any formal finding and even any allusion to the liability of an accused person for a particular infringement in a final decision unless that person has enjoyed all the usual guarantees accorded for the exercise of the rights of the defence in the normal course of proceedings resulting in a decision on the merits of the case."[541]

Furthermore, in the European Competition Law, following categorisation between burden and standard of proofs, as well as material subjective and objective evidential burdens the following notions play a central role:

> "[...] the standard of proof determines the requirements which must be satisfied for facts to be regarded as proven. It must be distinguished from the burden of proof. The burden of proof determines, first, which party must put forward the facts and, where necessary, adduce the related evidence ("*formelle Beweislast*", also known as the evidential burden); second, the allocation of that burden determines which party bears the risk of facts remaining unresolved or allegations unproven ("*materielle Beweislast*")."[542]

539 Jones and Surfin, EU Competition Law (n 450) 123.

540 The Latin maxim, meaning "The burden of the proof lies upon him who affirms not he who denies" Geradin, Ferrer, Petit, EU Competition Law (n 44) 391–4.

541 Jones and Sufrin (n 450) 123.

542 C. de la Torre 'Evidence, 'Proof and Judicial Review in Cartel Cases' (World Competition, Volume 32/ Issue 4, Kluwer Law International, 2009) 505–578.

As far as the standard of proof is concerned, the European Competition Law's jurisprudence competition law has been up to now requiring that 'sufficiently, precise and coherent proofs' must be established.[543] Furthermore, the European Courts in the competition law precedents require quality of evidences as follows: 'sufficiently precise and coherent [or consistent]'[544], 'precise and consistent'[545], 'solid, specific and corroborative'[546], 'firm, precise and consistent body of evidence'[547], 'convergent and convincing'[548], 'convincing'[549], or 'cogent'.[550] Furthermore, the Court of Justice in its recent decision, *Dresdner Bank* case, stipulated:

> "Any doubt in the mind of the Court must operate to the advantage of the undertaking to which the decision finding an infringement was addressed. The Court cannot therefore conclude that the Commission has established the infringement at issue to the requisite legal standard if it still entertains any doubts on that point, in particular in proceedings for annulment of a decision imposing a fine. [...] the Commission must show precise and consistent evidence in order to establish the existence of the infringement.[551]

Furthermore, the ECJ in the *Dresdner Bank* case stipulated that 'the Commission must adduce precise and consistent evidence to establish cartels agreement. On the one hand, the Commission should not establish precision and consistency as regards to each element of infringement, but merely globally.[552] On the other hand, the European courts in adjudicating competition law cases indicate a strong tendency to the principle 'beyond reasonable doubt' in terms of its eviden-

543 The standard of proof refers to "the standard of proof determines degree of conviction, which the judges must establish by considering the acceptable evidentiary instruments, in order to substantiate an allegation as truth and accept the evidences.The standard of proof determines the degree of conviction, the need to obtain the decision because of the admissible evidence ". cf. ibid.

544 Geradine, Ferrer, Petit, EU Competition Law (n 44) 128–130.

545 Schmidt in Immenga and Mestmäcker, *Wettbewerbsrecht (n 44)* 25–29. cf. Geradine, Ferrer, Petit, EU Competition Law (n 44), 128–130.

546 ibid.

547 ibid.

548 ibid.

549 ibid.

550 Ibid.

551 Geradine, Ferrer, Petit, EU Competition Law (n 44), 128–129.

552 ibid.

tiary standard. In the *Woodpulp* case, for example, the Court of Justice stipulated:

> "the evidence must be 'sufficiently precise and coherent [...] to justify the view that the parallel business [...] was the result of concerted action."

Equally important, Bellamy, the former Judge of the European Court, asserted as regards to evidentiary standard, as follows:

> "Thus, we have not yet articulated the difference known in common law systems between the criminal standard *of 'proof beyond reasonable doubt'* and the civil standard of 'balance of probabilities', a difference which is also known in civil law systems but not perhaps articulated in quite the same way. In practice, we are applying something very close to the criminal standard but perhaps subconsciously making some allowance in cartel cases for the inherent difficulty of proving collusion. "[553]

Equally important, *Schweitzer* explains that the European Competition Law requires the Commission to apply significanty higher evidentiary standards to prove cartels infringements under Article 101 TFEU, particulary in the decision imposing fines, similar to 'beyond reasonable doubt' in the common law system.[554] Accordingly, the GC argued in the Siemens case regarding the evidentiary standard thereof:

> "In competition matters, the Commission must ***show precise and consistent evidence in order to establish the existence of the infringement and to support the firm conviction that the alleged infringements constitute appreciable restrictions of competition within the meaning of Article 81(1) EC.*** However, it is not necessary for every item of evidence produced by the Commission to satisfy those criteria in relation to every aspect of the infringement. It is sufficient if the set of indicia relied on by the institution, viewed as a whole, meets that requirement. The existence of an anti-competitive practice or agreement may therefore be inferred from a number of coincidences and indicia which, taken together, may, in the absence of another plausible explanation, constitute evidence of an infringement of the competition rules."[555]

Consequently, by inferrence from the EU Competition Law's jurisprudences, Schweitzer emphasises that "if any doubt remains in the mind of the court on whether the Commission has established an infringement, it follows from the of innocence [in dubio pro reo] as established

553 OECD, 'Judicial Enforcement of Competition Law 1996' (Roundtable Policy, 1996) 105–107.

554 Schweitzer, *Judicial Review* (n 516) 501.

555 ibid. General Court, Case T-223/11 Siemens AG v European Commission.

by Article 6(2) ECHR and as accepted as a general principle of the Union law that the Commission's decision finding an infringement must be annulled."[556]

3.1.5.2 Evidentiary Evaluation and Category of Evidence

In the European competition law enforcement proceedings, evidences could be classified into: inculpatory and exculpatory evidences as well as direct and indirect (circumstantial) evidences. According to the Commission: "the notion of indirect or circumstantial evidences (...) comprise of evidence which is appropriate to corroborate the proof of existence of a cartel by way of deduction, common sense, economic analysis or logical inferences from demonstrated facts".[557]

Whilst direct evidence reveals directly the relevant facts, indirect evidences "prove a fact with which the relevant fact bears a logical relationship. Indirect evidence can rarely be used in isolation and usually requires corroboration or is itself used to corroborate other (possibly also indirect) evidence." For example, in proving cartels agreement, the Commission could not rely solely upon indirect evidences, such as economic evidences. Mere economic evidences, such as parallel price movements, could not serve as sufficient proof of a cartels' practice. These evidences ought to exist side-by-side with other evidences to corroborate other material indications regarding cartels practice. In other words, indirect (circumstantial) evidences on their own could be sufficient to prove cartels infringement, provided the judges review theses evidences in a holistic way and thus an overall indication of violation could be manifested.[558]

Equally important, the Commission can employ the direct evidences and the indirect (circumstantial) evidences to substantiate cartels infringement in accordance with Article 101 TFEU. However, in the practice of EU Competition Law, due to an absence of exact definitions of these evidentiary types, there has been a difficulty to make a clear distinction between the direct and indirect evidences. Further, as

556 Schweitzer, *Judicial Review (n 516)* 501.
557 Lianos and Genakos,' Econometric Evidence' (n 26) 55–57.
558 de la Torre, 'Evidence, Proof and Judicial Review' (n 541)505–578.

regards to the increasing importance of indirect (circumstantial) evidence, Buhart and Maulin report, as follows:

> "However, *direct evidence available to the competition authorities is increasingly rare due to the business community's growing awareness of European competition law and the risk of fines.* Given these developments, so as not to pose a burden on the Commission deemed "impossible", the Commission may prove, to some extent, its claims through the use of presumptions. The Community courts have thus validated the use of circumstantial evidence to corroborate the existence of a cartel based on deductions or economic analysis. This was especially the case in the *Wood Pulp* judgment, in which the ECJ appointed two expert economists responsible for determining whether the Commission's analysis concerning alleged parallel conduct was correct."[559]

3.1.5.3 The Application of Evidentiary Rules and Principle

In the context of application of evidentiary rules to Article 101 (1) TFEU, particulary the concerted practices, the real difficulties encountered by the EU Competition Authorithy (the Commission) are the informal market coordination by undertakings, which are committed within unlawfully secretive circumstances, such as by a price increase announcement leading to cartels. Herewith, Article 2 of the Regulation Number 1/2003 in correlation with Article 101 (1) TFEU, elaborates the so-called direct evidence, on the one hand, and the indirect (circumstantial) evidence on the other hand.[560]

According to *Schröter and van Vormizeele*, the direct evidences of unlawful market coordinations by undertakings, either in the form of the agreements, decisions of undertakings association, or of the concerted practices, include, among others, documents, that consist of agendas, participants' list, verbatims of meetings, logs or records of participating undertakings, exchange of correspondence, scripts on the future corporate actions and policies disbursed in medias, witness

559 J Buhart and R Maulin, 'Proof in Cartels: State of Play and Perspectives' (Concurrences N° 4–2011) http://awa2012.concurrences.com/academic/article/proof-in-cartels-state-of-play-and, accessed on 20th March 2016 51–64.

560 Emmerich in Immenga and Mestmäcker, *Wettbewerbsrecht: Kommentar (n 44) R. 98–102.*

statements or even personal confessions of the cartel participants.[561] In majority of cases, the Commission obtained the direct evidences by means of the Leniency programme.[562]

561 Schröter and van Vormizeele in von der Groeben, Schwarze, Hatje (eds.), *Europäisches Unionsrecht. Vertrag über die Europäische Union – Vertrag über die Arbeitsweise der Europäischen Union – Charta der Grundrechte der Europäischen Union* (7 Aufl. Baden-Baden (Nomos) 2015).

562 The Leniency programme refers to a general term for the total or partial reduction of fines applied to firms that co-operate with antitrust authorities in cartel investigations, which are currently enunciated in the 2006 Commission Notice on immunity from fines and reduction of fines in cartel cases, as amended in 2015. The Commission, Notice on Immunity from fines and reduction of fines in cartel cases, Official Journal C 298, 8.12.2006, 17.
According to the Commission, Directorate General for Competition (DG COMP): "In essence, the leniency policy offers companies involved in a cartel – which self-report and hand over evidence – either total immunity from fines or a reduction of fines which the Commission would have otherwise imposed on them. It also benefits the Commission, allowing it not only to pierce the cloak of secrecy in which cartels operate but also to obtain insider evidence of the cartel infringement. The leniency policy also has a very deterrent effect on cartel formation and it destabilizes the operation of existing cartels as it seeds distrust and suspicion among cartel members. In order to obtain total **immunity** under the leniency policy, a company which participated in a cartel must be the first one to inform the Commission of an undetected cartel by providing sufficient information to allow the Commission to launch an inspection at the premises of the companies allegedly involved in the cartel. If the Commission is already in possession of enough information to launch an inspection or has already undertaken one, the company must provide evidence that enables the Commission to prove the cartel infringement. In all cases, the company must also fully cooperate with the Commission throughout its procedure, provide it with all evidence in its possession and put an end to the infringement immediately. The cooperation with the Commission implies that the existence and the content of the application cannot be disclosed to any other company. The company may not benefit from immunity if it took steps to coerce other undertakings to participate in the cartel. Companies which do not qualify for immunity may benefit from a **reduction** of fines if they provide evidence that represents "significant added value" to that already in the Commission's possession and have terminated their participation in the cartel. Evidence is considered to be of a "significant added value" for the Commission when it reinforces its ability to prove the infringement. The first company to meet these conditions is granted 30 to 50% reduction, the second 20 to 30% and subsequent companies up to 20%. The Commission considers that any statement submitted to it within the context of its leniency policy forms part of the Commission's file and may therefore not be disclosed or used for any other purpose than the Commission's own cartel proceedings."

As far as the indirect (circumstantial) evidences are concerned, the Commission and the Court of Justice of EU could prove the unlawful market coordinations, notably by the concerted practices, through the indirect evidences obtained during the administrative and judicial proceedings. For example, the uniform market behaviour of undertakings could constitute an indirect evidence. However, the evaluation or appraisal of indirect (*circumstantial*) evidence must be subject to the considerations of peculiar characteristics of the market at hand.[563] Hence, such an irrational corporate actions or conducts, which are contrary to the economic interest of an undertaking at hand could be an indirect (*circumstantial)* evidence.[564]

Equally important, as regards the corroboration of indirect (*circumstantial*) evidences, according to Emmerich, the ambivalence of market behaviours of undertakings, notably in the oligopolistic market structure, must be carefully considered by the Competition Authority. Therefore, the Commission and the Court of Justice of EU, in order to reach the convicing and firm conclusion as to the cartel violation, must corroborate further the indirect evidences, the so-called "Plus factors" or the "Parallelism plus". Respectively, in the praxis of the European Competition law, Emmerich elaborates the 'Plus factors' as follows:

> "Such plus factors are, in particular, the participation of the participating companies in joint meetings with an anti-competitive objective and all other forms of information exchange, provided that there are other alternative courses of action open to the market. The same applies if the parallel behavior of the undertakings concerned creates competitive conditions The same is true if companies consistently demand identical prices in different national markets, even though the diverging market structures in the various Member States are the same Certain Member States may indeed allow or even suggest a differentiated price strategy or, if the circumstances of a common price increase, as in the past, are broadly similar imminent amounts of the price increase and the like more necessarily indicate a previous vote. Another such plus factor is the fact that the common and identical behavior of companies must remain incomprehensible for their individual interests and can therefore only be explained on the basis

---

The Commission, http://ec.europa.eu/competition/cartels/leniency/leniency.html, accessed 28th December 2018.

563 Schröter and van Vormizeele in von der Groeben, Schwarze, Hatje (eds) *Europäisches Unionsrecht (n 560)* R. 65–69.

564 ibid.

> of common goals and plans. For example, where producers from one Member State in other Member States also only supply to producers but refuse to supply to traders and end users, if they follow export prices higher local producer prices instead of price competition with their lower prices, if they refrain from exports and if they exaggerate on the export markets, clearly demanding prohibitively-priced prices. Again, of course, if companies are able to give other plausible reasons for their behavior. Other circumstances, depending on the peculiarities of the individual markets may indicate the existence of a behavioral vote, but are the simultaneous termination of the business relationship with a company by several competitors, of the common distribution of competitors through the same dealer or representative or a single distribution organization, co-operation in joint ventures or joint control of a competitor, as well as personnel links at the executive level."[565]

Whereas, according to *Kovavic*, in other perspective as regards the "Plus factors", the European Competition law and US Antitrust law's practices have since longtime developed this kind of indirect evidences for the purpose of distinguishing collusive agreements, and concerted practices from the oligopolistic interdependence, occuring ordinarily in an oligopoly market, by elaborating as follows:

> "Evidence of certain types of conduct strongly signifies market collusion. Examples include, as argued by Kovacic and others, 'super plus factors' such as evidence that competing firms share firm-specific production information.In the absence of such evidence, a decision to further investigate market players for potential collusion can be based on empirical analysis, including the use of empirical screens. For example, a decision to further investigate can also be justified when the data in question (e.g. price or quantity-related data) are clearly abnormal and completely different from a carefully chosen benchmark."[566]

565 Emmerich in Immenga and Mestmäcker, *Wettbewerbsrecht (n 44) R. 100–102.*

566 E Ghezzi; M Maggiolino, 'Bridging EU Concerted Practices With U.S. Concerted Actions' (Journal of Competition Law & Economics, Volume 10, Issue 3, Oxford Academic, 2014) 647–690.

3.2 Procedural Law pursuant to the German Cartel Law

3.2.1 Introduction

Principally, the German Act against Restraints of Competition (GWB) or the German Cartel Law) stipulates four main enforcement procedures of the prevailing cartel law.[567] First, the administrative proceeding (*Verwaltungsverfahren*) before the Competition governmental authorities (*Kartellbehörde, Bundeskartellamt*).[568] Second, the appeal or complaint proceedings (*Beschwerdeverfahren*) before the Courts.[569] Third, the imposition of fines proceedings (*Bußgeldverfahren*).[570] Fourth, the civil litigation (*Bürgerliche Streitigkeiten*) before the Courts.[571]

Furthermore, the German Cartel law stipulates that there are five Competition Authorities (*Kartellbehörden*), responsible for the implementation of the Law and share jurisdictions. *First,* the Federal Cartel Office (*Bundeskartellamt* or FCO), whose main duties are to apply GWB to all restraints of competition having an effect on Germany, irrespective the location of an infringement. The *Bundeskartellamt* is an independent higher federal authorithy assigned to the Federal Ministry of Economics and Technology and serves as the centre of the eGerman Leniency Progamme. The *Bundeskartellamt* establishes a cooperation with other competition authorities particulary the Directorate General of Competition of the European Commission.[572] *Second,* the Federal Ministry of Economics and Technology (*Bundesministerium für Wirtschaft und Technologie-BMWT*), whose main function is to issue a ministerial authorisation (*Ministererlaubnis*) whenever a concentration prohibited by the FCO has outweight benefits to the economy as a whole.[573] *Third,* the State Cartel Offices (*Landeskartellbehörden*), whose main duty is to deal with competition cases which af-

567 Bach, in Immenga and Mestmäcker, *Wettbewerbsrecht, Band.2* (CH Beck, München, 2012) 2160–65.
568 Pursuant to the Sec. 54–62 GWB. Bach in Immenga and Mestmäcker (n 566).
569 Pursuant to the Sec. 63–76 GWB. ibid.
570 Pursuant to the Sec. 81–86 GWB. ibid.
571 Pursuant to the Sec. 87–89a GWB. ibid.
572 Schneider in *Langen and Bunte*, Kommentar zum (n 99) 1133–1135.
573 Staebe in *Just and Schulte*, Kartellrecht (n 118), 381–399.

fect one Federal State (Land). However, the merger and acquisition cases are subject to FCO's examination.[574] *Fourth,* the other Authorities, for instance the Federal Network Agency (*Bundesnetzagentur*) and the Monopolies Commission (*Monopolkommission),* whose main responsibilities comprise, among others: to develop the electricity, gas, telecomunication, post and railway markets through the liberalisation and deregulation intruments.[575] *Fifth,* the District Court and the Federal Supreme Court (*Bundesgerichtshof*-BGH), whereas the Decision of the *Bundeskartellamt* is subject to the Higher Regional Court/Court of Appeals (*Oberlandesgerichte-OLG*). Furthermore, the Decision of the Higher Regional Court can be appealed to the *Bundesgerichsthof* in the following matters, notably: the questions of general importance, the development of law and the ensurement of uniform court practice.[576]

3.2.2 The Administrative Proceeding (*Verwaltungsverfahren*)

3.2.2.1 General Principles

In general, the administrative proceedings rules before the German Competition Authority (*Kartellbehörde*) are regulated in Sec. 54 until 62 of the GWB. Besides, there are common provisions for administrative proceedings, the complaint (*Beschwerde*) and the appeal of law (*Rechtsbeschwerde)* pursuant to Sec. 77 until 80 of the GWB. In addition, provisions of the Administrative Procedure Act (*Verwaltungsverfahrensgesetz – VwVfG*) complement the administrative proceedings of the German Cartel Law.[577]

The administrative proceedings rules before the *Kartellbehörde* have been very formal. The rules give the *Kartellbehörde* powers to make legally binding decision proportionally. However, the *Bundesgerichtshof had* in *the Pepcom case* made decision concerning the

574 ibid.

575 Schneider in Langen and Bunte, *Kommentar zum (n 99) 1133–1135.*

576 Bechtold and Denzel in Kokkoris, "Competition cases (n 460) 501–510.

577 Funke in Berg and Märsch, *Deutsches und Europäisches Kartellrecht (n 297)* 568–569.

Third-party's right to appeal, which was developed in accordance to the EU Competition Law.[578]

Systematically, the administrative proceeding provisions in Sec. 54 until 62 of the GWB shall not apply to other enforcement proceedings, such as the imposition of fines proceeding (*Bußgeldverfahren).* Accordingly, the rules concerning investigation and procedural rights of the Parties under the administrative proceeding largely differ with the other proceedings. Thus, the *Kartellbehörde* is obliged from the start of case to decide whether the administrative proceeding or the imposition of fines will apply to cases in question. However, the *Kartellbehörde* can shift the proceeding from one to another depending upon the discretion (Ermessen). Hence whenever the event shift from the administrative to the imposition of fine proceeding, the *Kartellbehörde* is able to re-employ previously obtained evidences in a proportional manner.[579]

As has been previously noted, in the administrative proceeding before the *Kartellbehörde* a set of general guiding rules of the Administrative Procedure Act (*VwVfG)* applies. First, the inspection of files and secrecy (privacy) rules according to Sec. 29 and 30 of the VwVfG. Second, the relevancy of procedural and/or formal mistakes. Third, the re-interpretation rule and ancillary provisions as stipulated in Sec. 36 of VwVfG. Fourth, the withdrawal and revocation of administrative acts according to Sec. 48 and 49 of VwVfG.[580]

Equally important, in the administrative proceeding of the German Cartel law, the principle of 'protection of legitimate expectation' prevails as well as legal certainty shall apply under Sec. 38 of VwVfG. In addition, Sec. 61 of VwVfG requires the immediate enforcement measure of the Decision of the *Kartellbehörde.*[581]

At the same time, the *Kartellbehörde* imposes also a set of informal administrative proceeding practices, which comprise among others: the publication of information, advocacy, informal information request, lecturing activities, and public relations matters.[582]

---

578 Peter in Just and Schulte, *Kartellrecht* (n 118) 408–410.

579 Bach, in Immenga and Mestmäcker, Wettbewerbsrecht (n 566) 2174–2177.

580 Ost in Säcker, et.al, *Europäisches und deutsches Wettbewerbsrecht (n 13)* 1000–1002.

581 Bach in Immenga and Mestmäcker, *Wettbewerbsrecht* (n 566) 2147–2150.

582 Ost in Säcker, et.al, *Europäisches und deutsches Wettbewerbsrecht (n 13) 1066–1070.*

In fact, the administrative proceedings before the *Kartellbehörde* consists of three main phases. Firstly, the initiation or opening phase. Subsequently, investigation and evidentiary phase. Eventually, the conclusion or decisional phase. In the opening or initiation of a case phase, the *Kartellbehörde* can initiate a case either by ex-officio (von Amts wegen) or upon request or application (Antrag) pursuant to Sec. 54 (1) of the GWB. However, the *Kartellbehörde* can initiate an investigation based on its own initiative having received request from complainants pursuant to Sec. 54 (2) of the GWB.[583] Accordingly, in this context the problematic of 'horse and rider' emerges.[584] Furthermore, in this phase the Opportunity principle (*Opportunitätsprinzip)* applies, which refers to the considerations of the *Kartellbehörde* as to whether and how it takes enforcement measures against the Cartel law infringement.[585]

Equally important, as regards to the participating Parties in the administrative proceeding, Sec. 54 (2) of the GWB elaborates that Parties to the proceedings before the *Kartellbehörde* are: *First*, those who have applied for the initiation of the proceeding. *Second*, the alleged cartels, undertakings, trade and industry associations or professional organisations against which the administrative proceedings are directed. *Third*, persons and associations of persons whose interests will be substantially affected by the decision and who, upon their application, have been admitted by the Competition Authority to the proceedings.Furthermore, the *Bundeskartellamt* shall also be the party to the proceedings before the supreme Land Authorities (Landesbehörde) as stipulated by Sec. 54 (3) of the GWB. In this context, the investigation phase recognises three courses of action: First, searching towards the alleged undertakings, second, compilation and third, an analysis of evidences and lastly examination of witnesses. Thus, according to Sec. 57 of the GWB, the taking of evidences is carried out following the court's proceeding practice.[586]

Even more, the provisions of Sec. 32 until 32 (e) and 34 of the GWB confer the *Bundeskartellamt* following decisional powers. Accordingly, its principally important powers are: First, the order con-

583 Bach, Immenga and Mestmäcker, *Wettbewerbsrecht (n 566)* 2162–216

584 Peter in Just and Schulte, *Kartellrecht (n 103)* 405–406.

585 Funke in Berg and Märsch, *Deutsches und Europäisches Kartellrecht (n 297)* 570.

586 Ost in Säcker, et.al, *Europäisches und deutsches Wettbewerbsrecht* (n 13) 1001–1014.

cerning termination and subsequent findings of infringements pursuant to Sec. 32 of the GWB. Second, the edict of preliminary injunctions according to Sec. 60 of the GWB. Third, the prohibition concerning the mergers by undertakings stipulated by Sec. 36 (1) of the GWB. Fourth, the order concerning skimming-off of benefits pursuant to Sec. 34 and 43 of the GWB. Thereby, in the conclusion phase, the provisions of Sec. 61 stipulate two elements: First, the issuance of an order (*Verfügungen)* and second, the notification (*Zustellung).*[587] Also, the provisions of Sec. 61 of the GWB reads:

> "1) Decisions of the cartel authority shall contain a statement of reasons and be served together with advice as to the available legal remedies upon the parties pursuant to the provisions of the Act on Service in Administrative Procedure [Verwaltungszustellungsgesetz]. Sec. 5 (4) of the Act on Service in Administrative Procedure and Sec. 178 (1) no. 2 of the Code of Civil Procedure shall apply mutatis mutandis to undertakings and associations of undertakings as well as to contracting entities within the meaning of Sec. 98. Decisions directed at undertakings with their registered seat outside the scope of application of this Act shall be served by the cartel authority upon the person who was named by the undertaking to the *Bundeskartellamt* as authorised to accept service. If the undertaking has not named any person authorised to accept service, the cartel authority shall serve the decisions by way of publication in the Federal Gazette.
> (2) If proceedings are not completed by way of a decision served upon the parties pursuant to paragraph 1, the parties shall be informed in writing of the completion of the proceedings."[588]

Within the administrative proceedings, the principle of administrative legality (*Gesetzmäßigkeit der Verwaltung*), embodied in Article 20 III of the Federal Republic of Germany's *Grundgesetz* (GG), applies. This principle means that any administrative action must be based on prevailing legislation.[589] Nevertheless, in the broad sense, this principle refers to two main characteristics: *First,* due to the principle of precedence of law (*Vorrang des Gesetzes*), all of the administrative actions must comply with the existing laws and regulations. Further, the administrative actions are not in contrary to respective superior rules. Had these principles been violated, the affected parties or the citizens

587 ibid. 1057–1067.

588 ibid.

589 Foster and Sule, *German Legal System (n 495)* 287–289. cf. Ost in Säcker, et.al, *Europäisches und deutsches Wettbewerbsrecht* (n 13) 1100–1102.

are able to file the judicial review due to an illegality of the administrative actions.[590] *Second*, the principle of subjection of law (*Vorbehalt des Gesetzes)*, requiring a prior authorisation of the prevailing laws. Thus, these rules will limit the administrative competence. In the second place, whenever the administrative decision violated the public rights and properties, thus the judicial review applies.[591]

Equally important, the administrative authorities have certain degrees of the discretionary competence (*Ermessen*) in making decisions. However, the discretionary competence is subject to certain limitations, notably: First, a non-use of discretion (*Ermessensnichtgebrauch)* take places. Second, exceeding discretion (*Ermessensüberschreitung*). Third, misuse of discretion (*Ermessensfehlgebrauch)*.[592]

Subsequently, the German Cartel Law's administrative proceedings are also equipped with the principle of proportionality *(Verhältnismäßigkeit)*. Basically, this principle refers to a basic principle of the Rule of law (*Rechtsstaat*) and mandates that every law, administrative act, and measures of public institutions must not go beyond that strictly required to achieve the legal purpose.[593] Whereas this principle has derived from the protection of fundamental rights and individual freedoms in European values, the German Constitutional and Administrative laws develop this principle into a test of three parts, which are: First, the administrative actions must be suitable (efficient) to achieve the aim they are used for (*Geeignetheit*). Second, the administrative actions must be necessary to achieve this aim (*Erforderlichkeit*). Third, the administrative actions must outweigh the individual interests or basic rights on a balance.[594]

3.2.2.2 Evidentiary and Inquisitorial Principles

Within the framework of German Cartel Law, the GWB enshrines three main aspects of the evidentiary and inquisitorial principles. These are: (1)

590 Foster and Sule, *German Legal System (n 495)* 287–289 (Article 19 IV 4 of the GG).

591 ibid. 290–293.

592 M Reimann and J Zekoll (eds.) *Introduction to German Law* (CH Beck, 2006), 95–97.

593 Foster and Sule, *German Legal System (n 495)* 291–300.

594 Reimann and Zekoll, *Introduction to German Law* (n 591) 90.

the investigatory principle; (2) the burden of proof; (3) the types of evidentiary instruments.[595]

Firstly, as to the investigatory principle, due to its inquisitorial system, the *Kartellbehörde* must comply with the inquisitorial principle (*Amtsermittlungsgrundsatz, Untersuchungsmaxime*). By virtue of Sec. 24 of the VwVfG, three inquisitorial principles prevail. First, "the Offical authority shall examine the facts of its own motion. It determines the nature and extent of the investigation and it is not bound by arguments and proof of evidence presented by the parties in the proceeding". Second, the official authority shall take into account all significant matters individually. third, the official authority may not refuse the use the receipt of declarations or applications that fall within compentency, because it holds the declaration or the request in the matter inadmissible or unfounded.[596]

Profoundly important in this respect, *Schmidt* emphasises that the inquisitorial principles have goals to find the substantive or material truth (*materielle Wahrheit*), by ensuring the legality (*Rechtmäßgikeit)* of the administrative acts at the same time. Also, the abovementioned principles mean that the establishment of the facts of a matter (*Sachverhalte*), which are complete and accurate determine directly the legality of administrative actions.[597]

Secondly, with respect to the material burden of proof, the German Cartel Law distinguishes between the inquisitorial principles and the officiality principle (*Offizialmaxime*).[598] Thus, the officiality principle means that the initiation, required investigations of the proceeding take place because of an *ex-officio* initiative.[599] Besides, the principle refers to a factual truth-finding process during the administrative proceedings.[600] Consequently, the rule on presentation of evidences by the parties

595 Schmidt „Sec. 57 GWB" in Immenga/Mestmäcker, Wettbewerbsrecht (n 566) R 1–38.

596 ibid.

597 ibid.

598 *Engelsing* in Säcker, et.al, *Europäisches und deutsches Wettbewerbsrecht* Band. 2 (n 13) 1026–1030. cf. Schmidt in Immenga and Mestmäcker, Wettbewerbsrecht (n 566) 2212–2217.

599 Reimann and Zekoll, *Introduction to German Law* (n 591).

600 Schmidt „Sec. 57 GWB" in Immenga/Mestmäcker, Wettbewerbsrecht (n 566) R 1–14.

(*Beibringungsgrundsatz*) is inapplicable. Whenever the Parties presented evidences in the administrative proceeding, these evidences do not have a binding effect and thus are unnecessary for the *Kartellbehörde*. Equally important, the administrative proceedings apply the principle of cooperation obligations (*Mitwirkungsobliegenheiten*), which considerably limits the *Kartellbehörde*'s obligation on burden of proof.[601]

Under the material burden of proof, pursuant to the German Cartel Law, by virtue of Sec. 24 of VwVfG, it could be inferred that the *Kartellbehörde* has the administrative obligation to inquire (investigate) the facts of a case. However, the *Kartellbehörde* has the discretionary competence (*Ermessen*) to decide which types of investigatory measures applied within the administrative proceeding.[602] Even more, the provision of Sec. 24 of VwVfG prescribes that during the administrative proceeding, the *Kartellbehörde* shall observe the guiding rules, as follows: First, the investigations (inquiries) must be comprehensive and shall not be redundant or superfluous. This means, the *Kartelllbehörde* investigates only whenever the information and knowledge obtained from the proceedings are insufficient to find the substantive truth. Second, the neutrality principle towards the Parties during the administrative proceeding.[603] On the other hand, the principle of proportionality applies to the collection of the evidence phase. Hence the *Bundesverfassungsgericht* is of the opinion that this principle consists of three main ingredients. First, suitability (*Geeignetheit*). Second, necessity *(Erforderlichkeit)*. Third, proportionality in a strict sense (*Zumutbarkeit)*.[604] In the second place, the *Kartellbehörde* must consider the intended administrative action and the significance of a case prudentially. Also, the *Kartellbehörde* must opt for the most moderate or lenient measures to collect evidences.[605]

Indeed, within the administrative proceedings, the *Kartellbehörde* must conduct investigations until two requirements have been fulfilled. First, the whole matters of fact are clarified. Second, until the *non-li-*

601 ibid.
602 Sec. 24 para.1 of VwVfG. cf. Schmidt „Sec. 57 GWB" in Immenga/Mestmäcker, Wettbewerbsrecht (n 566) R 1–14.
603 ibid.
604 ibid.
605 ibid.

quet situation ceases to exist. In other words, obscurities concerning legal facts are cleary explained.[606] Whenever an assumption emerges during the administrative proceeding, thus the principle of neutrality applies. This means the *Kartellbehörde* must examine the incriminating and acquitting evidences.[607]

At the same time, within the administrative proceeding, the principle of unfettered consideration of evidences (*freie Beweiswürdigung*) applies, which means, as follows: First, the *Kartellbehörde* is not allowed to do typification (*Verbot der Typisierung*). Put differently, the *Kartellbehörde* must examine the evidences from the beginning and factual circumstances comprehensively. Second, the *Kartellbehörde* could employ previous empirical knowledge (*Erfahrungssätze*) for the appraisals during the investigatory proceedings. However, the application of empirical knowledge must be very careful. In other words, this means that the empirical knowledge must be disclosed and thus supported by appropriate evidences. [608]

Moreover, as regards to the substantive burden of proof (*materielle Beweislast*) in proving the cartels infringement, the provisions of Sec. 1 and 2 of the GWB in conjuction with Article 2 of the Regulation Number 1/2003 applies. The substantive burden of proof refers to the Parties, who must prove factual circumstances in question. Accordingly, Article 2 of the Regulation Number 1/2003 reads as follows:

> "In any national or Community proceedings for the application of Articles 81 and 82 of the Treaty, the Burden of proving an infringement of Article 81 (1) or of Article 82 of the Treaty shall rest on the party or the authorithy alleging the infringement. The undertaking or association of undertakings claiming the benefit of Article 81 (3) of the Treaty shall bear the Burden of proving that the conditions of that paragraph are fulfilled."

---

606 In the European and German Cartel Laws, *non-liquet* is a situation where there is no applicable law. The *Latin* term of *non-liquet* means "it is not clear". According to Cicero this term was applied during the Roman republic to a verdict of "not proven" where the case was "not clear". Schmidt „Sec. 57 GWB" in Immenga/ Mestmäcker, Wettbewerbsrecht (n 566) R 1–14.

607 Accordingly, that in the case of presumption according to Sec.18 and 20 GWB thus the *Kartellbehörde* subject to the Neutrality principle (Sec. 24 Abs. 2 VwVfG). cf. Schmitd, 'Sec. 57 GWB' in Immenga and Mestmäcker, Wettbewerbsrecht (n 566) R 1–14.

608 ibid.

Thirdly, as regards the admissible evidences, pursuant to Sec. 26 para.1 of the Administrative Process Law (*Verwaltungsverfahrengesetzt – VwVfG*), the *Bundeskartellamt* as the Competition Authority can collect and corroborate varying types of evidences to obtain clarification of factual circumstances and thus the material (substantive) truth of a case at hand. In the administrative proceedings there is none of 'N*umerus clausus*' as regards to the admissible evidentiary instruments.[609] Nevertheless, the Decision of *Bundeskartellamt* in a cartel infringement shall be based on 'a high accuracy grade of plausibility' pursuant to Sec.61 of the GWB.[610] Moreover, both the *Oberlandsgericht* (OLG) and the *Bundesgerichtshof* put 'high importance to an economic analysis' in examining and deciding cartels law cases.[611]Whereas the provisions of Sec. 57 of the GWB requires the *Kartellbehörde* to follow the formal procedures in the taking of evidences, these provisions distinguish between the formalised and free evidences.[612]

Henceforth, during the administrative proceedings, the German Cartel Law acknowledges and thus can corroborate the following evidentiary instruments: First, the direct inspection (*Augenschein*) of cartel law enforcement authority, such as photographs, conversation records and videos.[613] Second, request for transmittal of official deeds or documents (*Beiziehung von Urkunden*), which means the *Bundeskartellamt* could demand from third parties an official assistance as to the documents or official deeds for the investigation processes.[614] Third, judicial interrogation (*Vernehmung*) of the involving parties and third ones as regards to collusive practices between undertakings.[615] Fourth, hearing of witnesses which have reliable and substantial infor-

609 Accordingly, in accordance with the general principle of Sec. 26 VwVfG. cf. Schmidt 'Sec. 57 GWB' in in Immenga/Mestmäcker, Wettbewerbsrecht (n 566) R 1–13.

610 Schneider in *Langen and Bunte*, Kommentar zum Kartellrecht (n 99) 1234–1240.

611 W. Kirchhoff, 'Requirements of proof in court – the economic approach: Introductory Statement' (Judge, Federal Court of Justice, Germany IKK Berlin April 15, 2011) 2–5.

612 Schmidt „Sec. 57 GWB", in Immenga/Mestmäcker, Wettbewerbsrecht (n 566) R 1–14.

613 Sec. 372 (1) ZPO. cf. Schneider in *Langen and Bunte*, Kommentar zum Kartellrecht (n 99) 1234–1237.

614 Sec. 142 ZPO. cf. Schneider in *Langen and Bunte*, Kommentar (n 99).

615 Sec. 57 of the GWB in conjunction to Sec. 26 para.1 (2) VwVfG. cf. Schneider in *Langen and Bunte*, Kommentar (n 99) 1235–1240.

mation to provide clarification of facts as to collusive arrangements between undertakings.[616] Fifth, hearing of persons with specialist knowledge (*Sachsverstädige*), this means both of *the Bundeskartellamt* and the Courts adjudicating cartels cases could seek expert opinions to assist them in understanding the factual circumstances as to the alleged cartels infringement. However, the value of this expert opinions is merely as facilitating instrument for the *Bundeskartellamt* and Courts in making judicial decisions as to the cartels cases at hand.[617] Sixth, dawn raids and forfeitures (*Beschlagnahme*), which means the *Bundeskartellamt* could perform on-site raids and forfeitures of documents and other relevant evidences for the purpose of proving the cartels infringement.[618] Seventh, requests for information (*Auskunftsverlangen*), whereas the *Bundeskartellamt* is able to request the other law enforcement authorities or state official institutions the information to obtain clearance of factual circumstances concerning the cartels cases. [619]

3.2.3 The Imposition of Fines Proceeding (*Bußgeldverfahren*)

3.2.3.1 General Principles

Within the German Cartel Law, *Emmerich* explains that the sanction mechanism against the cartel infringement has three pillars. First, the administrative enforcement proceedings particularly through the order to end the infringement under Sec. 32 of the GWB. Second, the civil litigation proceedings concerning claim for damages (*Schadenersatzanspruch*) stipulated in Sec. 33 of the GWB. Third, through the imposition of fines in the fining proceeding *(Bußgeldverfahren)* pursuant to Sec. 81 of the GWB.[620]

616 ibid.

617 Sec. 57 para.5 of the GWB. Schneider in *Langen and Bunte*, Kommentar zum Kartellrecht (n 99) 1235–1240.

618 Sec. 59 para 4 in conjuction to Sec. 58 of the GWB. Schneider in *Langen and Bunte*, Kommentar zum Kartellrecht (n 99) 1235–1240.

619 Sec. 59 para 1 of the GWB. cf. Schneider in *Langen and Bunte*, Kommentar (n 99) 1235–1240.

620 Sec. 81 GWB (vgl. Sec. Art. 7 und 23 VO 1/2003). V. Emmerich *Kartellrecht (n 619) 515–517.*

Furthermore, the provisions of Sec. 81 until 86 of the GWB enunciate the substantive rules of the fining proceeding (Bußgeldverfahren). Nevertheless, the prevailing procedural rules refer to the provisions stipulated in the German Act on Regulatory Offences (*Gesetz über Ordnungswidrigkeiten – OWiG*). However, the provision of Sec. 83 unitil 86 of the GWB prescribes rules concerning jurisdiction of the Appeal Court and Appeal to the Higher Courts on points of law. In accordance with the provisions of Articles 7 and 23 of the Regulation Number 1/2003, the imposition of fines proceeding aims not only to prevent and deter cartels practices, but also to skim-off profits gained from cartels offences.[621] In contrast to the US Antitrust Law (Sherman Act), *Schmidt* asserts that the GWB acknowledges merely the administrative offence proceedings with the imposition of fines *(Bußgeld)*, not the criminal law process. Thereby, an administrative offence is not a criminal delict.[622] Furthermore, Dannecker and Biermann explain that the imposition of fines proceeding has twofold functions: First, to supervise cartels (antitrust) practices in the market. Second, to guarantee the Rule of law *(Rechtsstaat)* principle.[623]

Whereas the imposition of fines proceeding under the GWB and OWiG concern primarily with the natural person liability due to the cartel offence, the rules of the fining procedure *(Bußgeldverfahren)* can permeate and thus apply to the legal person, such as corporations. Accordingly, the natural persons could subject to imposition of fines whether they act as perpetrator of cartel infringement or as the owner (Inhaber) of the violating undertaking.[624] Besides, according to the provision of Sec. 30 of OWiG the imposition of fines prevails to the natural persons who act: First, as a partner authorised to represent the undertaking with legal capacity. Second, as the authorised representative with full power of attorney or in a managerial position. Third, as another person responsible on behalf of the management of a undertaking.[625]

621 The Regulation Number 1/2003, Article 13. cf. Emmerich, *(n 619)* 515–517.

622 Schmidt in Immenga and Mestmäcker, *Wettbewerbsrecht (n 566) 225*.

623 Dannecker and Biermann „Sec. 81 GWB" *in* Immenga and Mestmäcker, Kommentar (n 566) R. 1–16.

624 ibid.

625 ibid.

Furthermore, whenever natural and legal persons commit bid-rigging cartels, thus the provision of Sec. 298 of the German Criminal Code (*Strafgesetzbuch – StGB*) applies. Consequently, in the investigation of bid-rigging cartels, two autonomous enforcement proceedings take place. First, the criminal proceedings, whereas the public prosecutor (*Staatsanwalt*) leads the prosecutorial proceedings against the natural person. Second, the *Kartellbehörde* performs the imposition of fines proceedings against the persons or undertakings. Hence, Sec. 298 of StGB applies to the natural persons committing cartel infringement. As regards the number of penal fines imposed, Sec. 40 StGB stipulates that the statutory maximum of this fine is calculated by multiplying the maximum number of daily instalments (Tagessätzen) with maximum value an instalment could have. Accordingly, the amount of fines imposed is subject to the considerations of personal and economic situations of the natural person.[626] Besides, Sec. 62 of StGB regulates that the natural persons committing bid-rigging cartel crimes can be disqualified from the profession in order to prevent re-occurrence of the cartels infringement. Nonetheless, this penal sanction is subject to the principle of proportionality considering the impact and degree of violation.[627]

Eventually, in the determination of fines's amount, the *Kartellbehörde* shall take into account the gravity and the duration of the infringement. Specifically, the *Kartellbehörde* must consider the following aspects: market impact, affected commerce, economic conditions of the undertakings involved, the period between infringement and fine.[628] For that reason, the *Bundeskartellamt* has issued in 2013 the Leitlinien für die Bußgeldzumessung in Kartellordnungswidrigkeitenverfahren. Equally important, the provisions of Sec. 81 (5) and 34 GWB prescribe that the *Kartellbehörde* can impose skimming-off fines

626 ibid.

627 M. Freese, *Sanctions in EU Competition Law: Principles and Practice* (1st Ed., Hart Publishing, 2014) 236–238.

628 Raum in Langen, Bunte, Kommentar zum (n 99) 1148–1152. cf. Freese, Sanctions in EU Competition Law (n 626) 206.

to the undertakings because of 'illegal economic benefits' resulted from cartel practices. [629]

3.2.3.2 Evidentiary and Investigatory Principles

The main objective of the impositition of fines proceedings is to find the material truth (*materielle Wahrheit*).[630] Therefore, during the processes of this proceeding, the investigation principle (*Untersuchungsgrundsatz*) plays a very important role. This is to say that, the German Competition Authority (*Kartellbehörde),* will determine by itself the scope and feasible instruments to be applied on the case at hand. Thereby, the *Kartellbehörde* is free to perform whatever it considers necessary to conduct the investigation and prosecution. Moreover, the *Kartellbehörde* can verify all information and seek more information and is not bound by the statements or testimonies of the parties. Nevertheless, the *Kartellbehörde* must assure that all necessary measures have been taken to reach a just and correct decision in order to find the material or substantial truth *(materielle Wahrheit)* of the case in question. [631]

3.2.3.2.1 Principle of the Unfettered Consideration of the Evidence (*Grundsatz der freien Beweiwürdigung*)

Pursuant to Sec. 261 StPO the Court must find evidences on the basis of its own opinion during the trial proceedings in a freely manner. Thereby, the Court is not subject to old medieval rule 'ordeal by fire 'and the Judge must personally be convinced as to the existence of facts presented before the Court. According to Roxin, the subjective conviction of a judge must be objectively convincing to other judges. Further, the provision of Sec. 274 StPO limits this principle, which stipulates that breach of essential formal requirement in the main proceeding must be proven by a protocol. Further, the prohibition of wrongfully

629 Dannecker and Biermann „Vorbemerkung vor § 81" in Immenga and Mestmäcker (n 566). Freese, Sanctions in EU Competition Law (n 626) 206.

630 Dannecker and Biermann, „Vorbemerkung Sec. 81" in Immenga and Mestmäcker (n 566). R 1–308.

631 Reimann and Zekoll, *Introduction to German Law (n 591)* 433. cf. Foster and Sule, *German Legal System (n 495)* 384–385.

obtained evidence (*Beweisverwertungsverbot*) confines this principle.[632] Furthermore, under this principle it is prohibited to take negative inferences from the choice of accused to be remain silent.[633]

3.2.3.2.2 Principle of Presumption of Innocence (*In Dubio Pro Reo*)

In the German Legal system, according to *Holtappels,* historically the *in dubio pro reo* principle originates from the Roman civil and subsequently penal laws.[634] By virtue of the reception process in the German legal system, initially in the penal proceedings during the Frankish Kings in the 5th until 6th Centuries, continued by the medieval period's criminal law, this principle has evoluted progressively.[635]

Altough the principle of *in dubio pro reo* has not been explicitly stipulated in the European Competition legislations, the provisions of Article 6 para. 2 of the European Convention of Human Rights (ECHR) and Sec. 261 of the German Code of Criminal Procedure (StPO) enunciated this principle.[636] *Lianos and Genakos* emphasise that the principle of 'in dubio pro reo' has been embodied in Article 48 (1) of the Charter of Fundamental Rights of the EU (CHFR-EU), which prescribes that 'any doubt in the mind of the Court must operate to the advantage of the undertaking to which the decision finding an infringement was addressed'.[637]

---

632 C. Roxin and E. Kern, Strafverfahrensrecht: Ein Studienbuch (25 Aufl, Rechtsstand: 1. Mai 1998 Taschenbuch) 384–385.

633 Reimann and Zekoll, *Introduction to German Law (n 591)* 434

634 The manuscripts (Edict) of Roman laws stipulated accordingly:
Inter pares numero iudices si dissonae sententiae proferantur, in liberalibus quidem causis, secundum quod a divo Pio constitutum est, pro liberiate statutum optinet, in aliis autem causis pro reo. Quod et in iudiciis publicis optinere oportet, 14). Holtappels, *Die Entwicklungsgeschichte des Grundsatzes "in dubio pro reo" (n 489)* 2–5.

635 In the *Constitutio Criminalis Carolina, notably the Halsgerichtsordnung Karls V.,* stipulated „und daß... an viel orten offter mais wider recht und gute vernunfft gehandelt und entweder die unschuldigen gepeinigt und getötet... werden. Im Artikel 150 heißt es dann, die Richter sollten ja nicht eigene unvernünfftige Regel oder Gewohnheit. [...] sprechen machen, die den Rechten widerwärtig seynd als je Zeiten an den peinlichen Gerichten hißhero geschehen." Holtappels (n 489).

636 Foster and Sule, *German Legal System and Laws (495)* 139–140.

637 ibid 140–142.

In the Competition Law enforcement proceedings, the Advocate General Vesterdorf strongly advocated the application of 'in dubio pro reo' principle, as follows:

> "Considerable importance must be attached to the fact that the competition cases of this kind (cartels) are in realityof a penal nature, which naturally suggests that a high standard of proof is required (…). There must be a sufficient basis for the decision and any reasonable doubt must be for the benefit of the applicants according to the principle of *in dubio pro reo*."[638]

Reimann and Zekoll assert that the principle of *in dubio pro reo* applies to all issues concerning the questions of guilt or innocence of the persons or undertakings, for instance alibis, justifications, excuses or immunities.[639]

Pursuant to Sec. 46 para. 1 of OWiG in conjuctions with the provisions of Sec. 160 and 163 StPO, the inquisitorial principles apply to the imposition of fines proceedings.[640] Furthermore, as regards to the scope of the evidence's collection, the principle of discretionary competence (*pflichtgemäßen Ermessen*) applies pursuant to the provision of Sec. 77 OWiG. Thereby, the *Kartellbehörde* is not subject to stringent evidentiary rules stipulated in Sec. 224 StPO.

Furthermore, the consideration of evidences (*Beweiswürdigung*) is oriented to the court's evidentiary considerations.[641] Accordingly, there are five principles which are important. First, the role of personal certainty (*persönliche Gewissheit*). Second, empirical knowledge (*Erfahrungssätze*). Third, the significancy of confessions. Fourth, the admissible evidentiary instruments. Fifth, the role of indirect evidences (*Indizienbeweis*).[642]

In the imposition of fines proceedings, the personal certainty (*persönliche Gewissheit*) refers mainly to a subjective conviction. Thereby, the adequacy assumption that the personal certainty has probability value is deemed as incorrect and harmful. Moreover, the employment of personal certainty must be able to convince not only the Judges or

638 Lianos and Genekos, "Econometric Evidence" (n 26) 86–87.

639 Reimann and Zekoll, *Introduction to German Law (n 591)* 434.

640 Dannecker and Biermann, „Vorbemerkung Sec. 81 GWB" in Immenga and Mestmäcker (n 5669 R. 287–303).

641 ibid.

642 ibid.

Adjudicators but also the third Parties logically.[643] Furthermore, as regards to the empirical knowledge (*Erfahrungssätze*), the imposition of fines proceedings distinguishes between the scientific knowledge (*wissenschaftliche Erkenntnisse*) and ordinary empirical knowledge. Equally important, the knowledge concerning typical symptoms and connectives within the economic processes is highly important in the imposition of fines proceedings. In the cartel enforcement proceedings, the scientific and economics theories or statements were not qualified as the empirical knowledge. These theories and statements must be applied with other evidences in order to convince the Judges or Adjudicators, such as the interest of the undertakings in the cartel enforcement proceedings.[644]

Furthermore, during the imposition of fines proceedings, Sec. 46 para. 1 OWiG concerning admissibility of evidences applies. Thus, the opinion of the *Kartellbehörde* is not an evidence before the Court. Additionally, the confession of the Parties is deemed as an additional evidence as stipulated by Sec. 46 para.1 OWiG. Moreover, in the imposition of fines proceedings, the confessions of the Parties do not have binding effects for the court and the *Kartellbehörde*. Thereby, the courts and *Kartellbehörde* must cross-examine the confessions with other parties.[645]

Equally important, as regards to indirect evidences, the Court and *Kartellbehörde* are able to conclude the merits of a case in question from the indirect factual circumstances by means of judicial inferences. Hence the indirect evidences encompass: First, indirect witness testimony. Second, written documents such as certificates (*Urkunde)* and visual inspection properties (*Augenscheinobjekte).* Third, written documents on cartel agreements, such aas protocols and notices. However, each of this written document must lead to the compulsive conclusions. Third, the decryption of coding mechanism in the bid-rigging cartels. Fourth, the "plus-factors" are essential evidence in the concerted practice. Fifth, the private control measures in order to punish mutual cheatings, for example the price-cutting strategy. Finally, the exchanges of contracts, the notification of contracts to the neutral parties like the

643 ibid.

644 ibid.

645 ibid.

Notary constitute the indirect evidences to substantiate the cartels infringements.[646]

3.2.3.2 The Appeal (Objection) Proceedings before the *Oberlandesgericht* (*Kartell-OLG*)

In the imposition of administrative fines proceedings, the *Oberlandesgericht* (*Kartell-OLG*) constitutes an important function, whereby Sec. 83 of the GWB stipulates:

> "Jurisdiction of the Higher Regional Court (Oberlandesgericht-OLG) in Judicial Proceedings
> (1) The Higher Regional Court in whose district the competent competition authority has its seat shall decide in judicial proceedings concerning an administrative offence pursuant to Sec. 81; it shall also decide on an application for judicial review (Sec. 62 of the German Administrative Offences Act) in the cases of Sec. 52(2) sentence 3 and Sec. 69(1) sentence 2 of the German Administrative Offences Act. Sec. 140(1) no. 1 of the German Code of Criminal Procedure in conjunction with Sec. 46(1) of the German Administrative Offences Act shall not be applicable.
> (2) The decisions of the Higher Regional Court shall be made by three members including the presiding member."[647]

Primarily, the judicial philosophical backgrounds for the appeal process of the Antitrust Decisions to the Oberlandesgerichtin the imposition of administrative fines proceeding, *Dannecker and Biermann* argue, as follows:

> "In deviation from Sec. 68 OWiG, the provision of Sec. 83 (Sec. 82 to the sixth GWB amendment) regulates the material (and local) jurisdiction of the Higher Regional Court as the first judicial authority in the appeal procedure. This reflects the legislator's aim to concentrate antitrust case law on as few courts as possible. By assigning jurisdiction to the Higher Regional Court, the court which already acquires antitrust expertise when deciding on appeals in administrative proceedings, also takes part antitrust proceedings. With regard to this purpose of the law and the general reference in Article 83 (1) to offenses under Section 81, the validity of

646 ibid.

647 The German Act against Restraints of Competition (Gesetz gegen Wettbewerbsbeschränkungen 9. Novelle) (Bundesgesetzblatt (Federal Law Gazette) I, 2013, p. 1750, 3245), as last amended by Article 1 of the law of 1 June 2017 (Federal Law Gazette I, p. 1416). ‹https://www.gesetze-im-internet.de/englisch_gwb/englisch_gwb.html#p0962› accessed 27th December 2018.

> the jurisdiction clause in Section 83 must also be considered as the fine proceedings for which the Bundeskartellamt or Bundesnetzagentur acts as the market transparency agency acted. Furthermore, Sec. 83 applies to administrative offenses in connection with infringements in the field of mergers of health insurance companies. The assignment of jurisdiction to the Landessozialgericht in Sec. 202 sentence 3 SGG concerns only appeal proceedings.
> For judicial acts before objection, for example,in the preliminary proceedings of the antitrust authority, it remains with the general jurisdiction of the other courts of criminal justice (Sec. 46 Abs. 1 OWiG).This is especially true for judicial jurisdiction in connection with searches and seizures (Sec.Sec. 105, 98 StPO) and other coercive measures (Sec. 162 StPO). With regards to the competence for the general judicial review of "measures" (investigations) of the antitrust authority, Sec. 62 (2) OWiG refers to the court named in Sec. 68 OWiG, which is competent to decide on an objection to the fine. However, in this respect, the district court is also responsible for the fine proceedings for antitrust violations, since Sec. 83 in total only applies to the judicial procedure after opposition. In these cases, the district court in whose district the administrative authority has its seat is competent."[648]

Nevertheless, in the proceedings before the Oberlandesgericht-Kartell-OLG, there is no particular requirement for the cooperation of a defense counsel.[649] Provided that there is compelling necessity due to the difficulties of the factual and legal situations, thus the appointment of a defense counsel can take place pursuant to Sec. 140 para 2 and Sec. 46 (1) OWiG therefore only takes place if deemed necessary because of the difficulty of the factual or legal situation.[650]

Principally, the *Oberlandesgericht-Kartell-OLG* exerts its judicial powers based upon two main jurisdicitions and one additional jurisdiction, which encompass: First, the subject-matter jurisdiction (*Sachliche Zuständigkeit*) and occupation of Kartellsenat-OLG.[651] Second,

648 Dannecker and Biermann, „Sec.83 GWB" in Immenga/Mestmäcker, *Wettbewerbsrecht (n 566).*

649 ibid.

650 ibid.

651 According to *Dannecker and Biermann* as to the subject-matter jurisdiction of the *Kartell-Oberlandesgerichshof:*
"The Higher Regional Court has jurisdiction over the decision on the appeal against the antitrust authority's fine. It is in accordance with the law of criminal law to designate the "entrance competence" of the Higher Regional Court in rela-

geographical (territorial) jurisdiction *(Örtliche Zuständigkeit)*.[652] Third, the jurisdiction in the event there are: (1) Request to decide the Appeal for the Court Decision against the Dismissal application to re-establish the applicant's rights and dismissal of its appeal ("Restitutio in integrum") pursuant to Sec. 62, Sec. 52 para. 2 (3) OWiG, and (2)

---

tion to the district court and district court as factual and not merely as functional competence. According to Sec. 95, this material jurisdiction is exclusive. In the opinion of the Bundesgerichtshof, 9 the establishment of an auxiliary cartel senate is generally permissible if there is a temporary charge on a certain permanent court. It can thereby be achieved that the acceleration principle is taken into account and that the procedures can be completed within a reasonable time. The Higher Regional Court decides on the appointment of three members including the chairperson (Sec. 83 para. 2). This express regulation was required for clarification in relation to section 122 GVG (see section 2) and corresponds to the composition foreseen in section 122 (1) of the GVG in the case of non-first instance jurisdiction of the Higher Regional Court. The law (Sec. 91) speaks only of the cartel senate at the higher regional courts, without clarifying whether the cartel senate should be considered as a criminal tribunal when deciding on fines.10 The provision of Sec. 116 (1) sentence 1 GVG is not exhaustive. The Cartel Senate at the Higher Regional Court is therefore similar to the "senate for fines" provided by Sec. 46 para. 7 OWiG neither civil nor criminal senate, but its own specialized court body.11 This specialization and concentration can with the peculiarities and difficulties of anti-trust law this sentence is not complete. (with its close connection with antitrust law)." cf. Dannecker and Biermann, „Sec.83 GWB" in Immenga/Mestmäcker, *Wettbewerbsrecht (n 566)*.

652 According to *Dannecker and Biermann* as to the geographical (territorial) jurisdiction of the Kartell-OLG:
"The local jurisdiction of the Higher Regional Court is determined in accordance with. Sec. 83 according to the seat of the "competent" antitrust authority. Despite this deviation from the wording of Sec. 68 (1) OWiG, Sec. 83 (1) is also to be interpreted as meaning that the jurisdiction of the Higher Regional Court is determined by the seat of the antitrust authority which issued the penalty notice the antitrust authority was locally (and objectively) responsible for the prosecution and punishment, thus irrelevant to the local jurisdiction of the Higher Regional Court. In addition to Sec. 83, Sec.Sec. 7 to 11 StPO do not apply (correspondingly) (Sec. 95). However, in case of a jurisdiction clause Sec. 14 StPO applies accordingly (see Sec. 46 (1) OWiG). For federal states with several higher regional courts, Sec. 92 contains the authorization of the state governments to assign cases according to Sec. 83 to a higher regional court or to several higher regional courts. In particular, the Land Nordrhein-Westfalen has made use of this authorization, which the Düsseldorf Higher Regional Court has declared responsible. Since its relocation from Berlin to Bonn, the competent higher regional court for the Bundeskartellamt is no longer the Kammergericht, but the Düsseldorf Higher Regional Court." Dannecker and Biermann, „Sec.83 GWB" in Immenga/Mestmäcker, *Wettbewerbsrecht (n 566)*.

Request to decide the appeal for the Court Decision against the rejection of an objection through the Kartellbehörde according to Sec. 62, 69 para. 1 (2) OwiG.[653]

3.2.4 The Civil Litigation Proceeding (*Bürgerliche Streitigkeiten*)

3.2.4.1 General Principle

The provisions of Sec. 87 until 90 of the German Act against Restraint of Competition (GWB) provides rules concerning the civil law proceedings resulted from cartels infringement, for example claim for damages. According to Schmidt, the provisions concerning the civil litigation proceedings aim to provide compensation of damages due to cartel infringements.[654] Accordingly, the civil litigation proceeding enables the *Kartellbehörde* and the associations to claim for skimming-off the illegal benefits resulted from cartels infringement pursuant to the provisions of Sec. 34 and 34a of the GWB.[655]

In contrast to the administrative appeal proceedings, the civil law proceedings in Sec. 87 until 90 of the GWB concerns mainly with the civil disputes stipulated by Sec. 13 of the Courts Constitution Act (*Gerichtsverfassungsgesetz* – *GVG*) in conjunctions with the provisions of

653 ibid. R. 2–14.

654 Schmidt and Haucap, *Wettbewerbspolitik und Kartellrecht (n 260)* 277–279.

655 Further, the provision of Sec. 34 of GWB concerning the skimming off of benefits by the Kartellbehörde:
"(1) If an undertaking has intentionally or negligently violated a provision of this Act, Article 81 or 82 of the EC Treaty or a decision of the cartel authority and thereby gained an economic benefit, the cartel authority may order the skimming off of the economic benefit and require the undertaking to pay a corresponding amount of money."
Furthermore, the provision of Sec. 34a of GWB provides
"(1) Whoever intentionally commits an infringement within the meaning of Sec. 34 (1) and thereby gains an economic benefit at the expense of multiple purchasers or suppliers may be required by those entitled to an injunction under Sec. 33 (2) to surrender the economic benefit to the federal budget, to the extent that the cartel authority does not order the skimming off of the economic benefit by the imposition of a fine, by forfeiture or pursuant to Sec. 34 (1)." See Emmerich, Kartellrecht (619) 517 518.

Sec. 87 and 91 of the GWB.[656] Whereas the provision of Sec. 13 of GVG reads:

> "The ordinary courts shall have jurisdiction over the civil disputes, family matters and non-contentious matters (civil matters) as well as criminal matters for which neither the competence of administrative authorities nor the jurisdiction of the Administrative Courts (*Verwaltungsgerichte*) has been established and for which no special courts have been created or permitted by provisions of federal law."

In the civil law litigation proceeding, the District Courts (*Landgerichte*) has exclusive jurisdictions to implement the competition rules stipulated in Articles 101 and 102 TFEU as well as in Articles 53 and 54 of the Convention on the European Economic Area. Thus Sec. 95 of the GWB reiterates the exclusive jurisdiction of the *Landgericht*. Moreover, with respect to the judicial review of the decision of the *Landgericht*, the Cartel Division (*Kartellsenat*) of *Bundesgerichtshof (BGH)* has the exclusive jurisdiction. Hence the provision of Sec. 94 (1) of the GWB stipulates:

> "(1) The Federal Court of Justice shall establish a cartel division; it shall decide on the following judicial remedies:
> 1. in administrative matters, on appeals on points of law from decisions of the Courts of Appeal (Sec. 74, 76) and on appeals from the refusal to grant leave to appeal (Sec. 75);

---

656 Further, Sec. 87 of GWB provides as regards to the exclusive jurisdiction of the District Court:
"Regardless of the value of the matter in dispute, the District Courts [Landgerichte] shall have exclusive jurisdiction in civil actions concerning the application of this Act, of Articles 81 or 82 of the EC Treaty or of Articles 53 or 54 of the Convention on the European Economic Area. Sentence 1 shall apply also if the decision in a civil action depends, in whole or in part, on a decision to be taken pursuant to this Act, or on the applicability of Articles 81 or 82 of the EC Treaty or of Articles 53 or 54 of the Convention on the European Economic Area. Sentence 1 shall not apply to civil actions arising from the legal relations mentioned in Sec. 69 of the Fifth Book of the Code of Social Law [Sozialgesetzbuch], also as far as rights of third parties are affected hereby."
Accordingly, Sec. 91 of GWB stipulates concerning the Cartel Division of the Court of Appeal:
"The Courts of Appeal shall establish cartel divisions. They shall decide on legal matters assigned to them pursuant to Sec. 57 (2) sentence 2, Sec. 63 (4), Sec. 83, 85 and 86, and on appeals from final judgments and other decisions in civil actions pursuant to Sec. 87 (1)."Schmidt in Immenga and Mestmäcker, *Wettbewerbsrecht, p.*2822–2829.

2. in proceedings concerning administrative fines, on appeals on points of law from decisions of the Courts of Appeal (Sec. 84);
3. in civil actions pursuant to Sec. 87 (1):
a) on appeals on points of law from final judgments of the Courts of Appeal including appeals from the refusal to grant leave to appeal,
b) on reviews from final judgments of the District Courts,
c) on appeals from decisions of the Courts of Appeal in the cases of Sec. 574 (1) of the Code of Civil Procedure."

In addition, the provision of Sec. 90 of the GWB prerequisites the court to inform the *Bundeskartellamt* concerning the whole legal actions in the civil litigation proceeding. Thereby, the courts shall forward copies of all relevant documents and the decision to the *Bundeskartellamt*, which include the civil litigation matters and the application of Articles 101 and 102 TFEU.[657] The *Bundeskartellamt* can participate in the court's processes whenever necessary.[658] Schmidt explains that in the civil law litigation proceedings the *Bundeskartellamt* acts as the "*Amicus curiae*". Put differently, the *Bundeskartellamt* will participate in the courts' proceedings, as the non-party, to provide opinions and give statements for assisting the court in making the decision. Whereas this *amicus-curiae* rule derives originally from the Common-law tradition, Sec. 27a of the Act concerning the Federal Constitutional Court (*Gesetz über das Bundesverfassungsgericht* – BVerfGG) that acknowledges and applies this rule. Eventually, as regards the institutional cooperation, Article 15 of the Regulation Number 1/2003 prescribes that the German courts are able to request the Commission to transmit information and opinions as to questions on the application of the European Competition law.[659]

657 Schmidt and Haucap, *Wettbewerbspolitik und Kartellrecht* (n 260) 227–228. The provision of Sec. 90 (1) of GWB provides:
"1) The Bundeskartellamt shall be informed by the court of all legal actions pursuant to Sec. 87 (1). The court shall, upon request, transmit to the Bundeskartellamt copies of all briefs, records, orders and decisions. Sentences 1 and 2 shall apply mutatis mutandis in other legal actions which concern the application of Articles 81 and 82 of the EC Treaty." Schmidt and Haucap, *Wettbewerbspolitik und Kartellrech (n 260) 227–228.*

658 ibid.

659 Furhter the provision of Article 15 of the Regulation 1/2003 stipulates concerning the cooperation with the national Courts:
"1. In proceedings for the application of Article 81 or Article 82 of the Treaty, courts of the Member States may ask the Commission to transmit to them infor-

3.2.4.1.1 Principle of Free Party-Dispositions (*Dispositionsgrundsatz*)

In the German Code of Civil Procedure (*Zivilprozessordnung – ZPO*) the principle of free party-dispositions reflects the procedural aspect of the general right of self-determination. Put differently, the Parties in the proceedings, instead the Court, who determine the beginning, the subject-matter and termination of the proceedings. Thereby, the Court does not have the competence to initiate the proceeding *ex-officio* as well as to preclude the Parties from surrendering the case at any stage of the proceedings.[660]

3.2.4.1.2 Principle of Party Representation (*Verhandlungsgrundsatz*)

Whereas the provisions of the ZPO have undergone several changes, this principle consistently refers to the concept that the Parties in the proceedings have freedom to present the legal facts and the relevant evidences before the Court. Thus, due to the adversarial procedure characteristic of the proceedings, the Court does not have obligation to conduct ex-officio inquiries towards the Parties during the proceedings.[661]

---

mation in its possession or its opinion on questions concerning the application of the Community competition rules.
2. Member States shall forward to the Commission a copy of any written judgment of national courts deciding on the application of Article 81 or Article 82 of the Treaty. Such copy shall be forwarded without delay after the full written judgment is notified to the parties.
3. Competition authorities of the Member States, acting on their own initiative, may submit written observations to the national courts of their Member State on issues relating to the application of Article 81 or Article 82 of the Treaty. With the permission of the court in question, they may also submit oral observations to the national courts of their Member State. Where the coherent application of Article 81 or Article 82 of the Treaty so requires, the Commission, acting on its own initiative, may submit written observations to courts of the Member States. With the permission of the court in question, it may also make oral observations." Schmidt and Haucap, *Wettbewerbspolitik und Kartellrecht (n 260) 227.*

660 Reimann and Zekoll, Introduction to German Law (n 591) 365–366.

661 ibid.

3.2.4.1.3 Principle of the Party's Right to Due Process (*ordnungsgemäßes Verfahren*)

Article 103 I of the *Grundgesetz* concerning the fair trial stipulates that the Parties have the right to due process. This means the Parties shall be entitled to the fair-hearing in accordance with the law. In other words, the Parties have the right to make motions, present the facts, and thus present the evidences in the civil litigation proceeding. Additionally, the Parties have the opportunity to be appraised as to the opponent's allegations and to comment as well as to refute the opponent's opinions and statements. Eventually, the rule of fair hearing denotes also that the Parties have the rights to present legal arguments and rebuttals, whereas the Court is obliged to make deliberations of the arguments and rebuttals.[662]

3.2.4.2 Evidentiary for Finding Material Truth Principles

In the German Civil Law's proceeding, based upon the principle of parties' disposition *(Beibringungsgrundsatz)*, the Parties must present the holistic chain of evidences to support their legal claims before the court. In the claim for damages due to the cartels infringement, the parties must prove not only the cartel infringement, but also the facts that the cartels infringement cause harms and damages.[663] Conversely, the undertaking acting as the defendant must rebut the legal claim by submitting the counter evidences. For example, the defendant could argue that the claiming undertakings have not done efforts to find alternative supplier.[664]

On the one hand, in the German Civil Law's proceedings, two evidentiary requirement rules are of importance. First, the shifting of the

662 ibid.

663 Reimann and Zekoll, Introduction to German Law (n 591). cf. Foster and Sule, German Legal System and Laws (n 495) 139–140. cf. Wach, et.al, Germany Report on Competition Law, at. 9–10 ‹http://ec.europa.eu/competition/antitrust/actionsdamages/national_reports/germany_en.pdf,› accessed 4th October 2017.

664 ibid.

burden of proof.[665] Second, the relaxation of the burden of proof.[666] With regards to the evidentiary instruments, Sec. 291 of ZPO provides that facts which are obvious (*Offenkundig*) do not have to be proved. This means that the facts are deemed as common knowledge or have been known by the Parties through the court's jurisprudences. On the other hand, as regards the evidentiary value of documents, the provisions of Sec. 416 until 418 of ZPO prevails.[667] Specifically, as regards

665 This rule refers to:
"The burden of proof is shifted from the party on whom it normally falls to the opposing party. In some cases, this is known in legal parlance as the rule-exception relationship. The burden of proof then falls on the party invoking the exception. The legislator, for example, assumes the buyer's good faith under Sections 932(1)(1), 892(1)(1) and 2366 of the German Civil Code. The shifting of the burden of proof is of particular significance in cases involving liability under the law on defective performance, where the debtor (defendant) must prove that he is not liable for the failure to comply with an obligation under Section 280(1)(2) of the Civil Code.
ECN, European Judicial Network, Taking of evidence and mode of proof – Germany, ‹http://ec.europa.eu/civiljustice/evidence/evidence_ger_en.htm,› accessed on 4th October 2017, 2–5.

666 This rule refers to:
First, "Statutory presumptions are a relaxation for the party on whom the burden of proof falls as the latter simply has to demonstrate and prove the facts on which the presumption is based (Section 292 of the ZPO (Code of Civil Procedure)). Statutory presumptions may apply to facts such as the presumption that a mortgage certificate is transferred to the creditor by virtue of possession of the certificate (Section 1117(3) of the Civil Code). They may also relate to rights such as presumption that the holder of the certificate of inheritance has the status of heir (Section 2365 of the Civil Code). Legal presumptions can, in principle, be rebutted in accordance with Section 292 of the ZPO provided no other legal provisions apply."
Second, "Statutory presumptions are comparable a priori to actual presumptions on which prima facie evidence is based. Prima facie evidence is where a fact to be proved is a typical occurrence in the normal course of events where all the undisputable and established circumstances of the case are taken into account. Prima facie evidence can be used in particular to establish causality and fault, e.g., fault where a car is driven into a tree. The opposing party can challenge the presumption on the basis of facts which cast serious doubt on whether a typical occurrence is involved."
Third, "Case law is increasingly defining the burden of proof by specific area of risk on the grounds of equity and fair balancing of interests." ECN, European Judicial Network, Taking of evidence and mode of proof – Germany

667 Sec. 416, 416 (a), 417 and 418 of ZPO. cf. Wach, *et.al*, Germany (n 662) 9–10.

the evidentiary value of private records and documents, Sec. 416 of ZPO prescribes:

> "To the extent that private records and documents are signed by the parties issuing them, or have been signed using a mark that has been certified by a notary, they shall establish full proof that the declarations they contain have been made by the parties who prepared such records and documents."

Moreover, with respect to the evidentiary evaluation and conviction (Überzeugung) of the Court, the provisions of Sec. 286 of ZPO regulate as follows:

> "(1) The court is to decide, at its discretion and conviction, and taking account of the entire content of the hearings and the results obtained by evidence being taken, if any, whether an allegation as to fact is to be deemed true or untrue. The judgment is to set out the reasons informing the conviction of the judges.
> (2) The court shall be bound to statutory rules of evidence only in the cases designated in the present Code."

Put differently, in the civil litigation proceedings, principle of unfettered consideration of evidences (*Prinzip der freien Beweiswürdigung*) applies. Thereby, the court has judicial discretion both in the admission and weighing the evidences. Also, the judicial review over this judicial discretion is restricted to determine whether the violation of fair hearing (*Recht auf rechtliches Gehör*) and arbitrariness during the proceedings exist.[668] Moreover, the evidentiary standards in the civil litigation proceeding relate with the provision of Sec. 261 of the German Code of Criminal Procedure (StPO) on the free evaluation of evidences, that is to say, the 'beyond reasonable doubts' is inapplicable in the civil litigation proceeding.[669]

Moreover, the German Civil Law's proceeding acknowledges principally five types of the admissible evidences. First, the judicial inspection pursuant to the provisions of Sec. 371 until 372a of ZPO. Mainly, this evidence refers to a direct physical inspection of the evidence by the Judges through the human senses. Further, this includes the in-

668 Wach, *et.al,* Germany Report. p. 9–10.

669 The provision of Sec. 261 of StPO concerning the Free evaluation of evidences reads:
"The court shall decide on the result of the evidence taken according to its free conviction gained from the hearing as a whole."

spected sound, video recordings and computer records.[670] Second, the witnesses' testimonies, which are regulated in the provisions of Sec. 373 until 401 of ZPO. Principally, this evidentiary instrument refers to the persons which can confirm events occurred in the past which they themselves have witnessed and thus can not be replaced. Thus, witnesses are not the Parties in the proceedings.[671] Third, expert evidence, which can be classified into: experts appointed by the Court, expert witnesses and private expert opinions. Hence, the provisions of Sec. 402 until 414 of ZPO enshrines the rules on expert evidences.[672] Accordingly, the Judges appoint the experts having the specialist knowledge in order to evaluate the facts in the proceedings. However, the experts have functions to give a value judgement over the established facts and thus do not constitute the fact themselves. For example, the

670 Schmidt 'Vorbemerkung vor § 87 GWB' in Immenga and Mestmäcker (n 566) R. 55–58.

671 The provisions of Sec. 373 until 401 of ZPO prescribes:
"Sec. 375 ZPO; Taking of evidence by a judge correspondingly delegated or requested
(1) The task of taking evidence by hearing witnesses may be allocated to a member of the court hearing the case or to another court only if, and to the extent, that it is to be assumed from the outset that the court hearing the case will be able to properly evaluate the results obtained in taking the evidence, without obtaining a direct impression of the course of the taking of evidence, and:
1. If it seems expedient, by way of assessing the truth, to examine the witness on site or if, according to the stipulations of the law, the witness is not to be examined at the seat of the court, but instead at a different location;
2. If the witness is prevented from appearing before the court hearing the case and the witness is not examined in the form governed by section 128a (2);
3. If, in light of the great distance the witness would have to travel, and taking account of the significance of his or her statement, it cannot be reasonably expected of the witness to appear before the court hearing the case, and the witness is not examined in the form governed by section 128a (2).
(1a) The task of taking evidence by hearing witnesses may be allocated to a member of the court hearing the case also in those cases in which this seems suitable for the purpose of simplifying the oral argument before the court hearing the case, and if, and to the extent, that it is to be assumed from the outset that the court hearing the case will be able to properly evaluate the results obtained in taking the evidence without obtaining a direct impression of the course of the taking of evidence."
(2) The President of the Federal Republic of Germany is to be examined in his residence.

672 The provisions of Sec. 402 until 414 of *Zivilprozessordnung* (ZPO).

medical diagnosis of a doctor to assist the Judges to find conclusions of the case in question. Besides, the Parties could designate a private expert report to be presented before the Court only in exceptional circumstances and this is subject to the mutual consent of the Parties.[673] Fourth, the documents. this type of is regulated by the provisions of Sec. 415 until 444 of the ZPO.[674] Eventually, the documents refer to the written declarations. Thus, the German Civil Law's proceeding distinguishes between evidentiary values of the public documents and the private documents. Fifth, the questioning of the Parties. This evidence refers to the subsidiary forms of evidences. Accordingly, this type of evidence merely serves the main evidences pursuant to Sec. 445 (2) of the ZPO. Nevertheless, the application of this type of evidence has been subject to the court's approval as well as the other Parties'agreement.[675]

3.3 Procedural Law pursuant to the Law Number 5/1999

3.3.1 Introduction

Since the inception of the Law Number 5/1999, the procedural laws to be applied within the Indonesian Competition Office (KPPU) as well as the Indonesian Courts, have been undergone gradual amendments. Intially, the Presidential Decree Number 75/1999 concerning the Com-

673 European Judicial Network (EJN), Taking of evidence and mode of proof (n – Germany, http://ec.europa.eu/civiljustice/evidence/evidence_ger_en.htm, accessed on 4th October 2015.

674 The provisions of Sec. 415 until 444 ZPO reads as follows:
"Evidentiary value of public records and documents regarding declarations
(1) Records and documents that have been prepared, in accordance with the requirements as to form, by a public authority within the scope of its official responsibilities, or by a person or entity vested with public trust within the sphere of business assigned to him or it (public records and documents), shall establish full proof, provided they have been executed regarding a declaration made before the public authority or the public official issuing the deed.
(2) Evidence proving that the transaction has been improperly recorded is admissible.

675 European Judicial Network (EJN), Taking of evidence (n 664).

mission for Supervision of Business Competition (hereinafter referred to as "KPPU").

Subsequently, the KPPU Decree Number 05/KPPU/KEP/IX/2000 (SK 05), which amended into the KPPU Regulation *("Peraturan Komisi or Perkom")* Number 1/2006 regarding the Procedures for Settlement of Cases. Afterwards, the Perkom Number 1/2006 has been amended into the Perkom Number 1/2010 on the Handling of Cases, which took into effect on 5th April 2010 until now.[676]

As a matter of fact, there had been delicate debates as to the applicability of the provisions of Indonesian Criminal Procedural Code (Kitab Undang-Undang Hukum Acara Pidana-KUHAP) upon the the Indonesian Competition law's enforcement proceedings. There had been an ongoing question, if the enforcement procedural provisions in the Law Number 5/2000 as well as the Perkom would not be adequate, KPPU could invoke partially the provisions of criminal proceedings under the KUHAP.[677] Accordingly, there are several reasons for the applicability of the KUHAP's provisions in the Indonesian Competition law's enforcement proceedings, among others: Firstly, the functions of inquries (Penyelidikan) as well as examination (Pemeriksaan) have not been acknowledged and prescribed in the Indonesian Civil Procedural Code ("Kitab Undang Undang Hukum Acara Perdata-KUH Perdata"). Secondly, the main objective of the Competition law's enforcement proceedings before the KPPU is the material or substantive truth. In contrast, in the Indonesian Civil Procedural Code (KUH Perdata), the main purpose thereof is to discover the formal truth (*formelle Wettelijk*). In this sense, the material or substantive truth refers to following notions:

> "In seeking material truth, it is necessary for the existence of KPPU's conviction that an alleged business actor commit or do not carry out actions that cause monopolistic practices or unfair business competition. To create conviction, KPPU must ensure that there are actions that cause monopolistic practices or business competition."[678]

Furthermore, in the processes of discovering the material or substantive truth, KPPU must rely upon the concrete evidences as well as sup-

676 Lubis and Sirait (eds), Hukum Persaingan Usaha *(n 225)* 389–391.
677 ibid.
678 ibid.

ported by the unrebuttable conviction during the competition enforcement proceedings, as correctly explained by the following notions:

> "In the process of seeking material truth, KPPU has the authority to summon business actors who, for reasons that are reasonably suspected, have committed violations. A reasonable reason is the allegation that resulted from the investigation process carried out by the Commission. The business actor is given the right to express his opinion as an effort to defend himself against the accusations of KPPU. After the suspicion and listening to the defense of the business actor, in order to obtain material truths, KP-PU can carry out verification by summoning witnesses, expert witnesses and everyone who is considered to know the violation. In addition, the written Deed can also be used as evidence. After conducting the investigations, listening to the defenses of the business actor and carrying out evidence, KPPU could make a decision. Decisions are in the form of the existence of violations committed by the business actor being examined as well as the presence or absence of losses on the part of other business actors as a result of the violation. By looking at the investigation process up to the decisions made by the Commission, it is clear that the truth sought in monopoly cases and business competition is material truth based on tangible evidence, and the undisputed beliefs of the KPPU. "[679]

Accordingly, the addressee of these enforcement procedural laws and regulations are all business actors as defined by Article 1 (5), notably "individual(s) or business entities either incorporated as legal entities or not, established and domiciled or conducting business activities within the jurisdiction of the Republic of Indonesia, either independently or jointly based upon an agreement, conducting various business activities in the economic fields". Thereby, these legislations prevail towards any business actor engaging businesses in Indonesia, including, amongst other, state-owned enterprises and subsidiaries of foreign companies.[680]

Equally important, according to the Law Number 5/1999 and regulations abovementioned, KPPU acts as the principal Competition Authority (CA). Moreover, KPPU is an independent public institution, that is to say, KPPU does not subject to the Government and other stakeholders' political and business influences.[681] Thereby, KPPU is

679 ibid.

680 The Indonesian Competition Law Number 5/1999 concerning Prohibition of Monopolistic Practices and Unfair Business Practices, Article 5, ‹ www.aseancompetition.org/aegc/aegc-members/indonesia.› accessed on 30th September 2017.

681 ibid.

only accountable to the President. Accordingly, its Members ("Commissioners") are appointed and dismissed by the President upon prior approvals of the House of Representatives ("DPR").[682]

According to the Presidential Decree Number 75/1999 and *Sauter*, KPPU will perform following responsibilities: First, law enforcement which encompasses investigating, interpreting, and enforcing provision of the Law No.5/1999 as outlined by Article 35 a, b, c and d. Second, competition advocacy which provides advisory opinions on government policy and laws related to, or affecting, monopolistic practices and unfair business competition as prescribed by Article 35 e. Third, generating guidelines and competition policy notices to assist business and the public to understand and comply with the Law No.5/1999 as mandated by Article 35 f.[683]

In the practice of the Law Number 5/1999, KPPU has been frequently considered as "quasi-judicial body", which means that it has been conferred with civil remedial as well as penal remedial competencies. More important are the institutional relationships of KPPU with the District Court (Pengadilan Negeri) and the Indonesia Supreme Court (Mahkamah Agung Republik Indonesia-MARI), whereas based upon the appeal processes either by KPPU or by the business actors the District Court frequently compete with KPPU in the adjudications of competition law matters. In addition, in the last instance the Supreme Court has the authorithy to uphold or to hand down previous KPPU and the District Court's Decisions over the competition law disputes.[684]

Accordingly, Sirait posed critism as to KPPU's existence, as follows:

> "Another foreign import to the Indonesian legal system was that the Law introduced a self-regulatory agency (KPPU) as the primary law enforcer. The Commission is an independent and quasi-judicial agency with a variety of powers. Initially, many were skeptical about the existence of such a Commission and raised questions about its position in the structure of the legal system and whether KPPU should be treated as a court at first

682 ibid.

683 *Sauter* in Säcker, et.al, *Law Concerning Prohibition of Monopolistic Practices (n 39) 691.*

684 Lubis and Sirait, *Hukum Persaingan Usaha (n 225)*.369–370. cf. *Sauter* in Säcker, et.al, (n 3) 369–370.

instance or merely as an administrative body. The Commission's decisions may be appealed to the District Court by the Reported Party if they disagree with a decision. This is the first stage where the court is involved and takes a role in enforcing Law No. 5 of 1999. It should also be understood that in a civil law system, judges and administrative agencies have less ability to influence the development of legal doctrines because the judges' role in developing doctrine is relatively limited; they merely apply the law and give explanations of the written law but they do not make it. When compared to a common law system where judges have greater opportunities to develop the law, Indonesian courts have taken time to adapt to this new mechanism to enforce the competition law. Both the judiciary and the Commission realized that by relying on the traditionally mandated enforcement structure, improvements in enforcement would be retarded. As a result, both were persuaded to collaborate to find a resolution to the need to harmonize procedural standards between the two institutions which had been a source of considerable friction."[685]

3.3.2 Administrative Proceedings before KPPU

According to KPPU Regulations Number 1/2006 and KPPU Regulation Number 2/2008 in conjunctions with KPPU Decision Number 05/KPPU/KEP/IX/2000, the enforcement proceedings in KPPU consist of the following phases: First, the reporting or collecting indications phase. Second, the preliminary investigation phase. Third, the advance investigation phase. Fourth, the decision phase. Fifth, the after the decision phase.[686]

Whereas in the reporting phase, KPPU is able to receive reports concerning infringement against the Law Number 5/1999, both from every natural person knowing the alleged violations and the affected parties, KPPU could also conduct its inquiry initiative as to alleged vi-

685 Sirait, *Overview of the Indonesia Competition Law Number 5 of 1999 concerning the Prohibition of Monopolistic Practices and Unfair Business Competition*, http://www.jftc.go.jp/eacpf/05/AOTS/indonesia_ningrum.pdf, accessed on 22th March 2016.

686 Lubis and Sirait, *Hukum Persaingan Usaha* (n 225) 361–369.

olations of the Law Number 5/1999.[687] Further Article 40 of the Law Number 5/1999 reads:

> "The Commission (KPPU) may conduct investigations of business actors if there is an allegation of the occurrence of violations of this Law even though no report is filed."

According *to Sirait and Lubis*, KPPU could initiate the preliminary investigation phase after the Decree on admissibility of preliminary investigation is issued. Pursuant to Article 39 (1) of the Law Number 5/1999 the time limit for the preliminary investigation is 30 days as of the issuance date of the Decree. However, upon receiving reports from the persons and affected parties, KPPU is required to examine the completeness and clarity of reports previously.[688]

Subsequently, in the advance investigation phase, KPPU could begin the investigation provided: Firstly, there had been indications concerning violations of the Competition Law Number 5/1999; Secondly, KPPU requires more investigatory time to examine the competition cases in questions. Additionally, KPPU will issue the Decision regarding initiation of the advance investigation. Moreover, as regards to the time limit of advance investigations, Article 43 of the Competition Law Number 5/1999 stipulates:

> "(1) The Commission shall be obligated to complete an advance investigation within 60 (sixty) days from the start of the advance investigation as intended in Article 39 paragraph (1).
> (2) If required, the time limit for an advance investigation as intended in paragraph (1) may be extended by not more than 30 (thirty) days."[689]

Moreover, in the advance investigation proceeding, KPPU distinguishes the two types of legal status of business actors, which are: the report-

---

687 Article 38 (1) and (2) of the Law Number 5/1999 reads:
"Any person having knowledge of the occurrence of or reasonably suspecting that a violation of this Law has occurred, can report it in writing to the Commission with a clear statement concerning the occurrence of violation, attaching the identity of the reporting party. A party suffering loss as a result of violations of this Law may file a written report to the Commission with a complete and clear statement regarding the occurrence of violation and the losses inflicted, attaching the identity of the reporting party."

688 Lubis and Sirait, *Hukum Persaingan Usaha* (n 225) 324–325.

689 ibid.

ed and the witness.[690] Afterward, in the advance investigation phase, KPPU will summon the Parties to attend the administrative proceedings. Besides, Article 41 (3) of the Competition Law Number 5/1999 requires that the summoned parties are obliged to attend the administrative proceedings. Thereby, the summoned parties are subject to criminal prosecutions they had refused to fulfil their obligation of attending the administrative proceedings before KPPU.[691]

Equally important, the KPPU's advance investigation proceeding comprises mainly three aspects. First, the administrative inquiries procedure. Second, the adjudication of principal legal matters. Third, the evidentiary or substantiation processes.[692] Whereas in the administrative inquiry procedure, KPPU will examine the parties' identities and their legal rights, Article 65 (2) of KPPU Regulation Number 1/2006, the parties have the right to be escorted by or come along with their Barrister or Advocate.[693] The adjudication of main legal matters, moreover, consists of two proceedings. On the one hand, KPPU is authorised to question the parties unilaterally, that is to say, the parties are not able to refute or comment as regards to the documents and witnesses acquired by KPPU. On the other hand, the parties are given op-

690 Article 1 (5) of the Law Number 5/1999 stipulates:
"Business actors shall be any individual or business entity, either incorporated or not incorporated as legal entity, established and domiciled or conducting activities within the jurisdiction of the Republic of Indonesia, either independently or jointly based on agreement, conducting various business activities in the economic field." ibid.

691 Article 41 of the Law Number 5/1999 reads:
"(1) Business actors and or other parties examined shall be required to submit instruments of evidence required in the investigation and or hearing.
(2) Business actors shall be prohibited from refusing to be heard, from refusing to provide information required for investigations and or hearings, or from impeding the investigation and or hearing processes.
(3) Violations of the provisions of paragraph (2) shall be submitted by the Commission to investigators for conducting investigations in accordance with the prevailing provisions."
Indonesian Law regarding the Prohibition of Monopolistic Practices and Unfair Business Competition Number 5/1999. http://eng.kppu.go.id/competition-law/, accessed on 7th January 2019.

692 Lubis and Sirait, *Hukum Persaingan Usaha (n 225)* 324–327.

693 This principle has also been stipulated by the Indonesian Law Number 18/2000 concerning Advocates and Legal Aid. Lubis and Sirait, *Hukum Persaingan Usaha (n 225)* 325–327.

portunities to submit either documents or information related to the case in question to KPPU. Further, the parties are given an opportunity to confer additional documents or information to KPPU both in the preliminary and in the advance investigations. This opportunity has been to a large extend regarded as another form of defense of rebuttal rights. Also, in the adjudication of main legal matters, KPPU provides the parties an opportunity to give corrections as to the procès-verbal("Berita Acara Pemeriksaan-BAP") upon the prior approval of KPPU.[694]

Equally important, in the evidentiary or substantiation proceedings, KPPU attempts to find and verify the material truth as to the case in question. Accordingly, the evidentiary requirement rules pursuant to Article 42 of the Competition Law Number 5/1999 prescribes:

> *"Evidence used by the Commission for investigation and examination are: (a) Witness or Testimony's explanations, (b) Expert explanations, (c) Letters and/or Documents, (d) Indications, (e) Explanations from the business actor".*[695]

Whereas the evidentiary requirement rules of Article 42 of the Competition Law Number 5/1999 apply primarily to the administrative proceedings before KPPU, these rules apply simultaneously as the judiciary proceedings before the Courts according to the principle of *Lex specialis derogat legi generali.*

With respect to the decision phase, pursuant to Article 43 (3) of the Competition Law Number 5/1999 KPPU must decide whether an infringement of competition law had been existed or not existed within 30 days. Accordingly, Article 43 (4) prescribes that the Commission's Decision abovementioned must be announced in an open hearing to the public and followed by the notification to the parties. Taking into account the principle of transparency and efficiency, KPPU is obliged to deliver thedDecision abovementioned without delay, that is to say, not only through direct submission to the business actors (in person) but also through e-mail or facsimile.[696]

694 ibid.
695 ibid.
696 ibid.

Eventually, in the after-decision phase, three scenarios are possible to take place according to the Competition Law Number 5/1999.[697] Firstly, the business actor voluntarily accepts the decision of KPPU and is thus willingly to implement the decision and submit the implementation report. Article 44 (1) of the Competition Law Number 5/1999 provides:

> "Within 30 (thirty) days from the time the business actor concerned receives notice about the Commission's Decision as intended in Article 43 paragraph (4), the business actor concerned shall be obligated to implement such decision and to submit an implementation report to the Commission."

Secondly, the business actor refuses the Decision of KPPU and thus subsequently appeals to the District Court ("PN"). Whereas, Article 44 (2) of the Competition Law Number 5/1999 stipulates:

> "Business actors may appeal to the District Court by no later than 14 (fourteen) days after receiving notification of the Commission's Decision."

Thirdly, the business actor is neither willing to implement the decision of KPPU nor to appeal the District Court. In this scenario, Article 44 (4) of the Competition Law Number 5/1999 provides:

> "In the event that the provisions of paragraph (1) and paragragph (2) are not implemented by the business actor concerned, the Commission shall submit such decision to an investigator for conducting an investigation in accordance with the provisions of the prevailing laws and regulations."

Accordingly, the KPPU's decision serves as the sufficient initial evidence for the investigators to conduct criminal investigations as regulated by Article 44 (5) of the Competition Law Number 5/1999.[698]

2.3.3 Judiciary Review (Judicial Supervision)

Within the judicial proceedings before the District Courts (PN) as well as the Supreme Court of Republic of Indonesia (MARI), Article 45 and Article 46 of the Competition Law Number 5/1999 in conjunction with the Regulation of Indonesian Supreme Court ("MARI") Number

697 ibid.
698 ibid.

3/2005 ("Perma No.3/2005") and Number 1/2003 ("Perma No.1/2003) prescribe the procedural rules which are primarily important.[699]

In contrast to the previous rule on judicial appeal, the Law Number 5/1999 as well as Perma No. 3/2005 introduce "the judicial complaint" to counter administrative decisions of KPPU.[700] Article 1 of the Perma No.1/2003 defines "the judicial complaint" as a legal endeavor provided to the business actor, who refuses the decision of KPPU. Further, Article 2 (1) of the Perma No.3/2005 stipulates that the business actor affected by KPPU decision can only file a judicial complaint to the District Court, in which the domicile (corporate seat) of business actor locates.

With regard to the jurisdictional forum, the Perma No.3/2005 clearly stipulates two possibilities. First, the business actor must file a judicial complaint to the District Court (PN), in which the business actor's corporate seat locates. Whenever, there is more than one business actor, with the same corporate seat, filing judicial complaints against a same decision of KPPU, thus the District Court must register the complaints with a similar register number. Second, whenever the business actors subject to different jurisdictions of the District Court, thus KPPU is able to propose the Supreme Court (MARI) to appoint a certain District Court to adjudicate the judicial complaint. This rule aims to guarantee a legal certainty as to the Court's Decision over the judicial complaint.[701]

As has been noted by the Perma No.3/2005, as regards KPPU's legal position in the judicial complaint, the District Court considers KPPU as the parties to this adjudication. Principally, there are two juridical reasons behind this rule: Firstly, to ensure the principle of objectivity, proportionality and equity pursuant to the principle of "audi alteram et partem". Second, to prevent or to minimalise evaluation bias of KPPU during the evidentiary proceeding before the District Court.[702]

Furthermore, in judicial proceedings in the District Court, Article 45 (1) requires the District Court to adjudicate the complaints within

---

699 Peraturan Mahkamah Agung RI Nomoer 1/2003 ("Perma No.1/2003) ‹http://www.kppu.go.id/id/produk-hukum/perma/› accessed on 23th March 2016.

700 Lubis and Sirait, Hukum Persaingan Usaha (n 225) 331–337.

701 ibid.

702 ibid.

the time limit of 14 days as of the registration of judicial complaint. Accordingly, the Chairman of the District Court must appoint the Judges, who have sound knowledge in the Competition law, to adjudicate the judicial complaint.[703] Also, pursuant to Article 5 (3) of the Perma No.3/2005, the District Court does not employ the mediation process in adjudicating the judicial complaint.[704] Moreover, the District Court, by means of an interlocutory (provisional) decision, can issue an order for KPPU to carry out additional examinations of the case in question.[705] It must be observed, that the District Court must decide the judicial complaint within the time limit of 30 days as of an initiation of trial over the judicial complaint.[706]

Finally, with respect to the cassation proceedings before the Supreme Court (MARI), Article 45 (3) of the Competition Law Number 5/1999 regulates that KPPU and the business actors could file the cassation to the Supreme Court (MARI) within the time limit of 14 days as of the decision of District Court delivered. In this respect, the Supreme Court (MARI) acts as the Court of last resort both for KPPU and the business actors. Equally important, according to Article 45 (4) of the Competition Law Number 5/1999, the Supreme Court (MARI) is obliged to decide on the case within the time limit of 30 days as of the cassation is received.[707]

3.3.3 Judiciary Review (Judicial Supervision)

In the Indonesia competition law, in the event of a cartel infringement, KPPU shall employ evidentiary requirements as prescribed in the Law Number 5/1999. Nevertheless, in the law enforcement proceedings of

---

703 Article 5 (2) of the PERMA No.3/2000. ‹http://www.kppu.go.id/id/produk-hukum/perma/›, accessed on 5th January 2019.

704 Lubis and Sirait, Hukum Persaingan Usaha (n 225) 334.

705 Article 6 (1) of the Indonesian Supreme Court Regulation (PERMA) No.1/2003. See ‹http://www.kppu.go.id/id/produk-hukum/perma/› accessed on 5th January 2019.

706 Article 45 (2) of the Law Number 5/1999. Law regarding the Prohibition of Monopolistic Practices and Unfair Business Competition. ‹http://www.kppu.go.id/id/produk-hukum/perma/› accessed on 5th January 2019.

707 Lubis and Sirait, Hukum Persaingan Usaha (n 225) 324–327.

the Law Number 5/1999 the Indonesia District Court and the Supreme Court also apply the general evidentiary requirement rules, namely civil law and criminal law ones, to adjudicate competition law violation cases. Hence, it is necessarily important to understand the general evidentiary requirement rules to conduct analysis of the Indonesia competition law optimally.

3.3.4 Evidentiary Rule and Principle

3.3.4.1 General Evidentiary Rule

From a theoretical standpoint, there are four approaches with regard to the evidentiary requirement rule, which are as follows:[708]

3.3.4.2 Evidentiary Principle According to the Judge's Conviction (*Conviction Intime*)

According to this approach, the judges in adjudicating cases could make dictum in the end of trial proceedings based upon merely their personal conviction, in spite of inadequacy of evidences. Thus, the judges have a wide discretion or judicial freedom in deciding cases. However, this approach has drawbacks, notably the judges could be largely subjective and arrive to decisions which are contrary to the principle of justice.

Although this evidentiary has been derived from the French legal system, Article 294 (1) of the Indonesia Civil Procedure Law (*Herziene Indische Regeling-HIR*) stipulates as follows:

> "None of persons can be punished, unless the judges have obtained personal conviction with legally evidentiary instruments, which confirm the wrongful of an alleged offence and the alleged person, that he or she commits the offence."[709]

708 M. Y. Harahap, *Pembahasan permasalahan dan penerapan KUHAP* (Ed. 2, Sinar Grafika, Jakarta, 2000) 71–77.

709 M. Y. Harahap, *Hukum acara perdata: Tentang gugatan, persidangan, penyitaan, pembuktian, dan putusan pengadilan* (Cet. 2 Sinar Grafika, Jakarta, 2005) 55–58.

3.3.4.3 Evidentiary Principle According to the Positive Law (*Positife Wettelijke Bewijstheorie*)

This principle has been often depicted as 'the formal evidentiary approach' (formule bewijstheorie), whereas according to this approach 'whenever all elements of statutory act are proved in the trial proceedings, thus the judges' conviction becomes insignificant and the judges are obliged to decide the cases immediately'. However, this principle has a prominent drawback, notably the judges decide cases although the evidences are insufficient.

Article 138 (2); 150 (3); 153 (3); 154 (1); 155(1); 156 (1) of the HIR embody this evidentiary principle.[710]

3.3.4.4 Evidentiary Principle According to the Restricted Judges Conviction (*La conviction raisonee*)

This evidentiary is a modus vivendi for the dilemmatic evidentiary approaches aforementioned. Accordingly, in this approach the judges are able to make decisions based upon their personal conviction; however, this personal conviction must be based upon the rules concerning evidences either stipulated in the prevailing legislations or outside the prevailing legislations.[711]

3.3.4.5 Evidentiary Principle According to the Laws Negatively (*Negatief Wettelijke*)

According to this evidentiary approach, the judges in the trial proceedings are able to decide based upon evidence rules which are limited by the laws plus the judges' conviction. These two consideration factors are integrated and inseparable for the judges in the trial proceedings, notably in the criminal law proceeding. Furthermore, pursuant to Article 183 the Indonesia Criminal Procedural Code (KUHAP), the standard of proof for deciding cases for the judges has at least two evidentiary instruments, in which the judges' conviction is one of the instruments. This principle is profoundly important to establish 'beyond rea-

710 Harahap, *Pembahasan permasalahan dan penerapan KUHAP (n 707)* 71–77.
711 ibid.

sonable doubt' and achieve ultimate righteous truth (*materiele waarheid*).

With regard to the evidentiary instruments, the Indonesia civil law, criminal law and administrative law acknowledge the following instruments, which encompass as follows:[712]

1) Testimony (Witness and Expert testimony);
2) Written or documentary evidence;
3) Indicating evidence;
4) Information of the accused person;
5) Acknowledgement;
6) Allegation evidence;
7) Judge's knowledge;
8) Oaths[713]

3.3.4.2 Principle of Evidentiary Evaluation

According to Mertokusumo, the Indonesia procedural law scholar, from the adjudicators' perspective, there are three theories concerning evaluation and/or assessment of evidences, which are as follows:[714]

3.3.4.2.1 Free evidentiary theory

According to this principle, in the evaluation of evidences, the judges should not be restricted by certain rules. As a matter of fact, the judges shall have a wide discretionary power to make assessments or evaluations as to evidences in the trial proceedings. Nonetheless, this principle prerequisites the impartial, honest and reliable judges to adjudicate cases before the courts.[715]

---

712 I G Zega, ‚Tinjauan Mengenai Indirect Evidence (Bukti Tidak Langsung) sebagai Alat Bukti Dalam Kasus Dugaan Kartel Fuel Surcharge Maskapai Penerbangan di Indonesia (Tesis Magister Hukum, Pascasarjana Universitas Indonesia, Jakarta 2012) 51–57.

713 Harahap, *Pembahasan permasalahan dan penerapan KUHAP (n 707) 71–77*. cf. Zega, *(n 711)*.

714 Chazawi, *Hukum Pembuktian Tindak Pidana Korupsi, (Cet.1*, Penerbit Alumni, 2006) 7–9.

715 Zega, 'Tinjauan Mengenai Indirect Evidence (Bukti Tidak Langsung) (n 711) 51–55.

3.3.4.2.2 Negative evidentiary theory

According to Article 169 HIR and Article 1905 of the Indonesia Civil Code (*Burgerlijke Wetboek-BW*), the principle requires that the judges should be limited in their discretionary powers when evaluating or assessing evidences as stipulated by the evidentiary rules. Hence, the discretionary powers of the judges, notably in obtaining and evaluating of evidences, are to be limited through exceptional provisions.[716]

3.3.4.2.3 Positive-limited evidentiary theory

Pursuant to Article 165 HIR in conjunction to Article 1870 of BW, this principle mandates an instruction to the judges to evaluate evidences in the light of their discretionary powers, unless the prevailing laws stipulated otherwise. For example, Article 169 HIR stipulates that a notarial deed is to be regarded as an authentic document and thus has a full evidentiary value.[717]

3.3.4.3 Specific Evidentiary Requirement

With regard to the evidentiary requirements, Article 42 of the Law Number 5/1999 requires, as follows:

> *"Evidence used by the Commission for investigation and examination are: (a) witness explanations, (b) expert explanations, (c) letters and/or documents, (d) indications, (e) explanations from the business actor".*[718]

Pursuant to Article 42 of the Law Number 5/1999 these acceptable evidentiary instruments serve to find and to verify the material truth before the competition law authorities. According to *Hansen,* in the practice of Indonesian Competition Law Number 5/1999, indications or indirect evidence could serve as an acceptable evidentiary instrument in the adjudication proceedings. However, this requires that the indications or indirect evidences are 'coherent and consistent' with other available evidences in the cartels law enforcement proceedings. Nevertheless, the implementation of indirect evidences or indications in the

716 ibid.

717 ibid.

718 Lubis and Sirait, *Hukum Persaingan Usaha (n 225) 324–327.*

cartel's infringement cases could not be generalised, instead this should be subject to an individual and casuistic approach by the Courts.[719]

3.4 Application of the Indirect (Evidences) and the 'Plus Factors' (Parallelism Plus) within the Cartel Enforcement Proceedings

3.4.1 Application of the Indirect (Circumstantial) Evidences in the Cartel Enforcement Proceedings

In the majority of antitrust enforcements, the Competition Authorities in the European Union (EU), in Germany and in Indonesia, had experienced profound difficulties as to how to detect (conceal), deter and thus prosecute cartel infringements, because cartels involve various forms of agreement, arrangement or practices between the undertakings to eliminate and subvert the competition processes on the market. Altough cartels occur secretively, they cause detrimental effects, which are perceivable by consumers, for instance prices' increases of products ultimately reducing the consumers' welfare.[720] Equally important, *Ruky* emphasises that cartels are the most dangerous infringement against competition law, compared to other violations. In fact, the Competition Authority (CA) faces an intensive enigma as to 'who commits cartels and what types of cartels occur?'[721] Likewise, *Beaton-Wells, et.al*, explains that difficulties in detecting, prosecuting and deterring cartels violations rest upon the fact that cartels infringement frequently involve so-called 'multiple-cheatings'. Put differently, the undertakings participating in cartels (cartelists) initially cheat the Competition Authorithy by presenting themselves as competitors, but in fact they do not compete against each other. Thus, the undertakings participating in cartels cheat other competitors, consumers and public as well (first-level cheating). Subsequently, the cartelists cheat the operation of cartels, secretly operate against the agreement not to compete when it may be to their economic advantage to initiate competition again, thus cheating between the

719 ibid., 324–325.
720 *Silalahi* 'Circumstantial Evidence' (n 14) 1–3.
721 *Ruky* 'Economic Evidence' (n 16) 1–5.

cartelists (second-level cheating). Afterwards, the ex-cartelists who act as the "whistle-blowers" and informants to the CA in the Leniency program, cheat the other cartelists by deserting to the law enforcement authorities (third-level cheating). Eventually, the former cartelists who act as the 'whistle-blower' and informants to the Competition Authority (CA), cheat the law enforcement officials by not giving the evidences optimally (fourth level cheating).[722] Moreover, *Heineman* maintains that the access to evidences isa main problematic matter in the competition law enforcement.[723] Accordingly, cartels practices are therefore difficult to uncover due to their secretive nature and the lack of availability of evidences. In fact, according to *Andrews*, the harder the CA investigates on cartels, the craftier the undertakings can commit cartels.[724]

In the second place, according to *Silalahi*, cartels frequently occur in an oligopolistic market due to their characteristics. Therefore, *Jones and Sufrin* are of the opinion that in an oligopolistic market, cartels (explicit collusion) as well as tacit collusion could emerge consecutively.[725] For that reason, *Silalahi* emphasises that the undertakings operating in an oligopolistic market are subject to the oligopolistic interdependences ('conscious parallelism').[726] Hence, *Kerber and Schwalbe* describe that these oligopolistic interdependences between undertakings had been derived from and could be explained by the game-theory approach.[727] Inded, *Jones and Sufrin* explain that based upon the economic theory, the undertakings in an oligopolistic market would recognise that the profitability of their conduct (behaviour) will depend on the other competitors' conduct (behaviour) in a market. Put differently, they would be better-off if they imposed higher prices and obtained higher profits. Thus, they could coordinate their conduct (behaviour) in a similar way to those committing cartels infringement, without an explicit collusive

---

722 C Beaton-Wells and C Tran (eds) *Anti-Cartel Enforcement in a Contemporary Age: Leniency Religion* (Hart Studies in Competition Law Book (Hart Publising 2015) 249.

723 Heinemann, 'Access to Evidence and Presumptions- Communicating Vessels in Procedural Law', in Schweitzer and Hüschelharth, *Public and Private Enforcement of Competition Law in Europe: Legal and Economic Perspectives* (Springer Verlag, 2014) 167–170.

724 *Ruky*, 'Economic Evidence' (n 16) 3.

725 *Jones and Surfin, EU Competition Law (n 46) 510–512.*

726 *Silalahi*, ‚Circumstantial Evidence' (n 14) 2–3.

727 Kerber and Schwalbe, in Säcker, et.al, *Europäisches Wettbewerbsrecht (n 13) 116–117.*

agreement.[728] *Posner* categorises such behavioural interdependencies on the markets as 'tacit collusion'.[729]

Thereby, *Silalahi* suggests that the Competition Authorithy (CA) requires not only the direct evidence, but also the indirect (circumstantial) evidence in order to substantiate cartels infringement, notably in an oligopolistic market.[730] In addition, *Ruky* reiterates that the substantiation of cartels existence in the market prerequisites a particular evidentiary instrument, namely the economic evidence.[731] As a matter of fact, according to the Organization for Economic Co-operation and Development (OECD), within the cartels' prohibition enforcement proceedings, the CA shall employ two types of evidences: First, the direct evidence, which refers to the evidence that identifies a meeting or communication between the subjects and describes the substance of their agreement. The most common form of direct evidence are: First, documents (in printed or electronic form) that identify an agreement and the parties to it, and oral or written statements by co-operative cartel participants describing the operation of the cartel.[732] Second, the indirect (circumstantial) evidence. The indirect (circumstantial) evidence is an evidence that does not specifically describe the terms of an agreement, or the parties to it. It includes evidence of communications among suspected cartel operators and economic evidence concerning the market and the conduct of those participating in it that suggest concerted action.[733]

Equally important, in the European Competition law, according to the Commission, the indirect (circumstantial) evidence is defined as follows:

> "[...] the notion of indirect or circumstantial evidence comprises of evidences which is appropriate to corroborate the proof of the existence of cartels by way of deduction, common sense, economic analysis or logical inference from the demonstrated facts."[734]

---

728 Jones and Sufrin, *EU Competition Law (n 46)* 534–537.
729 Posner, *Antitrust Law* (n 80) 53.
730 Silalahi,'Circumstantial Evidence (n 14)' 2–3.
731 Ruky, 'Economic Evidence' (n 16), 2–5.
732 OECD, 'Prosecuting Cartels Without Direct Evidence' (n 19) 2–10.
733 ibid.
734 ibid.

Even more, *Ruky* describes that the indirect (circumstantial) evidence can be classified into three categories. First, the communication evidence.[735] Second, the facilitating practice (*quasi-economic evidence*).[736] Third, the economic evidence.[737] According to the Commission, economic evidence refers to evidences which are derived from an economic reasoning employed in the competition law cases, notably in order to develop in a consistent manner or, conversely, to rebut facts due to their inconsistencies, the economic evidence and arguments in a case in question.[738]

---

735 According to the Organisation for Economic Co-operation and Development (OECD):
"Communication evidence is evidence that cartel operators met or otherwise communicated, but does not describe the substance of their communications. It includes, for example, records of telephone conversations among suspected cartel participants, of their travel to a common destination and notes or records of meetings in which they participated. Communication evidence can be highly probative of an agreement. Almost all of the circumstantial cases described by delegations included communication evidence; in some the evidence was compelling." OECD, 'Prosecuting Cartels (n 19) 10.

736 ibid.

737 According to the Organisation for Economic Co-operation and Development (OECD) as to the economic evidence:
"Economic evidence can be categorized as either conduct or structural evidence. The former includes, most importantly, evidence of parallel conduct by suspected cartel members, e.g., simultaneous and identical price increases or suspicious bidding patterns in public tenders. It can also include evidence of facilitating practices, though that conduct could also be characterised as ìquasi-communication evidence. Structural economic evidence includes evidence of such factors as high market concentration and homogeneous products. Of these two types of economic evidence, conduct evidence is considered the more important. Economic evidence must be carefully evaluated. The evidence should be inconsistent with the hypothesis that the market participants are acting unilaterally in their self interest. Economics, including the use of game theory, can be instructive on how to make this judgment. It appears that in most countries, however, that kind of analysis is not yet employed. But further, economic evidence can play an important role in the initial stages of a cartel investigation. A proper analysis of it could provide a basis for deciding which of several possible cases are likely to be the most fruitful to pursue, with the hope and expectation that better evidence of agreement, both direct and circumstantial, will be discovered." OECD; 'Prosecuting Cartels without Direct' (n 19) 10–12.

738 The Commission, Directorate General Competition, 'Best Practices on Submission of Economic Evidence and Data Collection in Cases concerning the Applica-

With regard to the economic evidences according to *Ruky*, they can be further divided into two types: First, the structural evidence. The structural economic evidence refers to the following economic variables: (1) high market concentration; (2) low concentration on the opposite side of the market; (3) high barriers to entry markets; (4) high degree of vertical integration; (5) standardised or homogeneous product. These economic variables could indicate the existence of cartels practice in a given market.[739] Second, the conduct evidence. The conduct evidence refers to the particular market behaviour of undertakings, *inter alia* 'parallel prices increases' and 'suspicious tender or bidding patterns', which could indicate whether the undertakings compete or not compete with each other on a relevant market.[740] *Kekevi and Göksin* argue that the economic evidences are able to prove cartels infringement based upon two reasons. First, the economic evidence can assist the Competition Authority (CA) to identify 'cartelised markets' by analysing outputs and price levels on a market. Secondly, the economic evidence supports the CA to prove cartels infringement by means of analysing the conducts (behaviours) of the undertakings in a market.[741]

Nevertheless, *Silalahi* observes that even though the economic evidence has been accepted in the most competition law jurisdictions, the Competition Authority views this type of evidene as ambiguous for the following reasons, that is to say, this category of evidence cannot exactly explain whether the undertakings have individually or collectively committed certain market conducts.[742] For that reason, *Kekevi* suggests that the CA must be cautious in implementing the indirect (circumstantial) evidences in order to prevent or minimalise the occurrence of the following catastrophic errors. First, to falsely condemn innocents, although what they carry out is subject to the oligopolistic interdependence or conscious parallelism ('False positive' or 'Type I er-

tion of Articles 101 and 102 TFEU and in Merger Cases' ‹http://ec.europa.eu/dgs/competition/economist/best_practices_en.html› accessed on 22nd May 2018

739 *Ruky*, 'Economic Evidence' (n 16) 3–4. See also OECD, 'Prosecuting Cartels Without Direct Evidence' (n 19) 5–7.

740 OECD, 'Prosecuting Cartels Without Direct Evidence' (n 19) *Ruky*, 'Economic Evidence' (n 16) 3–4.

741 ibid. OECD, 'Prosecuting Cartels Without Direct Evidence' (n 19) 5–7.

742 *Silalahi*, 'Circumstantial Evidence' (n 14) 2–3.

ror').[743] Second, to acquit cartel members by identifying their cartel behaviour as an oligopolistic interdependence ('False negative' or 'Type II error').[744]

Ultimately, whenever the Competition Authority (CA) encounters difficulties for finding direct evidences to prove concerted practices as well as for obtaining plausible explanations for parallel market behaviour (price parallelism), the CA could proceed to find additional circumstantial evidences, which are pervasively known as the "Plus factors".[745]

Particularly important, according to Judge *Posner*, in the *In re Text Messaging Antitrust Litigation* argued that "direct evidence of conspiracy is not *a sine qua non* and *[indirect] circumstantial evidence* could very well be used to establish an antitrust conspiracy."[746]

---

743 Type I Error refers to:
"the incorrect rejection of a true null hypothesis. It is also known as a false positive or an error of the first kind. For example, a fire alarm goes off indicating a fire breaking out when in fact there is no fire. Or a blood test result that shows a patient has a certain disease when in reality the patient does not have that disease. In antitrust cases, Type I error represents a false judgment in which the court condemns a conduct that was not anticompetitive. Type I error reflects an over-enforcement or over-regulation."
Kekevi, *Can Ecoomics Help Us with Cartel Detection' (n 20), 11–12. See also* New York Law School, 'European Competition Law: Unpacking a European Court of Justice Opinion' ‹https://www.eucomplaw.com/error-types/› accessed 5th January 2019.

744 Furthermore, Type II Error refers to the following notions:
"is defined as the failure to reject a false null hypothesis. It is also known as a false negative or an error of the second kind. For example, a fire breaking out and the fire alarm do not go off. Or a blood test fails to indicate that a patient has a certain disease. In antitrust cases, Type II error represents a false judgment in which the court fails to condemn a conduct that is anticompetitive. Type II error reflects under-enforcement or under-regulation." Kekevi, *Can Ecoomics Help Us with Cartel Detection' (n 20), 11–12. See also* New York Law School, 'European Competition Law: Unpacking a European Court of Justice Opinion' ‹https://www.eucomplaw.com/error-types/› accessed 5th January 2019.

745 M. Sadhya, 'Concerted action in an oligopoly and the role of plus factors' (LL.M Thesis, West Bengal University of Juridical Science, India, 2012) 8.

746 W. E. Kovacic et. al., 'Plus Factors and Agreement in Antitrust Law' (110 Mich. L. Rev. 393 2011), 393–400.

3.4.2 Application of the "Plus Factors" (Parallelism Plus) for Consolidating the Evidences of Cartels

On the one hand, in the current competition (antitrust) enforcement proceedings, the most difficult obstacle to solve is how to accurately distinguish, if the parallel market behaviour, such as the parallel pricing, in an oligopolistic market, is attributable to the concerted practices. On the other hand, if the parallel market behaviour is naturally the effect of market structure. Whereby, the first conduct is unlawful and is subject to the cartel prohibitions; the latter ("conscious parallelism" or "oligopolistic interdependence") is lawful, yet it demands particular Competition (Antitrust) law remedies.[747]

Whereas the concerted practices prohibition mandates the independence postulate, this would not deprive the rights of undertakings to intelligently adapt with other competitors' market conduct, that is to say, the parallel market behaviour.[748]

Primarily, in the European Competition law, the concerted practices under the prohibition of Article 101 (1) TFEU must be comprehended in the conceptual mindset inherent in the EU Treaty on competition policies:

> "[…] the criteria of co-ordination and co-operation […] must be understood in the light of the concept inherent in the provisions of the Treaty […] that each economic operator must determine independently the policy which he intends to adopt on the market. The Treaty thus lays down a requirement of independence. However, this requirement does not *prevent economic operators from adapting themselves intelligently to the conditions of the market; rather it prohibits any practice that may influence competitors' conduct on the market.*"[749]

Hence, the parallel conduct would not be, in itself, illegal and to prove the existence of a collusive agreement or concerted practices.[750] Respectively, the German Federal Cartel Office (*Bundeskartellamt*) inquired the parallel pricing on the fuel sector and found that there is no

747 Lettl, *Kartellrecht (n 138)*, 25–35.

748 ibid.

749 ibid.

750 D. Slobodenjuk, 'Parallel Behaviour under EU Antitrust Law' (Presentation Paper, IBA Conference 1st CIS Competition Law, Clifford Chance, London 8–9 December 2011) 1–3.

agreements or concerted practices, in spite of the parallel pricing therein. Thus, the FCO found that the oligopolistic market structure and a very transparent market had resulted in the parallel pricing.[751]

Accordingly, the Court of Justice in the *Ahlström Osakeyhtiö and others v Commission of the European Communities* case, argued as follows:

> „parallel conduct cannot be regarded as furnishing proof of concertation unless concertation constitutes the only plausible explanation for such conduct. It is necessary to bear in mind that, although Article [101] of the Treaty prohibits any form of collusion which distorts competition, it does not deprive economic operators of the right to adapt themselves intelligently to the existing and anticipated conduct of their competitors."

Furthermore, according to *Allendesalazar, Lage and Vallina*, indicating the legal stance of the Court of Justice of EU, has been as follows:

> "[...] it is perfectly justifiable for players in the market to adapt themselves to the existing or anticipated conduct of their competitors and as such parallel conduct is not caught by Article 101 and no presumption of collusion is created."[752]

Similar legal stance is found in the US Antitrust Law as regards the parallel pricing:

> "While a showing of parallel business behaviour is admissible circumstantial evidence from which the fact finder may infer agreement, it falls short of conclusively establishing agreement or [...] itself constituting the Sherman Act offense. Even conscious parallelism, a common reaction of firms in a concentrated market (that) recognize their shared economic interests and their interdependence with respect to price and output decision is not in itself unlawful [...]. The inadequacy of showing parallel conduct or interdependence, without more, mirrors the ambiguity of the behavior: consistent with conspiracy, but just as much in line with a wide swath of rational and competitive business strategy unilaterally prompted by common perceptions on the market."[753]

---

751 According to the President of *the Bundeskartellamt* (German Federal Cartel Office), Dr. Andreas Mundt:
"the market structures are such that agreements are not necessarily required as there is, so to speak, an implicit understanding between the companies. This leads to excessive prices." ibid. 13.

752 Allendesalazar, Lage and Vallina, 'Oligopolies, Consicous Parallelism, and Concertation' in C D Ehlermann, I. Atanasiu, *European Competition Law Annual 2006: Enforcement of Prohibition of Cartels* (Hart Publishing, Oxford: 2007) 119–122.

753 Sadhya 'Concerted Action in An Oligopoly and The Role of Plus Factors' (n 744) 8.

In the Competition law theory, the parallel pricing is not *Per-se Illegal* and it does not create a "presumption of *iuris tantum* of collusion"[754] In certain circumstances, parallel pricings could solely constitute 'indirect evidence' for 'concerted practices' by taking into account the overall competition parameters.[755]

Nevertheless, hitherto, the Competition Authorities have been experiencing perplexities to correctly distinguish between the legitimate conscious parallelism, on the one hand, and the illicit collusion, on the other hand.[756] Particularly, in an oligopolistic market, the blurry line of distinction between the two becomes manifested.[757] Put differently, how to correctly distinguish between conscious parallelism and the concerted practices in an oligopolistic market because of the market

754 Allendesalazar, Lage and Vallina, 'Oligopolies, Consicous Parallelism, and Concertation' (n 751) 119–122.

755 In the ICI ("Dyestuffs") case the Court of Justice of EU:
„*by its very nature, then, a concerted practice does not have all the elements of a contract but may inter alia arise out of coordination which becomes apparent from the behaviour of the participants.*
Although parallel behaviour may not by itself be identified with a concerted practice, it may however amount to strong evidence of such a practice if it leads to conditions of competition which do not correspond to the normal conditions of the market, having regard to the nature of the products, the size and number of the undertakings, and the volume of the said market.
This is especially the case if the parallel conduct is such as to enable those concerned to attempt to stabilize prices at a level different from that to which competition would have led, and to consolidate established positions to the detriment of effective freedom of movement of the products in the common market and of the freedom of consumers to choose their suppliers.
Therefore the question whether there was a concerted action in this case can only be correctly determined if the evidence upon which the contested decision is based is considered, not in isolation, but as a whole, account being taken of the specific features of the market in the products in question."
The EU Court of Justice C 48–69. *Imperial Chemical Industries Ltd. v Commission of the European Communities.*, Case 48–69 (ECLI identifier: ECLI:EU:C:1972:70), paras. 65–68.

756 Allendesalazar, Lage and Vallina, 'Oligopolies, Consicous Parallelism, and Concertation' (n 751) 119–122.

757 Sadhya 'Concerted Action in An Oligopoly and The Role of Plus Factors' (n 744) 5–8.

structure thereof becomes the utmost obstacle for the Competition Authorities.[758]

The European Competition and the US Antitrust laws' practices have provided viable solutions as regards to the methods for distinguishing between a collusive agreement or concerted practices as well as the conscious parallelism (an oligopolistic interdependence).[759] The European Competition and US Antitrust laws' practices have introduced the "Parallelism-plus doctrine" and "Plus factors" as well as the "inter-firm communications postulate" in order to distinguish between concerted practices (cartel); and the conscious parallelism (an oligopolistic interdependence).[760]

According to *Ghezzi and Maggiolino*, with regard to "plus-factors" and evidence of the concerted practices:

Evidence of certain types of conduct strongly signifies market collusion. Examples include, as argued by Kovacic and others, 'super plus factors' such as evidence that competing firms share firm-specific production information. In the absence of such evidence, a decision to further investigate market players for potential collusion can be based on empirical analysis, including the use of empirical screens. For example, a decision to further investigate can also be justified when the data in question (for example, price or quantity-related data) are clearly abnormal and completely different from a carefully chosen benchmark.

3.4.3 Elaborations of the Circumstantial (Indirect) Evidences in the EU Competition Law, German Cartel Law and Indonesian Competition Law

In the application framework of the indirect (circumstantial) evidences, notably the economic evidence constitutes the main ingredient of indirect (circumstantial) evidences in order to substantiate cartels in-

758 Allendesalazar, Lage and Vallina, 'Oligopolies, Consicous Parallelism, and Concertation' (n 751) 119–122.
759 Ghezzi and Maggiolino, 'Bridging EU Concerted Practices with U.S. Concerted Actions' (n 565) 651–666.
760 ibid.

fringement optimally. Accordingly, the economic evidence is the integral part of the indirect (circumstantial) evidences, which differs from the direct evidences such as contemporary documents, minutes or notes of meetings and corporate statements.[761] Further, according to *Lianos and Genakos*, the categories of economic evidence encompass economic theories, models of collusive conducts, evidences relating to market structures, natures of the product and economic theory on facilitating practices.[762]

Equally important, the implementation of indirect (circumstantial) evidences in the antitrust enforcement proceedings, must be considered within the evidentiary rules of the European Competition and the German Cartel laws. Whereas in the practice thereof, the standards of proof have been requiring that "sufficient, precise and coherent proofs" must be established. Furthermore, the Court of Justice of EU in the Competition law precedents requires quality of evidences as follows: 'sufficient precise and coherent [or consistent]', 'precise and consistent', 'solid, specific and corroborative', 'firm, precise and consistent body of evidence', 'convergent and convincing', 'convincing', or 'cogent'. Furthermore, the Court of Justice in its recent decision, *Dresdner Bank* case, stipulated:

> "Any doubt in the mind of the Court must operate to the advantage of the undertaking to which the decision finding an infringement was addressed. The Court cannot therefore conclude that the Commission has established the infringement at issue to the requisite legal standard if it still entertains any doubts on that point, in particular in proceedings for annulment of a decision imposing a fine. [...] the Commission must show precise and consistent evidence in order to establish the existence of the infringement."[763]

Furthermore, in the *Woodpulp* case, for example, the Court of Justice stipulated:

> "the evidence must be 'sufficient precise and coherent [...] to justify the view that the parallel business [...] was the result of concerted action."

761 OECD, 'Prosecuting Cartel without Direct Evidence' (n 19) 20.

762 Lianos and Genakos, "Econometric Evidence in EU Competition Law in Lianos and Geradin, *Handbook on European Competition Law (n 26)* 1–12.

763 Geradine, Farrar and Petit, *EU Competition Law* (n 33) 128–130.

On the one hand, the European Court's Judge, asserted as regards to evidentiary standard, as follows:

> "Thus, we have not yet articulated the difference known in common law systems between the criminal standard *of 'proof beyond reasonable doubt'* and the civil standard of 'balance of probabilities', a difference which is also known in civil law systems but not perhaps articulated in quite the same way. In practice, we are applying something very close to the criminal standard but perhaps subconsciously making some allowance in cartel cases for the inherent difficulty of proving collusion. "[764]

On the other hand, in the German Cartel law, the main objective of the competition enforcement proceedings, notably the administrative and the imposition of administrative fines, has been to find the material truth (*materielle Wahrheit*).[765] Hence, the German Cartel Authorities (*Kartellbehörde*) must assure that all necessary measures have been taken to reach a just and correct decision in order to find the material or substantial truth (*materielle Wahrheit)* of the alleged antitrust violation at hand. The *Kartellbehörde* is authorised to collect and corroborate varying types of evidences to obtain clarification of factual circumstances and thus the material (substantive) truth of a case at hand, including the indirect (circumstantial) evidences. For example, the *Oberlandsgericht* (OLG) and the *Bundesgerichtshof* (BGH) put "high importance to an economic analysis" in examining and deciding the alleged antitrust (competition) violation cases. In the administrative and imposition of fines proceedings, for example, the German Cartel Office (*Bundeskartellamt)* Decision must achieve 'a high accuracy grade of plausibility' pursuant to Sec.61 of the GWB.[766] In the antitrust enforcement proceedings before the German Court, there are several factors playing as key determinants for reaching the Decisions, notably, (1) the Judge's personal certainties (*persönliche Gewissheit*), (2) the Judge's empirical knowledge (*Erfahrungssätze*), (3) the significancy of

764 OECD, 'Judicial Enforcement of Competition Law 1996'(OCDE/GD(97)200) ‹https://www.oecd.org/daf/competition/prosecutionandlawenforcement/1919985.pdf› 105–107.accessed on 1st May 2018

765 Dannecker and Biermann, „Vorbemerkung Sec. 81" in Immenga and Mestmäcker, Wettbewerbsrecht (n 566) R 1–226.

766 Schneider in *Langen and Bunte*, Kommentar zum Kartellrecht (n 99) 1230–1234.

confessions,. (4) the role of indirect evidences (*Indizienbeweis*).[767] Particulary important, as to the indirect (circumstantial) evidences, the *Kartellbehörde* and the German Court could conclude the merits of a case in question from the indirect factual circumstances by means of judicial inferences (*facta concludentia*). Respectively, the "plus-factors" are the most important evidences for substantiating the concerted practices. Accordingly, the evidentiary standards in the German Cartel law enfocement proceedings shall establish the "beyond reasonable doubts" in accordance with Sec. 261 of the *German Code of Criminal Procedure* (*Strafprozessordnung* – StPO).[768]

3.4.3.1 In the European Competition Law

According to the Commission, economic evidences could be defined as "evidences which are derived from an economic reasoning employed in the competition law cases, notably in order to develop in a consistent manner or, conversely, to rebut facts due to their inconsistencies, the economic evidence and arguments in a case in question."[769] Further, according to Lianos, in the European Competition Law's enforcement proceedings, the economic evidence has been applied in the following three competition law cases. First, in the cartel violation cases; for example, to establish evidences of concerted practices under the Article 101 (1) TFEU and to determine the fines imposed. Second, in the merger cases; for instance, to identify market definition, anticompetitive harms, and unilateral effects. Third, the

767 Dannecker and Biermann, ‚Vorbemerkung Sec. 81' in Immenga and Mestmäcker, Wettbewerbsrecht (n 566) R 1–226.

768 "*§ 261 Grundsatz der freien richterlichen Beweiswürdigung*
Über das Ergebnis der Beweisaufnahme entscheidet das Gericht nach seiner freien, aus dem Inbegriff der Verhandlung geschöpften Überzeugung." ([Free Evaluation of Evidence] "The court shall decide on the result of the evidence taken according to its free conviction gained from the hearing as a whole."). Strafprozessordung – StPO ‹https://www.gesetze-im-internet.de/englisch_stpo/englisch_stpo.html#p1742› accessed on 5th January 2019.

769 The Commission: DG Competition, 'Best Practices on Submission of Economic Evidence and Data Collection in Cases concerning the Application of Articles 101 and 102 TFEU and in Merger Cases' 5.

abuse of dominant positions for example, in market definition and pricing abuses.[770]

Whereas the Commission has severally used economic evidences to prove and prosecute cartels infringement, the Courts of Justice of the EU, namely the Court of Justice of EU (ECJ), has adopted a very strict standard of proof in evaluating the economic evidence. In the case of *Wood-pulp*, the Commission based its decision on economic evidence as to parallel-behaviour of the alleged undertakings, but without carefully examining the market structure. Subsequently, the EJC decided that 'the Commission had no documents (direct evidences) which directly establish the existence of concertation between the producers concerned'. Further, the EJC dismissed the Commission's argument by deciding, that the Commission 'cannot rely on economic evidences (including econometric evidence) in order to prove cartels, but combines different pieces of evidences (direct and indirect)' and thus 'examined not isolation but in their entirety and never divorced from their context.'[771] Afterwards, in the case of Microsoft, the Courts of Justice of the EU argued that the Court "must not only establish whether the evidence put forward is factually accurate, reliable and consistent but must also determine whether that evidence contains all the relevant data that must be taken into consideration in appraising a complex situation and whether it is capable of substantiating the conclusions drawn from it."[772]

Furthermore, the ECJ annulled the Commission's decision by arguing that the economic evidences were not sufficient to prove concerted practices.[773] Specifically, the ECJ was of the opinion that "the Commission cannot rely on economic evidence only (including econometric evidence) in order to prove cartels infringement, but must combine different pieces of evidences (direct and indirect), examined not in isolation but in their entirety and never divorced from their con-

770 I. Lianos 'Economic evidence and econometrics in competition UNCTAD' (Faculty of laws University College London, Research Partnership Platform Geneva 7 July 2013) ‹file:///U:/RPP2013_Lianos_en.pdf› accessed on 15th October 2015.

771 Lianos and Genakos, "Econometric Evidence in EU Competition Law in Lianos and Geradin, *Handbook on European Competition Law (n 26)* 1–12.

772 ibid.

773 ibid.

text".[774] Nothwithstanding the opposing arguments of the Courts of Justice of the EU, in the PO/Copper plumbing tubes case, the Commission applied the economic evidence to prove a price fixing cartel in the European market for water, heating and gas tubes by means of price regression analysis to determine the effects to competition.[775] Subsequently, in the Ryan-air case, the Commission employed as well the economic evidence to analyse the effects of concentration in the air-transportation market.[776] However, in *the Ryan-air case*, the GC argued for the addition of a rigorous scrutiny of the economic evidence because of the protections of fundamental human rights, which are guaranteed by the EU. Accordingly, the Court stated "where the institutions have a power of appraisal, respect for the rights guaranteed by the legal order of the European Union in administrative procedures is of even more fundamental importance', whereas this means 'the duty of the Commission to examine carefully and impartially all the relevant aspects of the individual case, the right of the person concerned to make his views known and also his right to have an adequately reasoned decision."[777]

Equally important, according to *Holterhus*, pertaining the economic evidence, the practice of European Competition Law recognises the dichotomy of evidences, that is to say, the factual evidence and prognosis evidence, particularly in merger cases. Whereas the first type evidence the European Courts in the General Electric case stated:

> "As to the nature of the Community judicature's power of review, it is necessary to draw attention to the essential difference between factual matters and findings, on the one hand, which may be found to be inaccurate by the Court in the light of the arguments and evidence before it, and, on the other hand, appraisals of an economic nature."[778]

Thus, *Holterhus* emphasises that in cartels infringement cases, the factual evidence comprises, *inter alia:* agreements between undertakings, the existence of market transparency through information exchanges

774 ibid.

775 ibid.

776 ibid.

777 ibid.

778 Holterhus, *Beweisführung in der europäischen Fusionskontrolle: Regelungserfordernis und Regelungsbestand im Spannungsfeld von Wahrheit und Wahrscheinlichkeit* (Mohr Siebeck, 2014), 30–37.

between undertakings, the existence of punishment mechanism between the undertakings (Cartelists), and the existence of prices discounts between undertakings.[779]

As regards the prognostic evidence, whereas the Commission using evidences relating to the current and probable future state of competitions on the market to determine the 'significantly impediment of competition'. This prognostic evidence could be based, for example on structure and competitive dynamics of market. However, the Court of Justice in the case of *Bertelsmann and Sonny* decided that under the balance of probabilities standard, the prognosis evidence has none of strength and quality of supporting evidence. The Court adduced, that the Commission "must adduce adequate evidence of all facts on which its decision is based". Hence, the Court argued that such evidence must be "sufficiently precise and coherent proof" to sustain the Commission's conclusion in its decision. Thus, the quality of evidence of the Commission must go beyond the only assessment that factual proposition is "more likely than not". The Court of Justice imposed this high evidentiary requirement to prognosis evidence by taking into account the serious legal consequences for the alleged undertakings, namely the undertakings must pay the high fines and are liable for compensation of damages to the third parties.[780]

Nevertheless, the precedent of European Competition laws has indicated that the solely application of economic evidence will rarely, if ever, prove conclusive by themselves. Put differently, from the evidentiary standard requirement, the economic evidence had not been sufficient to prove cartels infringement against *the Article 101 (1) TFEU. In the case of Rhône Poulenc, the Advocate General Vesterdorf* convincingly asserted that:

> "Considerable importance must be attached to the fact that competition cases of this kind (cartels) are in reality of a penal nature, which naturally suggests that a high standard of proof is required [...]. There must be a sufficient basis of the decision and any reasonable doubt must be for the benefit of the applicants according to the principle *in dubio pro reo*."[781]

---

779 ibid.

780 N Levy, 'Evidentiary Issues in EU Merger Control in Hawk', (Fordham Competition Law Institute, 2008) 87–93.

781 I Kokkoris, I Lianos, The reform of EC competition law: new challenges (Kluwer Law International, 2010) 312–314.

Furthermore, as regards to the inconclusive value of economic evidence, the GC stipulated, as follows:

> "It is the Commission's task to make an overall assessment of what is shown by the set of indicative factors used to evaluate the competitive situation. It is possible, in that regard, for certain items of evidence to be prioritised and other evidence to be discounted. That examination and the associated reasoning are subject to a review of legality which the Court carries out in relation to Commission decisions on concentrations".[782]

Accordingly, learning from the previous failures, the Commission has issued the Best Practices for the Submission of Economic Evidence and Data Collection in Cases concerning the Application of Articles 101 and 102 TFEU and in Merger Cases (the Best Practice of Economic Evidence).[783] Equally important, in Recitals 2, 3 and 4 of the Best Practice of Economic Evidence, the Commission is of the following opinion:

> "It is therefore necessary to: (i) ensure that economic analysis meet certain minimum technical standards at the outset, (ii) facilitate the effective gathering and exchange of facts and evidence, in particular any underlying quantitative data, and (iii) use in an effective way reliable and relevant evidence obtained during the administrative procedure, whether quantitative or qualitative."

> "First, in order to determine the relevance and significance of an economic analysis for a particular case, it is first necessary to assess its intrinsic quality from a technical perspective, i.e. whether it has been generated and presented in a way that meets adequate technical requirements prevalent in the profession. Second, one must assess the congruence and consistency of the economic analysis with other pieces of quantitative and qualitative evidence (such as customer responses, or documentary evidence)."[784]

Equally important, Röller maintains that the application of economic evidence is subject to the judicial supervision of the European Courts.

782 General Court, Case T-342/07, Ryanair v Commission, [2010], para.136. cf. Holterhus, *Beweisführung in der europäischen Fusionskontrolle: (n 777) 30–37.*

783 The Commission: DG Competition, "Best Practices on Submission of Economic Evidence and Data Collection in Cases concerning the Application of Articles 101 and 102 TFEU and in Merger Cases" 3–5.

784 *ibid.*

In the case *of Aalborg Portland and Others v. Commission,* the Court stated:

> "Examination by the Community judicature of the complex economic assessments made by the Commission must necessarily be confined to verifying whether the rules on procedure and on the statement of reasons have been complied with, whether the facts have been accurately stated and whether there has been any manifest error of appraisal or misuse of powers."

Subsequently, in the *Tetra case*, the Court argued, as follows:

> "the fact that the Commission has a margin of discretion with regard to economic matters, […] does not mean that the Community Courts must refrain from reviewing the Commission's interpretation of information of an economic nature. Not only must the Community Courts, inter alia, establish whether the evidence relied on is factually accurate, reliable and consistent but also whether that evidence contains all the information which must be taken into account in order to assess a complex situation and whether it is capable of substantiating the conclusions drawn from it."[785]

3.4.3.2 In the German Cartel Law

According to *Burrichter and Paul*, in the German Cartel Law's enforcement proceedings, the economic evidence has an important function. This type of evidence has been mainly provided by the expert testimony, which serves as 'aides to the judge' by assisting the judges with their specific knowledge. For example, the economic evidence supports the parties before the Court to establish adequate and sufficient evidences in the two main matters, namely the causation and the quantum.[786] Also, this prerequisites rigorous analysis of the economic variables, such as input cost, demand-fluctuations, market entries and the exit by competing undertakings, and prices.[787] As it has been described previ-

785 See LH Röller 'Economic Evidence and Analysis in Competition Policy: some remarks' (Government Economists in Competition and Regulation 2005 Conference Wednesday, 9 November 2005, DTI Conference Centre). ‹http://ec.europa.eu/dgs/competition/economist/eeac.pdf,› accessed on 19th October 2017.

786 Burrichter and Paul, 'Economic Evidence in Competition Litigation in Germany' in Schweitzer and Hüschelrath, *Public and Private Enforcement of Competition Law in Europe (n 722) 193 194.*

787 *ibid.*

ously, the Court's appointed experts (*Gerichtssachverständige*) and the expert counsel for the parties (*Privatgutachter*) can provide the economic evidence. Hence, these experts are designated by the Court and must provide neutral legal opinions. Besides, their duty is mainly to accord advisory assistances to the Judges in the verification of facts or foreign law rules. Nonetheless, their legal opinions are absolutely subject to the Court's decision-making competence.[788]

In the German Cartel Law, the Court relies mainly upon the principle of unfettered consideration of evidences (*freie Beweiswürdigung*), which is applied in the Criminal Law's enforcement procedure. Therefore, the Court is supposed to decide based upon its independent conviction by taking into account the entire courses of proceedings to establish 'personal certainty or assurance (*persönliche Gewissheit*) and thus be able to prove cartels infringement[789]. Equally important, in the substantiation of cartels infringement, the *Bundesgerichtshof* requires the existence of cartels overcharge, whereas the *Bundesgerichtshof* stipulated, as follows:

> "According to economic principles, cartels will typically involve a cartel overcharge. It is therefore highly likely […] that a cartel being formed and maintained because it leads to higher prices than could otherwise be obtained in the market".[790]

Nevertheless, the economic evidence is rebuttable whenever the opposing parties can argue for other reasonable economic reasons before the Court.[791] In addition, cartels infringement can be substantiated by means of a time series analysis to establish the 'structural-break', which indicates cartels existence.[792] This method was applied before the *Oberlandesgericht (OLG)* Düsseldorf.[793] In fact, the OLG Düsseldorf, in the cement cartel case, carried out a 'full and comprehensive judicial review' as to the *Bundeskartellamt*'s arguments through the rigorous analysis of economic evidence at hand. Even more, the OLG Düssel-

788 Reimann and Zekoll, *Introduction to German Law* (n 591) 374.

789 *ibid.*

790 Burrichter and Paul, "Economic Evidence in Competition Litigation in Germany in Schweitzer and Hüschelrath, *Public and Private Enforcement* (n 722) 205.

791 ibid.

792 ibid. 213.

793 ibid. 216.

dorf applied a 'broad discretion' as regards the economic evidence at hand. Put differently, the Court requires through analysis by appointing reliable experts to provide economic analysis over time series data in the market (model-based approach) in order to attain an accurate decision.[794] Nevertheless, from the German Cartel Law's perspective, the application of economic evidence alone is inadequate to substantiate cartels infringement between the cartelists. Arguably, there is a large possibility that the oligopolistic interaction (conscious parallelism) exists, instead of cartels (collusive agreement). Thus, both phenomena have been difficult to differentiate by applying solely upon the economic variables' analysis.[795]

Equally important, in the German Cartel Law's enforcement proceedings, the application of economic evidence has been considerably problematic. According to Burrichter and Paul, there are several reasons for this proposition. First, the difficulties concerning access to economic-related data. For example, *the Bundeskartellamt* could hesitate to give its economic-related data upon the parties' request. This request is considered as 'administrative assistance' (*Amtshilfe*) and thus could be refused for confidentiality reasons pursuant to the Sec. 5 (2) of the Act on Administrative Procedure (VwVfG). Second, the constitutional limitation regarding confidentiality of economic-related information (data). Hence, the provisions of Article 20 (3) and (4) of *the Grundgesetz* prerequisite the citizens' right of resistance against any acts trying to obstruct their constitutional (fundamental) rights. For example, whenever the parties before the Court refuse to provide their underlying (raw) data as the economic evidence due to the confidentiality reason. Third, the reconciliation of dissenting economic experts' statements (opinions). Accordingly, *Burrichter and Paul* describe that there have been none of the intrinsic economic thresholds to evaluate expert's opinion, to decide whether the opinion (statement) is sufficient and reliable.[796] For that reason, the *Bundeskartellamt* has issued *the Notice on Best Practices for Economic Expert Opinions*, which aims

794 Lianos and Genakos 'Econometric Evidence' (n 26) 72–73.

795 Burrichter and Paul, "Economic Evidence in Competition Litigation in Germany" in Germany in Schweitzer and Hüschelrath, *Public and Private Enforcement* (n 722) 205.

796 ibid. 225.

to attain two functions. First, to assist the cartel law practitioners to develop and present evidences in a way to enable the Judges to determine their probative weight. Second, to support the Competition Authority (CA) in identifying and discarding baseless or unreasonable economic opinions and thus disregarding contradictory economic opinions.[797] As a matter of fact, *the Bundeskartellamt*'s Best Practices prescribe the following requirements as regards to the economic opinion for the purpose of the economic evidence: First, relevance; this refers to a requirement that an economic opinion must be clear from the opinion which competition issues are dealt with, which methods are used and what the conclusions and their implications are. These must be relevant to the case. Second, completeness; this means that "an expert opinion must be written to be comprehensible within a reasonable period of time. Opinions which do not contain the information necessary to understand and to replicate results are incomplete. Results of economic analyses which are not comprehensible cannot be considered as evidence." Third, transparency; thus, this refers to a requirement that an economic analysis, based on simplifying assumptions, to disclose the assumptions and being assessed for their compatibility with the relevant facts of the case under competition law. Fourth, consistency; this means that whenever an economic opinion contains analysis of similar or different circumstances, each of the assumption and result of the analysis isnot contradictory. Hence, any inconsistencies in the economic assumptions or results must be acknowledged and explained properly.[798]

3.4.3.3 In the Indonesian Competition Law Number 5/1999

Until now, on the one hand, there has been juridical obscurities concerning the implementation of indirect (circumstantial) evidences for proving cartels infringement in the Indonesia Competition Law Number 5/1999. Equally important, according to *Hansen,* in the framework of the Law Number 5/1999, indications are considered and could be

797 C A Melischek, *The Relevant Market in International Economic Law: A Comparative Antittrust and GATT Analysis,* (OUP,2013) 205.

798 The Federal Cartel Office (*Bundeskartellamt*), "Best practices for expert economic opinions 20 October 2010".

admitted as the indirect (circumstantial) evidence in the Law Number 5/1999's enforcement proceedings. However, Hansen argues that the indications must be 'coherent and consistent' with the other evidences. On the other hand, the implementation of indirect evidences (indications) in the cartels infringement cases could not be generalised, instead this should be subject to case by case approach before the Courts.[799] Article 42 (d) of the Law Number 5/1999, provides none of the elaborative explanations regarding indications. For that reason, KPPU released the Regulation No.1/ 2006, as amended by KPPU Regulation No.1/2010 concerning Procedure for Cartel Enforcement Proceeding, stipulating the indirect evidence. Subsequently, KPPU issued Regulation No. 1/2010 concerning implementation of Article 11 the Law Number 5/1999 regarding cartels prohibition enforcement. Hence, Article 36 the Regulation No.1/2010 prescribes that the indirect evidence comprises, among others: First, documents or verbatims of meetings as to the price, quota and market zone cartel agreements. Second, comparison of conscious parallelism towards the price, quota and market zone cartels. Third, testimonies of the employees and relevant parties knowing the cartel practices.[800] Furthermore, KPPU issued Regulation No.4/2011 on Implementation of Article 5 the Law

799 Lubis and Sirait, *Hukum Persaingan Usaha* (n 225) 329.

800 Article 36 of the KPPU Regulation No.4/2010 mentions following circumstantial evidences:
Documents or verbatims of meetings as to the price, quota and market zone cartels;
Documents or Prices list records by the business actors;
Data on the prices, production volume and total sales fluctuations;
Production capacity data;
Data on operational profits and excessive profits
Data results on conscious parallelism towards the prices coordination, quota production, market zone partitions;
Financial statements of the alleged companies in the cartel infringement;
Testimonies of relevant parties knowing the communication and coordinations and information exchanges between the cartel participants;
Testimonies of Kesaksian para pelanggan atas keseragaman dan keselarasan harga;
Kesaksian karyawan atau mantan karyawan perusahaan.
A M T Anggraini, 'Indirect Evidence Dalam Pembuktian Kartel' (UPH Law Faculty National Seminar "Eradicating Cartel Practices in Indonesia: The Challenges of Indirect Evidence", Lippo Karawaci, 20th January 2012) 2–8.

Number 5/1999 concerning price fixing. In the Regulation No.4/2011, KPPU asserts that evidentiary rules of Article 5 the Law Number 5/1999 largely applicable to Article 11 the Law Number 5/1999 on the rules of evidences for cartels infringement. According to Section 4.4 the KPPU Regulation No.4/2011 there are two types of evidences to substantiate Article 5 the Law Number 5/1999, namely: First, direct evidences. Second, indirect or circumstantial evidences.[801] Equally important, the implementation of indirect (circumstantial) evidences in the Indonesia Competition Law Number 5/1999 has been largely introduced and developed in the KPPU's decisions and the judicial practices, elaborated below.

3.4.4 "Plus-factor" for Consolidating the Circumstantial (Indirect) Evidences

3.4.4.1 Introduction

As has been noted previously, in the cartel prohibition enforcement proceedings, the so-called 'plus-factors' have a prominent function to corroborate other indirect (circumstantial) evidences, such as the economic evidence. Accordingly, Blanco asserts that to prove a cartel infringement, the Competition Authorithy (CA) could not solely base on the economic evidence.[802] Equally important, in the US Antitrust Law, the provision of Section 1 the US Sherman Act (1980) stipulates:

> *'Every contract, combination in the form of thrusts or otherwise, or conspiracy, in restraint of trade or commerce amongst the several States, or with*

801 According to the KPPU Regulation No.4/2011:
"Indirect or circumstantial evidences are evidence instruments which indicate the price fixing agreement. This type of evidences can be used as the admissible evidences to support an allegation on cartel infringements. The circumstantial evidences comprise: Firstly, Communication evidence but which directly shows a concurrence of wills. Secondly, Economic evidence, whose aims are to dismiss the possibility of an independent price fixing by the business actors. Thus, the circumstantial evidences which are appropriate and consistent with the market conditions and collusion can not serve as the complete evidence to the infringement against Article 5 of the Law No.5/1999." cf. Rizkiyana and Iswanto, '*Eradicating Cartel: The Use of Indirect Evidence' (n 28) 2–5*.

802 Blanco, *Market power in EU Antitrust Law* (n 57) 173–190.

> *foreign nations, is declared to be illegal. Every person who shall make any contract or engage in any combination or conspiracy declared by Sections 1 to 7 of this title to be illegal shall be deemed guilty of a felony'.*

Hence, whenever the parallel conduct on the market takes place, the US Supreme Court argued in the case of *Monsanto v. Spray-Rite* that "there must be direct or circumstantial evidence that reasonably tends to prove that the parties had a conscious commitment to common a scheme designed to achieve an unlawful objective". Accordingly, the plus-factors could tackle the existing ambiguitiy as to the undertakings' parallel market behaviour to prove the existence of cartels infringement.[803]

Furthermore, in the US Antitrust laws, in order to fulfill the evidentiary requirement standard of excluding the possibility that the undertakings behave independently in the market, the US Court prerequisites that "the evidence of a defendant's parallel pricing [should] be supplemented by so-called plus-factors, only when these additional factors are present does the evidence tend to exclude the possibility that the defendants acted independently." Hence, according to *Areeda*, the plus-factors refer to "the additional facts or factors required to be proved as a prerequisite to finding that parallel action amounts to conspiracy."[804]

In the EU Competition Law's jurisprudence, as regards the importance of plus-factors, in *the CISAC v. Commission case,* the Commission failed to substantiate the existence of cartels resulting from concerted practices on the market. Put differently, the Commission could not prove the concerted practice by using factors other than the parallel behaviour of the undertakings. Consequently, it was adequate for the undertakings to rebut the Commission's allegations by providing reasonable explanations for the parallel market conduct.[805] For that reason, the ECJ required a high burden of proof by argumenting "any doubt […] must benefit the undertakings" regardless of the decision

803 465 U.S. 752 Monsanto Co. v. Spray-Rite Svc. Corp. (1984). para 768. See also Silalahi 'Circumstantial Evidence' (n 14) 3–5. cf. ABA Section Antitrust Law, *Proof of Conspiracy under Federal Antitrust Laws* (American Bar Association, 2010) 24.

804 Stroux, *US and EC Oligopoly Control* (n 51) 47. cf. Kovavic et.al 'Plus Factors and Agreement in Antitrust Law' (*Michigan Law Review* Vol. 110:393) 393–400.

805 Stroux, *US and EC Oligopoly Control (n 51) 47.*

finding a cartels infringement involving the imposition of fines." Hence, *Ezrachi* argues that the CA must analyse the presence of plus-factors, that is to say, the evidence that is inconsistent with the unilateral action on the market in order to prove cartels infringement.[806]

On the other hand, from the other competition law perpectives, Johri is of the opinion that the plus-factors could be understood as "economic actions and outcomes, above and beyond parallel conduct by oligopolistic firms, which are largely inconsistent with unilateral conduct but largely consistent with coordinated action. Possible plus factors are typically enumerated without any attempt to distinguish them in terms of a meaningful economic categorisation or in terms of their probative strength for inferring collusion.[807] Indeed, Bohra argues:

> „Plus factors provides that if an inference of conspiracy has to be drawn from the concerted action the proof should include that defendants priced uniformly where price uniformity was improbable without an agreement; committed past antitrust violations involving collective action; directly communicated with competitors and then made simultaneous, identical changes in their behavior; or agreed to adopt common practices, such as product standardization whose implementation helped achieve pricing uniformity".[808]

Within the Competition Law or Antitrust Law' enforcement framework, the plus-factors have the function to prevent and even minimalise the two type of errors faced by the Competition Authority (CA).[809] First, False positive (Type I error), whereas the competition authority imposes sanction to innocent firms, merely because they perform natural reactions in an oligopoly market due to the oligopolistic interdependence therein. In other words, this type of error 'is to falsely convict innocent firms although what they do falls into the category of oligopolistic interdependence'[810] Second, False negative (Type

806 Ezrachi, *EU Competition Law* (n 239) 75–76.

807 S Johri 'Attribution of Price Parallelism as Cartels under the Competition Act, 2002' (Dissertation submitted to Competition Commission of India, Nirma University 2012) ‹http://citeseerx.ist.psu.edu/viewdoc/download?doi=10.1.1.649.6978&rep=rep1&type=pdf› accessed on 30th December 2017, 426–423.

808 M Bohra, '*Increasing Role of Economic Evidences In Prosecution Of* Cartels' (Research Paper, National Law Institute University India, 2011) 16–18.

809 *Ruky*, 'Economic Evidence' (n 16) 2–7.

810 Kekevi, 'Can Economics Help Us with Cartel Detection?' (n 20) 6–7

II error), whenever the competition authority is to acquit cartel members by identifying their cartel behavior (collusion) as an oligopolistic interdependence.'[811]

3.4.4.2 The Catalogue of Plus-Factors

In the competition law's practices, there are several factors, which constitute the plus-factors, which are the following:[812]

3.4.4.2.1 Motive to Conspire

Principally this refers to "that there must generally exist both a motive to act in concert and some reason why such action might not occur absent sufficient coordination among rivals." Further, Areeda outlines that "the presence of a benefit from, and therefore a motive for, common action is a prerequisite to the inference of an agreement, although it does not in itself demonstrate that the parties have formed an agreement."[813]

In the Venzie case, the US Court required a two-tier test to permit an inference of a collusive agreement from a conscious parallelism. First, the existence of a showing of acts by defendants in contradiction to their own economic interests. Secondly, the existence of a satisfactory demonstration of motivation for an entering into an agreement. Eventually, the Court held that the requirement of a motive for conspiracy had to be demonstrated by showing that an individual firm was in a position to benefit from a specified concerted conduct.[814]

3.4.4.2.2 Behaviour against Self-Interest

In the case of *Milgram v. Loew's Inc.*, the US Court maintained that "conduct in apparent contradiction to [each defendant's] own self-interest [...] considerably strengthens the inference of conspiracy.

811 ibid 11–12.

812 Stroux, *EC and US Oligopoly Control (n 51)* 48–50. cf. *Kovavic*, et.al.'Plus Factors and Agreement in Antitrust Law' (n 803). 426–433. See also Johri, 'Attribution of Price Parallelism as Cartels under the Competition Act' (n 806) 28–33.

813 Stroux, *EC and US Oligopoly Control* (n 51) 48–50.

814 ibid.

However, there has been disputes as to the definition of the requirement 'conduct against self-interest.'.[815] Furthermore, the other Court argued that "the presence of behavior contrary to the firm's own interest and a motive to conspire lead to the conclusion that the inference of conspiracy is more probable than the inference of independent action." In the *Baby Food Antitrust Litigation Re.*, the Court was of the opinion that "in order to prove conspiracy based on the theory of conscious parallelism, evidence of action that is against self-interest or motivated by profit must go beyond mere interdependence; 'parallel pricing must be so unusual that in the absence of an agreement, no reasonable firm would have engaged in it."[816]

However, in the Antitrust Law practice, Stroux contended that "the motive and against individual-self-interest" plus-factors are ambiguous plus-factors for the finding of collusion in an oligopolistically structured markets, often other plus-factors have to be relied upon in order to infer conspiracy."[817]

3.4.4.2.3 Factual Plus-Factors

Within the Antitrust Law's practice, the US Court acknowledges the factual evidences, *inter alia* high level of inter-firms communications, committed past antitrust violations involving collective actions, and identical sealed bids on a complex, made to order product; apart from extremely improbable coincidence, such uniformity could not occur without express *collusion.* Generally, showing that competitors had the opportunity to collude does not suffice as the plus-factors.[818]

3.4.4.2.4 Economic Plus-Factors

With regard to this type of evidence, *Posner* argues that the following economic evidences, hand in hand with the two-tier test abovementioned, could indicate the existence of cartels. For example, the econo-

815 ibid.

816 *Kovavic,* et.al.'Plus Factors and Agreement in Antitrust Law' (n 803) 426–433. Johri, 'Attribution of Price Parallelism as Cartels under the Competition Act' (n 806) 28–33.

817 Stroux, *EC and US Oligopoly Control* (n 51) 51.

818 ibid.

mic plus-factors, which include: pervasive parallel conduct in a market otherwise characterised by intense competition or where factors make tacit coordination implausible, poor economic performance in an industry bears on the existence of conspiracy, excessive prices or restricted output and "industry-wide saw-tooth pattern of pricing."[819]

According to Stroux, in the Antitrust Law, the US Court experiences dissenting opinions and approaches as to the economic plus-factors, namely the persistent extraordinarily high profits. *Posner* argued that this economic evidence is probative. Furthermore, the US Federal Trade Commission (FTC) argued that "the evidence of parallel conduct together with high profit margins should, by themselves, be sufficient to establish conspiracy."[820]

3.4.4.2.5 Facilitating Practices as the "Plus-factors"

In the Antitrust laws' practice, the US Court considers the adoption of facilitating practices by competing firms as the inference to cartels. For example, an adoption of delivered pricing, an adoption of two-tiered pricing, and an artificial product's standardisation. In the case of *Petroleum Prods.*, the US Court viewed that the price announcements "when considered together with the evidence concerning the parallel pattern of price restorations, is sufficient to support a reasonable and permissible inference of an agreement, whether express or tacit, to raise or stabilize price." However as regards the information exchange between the competitors, the US Court argued that "there must be evidence that the exchanges of information had an impact on the pricing decisions". Put differently, the Court restrict the inference of the cartels existence by merely using the information exchange, such as price announcements.[821]

On the one hand, as regards the main plus-factors, Gavil et. al, explains that these evidences include, but are not limited to: First, actions contrary to each defendant's self-interest unless pursued as part of a

819 ibid.

820 ibid.

821 *Kovavic*, et.al.'Plus Factors and Agreement in Antitrust Law' (n 803) 426–433. cf. Johri, 'Attribution of Price Parallelism as Cartels (n 806) 28–33. cf. Stroux, *EC and US Oligopoly Control* (n 51) 49–50.

collective plan. Second, phenomena that can be explained rationally only as the result of concerted action. Third, evidence that defendants created the opportunity for regular communication. Fourth, industry performance data, such as extraordinary profits, that suggest successful coordination. Fifth, the absence of a plausible, legitimate business rationale for suspicious conduct (such as certain communications with rivals), or the presentation of contrived rationales for certain conduct.[822]

On the other hand, *Posner* emphasises that the facilitating practices, serving as the plus-factors, consist of: First, the defendant's participation in past collusion related offences; second, evidence that the defendants had the opportunity to communicate or actually did so; third, the use of facilitating devices like a delivered pricing or most favoured nation clauses; Fourth, industry characteristics (product homogeneity, frequent transactions, readily observed price adjustments, high entry barriers, and high concentration) that are conducive to successful coordination.[823]

3.4.4.2.5.1 Facilitating Practices in an Oligopolistic Market as the Plus-Factors

In terms of the strategic interactions in an oligopolistic market, undertakings are able to develop the facilitating practices by means of increasing transparency, reducing uncertainty of the competitors' behaviour in a market, which enables them to achieve collussions and support collusive outcomes and to restrict destabilising factors for the cartels. Accordingly, *Schelling* points out that the facilitating practices serve as the 'focal points' and 'focal rules' for other competitors in the market to reach collusive outcomes. In brief, the focal points refer to tacit communications and certain signals, which can inform the competitors to reach the preferred outcomes and thus become the self-evident way to behave in a market. Whereas the focal rules refer to, for

822 Johri, 'Attribution of Price Parallelism as Cartels under the Competition Act' (n 806) 28–30.

823 Posner, *Antitrust Law (n 80) 79–81.*

example, basing point pricing, preserving existing price differences or existing market shares.[824]

Nevertheless, the facilititating practices cause dilemma to the Competition Authorithy (CA). Put differently, according to Stroux, on the one hand, facilitating practices could generate beneficial competitive effects; whereas on the other hand, they could incur detrimental effects to competition as 'they can facilitate the achievement of, and the monitoring and detection of deviations form oligopolistic pricing, thus helping to prevent a breakdown in oligopolistic discipline.'[825]

Equally important, the facilitating practices in terms of the competition law can be classified into five categories, which are: First, price leadership. Second, exchange of information. Third, product standardisation. Fourth, geographical pricing sytem.

3.4.4.2.5.2 Price leadership

According to the Organisation for Economic Co-operation and Development (OECD), a price leadership "refers to a situation where prices and price changes established by a dominant firm, or a firm are accepted by others as the leader, and which other firms in the industry adopt and follow"[826] In the Bain's analysis as regards to price leadership:

> "in an oligopolistic market any independent price change by a single oligopolist tends to be read as an 'offer' by his rivals, and an acceptable reaction to the price change that may be interpreted as an acceptance of the offer of the first firm. Thus, negotiation can perhaps take place through a series of public announcements rather than through a meeting of persons, and the meaning of true consensual action becomes vague".[827]

824 Stroux, *EC and US Oligopoly Control* (n 51) 27–28. cf. Kovavic et.al 'Plus Factors and Agreement in Antitrust Law' (n 803) 426–432.

825 Stroux, *EC and US Oligopoly Control* (n 51) 27–28.

826 However according to *Seaton and Waterson* "*Price leadership* occurs when one firm makes a change in a *price* (or set of prices) that is followed within a *predetermined short period* by the other (more generally, another) firm making a *price* change of exactly the same monetary amount in the same direction on the *same product(s)*, and doing so *significantly more often than would be expected by chance*." cf. Khemani and Shapiro, *Glossary of Industrial Organisation Economics and Competition Law(n 39)*.

827 Stroux, *EC and US Oligopoly Control* (n 51) 27–28. cf. *Kovavic*, et.al. 'Plus Factors and Agreement in Antitrust Law' (n 803) 426–433.

According to *Markham*, there are three categories of a price leadership, which are: First, a dominant price-leadership 'whereas one dominant competitor, the only firm large enough to significantly affect the market, imposes its prices upon the industry, and the other competitors follow, as they will have little to gain from diverging from the dominant firm's prices'.[828] Second, a barometric price leadership, whereas an undertaking as the leader is not dominant but is widely accepted as the best performing undertaking which is able to meet the demand and to adapt to evolving market conditions, such as cost increases.[829] Third, collusive price leadership, either an explicit or a tacit one, where the competitors commit themselves to adapt to price increases initiated by one of them, acting as the price leader.[830]

3.4.4.2.5.3 Exchanges of Information

In an oligopolistic market, exchange of information between firms could lead to an increase of market transparency. The more transparent the market is, thus easier it is for firms to detect deviating firms, what shortens detection lags and the increase of the possibility of punishing deviating firms adequately.

The Organisation for Economic Co-operation and Development (OECD) explains as to the information exchanges:

> "*Information exchanges among competitors increase transparency in the market, which can lead to efficiency enhancing benefits but may also present competition risks. The challenge for competition enforcers is how to approach this conduct within the context of traditional competition laws since generally jurisdictions around the world do not have specific rules dealing with exchanges of information.*"[831]

828 Stroux, *EC and US Oligopoly Control* (n 803) 28–29.

829 According to Stigler, in the barometric price leadership, the barometric firm commands the adherence of rivals to this price only because, and to the extent that, its price reflects market conditions with tolerable promptness. cf.
Deneckere and Kovenock (n 212). See also Stroux, *EC and US Oligopoly Control* (n 803) 28–29.

830 ibid.

831 OECD, '*Information Exchanges Between Competitors under Competition Law*' (DAF/COMP 2010 37, 2010) 9–12.

Furthermore, OECD elaborates:

> *"[...] information exchanges among competitors may fall into three different scenarios under competition rules: (i) as a part of a wider price fixing or market sharing agreement whereby the exchange of information functions as a facilitating factor; (ii) in the context of broader efficiency enhancing co-operation agreements such as joint venture, standardization or R&D agreements; or (iii) as a stand-alone practice, whereby the exchange of information is the only cooperation among competitors."*[832]

Even more, in order to determine the detrimental effects of information exchanges, several factors are important, which are: First, market structure. Second, information contents being exchanged. Third, ways information being exchanged. Fourth, the frequency of information exchanges.[833]

Eventually, according to Stroux the information exchanges as to future conducts of firms constitute an anticompetitive practice. Communications between firms, which contain promises to adhere to an agreement, which is not a firm's best choice, is just 'cheap-talk' and does not affect the firms' oligopolistic interactions. However, whenever communication between firms as to future behaviours contains commitments, these would affect the firms' oligopolistic interactions and thus increase the probability of collusion. For example, by means of 'meeting competition' and 'most-favoured customer', the cheap talks could transform into 'the less cheap talk'. In addition, as regards the content of the exchanged information, this can be classified into three categories: First, data concerning prices, sales conditions, sales and outputs. Secondly, data concerning current costs, demand and capacity, which assist to identify possible collusive equilibrium and to determine

832 ibid.

833 The exchange of aggregate data as to the whole market is less likely to enhance collusion than information concerning individual companies, enabling the compliance monitoring to collusion, thus decreasing the incentives to deviate from collusions. Furthermore, the information exchanges concerning actual information, could alter incentives for firms and thus increase the likehood of collusions. These kind of information exchanges informs who is defecting and consequently allows for immediate sanctions. The frequency of information exchanges influences lapses of time evolving betwenn cheating and punishment and thus the profitability of cheating. Accordingly, the competition authorithy should concentrate on frequent, detailed and actual information exchanges. Stroux, EC and US Oligopoly Control (n 803) 28–31.

availability of effective punishment strategies. Thirdly, exchanges of data on investment, research and development (R&D), future costs and demands, reducing the long-term uncertainty, which could jeopardise a collusive equilibrium. From a game theory perspective, the first and second categories of information exchanges could largely lead to collusions and thus require more careful observation of the competition authorities.[834]

3.4.4.2.5.4 Product standardisation

Notwithstanding its beneficial competitive effects, the product standardisation could cause detrimental effects to competition by facilitating collusion through increasing market transparency, thus making it easier for firms to collude on price and detect deviations from collusive agreements. Further, the product standardisation could slow down the innovations in market. [835]

3.4.4.2.5.5 Regional Price Systems

In order to facilitate collusion on the market, firms employ the geographical pricing system as well, which comprises among others: delivered pricing system, basing point and zone pricing systems. The geographical pricing systems had been frequently found in industries whose products are generally homogenous, transportation costs are high in proportion to the commodity's values, and producers or buyers are dispersed geographically.[836]

According to *Carlton* 'the geographical pricing systems could facilitate collusions in two ways: Firstly, the systems would remove price discretion on shipping or transportation charges. Secondly, firms' adherence to the pricing systems could enable firms in the low demand area to penetrate the high demand market without costly and potentially destabilising revisions to the price schedule'.[837]

834 Kovavic et.al 'Plus Factors and Agreement in Antitrust Law' (n 803) 426–432. cf. Stroux, *EC and US Oligopoly Control* (n 803) 29–31.
835 Johri, 'Attribution of Price Parallelism as Cartels under the Competition Act, 2002' (n 806) 28–33.
836 ibid.
837 ibid.

3.4.4.2.5.6 Contingency Contract Provisions

According to *Stroux*, 'long-term sales contracts often include contingency clauses, "Most-Favoured Customers" (MFC) clauses, which provide the buyer with the insurance protection against the contingency that the seller may offer a lower price to another customer'.[838]

However, an inclusion of MFC clauses in contracts could facilitate collusion and lead to supra-competitive pricing by constituting information exchange through customers policing price levels. Furthermore, according to Cooper, MFC clauses contribute to the achievement and maintenance of a tacitly collusive pricing structure. He argued that for firms to choose to adapt MFC clauses unilaterally, there need not be any explicit agreement among the rival producers to include these provisions in their sales contracts. Moreover, through MFC, all firms could profit from higher prices due to these clauses even if not all firms introduce them into their contracts.[839] Evenmore,, the "meeting competition" clause (MC) in a long-term supply contract provides the buyer with insurance protection against a lost opportunity of being offered a lower price by another seller, as the original seller commits himself to match the lower price offered by any other seller. A common variant is the meet-or-release (English clause), which provides sellers the chance to meet a lower price, offered to the buyer by a rival seller, or to release the buyer from the contract. The inclusion of MC clauses into a contract could serve as an information exchange device, buyers controlling adherence to consensus pricing by oligopolists. Thus, the cooperative joint profit outcome is made relatively more credible.[840]

3.5 Chapter Interim Result

Pursuant to the European Competition and German Cartel Laws as well as the Indonesian Competition Law, the procedural law of cartels

838 Kovavic et.al 'Plus Factors and Agreement in Antitrust Law' (n 803) 426–433.

839 Johri 'Attribution of Price Parallelism as Cartels under the Competition Act, 2002' (n 806) 28–33.

840 Stroux, *EC and US Oligopoly Contro*l (n 51) 33–35. cf. Johri, "'Attribution of Price Parallelism as Cartels under the Competition Act, 2002' 28–33.

prohibition enforcement proceedings has been profoundly important in order to ensure the establishment of the due process of law. This concept refers to the notion of constitutional right guarantee:

> "that all legal proceedings will be fair and that one will be given notice of theproceedings and an opportunity to be heard before the public administration or government acts to take away one's life, liberty, or property. Also, a constitutional rights guarantee that a law shall not be unreasonable, arbitrary or capricious."

In the context of European and German Competition Laws, the guiding principles of the procedural law play a very important role and are regarded as the commonly accepted legal foundations of the EU Laws. These principles have been developed both by the Court of Justice of the EU in their duties of guaranteeing that 'the law is observed' pursuant to Article 19 (1) TEU as well as by other EU Organs through the respective legislations. Principally, according to Article 2 TEU (Article 6(1) EU) stipulating that "Union is founded on the values of respect for human dignity, freedom, democracy, equality, the rule of law and respect for human rights, including the rights of persons belonging to minorities. These values are common to the Member States in a society in which pluralism, non-discrimination, tolerance, justice, solidarity and equality between women and men prevail". For example, the presumption of innocence *('in dubio pro reo')* principle, whereas "Considerable importance must be attached to the fact that the competition cases of this kind (cartels) are in the reality of a penal nature, which naturally suggests that a high standard of proof is required (...). There must be a sufficient basis for the decision and any reasonable doubt mustbe for the benefit of the applicants according to the principle of in dubio pro reo." This principle is essentially important in the competition case presenting indirect (circumstantial) evidences of a concerted practice, such as parallel conducts of alleged undertakings. In the German Cartel Law, the procedural law ensures that the obligation to find the substantive truth (*materielle Wahrheit*) as well as the respect of legality of an administrative act (*Rechtmäßgikeit)* are fulfilled. In the German Cartel Law, the German Courts rely on the principle of unfettered consideration of evidences (*freie Beweiswürdigung*), which is largely similar to the criminal proceedings. Accordingly, the Court will decide, according to its independent conviction by taking into account the entire course of proceedings, to establish 'personal certainty or assurance (*persönliche Gewissheit*). In the German Cartel law, pursuant to the principle of unfettered consideration of evidences (*freie Beweiswürdigung*), to successfully prove an existence of cartels, a 'probable' or a 'large probability' were not adequate or insufficient, instead there must be 'personal certainty or assurance (*persönliche Gewissheit*)' as to the elements of cartels violation.

Principally, these procedural law principles have profound substantial roles in the implementation of the EU Competition laws because of three reasons: First, the principles provide the basis for the fair and efficient administrative decision-making processes by ascertaining that the officials perform their duties independently and make decisions rationally and proportionally. Second, the principles shall operate as the guarantee for individuals or affected parties against arbitrary administrative acts by imposing the duty to provide reasons and the protection of fundamental and human rights. Third, the principles shall promote the accountability of the administrative acts towards the public, for example accessibility and transparency principles.

Furthermore, the European Competition, the German Cartel laws in conjucntions with the US Antitrust Law apply the so-called "Plus factors" or "Parallelism plus" for consolidating the indirect (*circumstantial*) evidences, whereby according to *Kovavic*:

> "Plus factors are economic actions and outcomes, above and beyond parallel conduct by oligopolistic firms, that are largely inconsistent with unilateral conduct but largely consistent with explicitly coordinated action. Possible plus factors are typically enumerated without any attempt to distinguish them in terms of a meaningful economic categorization or in terms of their probative strength for inferring collusion. In this Article, we provide a taxonomy for plus factors as well as a methodology for ranking plus factors in terms of their strength for inferring explicit collusion, the strongest of which are referred to as "super plus factors."[841]

841 Kovavic et.al 'Plus Factors and Agreement in Antitrust Law' (n 803) 394–400.

Chapter Four Conceptual and Judicial Praxis of the Indirect (Circumstancial) Evidence in the EU Competition Law, the German Cartel Law and the Law Number 5/1999

4.1 Introduction

According to *Silalahi*, the Competition Authorities would, in the majority of antitrust cases, encounter profound difficulties in order to uncover, deter and thus prosecute cartel infringements, because cartels involve various forms of agreement, arrangement or practices between the undertakings to eliminate and subvert the competition processes on the market. Altough cartels occur secretively, they cause detrimental effects, which are perceivable by consumers, for instance prices' increases of products ultimately reducing the consumers' welfare.[842] Equally important, *Ruky* emphasises that cartels are the most dangerous infringement against competition law, compared to other violations. In fact, the Competition Authority (CA) faces an intensive enigma as to 'who commits cartels and what types of cartels occur?'[843] Likewise, *Beaton-Wells, et.al*, explain that difficulties in detecting, prosecuting and deterring cartels violations rest upon the fact that cartels infringement frequently involve so-called 'multiple-cheatings'. Put differently, the undertakings participating in cartels (cartelists) initially cheat the Competition Authorithy by presenting themselves as competitors, but in fact they do not compete each other. Thus, the undertakings participating in cartels cheat other competitors, consumers

842 *Silalahi*, 'Circumstantial Evidence' (n 14) 2–5.
843 *Ruky*, 'Economic Evidence' (n 16) 1–4.

and public as well (first-level cheating). Subsequently, the cartelists cheat the operation of cartels, secretly operate against the agreement not to compete when it may be to their economic advantage to initiate competition again, thus cheating between the cartelists (second-level cheating). Afterwards, the ex-cartelists who act as the 'whistle-blowers' and informants to the CA in the Leniency program, cheat the other cartelists by deserting to the law enforcement authorities (third-level cheating). Eventually, the former cartelists who act as the 'whistle-blower' and informants to the Competition Authority (CA), cheat the law enforcement officials by not giving the evidences optimally (fourth level cheating).[844] Moreover, Heineman maintains that the access to evidences were a main problematic matter in the competition law enforcement.[845] Accordingly, cartels practices are therefore difficult to uncover due to its secretive nature and lack of availability of evidences. In fact, according to Andrews, the harder the CA investigate cartels, the craftier the undertakings can commit cartels.[846]

In the second place, according to *Silalahi* cartels frequently occur in an oligopolistic market due to characteristics thereof. Therefore, *Jones and Sufrin* are of opinion that in an oligopolistic market, both of cartels (explicit collusion) and tacit collusion could emerge consecutively.[847] For that reason, *Silalahi* emphasizes that the undertakings operating in an oligopolistic market are subject to the oligopolistic interdependences (conscious parallelism).[848] Hence, *Kerber and Schwalbe* describe that these oligopolistic interdependences between undertakings had been derived from and could be explained by the game-theory approach.[849] Indeed, *Jones and Sufrin* explain that based upon the economic theory, the undertakings in an oligopolistic market would recognize the profitability of their conduct (behavior) will depend to the other competitors' conduct (behaviour) in a market. Put differently, they would be better-off if they impose higher prices and obtain higher profits. Thus,

844 Beaton-Wells and Tran (eds) *Anti-Cartel Enforcement in a Contemporary Age (n 721)* 249.
845 Heinemann, 'Accesss to Evidence and Presumptions (n 722) 167–170.
846 Ruky, 'Economic Evidence' (n 16) 3.
847 Jones and Surfin, *EU Competition Law* (n 46) 510–512
848 Silalahi, *Circumstantial Evidence' (n 14)* 2–3.
849 Kerber and Schwalbe, in Säcker, et.al, *Europäisches Wettbewerbsrecht* (n 13) 116–117.

they could coordinate their conduct (behaviour) in a similar way to those committing cartels infringement, without an explicit collusive agreement.[850] *Posner* categorizes such behavioural interdependencies on the markets as 'tacit collusion'.[851]

Thereby, *Silalahi* suggests that the Competition Authorithy (CA) requires not only the direct evidence, but also the indirect (circumstantial) evidence in order to substantiate cartels infringement, notably in an oligopolistic market.[852] In addition, *Ruky* reiterates that the substantiation of cartels existence in the market prerequisites a particular evidentiary instrument, namely the economic evidence.[853] As a matter of fact, according to the the Organization for Economic Cooperation and Development (OECD), within the cartels prohibition enforcement proceedings, the CA shall employ two types of evidences: First, the direct evidence, which refers to the evidence that identifies a meeting or communication between the subjects and describes the substance of their agreement. The most common form of direct evidences are: 1) documents (in printed or electronic form) identifying an agreement and the parties to it, and oral or written statements by co-operative cartel participants describing the operation of the cartel.[854] Second, the indirect (*circumstantial*) evidence. Circumstantial evidence is the evidence that does not specifically describe the terms of an agreement, or the parties to it. It includes evidence of communications among suspected cartel operators and economic evidence concerning the market and the conduct of those participating in it that suggest concerted action.[855]

Equally important, in the EU Competition Law, according to the Commission, the indirect (circumstantial) evidence is defined as follows:

> "the notion of indirect or circumstantial evidence comprises of evidences which is appropriate to corroborate the proof of the existence of cartels by

850 *Jones and Surfin, EU Competition Law* (n 450) 534–540.
851 Posner, Antitrust Law (n 80) 53
852 Silalahi, 'Circusmtantial Evidence' (n 14) 2–5.
853 *Ruky*, 'Economic Evidence' (n 16) 3.
854 OECD, '*Prosecuting Cartel without Direct Evidence of Agreement*' (n 19) 2–5.
855 ibid.

way of deduction, common sense, economic analysis or logical inference from the demonstrated facts."[856]

4.2 Judicial Praxis concerning the Indirect (Circumstantial) Evidence

4.2.1 In the European Competition and the German Cartel Laws

Henceforth, this section analyses the landmark of judicial decisions on antitrust cases, up to the writing of this work, concerning the implementation of indirect (*circumstantial*) evidences in the practice of the European Competition and the German Cartel Laws.

Due to the principle of the 'full and direct effect' of the EU Competition laws in accordance to the Articles 101 and 102 TFEU, Article 6 of the Regulation 1/2003, and the Sec. 2 of GWB concerning the relationship between German Cartel Law and Articles 101 and 102 TFEU, hence this section will analyse the judicial practices in European Courts and in the German Courts consecutively.[857]

4.2.1.1 Bayer AG v Commission of the European Communities-Bayer Adalat Case (ECJ Joined Cases C-2/01 P and C-3/01 P) [858]

In a landmark judgment, the Court of Justice (ECJ) conforming the previous GC's decision, which examined whether a unilateral policy of Bayer manufacturer toward the Spanish and French wholesalers to prevent parallel imports of the cardiovascular Adalat into the UK can be deemed as the agreement under Article 81 (1) EC [now Article 101 (1) TFEU].

Case Facts: During 1989–1993 there were wide price differences of the medical products to treat the cardiovascular-illness name Adalat (Adalate) produced by the Bayer Group, a pharmacy company having representatives in all European Community Member States, namely in France and in Spain. For example, in Spain the wide price differences

856 ibid.

857 de *Bronett*, Europäisches Kartellverfahrensrecht (n 529) 105–109.

858 *Case T-41/96 Bayer AG v Commission of the European Communities.* See also Jones and B. Sufrin, *EU Competition Law (n 46) 150–152.*

of -35 until 47% less than in the UK and in Spain 24% less than France. Those wide price differences of about 40% led Spanish wholesalers (from 1989) and French wholesalers (from 1991) to export a large quantity of that medicinal product to the United Kingdom. Additionally, Bayer had a system for identifying the exporting wholesalers in France and Spain. However, according to report of the Association of the British Pharmaceutical Industry of 1989 which stated the overall effects of parallel imports on the UK economy are harmful. Direct estimates of the value of domestic sales lost to parallel imports by UK manufactures in 1987/1988 was GBP 350, s. Moreover, in 1992 the Report of Bayer an estimated loss to the UK market through parallel imports would be GBP 1.4, if total free trade and unlimited supply in low cost countries. Therefore, Bayer wanted to inhibit or to block parallel imports into the UK from mainly Spain and France and thus Bayer had the power to impose that measure consistently to its French and Spanish wholesalers. In addition, Bayer France and Spain imposed this blocking of parallel imports to their wholesalers namely through the permanent threat of reducing quantities supplied, so they advised their costumers as follow: *"Apologize for being unable to supply to your company your order. The reason is that the laboratory that produces it (Bayer) does not deliver to us the quantities we ordered because they want to avoid any kind of export of this product and then, they deliver only the quantity that estimate we need for the internal market"* Thus this export ban became an integral aspect in the continuous commercial relations between the parties, namely Bayer and the wholesalers in France and Spain. Accordingly, the conduct of the wholesalers in France and in Spain showed that they not only understood the existence of the export ban applied by Bayer, but also, they aligned their commercial conduct on this export ban imposed by Bayer.

However, in January 1996 due to repetitious complaints by the wholesalers in France and Spain, the Commission adopted a decision requiring Bayer to change its policy deemed contrary to Article 8181) EC and fined Bayer 3 million Euros. However, in 2000 the Court of First Instance (CFI) annulled the Commission's decision (Case T-41/96) stating that:

> *"The CFI found that the Commission had not proved that there was an "agreement" within the meaning of Article 81(1) between Bayer and its*

Spanish and French wholesalers to limit parallel exports of Adalat to the United Kingdom."

Furthermore, CFI stated:

> *"An agreement centres around the existence of a concurrence of wills between at least two parties, the form in which it is manifested is unimportant so long as it constitutes the faithful expression of the parties' intention."*

Decision: On 6th January 2004 the ECJ ruled its final decision that there was no evidence for the Commission's finding in 1996 that Bayer had infringed Article 81 EC [Article 101 TFEU] Furthermore, the ECJ has spelled out its *ratio decidendi* supporting this decision, as follows:

First, the Court of Justice recognised that when a decision of a manufacturer, Bayer, constitutes unilateral action, namely by restricting supplies to distributors thus impedes parallel trade between the Member States, that decision escapes [Article 101 (1) TFEU] and did not infringed the EU competition law prohibition.

Second, the concept of agreement within the meaning of Article 101 (1) TFEU, as interpreted by case-laws of the Court, "*centres around the existence of a concurrence of wills between at least two parties, the form in which it is manifested being unimportant so long as it constitutes the faithful expression of the parties' intention."*

Third, the Court rebutted the Commission's Decision which stated that merely the continuous commercial relations between the manufacturer, the wholesalers and the dealers, following a unilateral decision of the manufacturer, will constitute an agreement within the meaning of [Article 101(1) TFEU].

4.2.1.2 Ahlström Osakeyhtiö and others v Commission (Woodpulp Case) (Joined Cases C-89/85, C-104/85, C-114/85, C-116/85, C-117/85 and C-125/85 to C-129/85, 31 March 1993)[859]

In this landmark case the Court of Justice elaborated and examined the Commissions' finding based upon investigations over the woodpulp producers and trade associations for allegedly committing concerted practices to fix the prices, which was contrary to Article 85(1) EEC Treaty [Now Article 101 (1) TFEU]. While there was no evidence

859 *Kokkoris, Competition cases from the European Union* (n 460) 10–12.

of expressed agreements, the Commission based its allegation upon the several indirect evidences. Furthermore, the Court also examined the jurisdictional question of EU Competition law and adoption of an effect test basis for applying Article 85 EEC Treaty [Now Article 101 (1) TFEU] to the parties abroad.

Case Facts: Prior to 1984, several Finnish, American, Swedish and Canadian companies and trade associations, engaging in woodpulp productions, established outside the EC jurisdiction, a price cartel, which will eventually cause detriment effects to their customers in the EC. The Commission found that at least 40 producers of bleached sulfate wood pulp used in paper manufacturing and 3 of their trade associations had committed a concerted practice. This collusion had manifested in the continuous parallel pricing of the woodpulp products. During the investigation the Commission had found that there had been a direct and indirect exchange of information between the woodpulp producers and the trade associations. This periodical information exchange comprises: *First,* a system of quarterly public price announcements by a substantial number of producers to the trade press or sales agents whereby "the producer could expect that the prices he announced would immediately reach his competitors, just as he himself would expect to be given details in the way of his competitor's prices." The fact that prices were published well in advance gave other producers 'adequate lead time' to announce their own corresponding new prices and apply them from the start of the quarter. *Second,* the information exchanges on prices were conducted at meetings and through faxes between several producers. *Third,* there had been information exchanges on prices between U.S producers within the two trade associations, in which the Commission considered as an independent infringement of EC competition law.

Furthermore, according to the Commission's view these exchanges of information caused the parallel pricing leading to anti-competitive effects in the relevant market. However, this parallel pricing was not explainable by the market's structure because the market was not particularly concentrated and there was no market leader setting the price for others to follow. Accordingly, the Commission decided on 19th December 1984 that these woodpulp producers and trade association, which covered 60 % of the total market share, had infringed [Article

101 TFEU] due to the alleged concerted practice and thus imposed fines in amount of ECU 50,000,00 to ECU 500,000,00 upon them. Consequently, a number of woodpulp producers opposed the Commission's Decision and brought the Decision on appeal to the ECJ for more elaborative analysis on several factors related to the alleged concerted practice.

Decision: The ECJ reversed the Commission's Decision upon the appeal by the alleged companies. On the first step, the Court stated in this factual case that 'each economic operator must determine independently the policy which he intends to adopt [...].' Subsequently, the Court ruled that the communications to users "constitute in themselves market behaviour which does not lessen each undertaking's uncertainty as to the future attitude of its competitors. At the time when each undertaking engages in such behaviour, it cannot be sure of the future conduct of others". The Court therefore found the system of announcing prices on a quarterly basis, did not amount to an infringement of [Article 101 (1) TFEU]. The Court, based on the expert opinions, confirmed that the announcement system was a commercial requirement in the relevant market. Moreover, the Court opined that as woodpulp accounted for up to three-quarters of the customers' input costs, the purchasers desired to ascertain their future costs immediately, in order to minimalise commercial risks. Furthermore, the Court held the opinion that the system of quarterly public price announcements by a substantial number of woodpulp producers *per se* was not contrary to [Article 101 (1) TFEU] because the producer could not ascertain that other competitors will follow. In contrast to other most organised cartels, in this case the allegation was "market behaviour which does not lessen each undertaking's uncertainty as to the future attitude of its competitors". In general, the Court ruled that the Commission had failed to provide sufficient evidences to rule out other plausible explanations for the parallel pricing. This Court's final ruling was founded among others upon following reasons: *First*, the system of quarterly prices announcements had to a large extent the legitimate purpose of giving customers relevant information for the forthcoming transactions in the woodpulp market. *Second*, the parallel timing of prices announcements could simply have resulted from the natural transparency in the woodpulp market, which is characterised by the free-flowing information exchanges, as buyers informed each other about prices and several agents act on behalf of other producers. *Third,* the Court based on further examination, found the relevant woodpulp markets were more oligopolistic that the Commission had believed, whereby this market structure provided a further explanation for the parallel prices and trends in the respective woodpulp market.

4.2.1.3 Toshiba Corp. v European Union Commission (Gas Insulated Switchgear-GIS Cartel (ECJ Case C-180/16 P)

In this case the European Commission adopted a Prohibiting Decision against corporations engaging in the *Gas Insulated Switschgear* (GIS) for conducting cartel practices, which consisted principally of market allocation, customer allocation and bid rigging for public tenders and thus infringing Article 101(1) TFEU. In this chief decision the Commission and later the Courts tried to proof the unwritten complex agreement and the concerted practice by employing the direct and circumstantial evidences as well as the implementation of the Leniency programme.[860]

Case Facts: As of 1989 for about 16 years, approximately 20 companies, mainly Siemens, Alstom, Areva, and two Japanese corporations, participated in cartel practices on the market for *gas insulated switchgear* (GIS). GIS is a major component to control energy flow in electricity grids and is sold globally as a component for turnkey power stations or as separate equipment for a turnkey power substation. Based on the so-called 'GQ Agreement' signed in Vienna on 15th April 1988, the 'E-Group Operation Agreement for GQ Agreement' followed by an unwritten agreement or 'the common understanding' these alleged undertakings committed a series of secretive measures, for instance: coding the names for the involving cartel companies and individuals as well as using anonymous e-mail addresses to conduct the following cartel practices: (1) sharing the GIS markets in Europe and

860 M L T Centella 'Indirect Evidence of a Cartel in the GIS Judgments Saga' (Journal of European Competition Law & Practice, Volume 3/ Issue 3, 2012) 258–260. cf. D. Bailey, 'Gas Insulated Switchgear' (Presentation Paper for the Workshop Milestone Judgement in Competition Law, States Network for Economic Development in collaboration with the Barbados Fair Trading, 30–31 July 2012).

Japan; (2) allocating quotas and maintaining historic market shares; (3) doing collusive tendering; (4) exchanging the sensitive market information in the GIS market in Europe and in Japan. However, in March 2004 ABB Ltd, one of the cartel participants, based on its initiative informed the European Commission about the existing cartel practices through the concerted practices in the respective GIS sector through an oral application and at the same time applying for immunity from fines pursuant to the Commission Notice of 19th February 2002 on Immunity from Fines and Reduction of Fines in Cartel cases ("the Leniency Notice"). Accordingly, the Commission sent the Statement of Objections to the alleged 20 companies for infringing the cartel prohibition pursuant to Article 101(1) TFEU and thus levied fines either individually or jointly and severally to each cartel participant, whereby the largest fines, in amount of € 396,562,500, was imposed on Siemens AG, as a cartelist's secretary. However, the Commission's Decision was appealed by the affected companies to the General Court, *inter alia* due to the excessive or unjustified fines imposed and insufficient evidences to confirm the involvement of the companies in the cartel practices.

Decision: Before the General Court there were three legal issues which must be examined and decided, which are: *First,* what is the correct approach to evidentiary requirements in a cartel infringement. *Second,* whether the Japanese companies factually participated in the concerted practices, notably through sharing the market of GIS. *Third,* whether the fines imposed by the Commission had been correct and fair. With regard to the first question, the General Court stated its arguments from paragraph 75 until 89, as follows: Firstly, the evidences in substantiating cartel infringement must be "precise and consistent" and must be evaluated based on the reliability principle, particularly "[…] the GQ Agreement cannot be regarded as constituting documentary evidence of the existence of a common understanding between the companies". Secondly, to proof a cartel infringement the Commission can use the leniency materials provided the causality between the facts is fulfilled. Thirdly, the General Court ruled the judgment:

> "*the Commission cannot be required to produce documents expressly attesting to contacts between the traders concerned […]. The existence of an anti-competitive practice or agreement may therefore be inferred from a number*

of coincidences and indicia which, taken together, can, in the absence of another plausible explanation, constitute evidence of an infringement of the competition rules."

Moreover, as regards the allegation of Japanese companies participating in the concerted practices in GIS markets in Japan and Europe, the General Court ruled its judgement:

> "*The existence of a mutual agreement necessarily implies the existence of a meeting of minds, even if there is no evidence which makes it possible to determine with precision the exact point in time that meeting of minds was manifested [...] the content of that understanding was understood, accepted and implemented by all the participants to the cartel without the need for any specific discussion on it.*" (*para.* 231)

4.2.1.4 Gemeinschaftsunternehmen für Mineralölprodukte (Texaco-Zerssen) [Bundesgerichtshof Kartellsenat, KVR 3/82, 04.10.1983)[861]

In this landmark case-law concerning cartels' practice within the oligopolistic market, the German courts establish mainly three guiding principles, which have been inferred from Sec. 22 para.2 of the Act against Restraints of Competition, which are as follows:

First, the determination of oligopoly power in the relevant market according to Sec.22 para.2 of the Act against Restraint of Competition, regardless of the presumption of market dominance, shall take into considerations: the number of firms engaging in the relevant market, the factual structures of market and competition relations between the firms in an oligopoly market.

Second, for the purpose of assessment or determination, whether between the firms in an oligopolistic market exists functionable competitions therein, prerequisites comprehensive analysis pertaining not only the structural requirements of competition but also competition relations between firms within the relevant market.

Third, whenever in an oligopolistic market not all of the competition instruments had been employed, thus this requires that the existing competition between firms would have appreciable intensity and significance for the relevant market. Accordingly, the existing competi-

861 F. J. Säcker and K. Boesche,'Vertikale Fusionen im Energiesektor gefährden wirksamen Wettbewerb' BB 2001 2329–2237

tions between firms could create a functionable competition in an oligopoly market.

Circumstance of the Case

In this leading case-law, the *Kartellgericht* (KG) had adjudicated case concerning prohibition decision by the *Bundeskartellamt* against a merger or fusion plan by the undertakings, which engaged in the mineral and petroleum industry. However, the alleged undertakings filed a law objection against the prohibition. The Court (KG) decided in favour of the undertakings. *The Bundeskartellamt* thus subsequently posed a law objection against the Court's decision, which was later refused.

Adjudication of the Court

The adjudicating Court, the *Kartellgericht (KG)*, was of the opinion that for the appropriate assessment and application of the market dominant oligopoly in accordance to Sec.22 para. 2 of the GWB in the mineral and petroleum sector, not only the numbers of undertakings that are active in the market should be considered, but also the factual market structural requirements as well as competition relationships between the firms in the relevant market.

Furthermore, the adjudicating Court (KG) argued that for the examination of corporate fusions, which could change the structure of competitions requirements due to corporate concentration, the examination of relevant market structures would become the primary parameter; that is to say to determine whether there were significant competitions between undertakings in an oligopolistic market. Consequently, the competition authority shall take into considerations whole relevant circumstances, particularly the competition relations which actually work in the relevant market.

Particularly important is the assessment in the market of a homogenous product, which has none of competition in terms of prices and qualities. As regards to the determination of restriction of competition, the Court and *the Bundeskartellamt* (FCO) should carry out comprehensive and elaborative analysis as to the impacts of market structures as well as the competition relations between undertakings within the relevant market.

4.2.1.5 Total/OMV Tankstelle The German Supreme Court Decision (*Bundesgerichtshof Beschluss vom 6. Dezember 2011 – KVR 95/10)*[862]

On 26th May 2011, *the Bundeskartellamt* (Federal Cartel Office) published the final report on its sector inquiry into competition for the German fuel market. The sector inquiry describes several important aspects:[863]

First, whether the five leading fuel suppliers (BP, Shell, ConocoPhillips, ExxonMobil, and Total) hold collectively dominant position on several regional markets for the retail sale of fuel (thorough petrol stations) in Germany, and whether retail fuel prices in Germany were accordingly higher than necessary. The principal conclusions in this report is that the five integrated oil majors, which together account for nearly of 65% of fuel sales in Germany, as holding a collectively dominant position on several regional retail fuel markets. It therefore disagrees with the Appeal Court, which found that the FCOs' decision cannot reasonably be accepted. The FCO, however, will continue its decisional practice based upon this report, provided the *Bundesgerichtshof* (Federal Court of Justice) decides conversely.

Second, the FCO is of the opinion that there was no effective internal competition in the oligopolistic fuel market, partly due to high market transparency. Furthermore, this market transparency is further increased by the suppliers' operation of a comprehensive price monitoring system, by vertical integration of the fuel suppliers (which operate both refineries and petrol stations) and by the national-wide presence, which enables the undertakings to observe price changes and

862 *Bundesgerichtshof* ‹http://juris.bundesgerichtshof.de/cgi-bin/rechtsprechung/document.py?Gericht=bgh&Art=en&nr=60376&pos=0&anz=1› accessed on 5th January 2019.

863 *Bundeskartellamt,* Sektoruntersuchung Kraftstoffe (B8–200/09) Abschlussbericht Mai 2011.

thus to react promptly. Moreover, the existence of an effective retaliatory mechanism, supported by several links and interdependencies between the undertakings, prevents the undertakings to deviate from consciously parallel behaviour.

Third, as regards the fuel barometric pricing at petrol stations. According to FCO observation over the collected pricing information, the oligopolistic fuel market structure in Germany favoures the establishment of quasi-uniform pricing practices, such as increasing prices at the beginning of holiday periods and during the weekend. In this uniform increased pricing practices, the market leader initiated the prices and then followed by other fuel undertakings a few hours later. However, the FCO would not investigate these quasi-uniform pricing practices, because pricing scrutiny on the upstream and downstream fuel and gasoline markets will be legally and practically difficult.

Hence, through this recent landmark case-law, the *Bundesgerichtshof* consentrates onthe following reference norms: Sec. 19 para.2 and para.3, Sec.37 para 1 German Act against Restraint of Competition (GWB). From this adjudication, the *Bundesgerichtshof* generated three main judicial issues, which are:

First, with regard to legal question whether acquisition of several separate assets of undertakings could be deemed as a single corporate fusion in the light of Sec.37 para.1(1) of the GWB, thus the Court determines firstly whether the asset acquisition was an unitary event or process which is able to influence the market structures.

Second, as regards to the indications of market structures in an oligopolistic market, which initially seem to be an existence of the parallel behaviour of undertakings in the market and thus to a market dominance could be rebutted or invalidated, provided there were effective competitions between undertakings on the market. Accordingly, the assessment of market interactions of undertakings requires comprehensive considerations of structural requirements on the market, which are of importance for economic considerations.

Third, whenever the observed market conducts of undertakings in an oligopoly market was ambiguous, but to manifest a uniform behaviour which aims to reduce or eliminate competitions in the market, thus these market behaviours were subject to the application of Sec.19 para 3(2) of the GWB.

In this landmark case-law the *Bundesgerichthof* examined the Decision of the *Bundeskartellamt* of 29th April 2008 to prohibit over the previously informed merger and acquisition plan of Total Deutschland GmbH, namely, to acquire 59 petrol filling stations of OMV in Sachsen and Thüringen particularly pursuant to Sec.36 para.1 GWB. The key legal issues in this case were: collective market dominance, substantiation of the prices cartel through a quantitative analysis of prices and the forbidden suppression prices in the petrol filling station in Germany.[864]

Case facts: Total Deutschland GmbH ("Total"), a subsidiary of the France holding company Total S.A. Paris, operates in the domestic market of Germany and has already operated more than 1,000 petrol filling stations, which majority is located in Thüringen and Sachsen and has positioned as the fourth biggest operator of petrol filling stations in Germany. Whereas, OMV, a subsidiary of the holding company OMV AG Wien, operates in the mineral oil sector and ownes petrol filling stations in South and East Germany. In addition, OMV operates the Refinery factory in Bayern. On 5th December 2008 Total informed the *Bundeskartellamt* about the plan to acquire about 59 petrol filling stations in Sachsen and Thüringen. However, the *Bundeskartellamt*, through the Decision Number B 8–175/08, dated on the 29th April 2009 prohibited the informed merger or fusion plan based on the legal of Section 36 para.1 GWB. Moreover, the *Bundeskartellamt* was of the opinion that previously market dominating oligopoly hasexisted, namely collectively handled by Total and other four gasoline companies (Shell, Aral/BP, ConocoPhillips, Exxon Mobil (Esso)). Thus, the concerned fusion plan could largely coagulate and aggravate the existing market dominating oligopoly. Subsequently, based on the legal complaint, *Oberlandesgericht* (OLG) Düsseldorf through the Decision 04.08.2010–VI-2 Kart 6/09 nullified the *Bundeskartellamt's* Decision, in particular: First, OLG Düsseldorf confirmed that there was a market separation between diesel petrol and automotive gasoline based on the accessibility test; Second, OLG Düsseldorf refused the *Bundeskartellamt's* argument about the existence of collective market dominance

864 S. Gleave, ‚*Benzinpreis – Marktmacht, Preissetzung und Konsequenzen*' (Bundeskartellamt Sitzung des Arbeitskreises Kartellrecht Benzinpreis – Marktmacht, Preissetzung und Konsequenzen 6th Oktober 2019

after considering two factors, namely the vertical integration and the Germany-wide network of the gasoline filling stations.

Table 1. Price Fixing in the Petrol Filling Station in Daily Operation (2007–2010)

Durchschnittspreise für Ottokraftstoff in Köln nach Wochentagen und Jahren					
		2007	2008	2009	2010
Montag	00:00 Uhr	1,332	1,378	1,256	1,371
Montag	06:00 Uhr	1,330	1,378	1,256	1,370
Montag	12:00 Uhr	1,323	1,369	1,247	1,385
Montag	18:00 Uhr	1,326	1,363	1,245	1,401
Dienstag	00:00 Uhr	1,347	1,395	1,277	1,408
Dienstag	06:00 Uhr	1,347	1,395	1,280	1,410
Dienstag	12:00 Uhr	1,345	1,393	1,280	1,404
Dienstag	18:00 Uhr	1,341	1,388	1,271	1,394
Mittwoch	00:00 Uhr	1,344	1,400	1,290	1,416
Mittwoch	06:00 Uhr	1,344	1,400	1,292	1,419
Mittwoch	12:00 Uhr	1,339	1,394	1,288	1,423
Mittwoch	18:00 Uhr	1,335	1,385	1,277	1,405
Donnerstag	00:00 Uhr	1,341	1,397	1,282	1,422
Donnerstag	06:00 Uhr	1,341	1,397	1,284	1,423
Donnerstag	12:00 Uhr	1,335	1,390	1,279	1,425
Donnerstag	18:00 Uhr	1,335	1,383	1,266	1,407
Freitag	00:00 Uhr	1,348	1,402	1,282	1,412
Freitag	06:00 Uhr	1,348	1,402	1,285	1,412
Freitag	12:00 Uhr	1,347	1,400	1,285	1,414
Freitag	18:00 Uhr	1,348	1,401	1,288	1,425
Samstag	00:00 Uhr	1,348	1,399	1,286	1,423
Samstag	06:00 Uhr	1,348	1,399	1,286	1,423
Samstag	12:00 Uhr	1,343	1,393	1,279	1,407
Samstag	18:00 Uhr	1,337	1,385	1,268	1,387
Sonntag	00:00 Uhr	1,336	1,384	1,266	1,382
Sonntag	06:00 Uhr	1,336	1,384	1,266	1,382
Sonntag	12:00 Uhr	1,334	1,381	1,261	1,376
Sonntag	18:00 Uhr	1,332	1,379	1,257	1,372

Graphic 1. Example of the Price Increase Round Practice

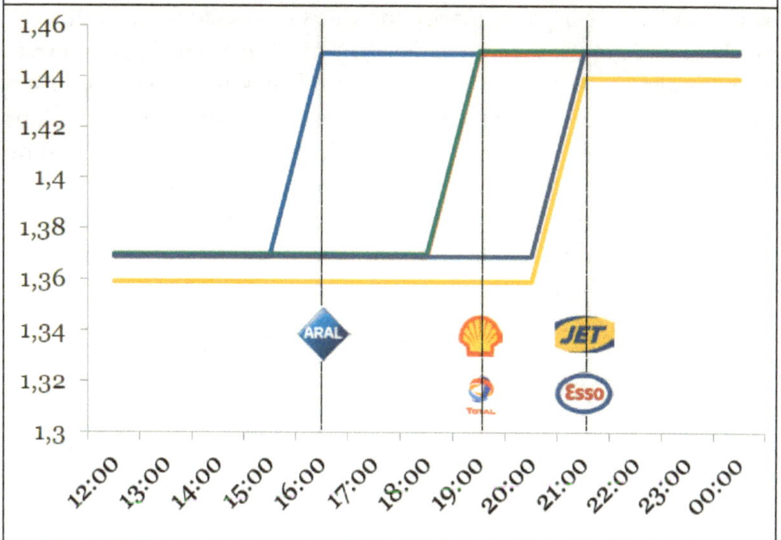

In the previous inquires over the gasoline and petrol filling station in Germany, the *Bundeskartellamt* had founded several salient market characteristics: (1) the homogenous product; (2) high market transparency; (3) a frequent direct and indirect communication between the companies; (4) relatively high interdependency; (5) the high entry barriers to the market, (6) no demand power. Furthermore, the *Bundeskartellamt* had also founded the price fixing practices in the petrol filling station sector, namely through the price increases and price decrease rounds. Firstly, the gasoline price increase was followed by petrol filling stations in the whole national market. Additionally, this price increase was initiated by Aral and operated wholly through the central pricing department. Secondly, in contract, the gasoline price decrease was only the reaction of petrol filling stations operated in the regional market, instead of the national market. Furthermore, these price increase and price decrease rounds had common ratio about three times higher or lower than the normal prices. More importantly the price increase and price decrease rounds were arranged through the following mechanism: First, the gasoline companies increased the prices in the whole domestic market; second, the petrol filling stations increased the prices periodically between Monday until Thursday at 18 o'clock and others began the price increases at 11 o'clock. The initiators for these price increases were either BP (Aral) or Shell. About 3 hours later, almost the other petrol filling companies increased the prices, and thus followed by Total within the next 3,5 hours. ConocoPhillips also increased the price after 5 interval hours. These increases and decreases of prices mechanisms were to be depicted as follows:[865]

Based on the prices data, the *Bundeskartellamt* was able to expose the price parallelism, which led to the prices cartel in the petrol filling station industry, based on the following *Edgeworth-cycle* method:

Graphic 2. Graphical Model of the Prices Trends in the Petrol Filling Station of 3 Operators

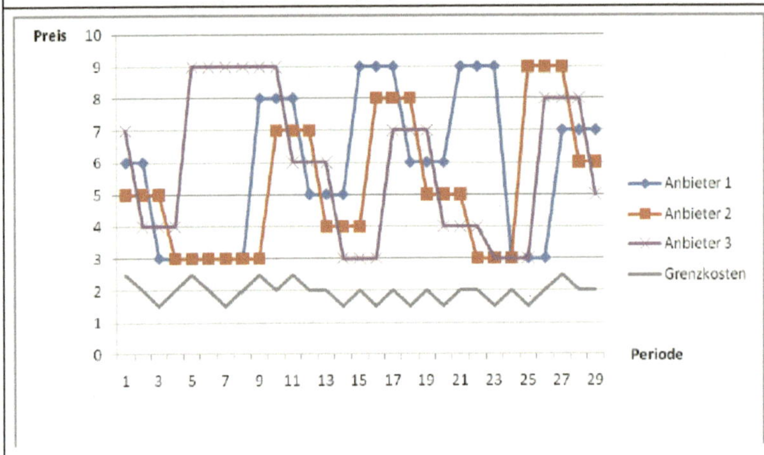

In addition, the *Bundeskartellamt* also perfomed the sectoral inquiries (*Sektoruntersuchung Kraftstoffe Abschlussbericht 2011*), whereby the *Bundeskartellamt* concluded that the existing five petrol filling station companies, namely: (1) Shell, (2) Aral/BP, (3) ConocoPhillips (Jet), (4) ExxonMobil (Esso), and Total implemented oligopoly in this lucrative sector, based on the following evidentiary factors: *First*, the restricted access to the gasoline refinery supply. *Second*, market transparency

865 *Bundeskartellamt*, Sektoruntersuchung Kraftstoffe (B8–200/09) Abschlussbericht Mai 2011.

particularly the price. *Third*, the product's homogeneity. *Fourth*, sanction mechanism for collective compliance. Accordingly, in this case the *Bundeskartellamt* firstly observed the periodical price parallelism which might indicate the absence of internal competition. Subsequently, the *Bundeskartellamt* examined the following indirect evidences of cartel, notably the routine direct and indirect communications between the companies which led to the market transparency. Additionally, the existence of any sanction instruments for ensuring compliances to the cartel practice was evaluated by the *Bundeskartellamt* as the other indirect evidence. Together with the observations over the market structures of the petrol filling station sector, the *Bundeskartellamt* concluded that the Total business plan to fusion or merger was to cause cartel infringement.

Decision: The *Bundesgerichtshof* refused the Decision of OLG Düsseldorf and thus confirmed the *Bundeskartellamt*'s arguments. Accordingly, the *Bundesgerichtshof* holds a final decision that the fluctuations of gasoline prices was not an indirect evidence and could not lead to conclusion about the existence of an internal competition in the petrol filling station companies. The *Bundesgerichtshof* was of the opinion that following evidentiary factors shall be considered to substantiate the existence of cartel practices, which were: the market structures, particularly the high concentration index, the existing vertical integration through the fusion of factory and refinery of the gasoline companies, the high market transparency notably the price, and lastly the product homogeneity in the petrol filling station sector comprehensively.

4.2.2 In the Indonesia Competition Law

Since the inception of the Indonesia Competition Law No.5/1999, several prominent cases related to infringement against cartel prohibition have been brought before the KPPU, subsequently before the District Court (PN) and finally before the Indonesian Supreme Court (MARI). Nonetheless, starting from the recent MARI Decision, up to now, the judicial practices on application of circumstantial (indirect) evidence have shown an inconsistency and leave some difficulties, among others how to harmonise the evidentiary rules of Article 42 of the Indonesia Competition Law No.5/1999 and evidentiary provisions of the Indonesia Criminal Procedural Law (KUHAP).[866] Accordingly, this section will expose the Decisions aforementioned, from the most recent Decisions up to the onset Decisions.

4.2.2.1 Cartels on Automotive Tire [The Indonesian Supreme Court-MARI Decision Number 221 K/Pdt.Sus-KPPU/2016][867]

Case summary

On 4th May 2018, the Indonesian Supervisory Commission for Business Competition (KPPU) obtained the formal notification (Relaas) of Decision from the Indonesian Supreme Court (Mahkamah Agung Republik Indonesia-MARI), Number Nomor 167-PK/Pdt.Sus-KPPU/2017 dated 25 January 2018, concerning the Supreme Appeal for Review (Peninjauan Kembali-PK) over the Decision of KPPU on automotive tire cartels. This *Peninjauan Kembali* or PK was lodged by the alleged companies, PT Bridgestone Tire Indonesia dan PT Sumi Rubber Indonesia, against KPPU in order to annul the previous KPPU's Decision, which found that both companies have violated the Cartels prohibition under the Law Number 5/1999. The contents of the Decision of Peninjauan Kembali (PK), is:

> "1. Rejecting the appeal for review from PT Bridgestone Tire Indonesia dan PT Sumi Rubber Indonesia, as the 1st appeallant and 2nd appeallant;
> 2. Punishing the 1st and 2nd appeallants, also as the appeallants for Cessation (Kasasi) and the appeallants for Objection, before the Indonesian Supreme Court (MARI) and the Higher Court (Pengadilan Tinggi)."[868]

Therefore, by virtue of this Supreme Appeal for Review (PK), the Decision of KPPU, stating that the alleged companies, PT Bridgestone Tire

866 *Lubis and Sirait,* Hukum Persaingan Usaha (n 225) 324–329. See also *Rizkiyana and Iswanto,* 'Eradicating Cartel' (n 28) 5–10.

867 Decision Number 221 K/Pdt.Sus-KPPU/2016, *PT. Bridgestone Tire Indonesia, dkk v. Komisi Pengawas Persaingan Usaha (KPPU) (The Indonesian Supreme Court -MARI)* ‹https://putusan.mahkamahagung.go.id/putusan/ab9d7a55d988324692cf5f22c8d35b01› accessed on 2nd January 2019.

868 KPPU, http://www.kppu.go.id/id/blog/2018/05/putusan-kartel-ban-inkracht/, accessed on 31st December 2018.

Indonesia dan PT Sumi Rubber Indonesia have committed cartels in the automotive tire industry, has become a final and binding decision (*inkracht van gewijsde*).

Prior to the issuance of the Indonesian Supreme Court Decision (MARI), KPPU has decided, after concluding the antitrust enforcement proceedings, that 6 automotive tire producers, namely PT Bridgestone Tire Indonesia, PT Sumi Rubber Indonesia, PT Gajah Tunggal, Tbk., PT Goodyear Indonesia, Tbk., PT Elang Perdana Tire Industry, and PT Deli Rubber Industry have legally and convincingly violated the Cartel Prohibitions in the Article 5 and Article 11 of Law Number 5 Year 1999 concerning Prohibition of Monopolistic Practices and Unfair Business Competition (the Law Number 5/1999). KPPU has also imposed pecuniary fines on each reported party (the six companies) in the amount of 25 Million Rupiah which must be paid to the Indonesian State treasury Office.[869]

The Decision

Equally important, in this case proceedings, KPPU has applied the indirect (circumstantial) evidences in order to determine that the alleged companies, PT Bridgestone Tire Indonesia and the other 5 car tire companies, have violated the Cartel prohibitions stipulated by Article 5 and Article 11 of the Law Number 5/1999. The Higher Court, and finally the Indonesian Supreme Court have thus confirmed the KPPU's Decision in the Decision Number 221K/PDT.SUS-KPPU/2016, that accepts the indirect (circumstantial) evidence. Nonetheless, in the legal considerations the Indonesian Supreme Court does not stipulate the legal basis on the receipt of indirect evidence as evidence in Law Number 5 of 1999. Besides, the consideration of the Indonesian Supreme Court does not contain the principle of evidentiary process which requires at least two valid evidences to prove the violation of Law Number 5 of 1999 pursuant to Article 42 thereof.[870]

---

869 ibid.

870 *Silalahi* and I C Edgina, 'Pembuktian Perkara Kartel Di Indonesia Dengan Menggunakan Bukti Tidak Langsung (Indirect Evidence) Kajian Putusan KPPU Nomor 17/KPPU-I/2010 dan Nomor 08/KPPU-I/2014 serta Putusan Nomor 294

In this respect, the Indonesian Supreme Court, confirming the previous KPPU's Decision, corroborated and thus accepted the indirect (circumstantial) evidences to prove cartels in the automotive tire sector. Specifically, KPPU applied the Economic evidences by means of the 'Harrington method of a cartel detection' The Harrington method refers to the analytical method between errors and recidual regressions between firms on a market, which is based on the estimation of panel data, in order to detect cartels on the market. Furthermore, KPPU used this Harrington method to discover, whether the prices of automotive tires stipulated independently and was not influenced unlawfully by other competing firms through an examination of contemporaneous correlation of prices.[871]

Furthermore, the Indonesian Supreme Court also confirmed the KPPU's Decision, that applied the communication evidences, in the form of: First, the minutes of meetings of APBI (Indonesian Automotive Tires Producents Association), which stated that the members of APBI are strongly banned from reducing the prices up to the bottom. Secondly, the verbatims of meetings of Presidium (chairing committee) of APBI, which stated:

> "All APBI members are asked to be able to hold back and continue to control their distribution according to the development of their (car-tire) demands."

Finally, in this Decision, the Assembly of Judge accepted the application of indirect (circumstantial) evidences by stipulating that in the re-

---

K/PDT.SUS/2012 dan Nomor 221 K/PDT.SUS-KPPU/2016' (Jurnal Yudisial Vol. 10 No. 3 Desember 2017) 311–330.

871 In the Indonesian Supreme Court Decision Number Nomor 221 K/Pdt.Sus-KPPU/2016, stipulated as follows:
Joseph Harrington by himself asserted in this scientific paper results that the application of the Harrington method of a cartel detection could not become the conclusive evidence of the cartel occurrence. Accodingly, the respective Harrington method means:
"high price-cost margins are not an adequate screening device";
"econometric evidence of structural change is far from conclusive evidence of collusion."
"A high price-cost margin (properly measured) is evidence of market power and does not imply collusion. Other reasons for a high pricecost margin are greatly differentiated products, production technologies, protected by patents and trade secrets and high search cost for consumers." paras. 13.1.–13.10.

al practices of business activities, agreements regarding prices, production, region (cartel) and agreements of anti-competitive practices were often done through the secretive (tacit) ways, so that the business competitions, the evidences which are not direct (indirect / circumstantial evidence), shall be accepted as the valid evidence insofar as the proofs are sufficient and constitue logical evidence, and there is no other stronger evidence, which could can weaken the indirect (circumstantial).[872]

4.2.2.2 Amlodipine Anti-Hypertension Pharmaceutical Cartel [Case NO. 17/KPPU-I/2010]

In this land-mark case law, KPPU had to intensively investigate in order to substantiate the infringements against the Law No.5/1999, as follows: Article 5: price fixing prohibition, Article 11: conspiracy prohibition, Article 16: prohibition over international agreement causing monopoly and Article 25 (a): prohibition of abuse of dominant position of the Law No. 5/1999. Moreover, during the proceedings KPPU intensively employed the circumstantial evidences to substantiate the existence of cartel agreements in the anti-hypertension medical products in Indonesia.

Case Facts: As of 2009 KPPU conducted investigation over the 6 pharmaceutical companies, which were: (I) PT. Pfizer Indonesia, (II) PT Dexa Medica, (III) Pfizer Inc., (IV) Pfizer Overseas LL.C, (V) Pfizer Global Trading, (VI) Pfizer Corporation Panama, notably over the cartel practices within the years 2004–2009. Furthermore, PT Pfizer Indonesia is a foreign investment company, whose majority of shares is owned by Pfizer International as the holding company. While PT Dexa Medica is a domestic investment company, whose majority of shares is owned by domestic investors. Both of these principal companies collectively engaged in the production and marketing of special anti-hypertension pharmaceutical product with a special component, Amlodipine Therapy in Indonesia. Moreover, between PT Pfizer Indonesia and PT Dexa Medica and the other companies there were special distribution relationships, as follows:

872 *Silalahi* and Edgina, „Pembuktian Perkara Kartel Di Indonesia Dengan Menggunakan Bukti Tidak Langsung (Indirect Evidence) (n 869) 326–328.

Graphic 1. Distribution Relationships of Amlodipine Therapy of the Six Companies (2004–2010) in Indonesia

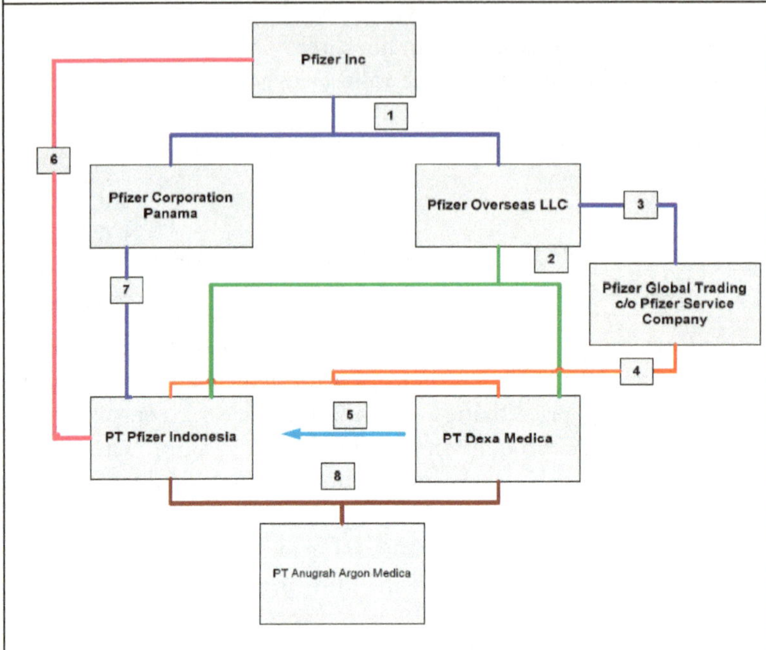

Notes:

1. Pfizer Inc. was the patent holder of Amlodipine Besylate and a parent company of Pfizer Overseas LLC in the supply agreement. Pfizer Inc. also was the parent company of Pfizer Corporation Panama, which was shareholder of 43% of PT Pfizer Indonesia;

2. Between Pfizer Overseas LLC and PT Dexa Medica, the Supply Agreement had been concluded;

3. In the operational, Pfizer Global Trading acted as the supplier of Amlodipine Besylate to PT Pfizer Indonesia and PT Dexa Medica;

4. In practice, PT Pfizer Global Trading instead of Pfizer Overseas LLC, which supplied the Amlodipine Besylate to PT Dexa Medica and PT Pfizer Indonesia. At that time, PT Global Trading was an affiliation company of Pfizer Overseas LLC;

5. The Supply Agreement required that all business communications between PT Dexa Medica and Pfizer Overseas LLC, namely the copies, must be forwarded

and attached to PT Pfizer Indonesia, in particular regarding the request for supply of Amlodipine Besylate, as the raw material;

6. In March 2007, PT Pfizer Indonesia and Pfizer Inc. concluded a license agreement over the patent right of Amlodipine Besylate, whereby this agreement was effective as the agreement of January 2007

7. Pfizer Inc. was the principal shareholder of PT Pfizer Indonesia through its proxy companies Pfizer Corporation Panama and Warner Lambert;

8. PT Anugrah Argon Medica is the main distributor company for the pharmaceutical products with Amlodipine Besylate for anti-hypertension, which were produced both by PT Pfizer Indonesia, with trademark Norvask and by PT Dexa Medica with trademark Tensivask

In the geographical market of anti-hypertension products in Indonesia, there were two main trademarks: the Norvarsk, produced and marketed by PT Pfizer Indonesia and the Tensivask, produced and marketed by PT Dexa Medica. Moreover, PT Anugrah Argon Medica ("AAM") as the main distribution company reported regularly following business information to its suppliers: (1) the forecasting of the market demands of the Amlodipine therapy, (2) the sales report of the Amlodipine therapy, (3) the expired products, (4) the flows of the Amlodipine therapy in the domestic market.

Subsequently, KPPU inquired the parallel price trends of the Norvarsk and the Tensivask in the domestic market between the years 2004–2009, as follows:

Graphic 2. Prices Trends of the Norvarsk per Unit (2004–2009) in Indonesia

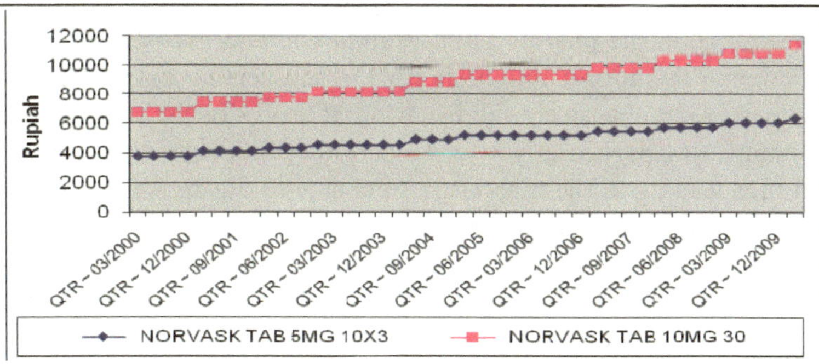

Graphic 3. Prices Trend of the Tensivask per Unit (2004–2009) in Indonesia

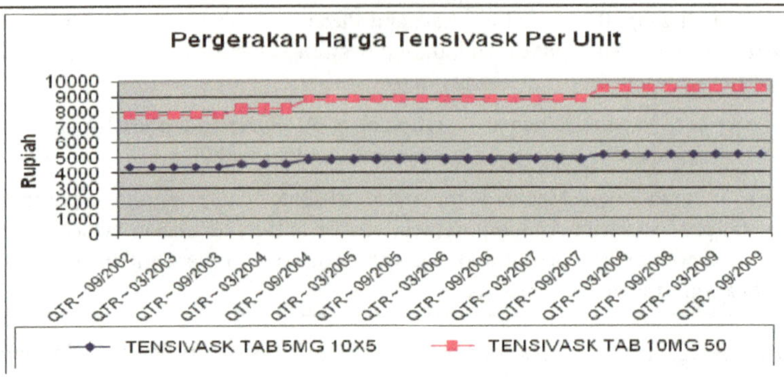

However, according to market survey conducted by the World Health Organisation (WHO) over the international prices of pharmaceutical anti-hypertension products with the Amlodipine Besylate, KPPU founded that the domestic prices of the Norvarsk was 51,13 % more expensive and of the Tensivask was 49,43 % more expensive than the international benchmark prices of similar products.

Based on the statistical information concerning the market shares, KPPU conducted furthermore analysis by employing the *HHI (Hefindahl-Hirschmann Index) and CR4* (the market shares of the four biggest companies) and founded the anti-hypertension pharmaceutical market in Indonesia was highly concentrated. Furthermore, KPPU also analysed several structural aspects, namely: products homogeneity, multimarket contacts, the high entry barriers such as technology and investment capital in the pharmaceutical product of anti-hypertension with amlodipine therapy in Indonesia. In the subsequent analysis, KPPU analysed comprehensively the behavioural aspect of the pharmaceutical companies, particularly over the periodical information exchanges and thus leading to the market transparency of the anti-hypertension amlodipine therapy in Indonesia.

Decision: *In the first phase* of analysis KPPU decided that there were several routine information exchanges from PT Dexa Medica and PT Pfizer Indonesia through Pfizer Global Trading as the principal supplier for the anti-hypertension medical product, notably Amlodipine Besylate leading to the relevant market transparency. In addition, this information exchanges were also facilitated by the sibling relationships between the director and the commissioner of PT Pfizer Indonesia and PT Dexa Medica, which provided a multi-market contact between PT Pfizer Indonesia and PT Dexa Medica. KPPU concluded that the main purpose of these information exchanges was to establish production cartel and the price cartel. *In the second phase*, KPPU analysed furthermore the price parallelism of the Norvask and the Tensivask between 2004 and 2009, the production volume parallelism of the Norvask and the Tensivask by using the homogeneity of variance test. Accordingly, KPPU examined the market concentration index, HHI and CR4, of the Amlodipine Besylate market in Indonesia and found that the relevant market was highly concentrated and had an inelastic market, which means the product prices remained high although there was a cheap generic pharmaceutical products programme from the government. In addition, the parallel pricing of the Norvask and the Tensivask had following characteristics: *First*, the increase trend within a certain period. *Second*, the increase trend was linear in similar percentages, around 3–6 %. Supported by the very high entry barriers to the anti-hypertension therapy market due to the huge investment capital and very expensive technology, KPPU strongly concluded based on these supporting factors that there had been a price fixing and production cartel practices which are prohibited by Article 5 and Article 11 of Law No.5/1999. Therefore, KPPU ruled out that the six pharmaceutical companies, chiefly PT Pfizer Indonesia and PT Dexa Medica as the main producers of the Amlodipine therapy for anti-hypertension in Indonesia, had committedly infringed Article 5 concerning price fixing prohibition and Article 11 regarding cartel pursuant to Indonesian Competition Law No.5/1999.

4.2.2.3 Cement Loco Cartel [Decision Number 01/KPPU-I/2010]

In this landmark case KPPU had to substantiate that the alleged 8 cement companies and the association had already infringed prohibition according to Article 5 and Article 11 Law No.5/1999 particularly concerning the price maintenance and cartel practices within the domestic cement industry. Although the evidences of written agreements were minimal, through the employment of circumstantial evidences in particular the economic and market analyses over the cement industry in a certain period, KPPU was able to substantiate the existence of cartel agreement between the alleged cement companies for committing the cartel on cement prices.

Case Facts: In 2004 KPPU initiatively began to conduct market monitoring and market investigation in the domestic cement industry in particular toward the existing eight cement companies in Indonesia, which were: (I) PT Indocement Tunggal Perkasa Tbk., (II) PT. Holcim Indonesia, Tbk, (III) PT. Semen Baturaja (Persero), (IV) PT. Semen Gresik (Persero) Tbk, (V) PT. Semen Andalas Indonesia, (VI) PT. Semen Tonasa, (VII) PT. Semen Padang, (VIII) PT. Semen Bosowa Maros. In the preliminary, KPPU monitored and inquired the market shares and total domestic consumptions of cement as well as the production capacities including the total sales volumes. Moreover, KPPU also noted that these eight companies periodically participated in a series of meetings under the auspices of the National Cement Association (ASI) among others to discuss and to monitor the prices and total production volumes of cement around 33 provinces.

The National Cement Association (ASI), as the main association for cement producers in Indonesia, established since 1960 in Jakarta, defined its function as follows: First, a forum for communication, consultation and coordination between the cement producers; second, a sole intermediary body for bridging the domestic cement producers with the government and other external parties. In ASI, there is the presidium, a highest organ whose tasks are the following: First, ASI is not the partner of the government, instead ASI has the function to lobby the government to follow the ASI's proposal; second, ASI is to check the illegality of information exchanges according to prevailing regulation; third, ASI is to check the illegality of the price maintenance against the price fluctuations according to government regulation; fourth, ASI lobbied the government, namely Directorate General of Agro and Chemistry Ministry of Trade and Industry, to impose import tax against the incoming cement (10 %) and clinker (15%). Furthermore, ASI conducted regular meetings to discuss following issues: (1) evaluation of distributions in every zoning area, (2) confirmation of realisation for cement supply per zoning area and per factory, (3) evaluation of cement procurements in every zoning area, (5) prognosis of domestic cement procurements. The Ministry of Industry and Trade also legalised the information exchanges meetings through the Letter Nr. 222/AK65/2010 for obtaining periodic and whole reports on the domestic cement market developments. The Ministry claimed that this practice was mandated by Law No.5/1984 on Industry.

Based on these preliminary circumstances, KPPU initiated further analysis and investigations by using the direct evidences, namely the existing blueprint of cartel process, and the indirect evidences. As to the indirect evidences, KPPU emphasised the analysis upon the structural and behavioural aspects of the cement market. The main indication of behavioural aspects is the cement prices in the domestic market, whereby KPPU evaluated the cement prices with a non-transitory trend in a certain period, notably the parallel prices and facilitating prices in the domestic market. The following tables show the prices parallelism of the cement product "Loco" in several zoning areas. In this price parallelism analysis, KPPU employed the *cost of goods sold/ COGS, Pearson correlation test, and homogeneity of variances test.*

Graphic 1. Market Prices Trends of "Loco" cement by 8 (I-VIII) Cement Producers (2004–2009)

The Cement prices fluctuations in the Zoning Area: **D.I Aceh**

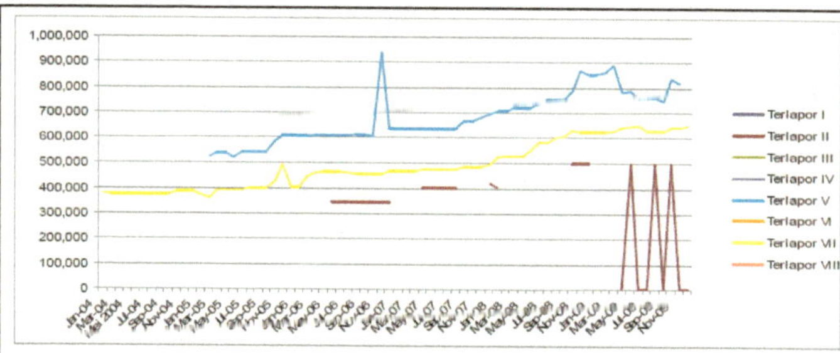

The Cement prices fluctuations in the Zoning Area: **North Sumatra**

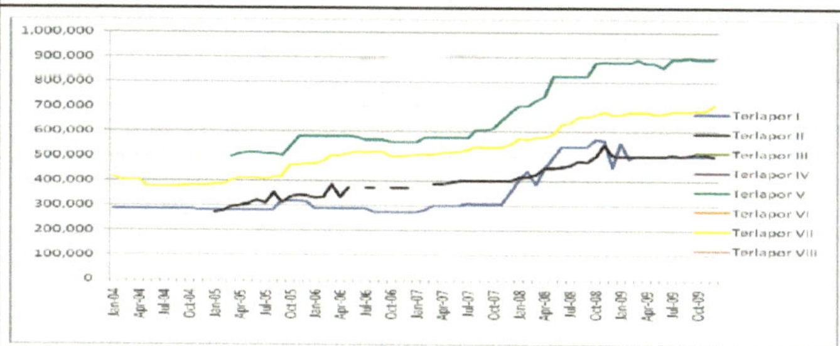

<table>
<tr><td>The Cement prices fluctuations in the Zoning Area: West Sumatra</td><td>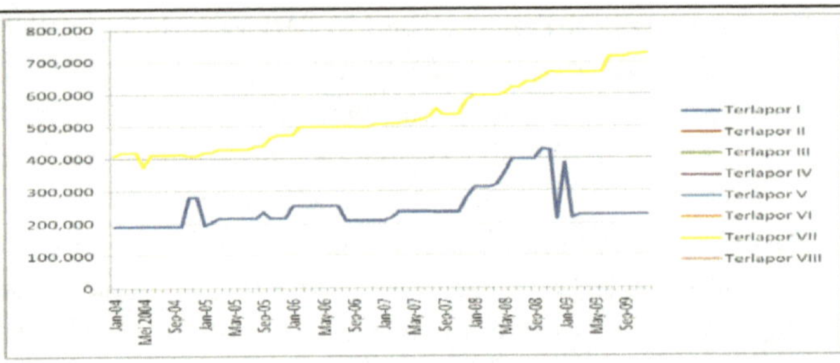
</td></tr>
<tr><td>The Cement prices fluctuations in the Zoning Area: South Sumatra</td><td>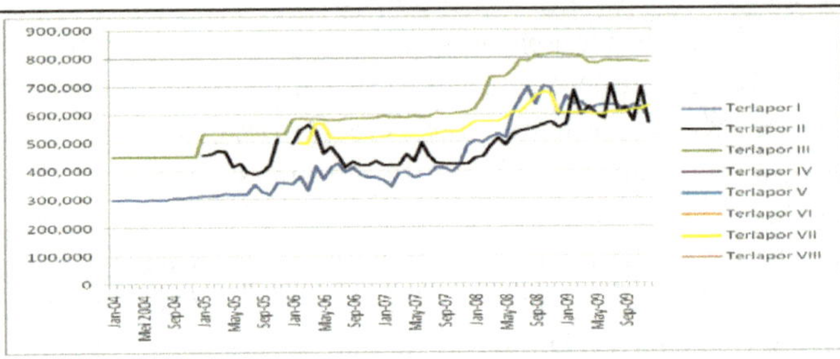
</td></tr>
<tr><td>The Cement prices fluctuations in the Zoning Area: Lampung</td><td>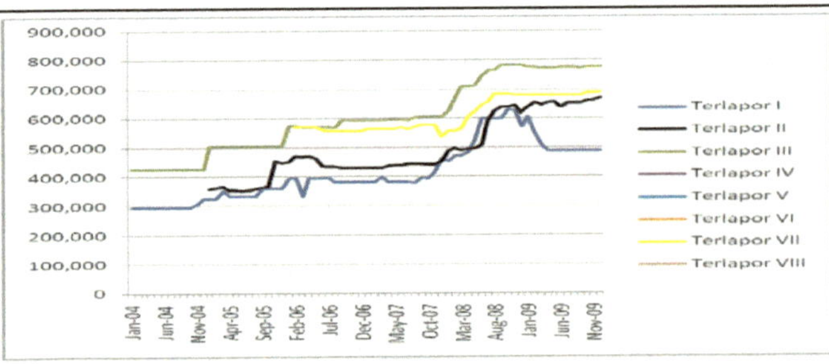
</td></tr>
<tr><td>The Cement prices fluctuations in the Zoning Area: DKI Jakarta</td><td>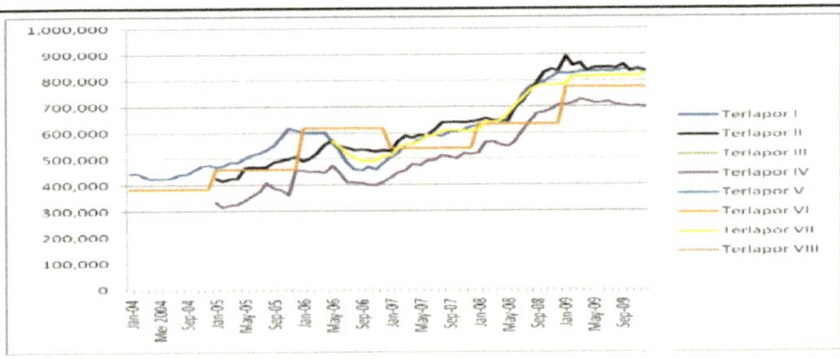
</td></tr>
</table>

The Cement prices fluctuations in the Zoning Area: **West Java**	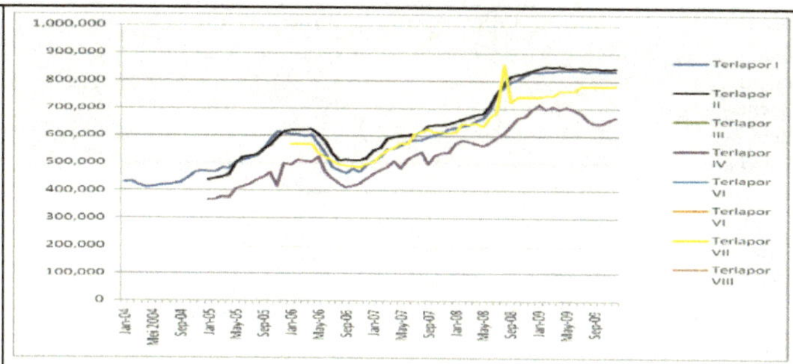
The Cement prices fluctuations in the Zoning Area: **Banten**	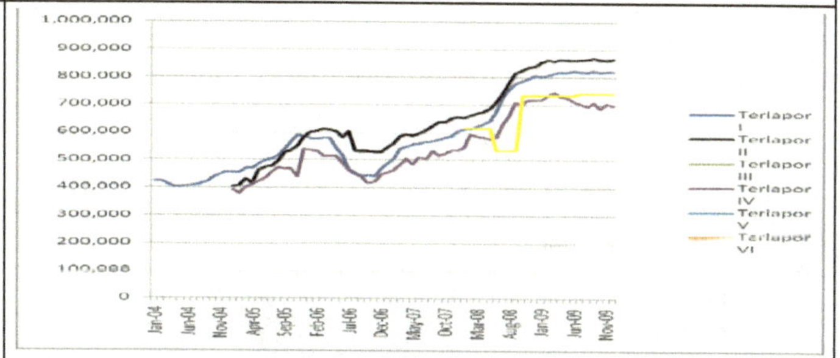
The Cement prices fluctuations in the Zoning Area: **Central Java**	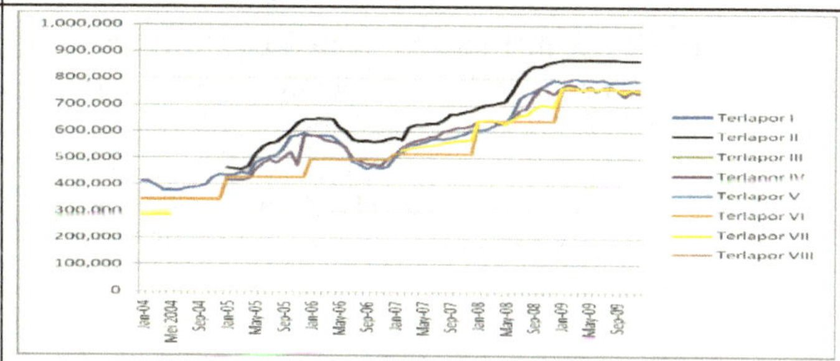
The Cement prices fluctuations in the Zoning Area: **East Java**	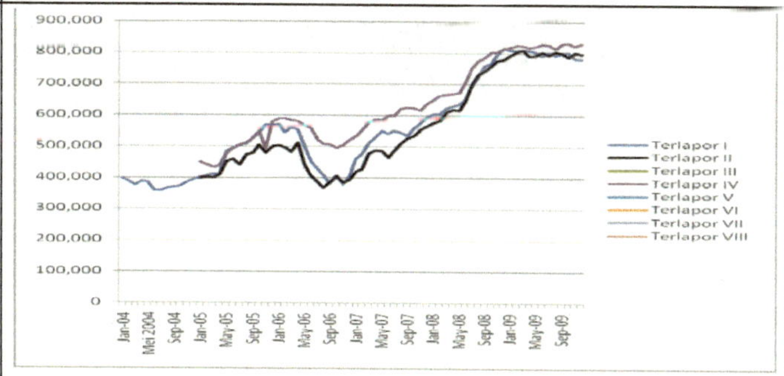

The Cement prices fluctuations in the Zoning Area: **South Sulawesi**	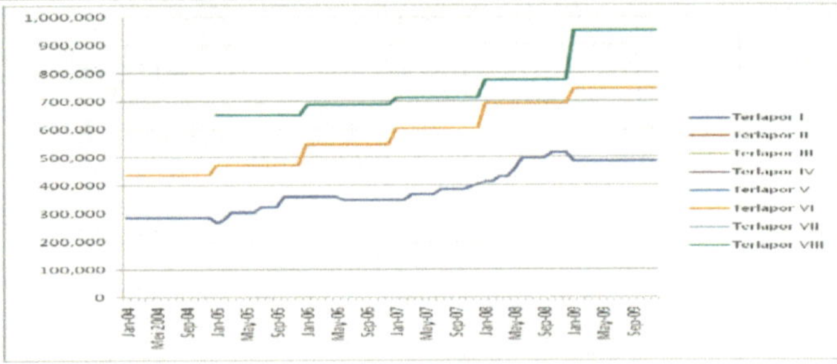
The Cement prices fluctuations in the Zoning Area: **East Kalimantan**	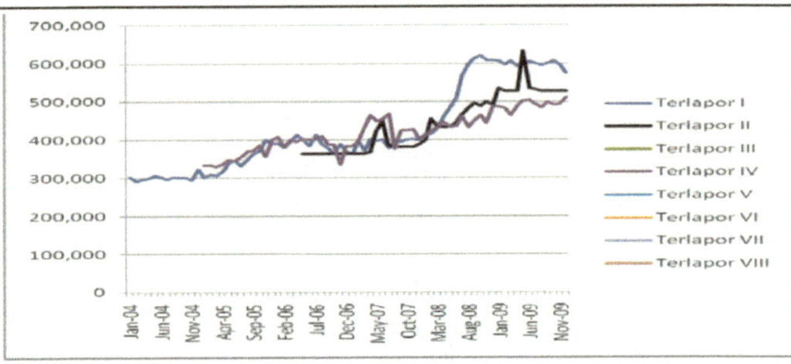

Furthermore, KPPU analysed the financial statements of each cement company between 2004 and 2009, notably the parallel increase of total profits of the cement companies, as follows:

Graphic 2. Trends of Total Profits of the 8 (I-VIII) Cement Producers (2004-2009)

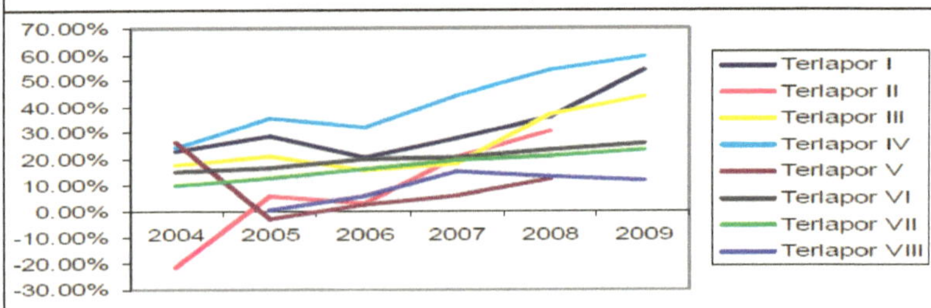

In the further analysis, KPPU examined the structural aspect of the domestic cement market notably the composition of market shares and the increases of market share of each cement company.

Graphic 3. Market Share and Increases of Market Shares of 8 Cement Companies (2004–2009)

Actual Market Shares of the Cement Companies (2004–2009)

	PT. Indocement Tunggal Prakarsa, Tbk.	PT. Holcim Indonesia, Tbk.	PT. Semen Baturaja (Persero)	PT. Semen Gresik (Persero) Tbk.	PT. Semen Andalas Indonesia	PT. Semen Tonasa	PT. Semen Padang	PT. Semen Bosowa Maros
2004	29.96%		3.02%	26.51%		8.12%		
2005	28.40%	14.78%	2.72%	24.05%	3.42%	8.34%	15.25%	3.04%
2006	29.35%	12.26%	2.80%	23.73%	3.83%	8.85%	16.10%	3.08%
2007	29.27%	13.80%	2.82%	20.52%	3.88%	9.17%	17.76%	2.78%
2008	30.73%	13.70%	2.71%	21.29%	3.95%	8.65%	15.48%	3.49%
2009	29.16%	13.44%	2.62%	23.[illegible]3%	3.90%	9.47%	13.88%	4.51%

Increases of the Market Shares of the Cement Companies (2004–2009)

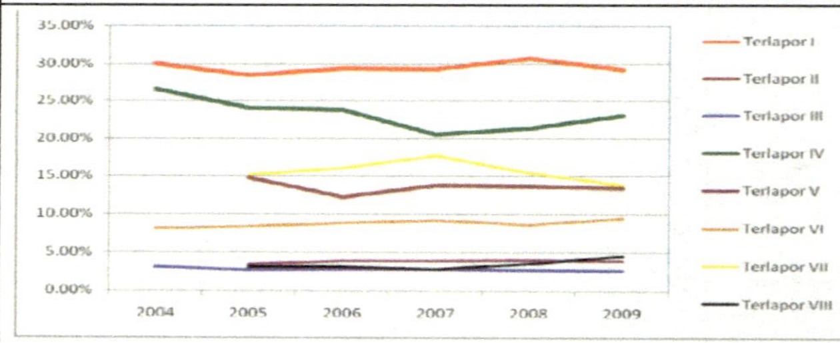

Furthermore, KPPU also found that PT. Indocement Tunggal Perkasa Tbk and PT. Semen Gresik (Persero) Tbk made special agreements with the local distributor:

Graphic 4. Distribution Lines of PT Indocement Tunggal Perkasa Tbk (Cement Company I)

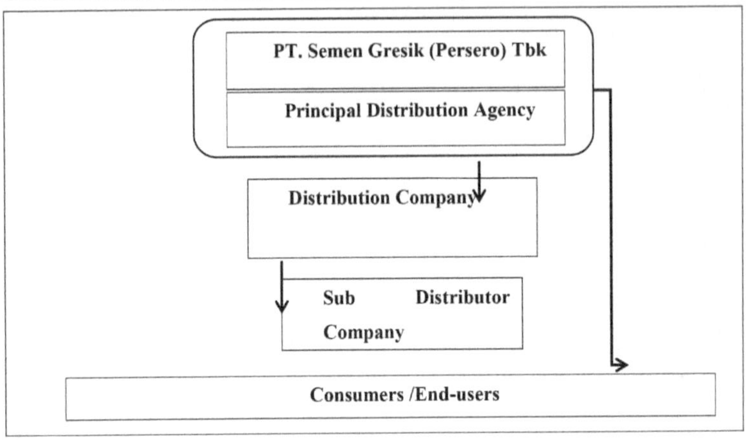

Decision: Embarking from the above mentioned legal and economic analysis of the domestic cement market and cement companies particularly according to Article 1 No.7 Law No.5/1999, the judicial committee ruled out following decisions: *First,* the eight cement companies (I-VIII) had not been proven to infringe cartel price prohibition pursuant to Article 5 Law No.1999. *Second,* the eight cement companies (I–VIII) had not been proven to infringe conspiracy prohibition pursuant to Article 11 Law No.5/1999. Furthermore, KPPU also recommended the government to dissolve the national cement association (ASI) due to its susceptibility for facilitating cartel practices as well as to stipulate the maximum retail prices for the domestic cement products.

4.2.2.4 Flight Airline Fuel Surcharges [Decision Number 25/KPPU-I/2009]

In this landmark decision, KPPU intensively examined the investigatory results over alleged infringement against Article 5 of the Law Number. 5/1999 concerning cartel prices committed by 13 domestic flight companies. For certain periods there had been cartel practice on the fuel surcharge prices between these companies, which were results of explicit agreement through the decision of the association (INACA) as well as the tacit agreements through series of internal meetings for prices coordination. Furthermore, these periodical meetings had been conducted under auspices of INACA, as the only authorised association of domestic flight companies in Indonesia. The agenda in those internal meetings *inter alia:* to adjust the prices of fuel surcharges. Fuel surcharge is an additional price, which is the result of the margin difference between the planned price and the actual price for purchasing avtur-oil for the airplanes. Between the years of 2004 and 2008, KPPU had monitored market trends of these flight companies particularly the market shares in the domestic flight market:

Graphic 1. Market Shares of the 12 Indonesian Flight Domestic Companies

Flight Companies	**2004**	**2005**	**2006**	**2007**	**2008**	**2009**
Garuda Indonesia (Persero)	34.00%	29.26%	24.15%	22.63%	20.68%	19.16%
Sriwijaya Air	3.73%	9.82%	10.90%	10.98%	12.76%	12.76%
Merpati Nusantara Airlines (Persero)	13.56%	7.72%	5.91%	8.15%	6.68%	6.24%
Mandala Airlines	11.81%	9.94%	5.83%	5.32%	9.31%	6.83%
Riau Airlines	0.00%	0.00%	0.34%	0.56%	0.63%	0.73%
TEAS	1.43%	1.36%	0.70%	0.79%	0.72%	0.58%
Lion Mentari Airlines	26.61%	22.81%	23.05%	20.07%	22.53%	22.53%
Wings Abadi Airlines	0.64%	7.47%	7.02%	7.22%	6.28%	7.71%
Metro Batavia Airlines	8.16%	8.27%	13.79%	16.32%	12.88%	15.50%
Kartika Airlines	0.00%	0.41%	0.91%	0.27%	0.65%	0.56%
Trigana Air Service	0.00%	0.00%	2.18%	2.26%	1.90%	1.83%

Indonesia Air Asia	0.06%	2.94%	5.23%	5.43%	5.55%	5.55%
Total	100%	100%	100%	100%	100%	100%

Furthermore, in 2005 the Ministry of Transportation issued a Ministerial Decree ("KepMenhub") allowing the domestic flight companies to stipulate the amount of fuel surcharge prices based on the market prices of avtur-oil. Accordingly, based on the compromise of the domestic flight companies, the INACA decided to set the price of fuel surcharges in amount of 20.000 rupiahs (IDR) for each passenger. However, in May 2006 KPPU issued an instruction for INACA to annul this decision and recommended that each domestic flight undertaking to decide price of fuel surcharges price individually. These instructions and recommendations were followed. In 2008, the Ministry of Transportation issued a further regulation, Decree Nr. AU/4603/DAU.1056/08, regarding the stipulation of prices for fuel surcharges, aimed to the existing domestic flight companies. In this regulation, the so-called Zoning method shall be used to formulate the prices for fuel surcharges, whereby the Zones around Indonesia are to be divided into 5 zones: a) Zone 1 (flight duration < 1hour), b) Zone 2 (flight duration < 2hour), c) Zone 3 (flight duration < 3hour), d) Zone 4 (flight duration 3–4 1hour), e) Zone 5 (flight duration > 4 hour). Accordingly, based on this regulation each of the domestic flight undertaking stipulate different formulas for airlines prices:

Graphic 2. Prices Calculation Formulas of the 12 Indonesian Domestic Airlines

No.	Domestic Airlines Companies	Prices Calculation Formula
1.	Garuda Indonesia (Persero)	Basic fare + PPN + IWJR (Rp 6,000,-) + FS
2.	Sriwijaya Air	Basic fare + PPN + IWJR (Rp 10,000,-) + FS
3.	Merpati Nusantara Airlines (Persero)	Basic fare + PPN + IWJR (Rp 6,000,-) + Administration Fee (Rp5,000,-) FS
4.	Mandala Airlines	Basic fare + PPN + IWJR (Rp 6,000,-) + FS + Biaya administrasi (Rp 4,000,-)
5.	Riau Airlines	Basic Fare + PPN + IWJR (Rp 6,000,-)
6.	TEAS	Basic fare + PPN + IWJR (Rp 6,000,-) + FS
7.	Lion Mentari Airlines	Basic fare + PPN + IWJR (Rp 6,000,-) + Insurance + FS

8.	Wings Abadi Airlines	Basic fare + PPN + IWJR (Rp 6,000,-) + Insurance + FS
9.	Metro Batavia Airlines	Basic fare + PPN + IWJR (Rp 5,000,-) + FS
10.	Kartika Airlines	Basic fare + PPN + IWJR (Rp 6,000,-) + FS
11.	Trigana Air Service	Basic fare + PPN + IWJR (Rp 11,000,-) + FS
12.	Indonesia Air Asia	Basic fare + PPN + IWJR (Rp 6,000,-) + FS (10th May 2006–11th November 2008) Basic Fare + PPN + IWJR (Rp 6,000,-) + Convenience Fee (latest)

Notes: a. PPN: Value Added Tax b. IWJR: Obligatory Life Insurance

c. FS: Fuel Surcharge d. Rp.: Rupiah currency (IDR)

Moreover, KPPU also noticed that between the years of 2004 and2009 there were significant price fluctuations of avtur-oil in Indonesia:

Graphic 3. Price Fluctuations of Avtur oil in Indonesia

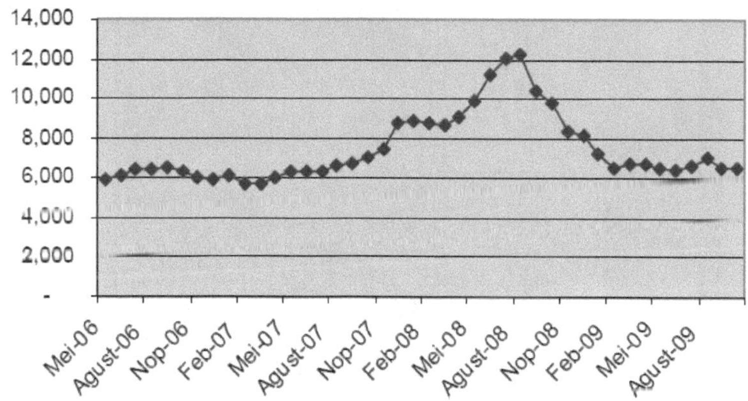

Note:
Vertical axis: Prices in Rupiahs
Horizontal axis: Observed Months

Although there had been significant differences in the formulas and the consumption levels, the prices of fuel surcharges between several airline companies remained similar. These price parallelisms, for instance can be showed as follows:

Graphic 4. Price Parallelisms of the Fuel Surcharges (FS) of the Indonesian 12 Domestic Airlines

Domestic Airlines Companies	FS Price Fluctuation (0–1 hour)	FS Price Fluctuation (1–2hour)	FS Price Fluctuation (2–3 hours)
Garuda Indonesia (Persero)	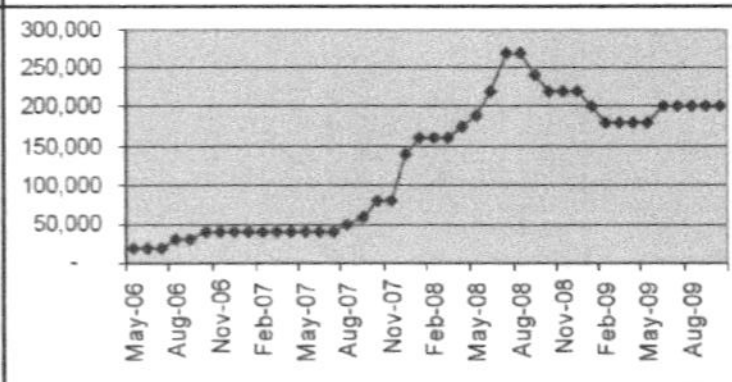	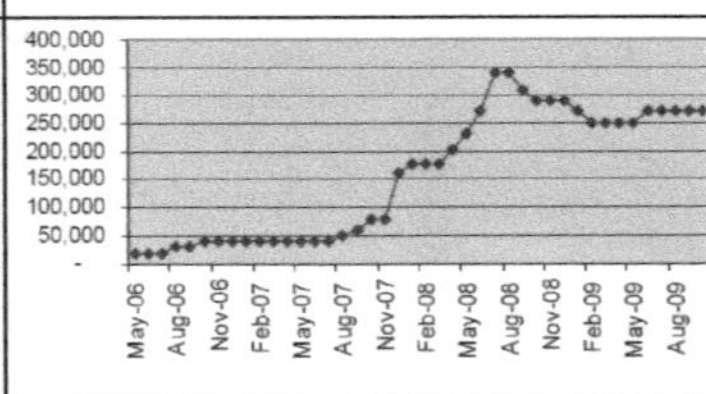	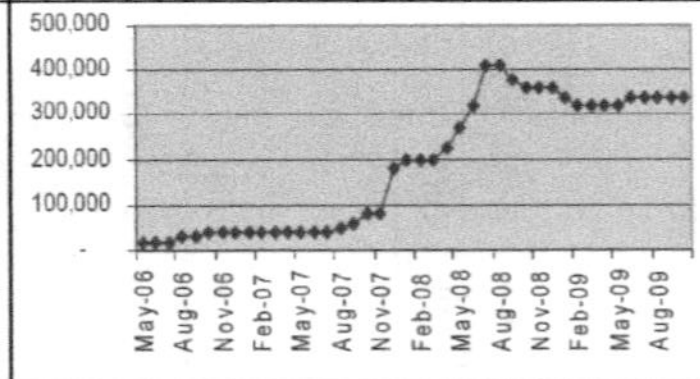
Sriwijaya Air	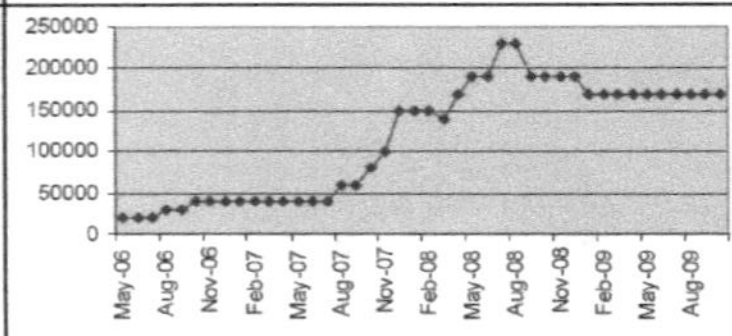	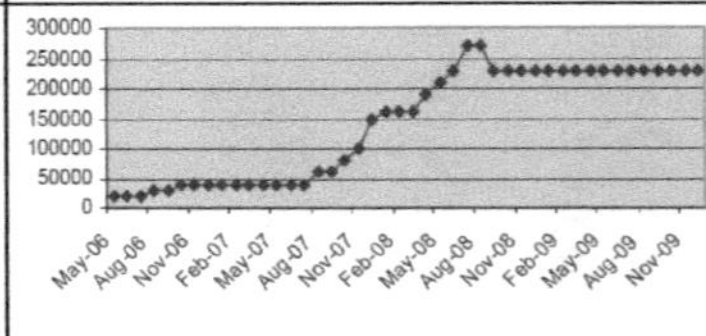	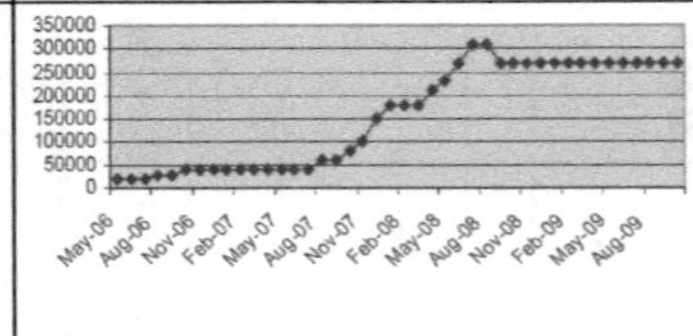
Merpati Nusantara Airlines (Persero)	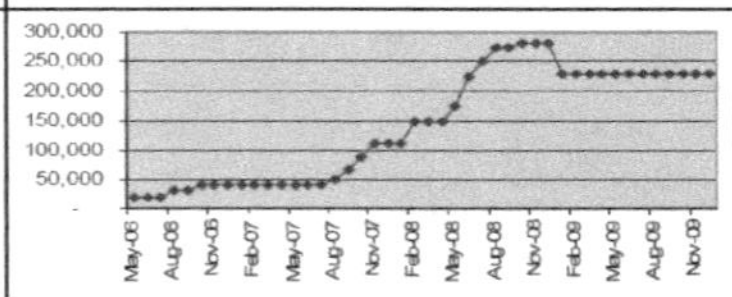	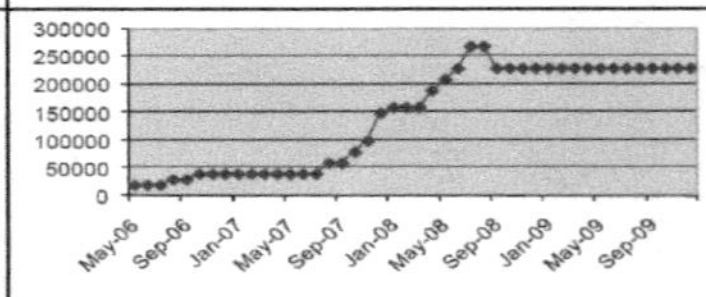	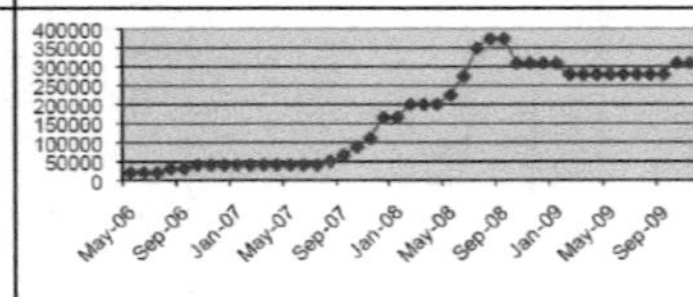

Lion Mentari Airlines	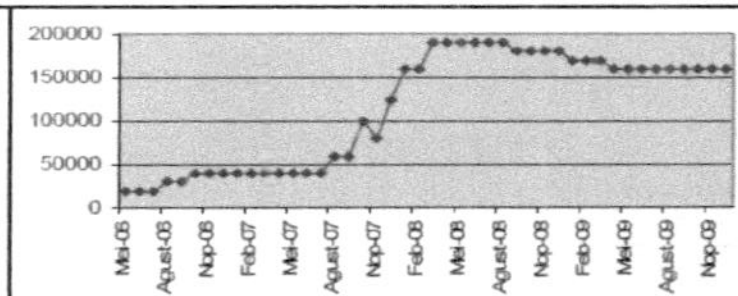	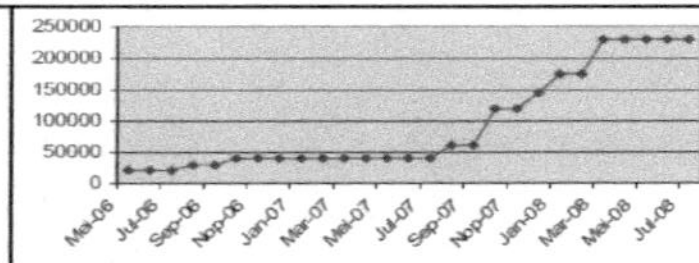	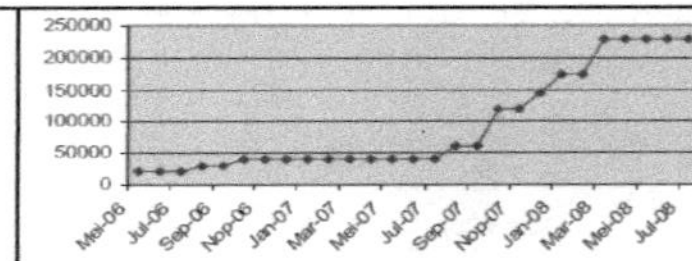
Wings Abadi Airlines	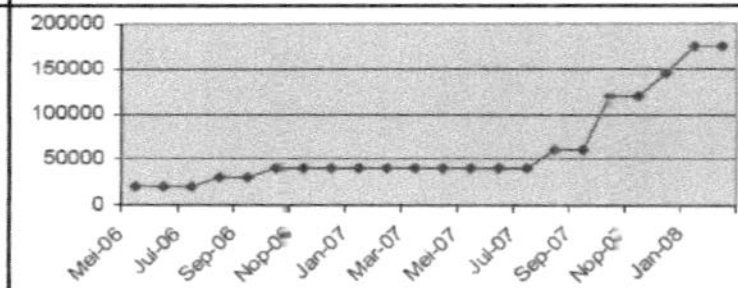	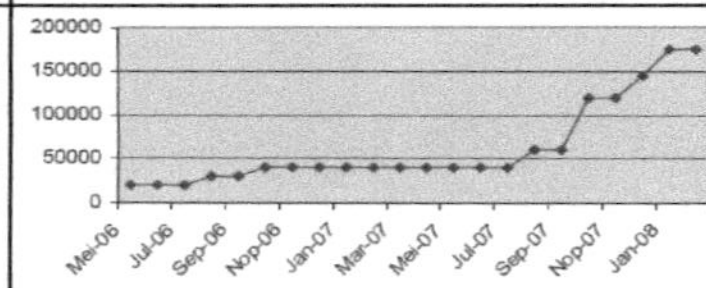	
Metro Batavia Airlines	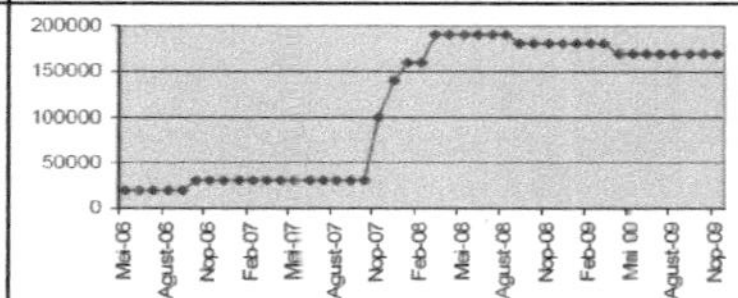	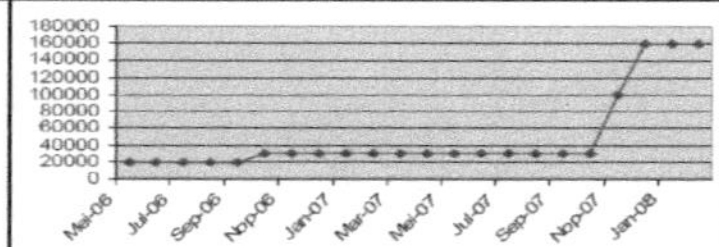	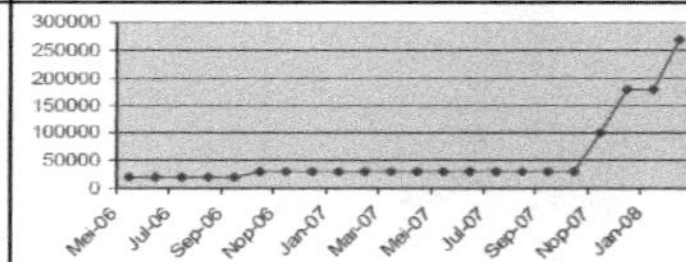
Indonesia Air Asia	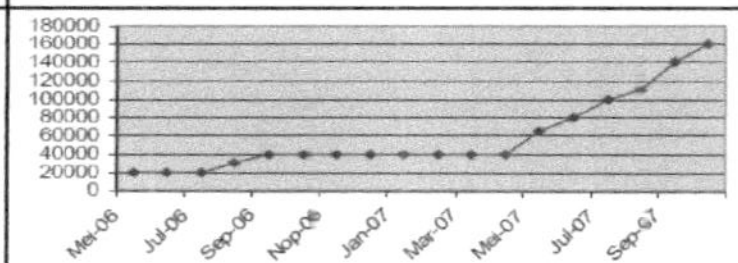	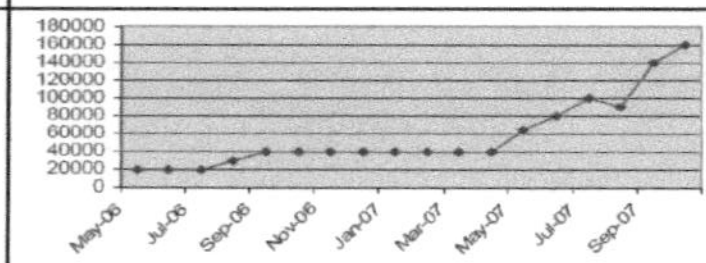	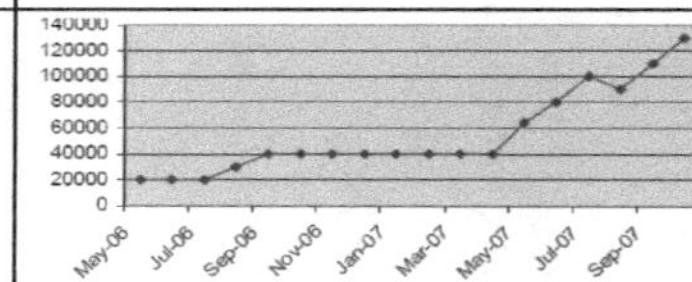

Subsequently, KPPU with the economic assistance from the statistical expert examined the causality between these prices for fuel surcharges to determine the existence of cartel prices practice after the annulment of association (INACA) decision for common fuel surcharge price. The method used was the correlation test and the homogeneity of variance test with the results as follows:

Graphic 5. Results of the Homogeneity Test of the FS Prices amongst the 12 Domestic Airlines

FS Price Fluctuation (0–1 hours) — Correlation Value (r) ≥ 0,90

	Sriwijaya	*Garuda*	*Mandala*	*Ekspress Air*	*Lion*	*Batavia*	*Kartika*	*Merpati*	*Wings*
Sriwijaya	1								
Garuda	0.981974	1							
Mandala	0.923059	0.955017	1						
Ekspress Air	0.980519	0.988032	0.957373	1					
Lion	0.963663	0.991556	0.971946	0.9755442	1				
Batavia	0.951784	0.969924	0.919332	0.9694725	0.948066	1			
Kartika	0.97582	0.987344	0.941961	0.9842514	0.972864	0.951313	1		
Merpati	0.960948	0.959447	0.978034	0.9727714	0.962488	0.929439	0.948065	1	
Wings	0.963663	0.991556	0.971946	0.9755442	1	0.948066	0.972864	0.962488	1

FS Price Fluctuation (1–2 hours) — Correlation Value (r) ≥ 0,90

	Sriwijaya	*Garuda*	*Mandala*	*Ekspress Air*	*Lion*	*Batavia*	*Kartika*	*Merpati*	*Wings*
Sriwijaya	1								
Garuda	0.993046	1							
Mandala	0.972223	0.98559	1						
Ekspress Air	0.988475	0.985138	0.983495	1					
Lion	0.973608	0.965744	0.952502	0.968962	1				
Batavia	0.968435	0.969687	0.957854	0.968775	0.943493	1			
Kartika	0.969977	0.964823	0.956135	0.974423	0.965464	0.947479	1		
Merpati	0.988282	0.979285	0.967557	0.990912	0.982715	0.958948	0.974337	1	
Wings	0.973608	0.965744	0.952502	0.968962	1	0.943493	0.965464	0.982715	1

FS Price Fluctuation (2–3 hours) — Correlation Value (r) ≥ 0,90

	Sriwijaya	*Garuda*	*Mandala*	*Ekspress Air*	*Lion*	*Batavia*	*Kartika*	*Merpati*	*Wings*
Sriwijaya	1								
Garuda	0.992584	1							
Mandala	0.971357	0.97637	1						
Ekspress Air	0.989441	0.982045	0.962812	1					
Lion	0.975925	0.959402	0.947762	0.968962	1				
Batavia	0.955953	0.96049	0.962909	0.966194	0.930562	1			
Kartika	0.980508	0.960801	0.940955	0.976508	0.963813	0.942611	1		
Merpati	0.992604	0.986143	0.959828	0.99419	0.979271	0.96793	0.977996	1	
Wings	0.978704	0.963876	0.955711	0.97824	0.986606	0.954725	0.966577	0.987366	1

In the following phases, KPPU also noticed that several internal meetings between these domestic airline companies occurred, as follows:

Graphic 6. Series of Internal Meetings between Domestic Airlines Companies, Association and the Ministry of Transportation

Nr.	Date	Venue	Agenda
1.	04th Mai 2006	Meeting room Pelita Airlines, Abdul Muis Jakarta Pusat	Discussing the Fuel surcharge due to increase of oil price
2.	30th Mai 2006	Meeting room Lion Air, Gajah Mada, Jakarta Pusat	Response to Press Release of KPPU on the prohibition of collective fuel surcharge prices
3.	19th September 2007	Meeting room of Gedung Cipta 3rd Fl.	Discussing the proposal for increasing FS due to Idul Fitri (Moslem religious big event)
4.	11th December 2007	Meeting room of INACA	Arrangement of Ceiling Prices (Max. Prices) of FS
5.	15th January 2008	Meeting room of INACA	Ceiling prices of FS
6.	07th Mai 2008	Meeting room of INACA	Discussing Justification of Elimination of PPN to FS
7.	15th September 2008	Meeting room of Garuda Indonesia	Discussing Ministerial Decree on FS
8.	05th August 2009	Meeting room of Mandala Airlines	Responding to Press Release of KPPU concerning Infringement Allegation
9.	03th November 2009	Meeting room, Merpati Nusantara Airlines	Revision of Ministerial Decree on FS
10.	17th November 2009	Meeting room, Merpati Nusantara Airlines	Revision of Ministerial Decree on FS

Decision: Embarking from those circumstantial facts and the existing legal evidences, KPPU decided as follows: *First,* although the written agreement through the decision of INACA to set cartel prices for fuel surcharges had been annulled, in fact there were significant prices parallelisms between May 2006 until March 2008. In addition, each of the alleged domestic airline company applied different formula for calculating the prices and the consumption volumes of avtur-oil. Based on the comprehensive analysis of circumstantial evidences using the economic statistical tests, the direct and indirect meetings between the companies and the association and the absence of reasonable economic justification from the companies for fuel surcharges prices stipulation, thus KPPU decided there had been tacit agreement between the domestic airline companies to commit cartel prices which is strictly prohibited by Article 5 Law No.5/1999. *Second*, KPPU decided that 4 airlines were not reasonably substantiated for infringing Article 5 Law No.5/1999 and thus acquitted.

4.2.2.5 Short Message Service (SMS) Telecommunication [Decision Number 26/KPPU-I/2007]

Case summary: Initially, after the implementation of Law No.5/1999, KPPU was faced by the challenge to substantiate the existence of prices cartel in the SMS cellular-tariff which is strictly prohibited by Article 5 Law No.5/1999. This prices cartel agreed between incumbent and new entrant companies engaging in the telecommunication sector in Indonesia. This prices cartel had been for several years realised through a several complex explicit and tacit agreement between 9 cellular operators.

Case Facts: Between the years 2004 and 2008 nine cellular operators, namely (1) Excelcomindo; (2) Telkomsel; (3) Indosat; (4) Telkom; (5) Hutschinson; (6) Bakrie Telecom; (7) Mobile-8; (8) Smart Telecom and (9) Natrindo Sel made several arrangements to set cartel prices particularly for the Short Message Services (SMS) for cellular-phone users. These cartel prices took place after the Government of Indonesia (GoI) issued the policies for elimination of telecommunication monopoly as well as the share cross-ownership requirements of telecommunication companies, as stipulated in the Law No.3 year of 1989 and the Telecommunication Minister Decision Nr. 72/1999. Consequently, there were only three principal telecommunication companies, namely: Telkomsel, Excelcomindo, and Indosat. Subsequently, there were other six new undertakins entering the telecommunication market. These nine telecommunication companies provided several telecommunication services, for instance: fixed line telephone, cellular phone, and fixed wireless access, and Multimedia Messaging Services

(MMS). However, all of these telecommunication companies offered one common service, namely SMS service. The SMS service market has several unique characteristics in terms of functionality, prices and characteristic. First, SMS service meanstext messages without voice and picture sent through a signaling canal. Second, the tariff for SMS service calculated based on the sums of sent messages and not levied on the SMS receiver. Additionally, the average tariffs of SMS service are lower than other telecommunication services. Third, the SMS service is for a unilateral communication and the volume of sent data is limited. In this case the SMS services were provided by all cellular operators within 33 provinces of Indonesia. Between the years of 2004 and2007 the basis tariffs of SMS services of the nine operators are as follows:

Table 2. Basis Tariff of SMS services

SMS Operator	Product	Destination	2004	2005	2006	2007
Telkomsel	Hallo	Off-net	250	250	250	250/350
	Hallo	On-net	250	250	250	250/350
	Simpati	Off-net	350	350	350	350
	Simpati	On-net	350	350	299	299
	Kartu AS	Off-net	300	300	300	299
	Kartu AS	On-net	300	150	150	149
Indosat	Matrix	Off-net	300	300	300	300
	Matrix	On-net	300	300	300	300
	IM 3	Off-net	350	350	350	350
	IM 3	On-net	N/A	150	150	150
	Mentari	Off-net	350	350	350	350
	Mentari	On-net	350	350	350	350
XL	xPlor	Off-net	250	250	250	250
	xPlor	On-net	250	250	250	250
	Bebas	Off-net	350	350	350	350
	Bebas	On-net	350	350	350	350
	Jempol	Off-net	299	299	299	299
	Jempol	On-net	99	99	99	99

Telkom	Flexi Classy	Off-net	N/A	N/A	N/A	250
	Flexi Trendy	On-net	N/A	N/A	N/A	350
Mobile 8	Fren post-paid	Off-net	N/A	N/A	N/A	250
	Fren pre-paid	Off-net	N/A	N/A	N/A	300
Bakrie	Esia pre-paid	Off-net	N/A	N/A	N/A	250
	Esia post-paid	Off-net	N/A	N/A	N/A	250
NTS	NTS pre-paid	Off-net	350	350	350	350

Note:
Off-net: SMS services between different operators
On-net: SMS services between same operators

At the outset, the prices parallelism of the SMS services was a result from the specific clause for prices maintenances of SMS services within the cooperation agreement of interconnection between the operators ("PKS Interkoneksi"). However, the Telecommunication Supervisory Body instructed the operators to revoke the agreement because it infringed the prohibition of Article 5 Law No.5/1999 pertaining cartel prices. Nevertheless, based on further inquiries of the KPPU as of 2004 until 2008, even without the existence of PKS Interkoneksi, the base tariffs of SMS services between the existing operators showed the prices parallelism. KPPU presumed that this prices parallelism could be either the main indication of the cartel practices or the result of market equilibriums. KPPU asserted further that, the share cross-ownership policy between the telecommunication companies in 1999 might largely cause the information exchanges chiefly amongst the principal operators: Telkomsel, Indosat and Excelcomindo. Accordingly, KPPU conducted further economic analysis of the SMS service tariffs using the methods called OVUM to determine whether there had been cartel prices even without the existence of written agreements.

Decision: KPPU examined firstly the case by invoking Article 1 No.7 of Law No.5/1999 pertaining the existence of an explicit and tacit agreement. KPPU was of the opinion that the tacit agreement to establish cartel prices in SMS services could be fully confirmed had two requirements fulfilled: First, the existence of prices parallelism for a certain period in the relevant market. Second, the information exchanges either directly or indirectly concerning the existing and future prices of SMS service between the operators. With regard to the prices parallelism, KPPU had concluded based on the legal and economic inquiries that the cartel prices had been existed before, during and after the PKS Interkoneksi agreement. The prices parallelism was not a result from the market equilibriums in the SMS service in Indonesia, but the result of the information exchanges between the principal operators as well as the secretive negotiations between the principal operators as the incumbent and the other six operators as the new entrants. Through these secretive negotiations the incumbent required the new entrants to abide with the recommended prices for SMS services for obtaining the cellular interconnections. Furthermore, the information exchanges activities between the incumbents were prompted by shares cross-ownership prescribed by the Law and the Ministerial Decision in 1999. Embarking from these juridical and economic enquiries in the relevant market of SMS service in Indonesia, KPPU finally could substantiate that 6 operators had infringed cartel prices prohibition according to Article 5 Law No.5/1999 both through the explicit "PKS Interkoneksi" agreement and secretive negotiations to maintain the cartel prices in the absence of written agreement. However, KPPU could not substantiate the other 3 operators for infringing cartel price prohibition pursuant to Article 5 Law No.5/1999 and thus acquitted these three operators.

4.3 Chapter Interim Result

Firstly, nowadays it has been generally accepted that cartels infringement is distinct from other types of competition law violations, namely due to its clandestine actors, secretive and lucrative practices. "The harder the investigations get, the smarter the suspects get" in cartel law enforcement efforts prompts competition law authority to employ special measures and impose a particular investigatory approach to detect cartels infringement. Thus, cartels frequently involve multiple cheatings. Further, cartels practice osften occurs in the oligopolistic market.

Accordingly, for the purpose of proving cartels infringement the competition law authorities have developed other types of evidences such as economic evidences to detect cartels practice. In a more advanced step, the Organisation for Economic Co-operation and Development (OECD) has introduced two categories of evidences in the detection and substantiation of cartels infringement nowadays, which are: Direct evidence and Indirect (circumstantial) evidences. The first type of evidence refers to *"Direct evidence of an agreement is that which identifies a meeting or communication between the subjects and describes the substance of their agreement. The most common forms of direct evidence are 1) documents (in printed or electronic form) that identify an agreement and the parties to it, and 2) oral or written statements by co-operative cartel participants describing the operation of the cartel.* Whereas, the second type of evidence refers to "*evidence that does not specifically describe the terms of an agreement, or the parties to it. It includes evidence of communications among suspected cartel operators and economic evidence concerning the market and the conduct of those participating in it that suggests concerted action.*" Nevertheless, the precedents of European Competition and German Cartel Laws have indicated that the indirect evidence (economic evidence) is not sufficient or adequate to substantiate cartels infringement, thus it requires the direct evidences as well, in the light of the high evidentiary standards, notably in the German Cartel Law.

Secondly, with regard to the 'plus-factors' and proving cartels infringement, the precedents of the Antitrust law have established that according to Section 1 of the Sherman Act, the Courts would not judge mere parallelism of actions of undertakings on a relevant market as cartels and thus punish these parallel behaviours. Furthermore, the Courts prerequisite the existences of evidences which '*tends to exclude the possibility that the alleged conspirators acted independently [...]. In other words, plaintiffs must show that the inference of conspiracy is reasonable in light of competing inferences of independent action or collusive action that could not have harmed plaintiffs.*' Hence, the Courts in the Antitrust cases, require the existence of 'plus-factors' in addition to the parallel actions on the relevant market in order to satisfactorily prove conspiracy or cartels by the undertakings. Moreover, the existence of 'plus-factors' has following drawbacks, as follows: *"two basic problems have attended judicial efforts to identify and evaluate plus factors. Firstly, courts have failed to establish any analytical framework that explains why specific plus factors have stronger or weaker evidentiary value or to present a hierarchy of such factors. Antitrust agreement decisions rarely rank plus factors according to their probative merit or specify the minimum critical mass of plus factors that must be established to sustain an inference that conduct resulted from concerted acts rather than from conscious parallelism. Nor do courts ordinarily devote great effort to evaluating the economic significance of each factor. This ad hoc approach makes judgments about the resolution of future cases problematic and gives an impressionistic quality to judicial decision making in agreement related disputes.* "[873]

Thirdly, the application of indirect (circumstantial) evidences and the Leniency programme for detecting cartels, which 'generally has secret nature of evidence' have not been an effective and comprehensive antitrust policy. An ideal Cartel law or policy aims both to provide deterrence effect and desistence impact to collusive practices by undertakings. The application of indirect (circumstantial) evidences and the Leniency programme were only complementary instruments to the cartels detection policy. Accordingly, the Cartel or Competition law Authorities should employ the proactive measures, for instance periodical market screenings focusing upon particular sectors (industries) and/or markets, in order to: identify alleged conduct on the market, determine competition rules violated and know groups of products or services concerned. Moreover, as regards to effective cartel detection policies or instruments, the Cartel or Competition law Authorities should take into considerations the following principles: First, they supposed to have potential capability to detect and deter cartels. Second, they could not be easily circumvented. Third, they shall take into consideration institutional capacities of competition law authorities. Fourth, they are supposed to consider a limited availability of public information.

Fourthly, in the Indonesian Competition Law, the implementation of circumstantial evidences creates a contradiction and legislative overlapping particularly with the rules of evidence in Article 184 section 1

873 Stroux, *EC and US Oligopoly Control* (n 51) 54–55.

of the Indonesian Criminal Proceedings Code (KUHAP) and Article 1866 of the Indonesian Civil Code (*Burgerlijk Wetboek* – KUHPerdata).[874] KUHAP and KUH Perdata provisions acknowledge the clues or indicators which correspond to circumstantial or indirect evidences. Nevertheless, for the District Court, this kind of evidence has insignificant evidentiary values and asserted that a mere evidentiary instrument is not an admissible evidence before the court in accordance with the *unus testis nullus testis* principle.[875] However, the Indonesia Supreme Court (MARI) Decision No. K/Pdt.Sus/2009 stated that "In Competition Law Perspective, a violation of the law could be based on some indirect evidence that correlated one another" Moreover, from the business practice point of view, the implementation of circumstantial evidences causes a misleading analysis in the cartel law enforcement.

Fifthly, as regards to the possibility of Leniency measure in the Indonesian Competition Law, although the Leniency has not been clearly regulated, the KPPU (the Commission for the Supervision of Business Competition) indeed employs the leniency programme. The legal basis of the KKPU was the Article 35 of the Indonesia Competition Law No.5/1999, whereas KPPU has been authorised to generate necessary legislation for implementing the provisions of the Indonesia Competition Law No. 5/1999, notably with regard to the implementation of the Leniency programme. In addition, by a systematic interpretation of Article 47 of the Indonesia Competition Law Number. 5/1999, which stipulates "*The Commission is authorized to impose administrative sanctions…* ", KPPU is able to implement the Leniency programme for cartel infringement.

874 The Indonesian Law No.8 year of 1981 on Criminal Procedural Law ('KUHAP') and the Indonesian Civil Code (Kitab-Undang-undang Hukum Perdata 1848).

875 Hukumonline, 'Proving Cartels Requires Extensive Investigations' ‹http://en.hukumonline.com/pages/lt4f1e5c482a5e9/proving-cartels-requires-extensive-investigations› accessed on 05th May 2012.

Chapter Five Conclusions

5.1 The Judicial Praxis in the European Competition and the German Cartel Laws

First, pursuant to the European Competition and German Cartel Laws as well as the Indonesian Competition Law Number 5/1999, the procedural law of cartels prohibition enforcement proceedings has been of profoundly important in order to safeguard 'the due processes of law'. This concept refers to the guarantee of constitutional and fundamental rights, which mandates that all legal proceedings will be fair and that one will be given notice of the proceedings and an opportunity to be heard before the public administration or governmental acts ('audi alteram et parte') to take away one's life, liberty, or property. Also, a constitutional rights guarantee that a law shall not be unreasonable, arbitrary or against the proportionality principle.

Principally, according to the European Competition and German Cartel Laws, the guiding principles of the procedural law play a very important role and have been regarded as the *acquis commune* constituting the legal foundations of the European Laws. These principles have been developed both by the Court of Justice of the EU in their duties of guaranteeing that 'the law is observed' pursuant to Article 19 (1) TEU as well as by other EU Organs through the respective legislations.

Furthermore, according to Article 2 TEU (Article 6(1) EU):

> "The Union is founded on the values of respect for human dignity, freedom, democracy, equality, the rule of law and respect for human rights, including the rights of persons belonging to minorities. These values are common to the Member States in a society in which pluralism, non-discrimination, tolerance, justice, solidarity and equality between women and men prevail".[876]

---

876 [876] Consolidated version of the Treaty on European Union,Title I Common Provisions OJ C 236, 7th August.2012

Thereby, these procedural law principles have profoundly substantial roles in the implementation of the EU Competition laws because of three reasons. First, the principles provide the basis for the fair and efficient administrative decision-making processes by ascertaining that the officials perform their duties independently and make decisions rationally a proportionally. Second, the principles shall operate as the guarantee for individuals or affected parties against arbitrary administrative acts by imposing the duty to provide reasons and the protection of fundamental and human rights. Third, the principles shall promote the accountability of the administrative acts towards the public, for example accessibility and transparency principles.

Equally important is the principle of presumption of innocence (*in dubio pro reo*). Although, the principle of *in dubio pro reo* is not enshrined in the Competition legislations, its application, however, has been emphasised in the provisions of Article 6 (2) of the European Convention of Human Rights (ECHR) and Sec. 261 of the German Code of Criminal Procedure (StPO).[877] Furthermore, according to Lianos and Genakos, the principle of 'in dubio pro reo' literary means 'when in doubt, in favour of the accused' or the presumption of innocence. This principles is incorporated in the Article 48 (1) of the Charter of Fundamental Rights of the European Union (ChFR-EU), which requires that 'any doubt in the mind of the Court must operate to the advantage of the undertaking to which the decision finding an infringement was addressed', in particular for decisions with fines in the competition law cases. Thus, in the Rhône-Poulenc case, it has been strongly argued as regards the 'in dubio pro reo' principle: "Considerable importance must be attached to the fact that the competition cases of this kind (cartels) are in reality of a penal nature, which naturally suggests that a high standard of proof is required (…). There must be a sufficient basis for the decision and any reasonable doubt for the benefit of the applicants according to the principle of *in dubio pro reo*." This principle is essentially important in the competition case presenting indirect (circumstantial) evidences, namely the economic evidences of a concerted practice of alleged undertakings. The European Courts

877 877 The German Code of Criminal Procedure (Strafprozeßordnung-StPO) of 23rd April 2014

have been reluctant to simply conclude the existence of concerted practices based upon merely price parallelism. Thus, the European Court demands a relatively higher standard of proof in order to prevent the false-positive error (type 1 error), by judging the oligopolistic interdependence as a cartel infringement against the Article 101 (1) TFEU.

Second, as regards to the evidentiary requirement standard in cartels cases, the German Cartel law in the civil, administrative and administrative fines (*Bußgeldverfahren*) prerequisites more sophisticated or higher evidentiary requirement standards than of the European competition law. In the German Cartel law, pursuant to the principle of unfettered consideration of evidences (*freie Beweiswürdigung*), to successfully prove an existence of cartels, a 'probable' or a 'large probability' were not adequate or insufficient, instead there must be 'personal certainty or assurance (*persönliche Gewissheit*)' as to the elements of cartels violation. Furthermore, in the German Cartel law, according to Sec. 81 of the GWB, the principle of '*in dubio pro reo*' has primacy over the European rules on burden of proof in the Regulation 1/2003. This juridical stance has been embraced by the Federal Republic of Germany in the Protocol to Article 2 of the Regulation 1/2003.[878] Nevertheless, the evidentiary requirement principles of the German Cartel law have invited several opposing opinions, that is to say, these could jeopardise or cause detrimental effects to the collectively 'coherent' implementation of the European competition laws. Accordingly, the European Court of Justice was of the opinion that the German Cartel law principles could be justified, provided these would not be contrary to the principle of "effectiveness" or "*effet utile*", which means the European laws shall be interpreted by the Member States 'as to ensure that the provisions retains their effectiveness', as has been stipulated in Article 4 para.3 of the Treaty European Union (TEU).

Third, with regard to the "plus-factors" and proving cartels infringement, the precedents of the Antitrust law have established that according to Section 1 of the Sherman Act, the Courts would not judge mere parallelism of actions of undertakings on a relevant market as

878 *Bundesrepublik Deutschland, ‚Protokollerklärung der Deutschen Delegation zu Art. 2 der Verordnung' (v. 10th December 2002, 15435/02 ADD 1, RC 22).*

cartels and thus punish these parallel behaviours. Furthermore, the Courts prerequisite the existences of evidences which '*tends to exclude the possibility that the alleged conspirators acted independently. In other words, plaintiffs must show that the inference of conspiracy is reasonable in light of competing inferences of independent action or collusive action that could not have harmed plaintiffs.*' Hence, the Courts in the Antitrust cases, require the existence of 'plus-factors' in addition to the parallel actions on the relevant market in order to satisfactorily prove conspiracy or cartels by the undertakings. Moreover, the existence of 'plus-factors' has following drawbacks, as follows:

> *"two basic problems have attended judicial efforts to identify and evaluate plus factors. Firstly, courts have failed to establish any analytical framework that explains why specific plus factors have stronger or weaker evidentiary value or to present a hierarchy of such factors. Antitrust agreement decisions rarely rank plus factors according to their probative merit or specify the minimum critical mass of plus factors that must be established to sustain an inference that conduct resulted from concerted acts rather than from conscious parallelism. Nor do courts ordinarily devote great effort to evaluating the economic significance of each factor. This ad hoc approach makes judgments about the resolution of future cases problematic and gives an impressionistic quality to judicial decision making in agreement related disputes."*[879]

Fourth, the application of indirect (circumstantial) evidences and the Leniency programme for detecting cartels, which 'generally has secret nature of evidence' have not been an effective and comprehensive antitrust policy. An ideal Cartel law or policy aims both to provide the deterrence effect and desistence impact to collusive practices by undertakings. The application of indirect (circumstantial) evidences and the Leniency programme were only complementary instruments to the cartels detection policy. Accordingly, the Cartel or Competition law Authorities should employ the proactive measures, for instance periodical market screenings focusing upon particular sectors (industries) and/or markets, in order to: identify alleged conduct on the market, determine competition rules violated and know groups of products or services concerned. Moreover, as regards to effective cartel detection policies or instruments, the Cartel or Competition law Authorities should take into considerations following principles: First, they sup-

879

posed to have potential capability to detect and deter cartels. Second, they could not be easily circumvented. Third, they shall take into account institutional capacities of competition law authorities. Fourth, they are supposed to consider a limited availability of public information.

Fifth, as regards to the European competition law, the ECJ, in the *Woodpulp* case requires a firm, precise and consistent body of evidences to substantiate the existence of agreement in the form of concerted practice.[880] This means: *First*, the parallel conduct of the undertakings like the prices parallelism in the market is not an evidence of concerted practice if the conduct of undertakings can be explained by market characteristics. Consequently, in accordance with the burden of proof principle the Court of Justice requires the Commission to demonstrate that the burden of proof cannot be shifted simply by finding of parallel conduct. *Second*, the Court of Justice asserted that cartel prohibition of Article [101 TFEU] "does not deprive economic operators of the right to adapt themselves intelligently to the existing and anticipated conduct of their competitors" or known as the oligopolistic interdependence.[881]

Third, the Court of Justice requires the comprehensive appraisal of plausible explanations to parallel conduct, which are: (1) price leader-

880 These evidentiary standards have been improved in the *Dresdner Bank Case v. Commission* (2002) whereas the General Court prerequisites a precise and and consistent evidence to substantiate a cartel infringement under Article 101 (1) TFEU. In other words, the more sophisticated economic analysis over the market structures and the behaviour of business operators together with the Plus factors such as network of joint ventures coordinated by a parent company, common board members, association of enterprises, and disclosure of decided course of conducts in the market to the competitors shall increasingly constitute the principal evidentiary requirements under Article 101 TFEU. *cf. Geradin, Farrar and Petit*, EU competition law and economics (n 33) 3.54 – 3.59.

881 In the *ratio decidenci* of the Court of Justice of the EU stated as follows:
[71] In determining the probative value of those different factors, it must be noted that parallel conduct cannot be regarded as furnishing proof of concertation unless concertation constitutes **the only plausible explanation of anticompetitive** conduct. It is necessary to bear in mind that although Article [101] of the Treaty prohibits any form of collusion which distorts competition, it does not deprive economic operators of the right to adapt themselves intelligently to the existing and anticipated conduct of their competitors.

ship and (2) market structures.[882] In the *Woodpulp* Case, the market structures comprise (1) nature of products, (2) the size and the number of undertakings and (3) the volume of the market in question were evaluated through the economic expertises for obtaining plausible explanation to determine the existence of concerted practices or conscious prices parallelism in the affected market.[883] Moreover, in the *Adalat* Case the Court of Justice required the 'requisite legal standards' to the existence of concurrence of wills.[884]

In the praxis of German Cartel law, the *Bundesgerichtshof* and the *Bundeskartellamt* have been very careful to implement the circumstantial evidences particulary the economic evidence to the concerted practice under Sec. 1 GWB.[885] In the *Benzinmarktoligopol* Case, the *Bundesgerichtshof* considered not only the periodical price parallelism in the petrol filling market as the primary *prima facie* evidence of cartel practice, but moreover the facilitating practices and the economic

882 In the competition theory the price leadership is classified into two parts: *First*, dominant price leadership. In this scenario an undertaking which having a dominant market share is able to act independently of its competitors, knowing that they would almost certainly follow suit. *Second*, barometric price leadership, whereas an undertaking as the leader is not dominant but is widely accepted as the best performing undertaking which is able to meet the demand and to adapt to evolving market conditions like cost increases. See Allenesalazar, Rafael, Oligopolies, Consicious Parallelism, and Concertation (n 751) 5–7.

883 In *the ratio decidendi*, the Court of Justice stipulates as follows:
[70] Since the Commission has no documents which directly establish the existence of concertation between the producers concerned, it is necessary to ascertain whether the system of quarterly price announcements, the simultaneity or near simultaneity of the price announcement and the parallelism of price announcements as found during the period from 1975 to 1981 constitute a firm, precise and consistent body of evidences of prior concertation.
[72] Accordingly, it is necessary in this case to ascertain whether the parallel conduct alleged by the Commission connot be explained otherwise than by concertation., by taking account of the nature of products, the size and the number of the undertakings and the volume of the market in question,

884 The Court of Justice repeals the Commission Decision and thus stipulated:
[77] In those circumstances, in order to determine whether the Commission has established to the requisite legal standard the existence of a concurrence of wills between the parties concerning the limitation of parallel exports, it is necessary to consider whether, as the applicant maintains, the Commission wrongly assessed the respective intentions of Bayer and the wholesalers. cf. Linklaters, A03700992/0.1/08 Jan 2004, p.1.

885 BGH, 06.12.11, KVR 95/10 *Benzinmarktoligopol* (n 861).

evidences prudently, which encompass: *Firstly*, the restricted access to the gasoline refinery supply. *Secondly*, market transparency particularly concerning the price. *Thirdly*, the product's homogeneity. *Fourthly*, sanction mechanism for collective compliance and also the direct and indirect communications such as about the prices between the competitors as one of the "Plus factor". Thus, the *Bundesgerichtshof* in the *Benzinmarktoligopol* Case dissented with the "partial examination" of the *OLG Düsseldorf* which not considered the market structures of the gasoline and petrol-filling stations within the affected period in Germany as a whole.[886]

5.2 The Judicial Practices in the Indonesian Competition Law Number 5/1999

Embarking from the judicial practices in Indonesia in particular amongst KPPU as the Competition Authorithy and the District Courts (PN) and the Indonesia Supreme Court (MARI), several comprehensions can be inferred which are as follows:

5.2.1 The Implementation of Circumstantial (Indirect) Evidence versus the Real Economic and Business Circumstances in Indonesia

According to *Iwantono*, a current representative from the Indonesian Chamber of Commerce (KADIN) and former KPPU Commissioner, argued that the implementation of circumstantial or indirect evidences of the Law No.5/1999 in the competition law enforcement could largely endanger the current economic and business activities because they do not reflect or explain the real business and economic conditions faced by Indonesian companies, notably as follows: First, prices parallelism. The real businesses conditions frequently show that price parallelism indicate an intensive competition, instead of cartel practice. The price parallelisms have often resulted from 'business shocks' from the

886 *Bundeskartellamt, Sektoruntersuchung Kraftstoffe* (n 864). See also Gleave, *Benzinpreise – Marktmacht, Preissetzung und Konsequenzen* (n 863).

demand and from the supply sides in the market. Second, the entry barriers to market. Due to the incredible 'sunk costs and fixed costs', several industries faced by huge natural entry barriers to market. Third, the excessive profits. Cartel practices are not, indeed the only viable way to obtain extraordinary profits, but moreover they largely resulted from efficiency, accurate business strategies, and profits from interests, *et cetera.* Fourth, the market multi-contacts. Naturally, companies with homogenous products will often make market multi-contacts with the competitors and *vice versa.* Fifth, production capacities and stocks. The companies often deliberately do not conduct full productions due to reserved industrial machineries. Sixth, the Common Board Members or Holding Company. It is reasonably normal for the companies integrated to a holding company to carry out business policies which are subject to instructive policies of a parent company.[887]

5.2.2 The Additional KPPU Regulation Related to Circumstantial or Indirect evidences to Complement Article 42 of the Law Number 5/1999

Article 42 of the Law No.5/1999, particularly letter (d) provides no elaborative explanations as to the clues or indications. Therefore, in 2006 KPPU released the Regulation No.1/ 2006 amended by KPPU Regulation No.1/2010 on Procedure for Cartel Enforcement Proceeding, which regulated the circumstantial or indirect evidences. Subsequently, KPPU issued Regulation No. 1/2010 concerning the Implementation of Article 11 on cartel infringement, whereas Article 36 of the Regulation No.1/2010 stipulates, among others: (1) documents or verbatims of meetings as to the price, quota and market zone cartel agreements, (2) comparation of conscious parallelism towards the price, quota and market zone cartels, (3) testimonies of the employees

887 S *Iwantono*, 'Kartel Dalam Perspektif Pelaku Usaha di Indonesia' (UPH Law Faculty National Seminar "Eradicating Cartel Practices in Indonesia: The Challenges of Indirect Evidence", Lippo Karawaci, 20th January 2012) 3–5.

and relevant parties knowing the cartel practices.[888] Furthermore, KPPU issued Regulation No.4/2011 on Implementation of Article 5 on price fixing, whereas KPPU is of the opinion that evidentiary rules of Article 5 largely applied to Article 11 rules of evidences on cartel. According to KPPU Regulation No.4/2011 section 4.4, there are two types of evidences to substantiate Article 5, which are: *First*, direct evidences. *Second*, indirect or circumstantial evidences.[889]

5.2.3 The Contentious Implementation of Indirect or Circumstantial Evidences in the Indonesian Legislation and Court Practice

From the normative point of view, the implementation of circumstantial evidences under the Law No.5/1999 creates a contradiction and legislative overlapping particularly with the rules of evidence in Article

888 Article 36 of the KPPU Regulation No.4/2010 mentions the following circumstantial evidences:
documents or verbatims of meetings as to the price, quota and market zone cartels;
documents or prices list records by the business actors;
data on the prices, production volume and total sales fluctuations;
production capacity data;
data on operational profits and *excessive profits*;
data results on conscious parallelism towards the prices coordination, quota production, market zone partitions;
financial statements of the alleged companies in the cartel infringement;
testimonies of relevant parties knowing the communication, coordinations and information exchanges between the cartel participants;
testimonies of Kesaksian para pelanggan atas keseragaman dan keselarasan harga;
Kesaksian karyawan atau mantan karyawan perusahaan.
See also *Anggraini*, 'Indirect Evidence Dalam Pembuktian Kartel (n 799) 2–8.

889 According to the KPPU Regulation No.4/2011:
"Indirect or circumstantial evidences are evidence instruments which indicate the price fixing agreement. This type of evidences can be used as the admissible evidences to support an allegation on cartel infringements. The circumstantial evidences comprise: Firstly, Communication evidence but which directly show a concurrence of wills. Secondly, Economic evidence, whose aims are to dismiss the possibility of an independent price fixing by the business actors. Thus, the circumstantial evidences which are appropriate and consistent with the market conditions and collusion can not serve as the complete evidence to the infringement against Article 5 of the Law No.5/1999." See Rizkiyana and Iswanto, *Eradicating Cartel (n 28) 5–8.*

184 section 1 of the Indonesian Criminal Proceedings Code (KUHAP) and Article 1866 of the Indonesian Civil Code (*Burgerlijk Wetboek* – KUHPerdata).[890] KUHAP and KUHPerdata provisions acknowledge the clues or indicators which correspond to circumstantial or indirect evidences. Nevertheless, for the District Court, this kind of evidence has insignificant evidentiary values and asserted that a mere evidentiary instrument is not an admissible evidence before the court in accordance with the *unus testis nullus testis* principle.[891] However, in the Indonesia Supreme Court (MARI) Decision No. K/Pdt.Sus/2009 stated that "In Competition Law Perspective, a violation of the law could be based on some indirect evidence that correlated one another [...]."[892] Moreover, from the business practice point of view, the implementation of circumstantial evidences causes a misleading analysis in the cartel law enforcement.[893]

5.2.4 The Premature and Anomaly Decisions of the Circumstantial or Indirect Evidences in KPPU and the Court Praxis

In the Pharmacy Cartel Case No. 17/KPPU-I/2010, KPPU made an erroneous decision which overly relied upon the prices parallelism of *Amlodipine antihypertension therapy* medicine between several pharmaceutical companies notably Pfizer as the indirect evidence, but not investigating comprehensively to substantiate the existence of prices

890 The Law No.8 year of 1981 on Criminal Procedure („KUHAP") and the Indonesian Civil Code (Kitab-Undang-undang Hukum Perdata 1848).

891 *Hukumonline*, Proving Cartels Requires Extensive Investigations (n 874).

892 In other words, for the Indonesian Supreme Court (MARI) the circumstantial evidences serve two functions in competition law case: First, to support the direct evidences. Second, as the preliminary evidence to cartel agreement whenever the direct evidences are absence. See *Rizkiyana and Iswanto*, 'Eradicating Cartel: The Use of Indirect Evidence' (n 28) 10.

893 According to Rizkiyana and Iswanto, "*Indirect evidence if the only evidence possessed in a cartel investigation has potentially negative consequences such as among others, in case of misleading analysis, may cause the contradiction between the result of economic analysis and the real fact or condition.*" ibid.

cartel agreement.[894] Subsequently, the KPPU's decision was recently annulled by the Indoneian Supreme Court (MARI) on June 2012.[895] In addition, this decision was in contrary with the KPPU decision on SMS Cellular Telecommunication Case No.26/KPPU-I/2007 whereby KPPU was initially able to substantiate the SMS interconnection agreements between the incumbent telecommunication operators and the new entrants companies. Subsequently, KPPU investigated the circumstantial or indirect evidences of cartel practices notably the periodical price increases and interlocking directory in Indosat and Telkomsel, which belonged to the same holding Singaporean company.[896] Nevertheless, in the Cement Cartel Case No. 01/KPPU-I/2010 KPPU made an unsual decision whereby KPPU found adequate indirect evidences such as prices parallelism and market zone partition facilitated by the Indonesian Cement Associaton (ASI) but not discovered sufficient documentary evidences to substantiate the allegation. KPPU deemed that price, production volume information exchanges and the marketing zone partition facilitated by ASI were allowed but instructed the dissolvement of ASI. Finally, KPPU decided that cartel infringement did not exist.[897]

5.2.5 The Leniency Programme's Implementation in the Indonesia Competition Law and the Institutional Strengthening of KPPU for Eradicating Cartels

Having comprehensively analysed and commentated on the jurisprudences concerning the cartel infringement substantiation, KPPU Commissioner and Indonesian competition law scholars have come to common argumentations, as follows:

894 KPPU stipulates in the Pharmacy Decision:
"That relates to parallel pricing, the Commission concludes there is a trend of rising prices the same between the Reported Party I (PT Pfizer Indonesia) and Reported Party II (PT Dexa Medica) against Norvask products and Tensivask", cf. *Rizkiyana and Iswanto*, 'Eradicating Cartel: The Use of Indirect Evidence' (n 28) 38–39.

895 Rizkiyana & Iswanto Number I/XII/ 02 ‹http://www.ri-advocates.com/files/R&I%20Newsletter%20I-XII-02.pdf› accessed on 20th July 2015.

896 KPPU Decision on the Short Message Service (SMS) Cartel (n 8).

897 KPPU Decision on the Industry Cement Cartel (n 6).

First, the Indonesian Competition Law No.5/1999 does not provide definitive and clear-cut provisions concerning the Leniency Programme.[898] The implementation of the Leniency Programme in Indonesian Competition Law is highly urgent because it has been very difficult to obtain a sound quality of direct evidences in cartel practices mainly due to 'reticence or silent code of ethic' between the cartel participating business actors. Thus, the Leniency Programme is the key to demolish this reticence practices by giving the proper incentives to the whistleblowers. Moreover, the implementation of Leniency Programme shall: (1) improve collection of intelligence and hard evidence, (2) increase difficulty of creating and maintaining cartels, (3) lower costs of adjudication, (4) provide restitution to injured parties. Second, the Indonesian Competition Law No.5/1999 shall give more judicial competences to obtain direct evidences for instance to seize, down raid, tape and power to search and to responsible mainly for the Leniency Programme's implementation.

898 Silalahi and Parluhutan, *Circumstantial Evidence in the Substantiation Mechanism against Cartel Infringements in Indonesia* (n 5) 12–17.

Bibliography

Books and Monographs

Agnew John H, Competition Law (1st Publ. Allen & Uwin 1985)

Akman Pinar, *The Concept of Abuse in EU Competition Law: Law and Economic Approaches* (Hart Publishing 2012)

Alese Femi, *Federal Antitrust and EC Competition Law Analysis* (1st Ed. Routledge Publishing 2008)

Alexander Christian, *Fälle zum Kartellrecht (Juristische Fall-Lösungen) Taschenbuch* (CH Beck, 2014)

Beaton-Wells Caron and Tan Christopher, *Anti-Cartel Enforcement in a Contemporary Age: Leniency Religion* (Bloomsbury Publishing, 2015)

Bechtold Rainer, *Kartellgesetz: Gesetz gegen Wettbewerbsbeschränkungen (§§ 1–96, 130, 131), Kommentar* (7 Aufl., CH Beck 2013)

Bidinger Ralph Müller, *Wettbewerbsrecht* (Berliner Wissenschafts-Verlag 2006)

Buccirossi Paolo, Deterrence in Competition Law (Wissenschaftszentrum Berlin für Sozialforschung 2009)

Boesche Katharina Vera, *Wettbewerbsrecht* (5 Aufl., C F Müller 2016)

Blanckenburg K von 'Detecting illegal activities: The case of cartels European journal of law and economics' (Vol.32(1) 2011)

Campbell Alan, *EC Competition Law: A Practitioner's Textbook (North-Holland Publishing Company*, 1980)

Damian Chalmers, Anthony Arnull, Alison Jones, *Competition Law Enforcement* (1, Oxford University Press 2015)

Dhall Vinod (ed.), *Competition Law Today: Concepts, Issues, and the Law in Practice (2nd Ed.* Oxford University Press 2007)

Dietze Philipp von and Janssen Helmut, *Kartellrecht in der Anwaltlichen Praxis* (CH Beck, 2015)

Drexl Josef, Idot Lauerence, Moneger Joel (eds.), *Economic Theory and Competition Law* (ASCOLA Competition Law Series, Edward Elgar 2009)

Dunne Niamh, *Competition Law and Economic Regulation: Making and Managing Markets* (Cambridge University Press 2015)

Emmerich Völker and Lange Kurt Werner, *Kartellrecht Juristische Kurz-Lehrbücher*, (CH Beck 2014)

Ezrachi Ariel, *EU Competition Law: An Analytical Guide to the Leading Cases (4th Edition.* Heart 2014)

Elhauge Einer and Geradin Damien, *Global Competition Law and Economics* (Hart 2008)

Ensthaler Jürgen, *Kartellrecht* (Springer 2013)

Faull Jonathan and Nikpay Ali, *The EU Law of Competition* (Oxford University Press 2017)

Frenz Walter, *Handbook of EU Competition Law* (Springer 2016)

Foster Nigel and Sule Sutish, *German Legal System & Laws* (4th Ed. Oxford University Press 2010)

Furse Mark, *Competition Law of the EC and UK* (6th Ed. Oxford University Press 2008)

Geradin Damien, Farrar Anne Layne, Petit Nicolas, *EU Competition Law and Economics.* (Oxford University Press 2012)

Gerber David *Global Competition: Law, Markets, and Globalization* (Oxford University Press 2010)

Gifford Daniel J and Kurdle Robert T., *The Atlantic Divide in Antitrust: An Examination of US and EU Competition Policy* (Chicago University Press, 2015)

Glader Marcus, *EU Competition Law and US Antitrust Law: New Horizons in Competition Law and Economics Series* (Edward Elgar 2006)

Götting Horst-Peter, Hetmank Sven, Marx Martin and Wündisch Sebastian, *Wettbewerbsrecht und Wettbewerbsprozessrecht* (C.H. Beck 2016)

Goyder DG, *EC Competition Law* (Oxford University Press 2003)

Gugerbaue Norbert, *Wettbewerbs- und Kartellrecht: [EU-Kartellrecht mit dem Kartell- und Wettbewerbsrecht in Deutschland Und Österreich]* (Linde 2015)

Harahap Muhammad Yahya, *Pembahasan Permasalahan dan Penerapan KUHA (Edisi* 2. Sinar Grafika 2000)

–,*Hukum Acara Perdata: Tentang Gugatan, Persidangan, Penyitaan, Pembuktian, dan Putusan Pengadilan (Edisi* 2 Sinar Grafika 2005)

Haucap Justus and Schmidt Ingo, *Wettbewerbspolitik und Kartellrecht: Eine interdisziplinäre Einführung (*10 Aufl., Oldenbourg Wissenschaftsverlag 2013)

Heidenhain Martin, *German Antitrust Law: An Introduction to the German Antitrust Law with German Text and Synoptic English Translation of the Act against Restraints of Competition (4th Ed Fritz Knapp Verlag* 1991)

Heße Manfred, *Wettbewerbsrecht: Schnell Erfasst* (Springer 2006)

Hönn Günther, *Klausurenkurs im Wettbewerbs- und Kartellrecht: Ein Fallbuch zur Wiederholung und Vertiefung (Schwerpunkte Klausurenkurs) Taschenbuch* – 9. (CF Müller 2013)

Hofmann Herwig C, Rowe Gerard C and Türk Alexander H, Administrative Law and Policy of the European Union (Oxford University Press 2011)

Hüschelrath Kai and Schweitzer Heike (Eds.), Public and Private Enforcement of Competition Law in Europe (ZEW Economic Studies Springer 2014)

Hofmann Herwig C, Rowe Gerard C and Türk Alexander H, Administrative Law and Policy of the European Union (Oxford University Press 2011)

Horst Albach, Collusion Through Information Sharing? New Trends in Competition Policy (Sigma Publishing 1996)

HolterhusTill Patrik, *Beweisführung in der Europäischen Fusionskontrolle: Regelungserfordernis und Regelungsbestand im Spannungsfeld von Wahrheit und Wahrscheinlichkeit* (Veröffentlichungen zum Verfahrensrecht 104, Mohr Siebeck Verlag 2014)

Jephcott Mark, *The Law of Cartels* (2th. Ed. Jordans Publishing 2011)

Jones Alison and Sufrin Brenda, *EU Competition Law: Text, Cases, and Materials* (4th Ed. Oxford University Press 2011)

–, *EU Competition Law: Text, Cases, and Materials* (5th Ed. Oxford University Press 2014)

Karenfort Jörg and Weitbrecht Andreas, *Entscheidungen zum Europäischen Kartellrecht: Die Entscheidungen des Europäischen Gerichtshofes, des Europäischen Gerichts und der Europäischen Kommission* (Mohr Siebeck 2010)

Kerse C.S. and Khan Nicholas, *EU Antitrust Procedure* (6th Ed., Sweet and Maxwell 2012)

Kingston Suzanne, *Greening EU Competition Law and Policy* (Cambridge University Press 2012)

Klees Andreas, *Europäisches Kartellverfahrensrecht: mit Fusionskontrollverfahren* (1 Aufl. Carl Heymanns Verlag 2011)

Kokkoris Ioannis, Competition Cases from The European Union: The Ultimate Guide to Leading Cases from the EU, Member States and EFTA (2nd Ed. Sweet and Maxwell 2010)

Krebs Peter and Becker Maximillian, *Lexikon des Wettbewerbsrechts: Kartellrecht und Lauterkeitsrecht-Taschenbuch* (CH Beck 2014)

Kling Michael and Thomas Stefan, *Kartellrecht* (Franz Vahlen Verlag 2016)

Korah Valentine, *An Introductory Guide to EC Competition Law and Practice* (9th Ed. Hart Publishing 2007)

Lianos Ioannis and Geradin Damien (eds.), *Handbook on European Competition Law Substantive Aspects* (Edward Elgar Publishing 2013)

–, *Handbook on European Competition Law: Enforcement and Procedure* (Edward Elgar Publishing 2013)

Monti Giorgio, *EC Competition Law*: Law in Context (Cambridge University Press, 2007)

Magen Albrecht, *Lizenzverträge und Kartellrecht Bücher des Betriebs-Beraters* (Verlag Gesellschaftsrecht und Wirtschaft 1963)

Nagy Csongor István, *EU and US Competition Law: Divided in Unity? The Rule on Restrictive Agreements and Vertical Intra-brand Restraints* (1st Ed. Routledge 2013)

Niels Gunner, Jenkins Helen and Kavanagh James, *Economics for Competition Lawyers* (2nd Ed, Oxford University Press 2011)

Noonan Chris, *The Emerging Principles of International Competition Law* (Oxford University Press 2008)

Kettler Stefan Hans *Wörterbuch gewerblicher Rechtsschutz und Urheberrecht: Englisch - Deutsch, Deutsch - Englisch = Dictionary of Intellectual Property and Unfair Competition Law* (CH Beck 20119)

Khemani R S A *Framework for the Design and Implementation of Competition Law and Policy* (World Bank 1999)

Law Jonathan, *Antitrust Law* (9th Ed. Oxford University Press 2018)

Lenaerts Koen, Maselis Ignace, Gutman Kathleen (eds.), *EU Procedural Law* (Oxford University Press 2014)

Lianos Ioannis and Sokol Daniel D, *The Global Limits of Competition Law* (Stanford University Press, 2012)

Lovdahl Gormsen Liza, *A Principled Approach to Abuse of Dominance in European Competition Law* (Cambridge University Press 2010)

Papadopoulos Anestis S., *The International Dimension of EU Competition Law and Policy* (Cambridge University Press 2010)

Posner Richard A., *Antitrust Law* (2nd Ed. University of Chicago Press 2001)

Reiner Schulze and Hoeren Thomas, *Dokumente zum Europäischen Recht (Band 3: Kartellrecht bis 1957* Springerlink, 2000)

Ritter Lennart Kurt, Braun W. David, *European Competition Law: A Practitioner's Guide* (3rd Ed. Kluwer Law International 2005)

Rosengarten Joachim, Burmeister Frank and Klein Martin, *Mergers &Acquisitions in Germany* (CH Beck 2016)

Ruffner Markus, *Neue Wettbewerbstheorie und Schweizerisches Kartellrecht: Möglichkeiten und Grenzen Einer Markt- und Institutionentheoretischen Fundierung der Wettbewerbspolitik* (Schulthess Polygraphischer Verlag 1990)

Schmidt Ingo *Wettbewerbspolitik und Kartellrecht: Eine Interdisziplinäre Einführung* (Oldenbourg 2012)

Schmidtchen Dieter, Albert Max, Voigt Stefan (eds) *The More Economic Approach to European Competition Law* (Mohr Siebeck 2007)

Schwalbe Ulrich and Zimmer Daniel, *Law and Economics in European Merger Control* (Oxford University Press 2009)

Schwintowski Hans Peter, *Wettbewerbs- und Kartellrecht (C.H.* Beck 2007)

Sibony Anne Lise, *Le Juge Et Le Raisonnement Économique En Droit De La Concurrence Judges and Economic Reasoning in Competition Law* (L.G.D.J. 2008)

Siragusa Mario, *EU Competition Law: III Book (2 Ed. Claeys & Casteels Publishing 2012)*

Stroux Sigrid *US and EC Oligopoly Control* (International Competition Law Series, volume 14, Kluwer Law International 2004)

van Bael and Bellis, *Competition Law of the European Community* (4 Ed., Kluwer Law International 2005)

van den Bergh Roger and Camesasca Peter D., *European Competition Law and Economics: A Comparative Perspective* (2 Ed. Sweet & Maxwell 2006)

Whish Richard and Bailey David, *Competition Law* (8th Ed, Oxford University Press 2017)

–, *Competition Law* (7th Ed. Oxford University Press 2012)

Commentaries

Säcker, Franz Jürgen, Bornkamm Joachim and Montag Frank, *Münchener Kommentar europäisches und deutsches Wettbewerbsrecht (Kartellrecht): Kartellrecht, Missbrauchs- und Fusionskontrolle Band 1: Europäisches Wettbewerbsrecht* (CH Beck, 2015)

–,*Münchener Kommentar europäisches und deutsches Wettbewerbsrecht (Kartellrecht): Kartellrecht, Missbrauchs- und Fusionskontrolle Band 2: Deutsches Wettbewerbsrecht* (CH Beck, 2015)

Säcker Franz Jürgen, *The Concept of the Relevant Product Market: Between Demand-side Substitutability and Supply-side Substitutability in Competition Law* (Peter Lang Verlag, 2008)

Säcker Franz Jürgen (ed), *Handbuch zum Deutsch-Russischen Energierecht* (1 Aufl. CH Beck 2010)

Säcker Franz Jürgen, Rixecker Roland, Oetker Hartmut, Limperg Bettina, *Münchener Kommentar zum Bürgerlichen Gesetzbuch: BGB, Band 7: Sachenrecht §§ 854–1296, WEG* (CH Beck 2017)

Säcker Franz Jürgen, Rixecker Roland, Oetker Hartmut, Limperg Bettina, *Internationales Wettbewerbs- und Kartellrecht (IntWettbR/IntKartellR). Münchener Kommentar zum BGB* (7. Aufl. CH Beck 2018)

Berg Werner and Mäsch Gerard (eds), *Deutsches und Europäisches Kartellrecht: Kommentar* (3 Aufl. Luchterhand 2018)

Berg Werner, *Deutsches und Europäisches Kartellrecht: Kommentar* (2 Aufl. Luchterhand, 2015)

Bechtold Rainer and Bosch Wolfgang (eds), *Gesetz gegen Wettbewerbsbeschränkungen: GWB §§ 1–96, 185, 186:* Kommentar (8 Aufl. CH Beck 2015)

Busche Jan and Röhling Andreas (eds), Kölner Kommentar zum Kartellrecht Bände 1–4, Band 1: Deutsches Kartellrecht §§ 1–34a GWB (Carl Heymanns Verlag 2017)

Calliess Christian and Ruffert Martin, *EUV/AEUV: Das Verfassungsrecht der Europäischen Union mit Europäischer Grundrechtcharta: Kommentar* (5 Aufl. CH Beck 2014)

Doehner Gerhard, Hoffmann Jochen, *Münchener Handbuch des Gesellschaftsrechts Bd. 2: 16 Wettbewerbsverbot* (5. Aufl. CH Beck 2019)

Godin Hans von and Hoth Jürgen, *Wettbewerbsrecht: Kommentar zum Gesetz gegen den unlauteren Wettbewerb nebst Warenzeichenverletzungen, Zugabeverordnung und Rabattgesetz (Sammlung Guttentag) Gebundenes Buch – 1. September 1974* (De Gruyter & Co Verlag, 2011)

Grabitz Eberhard, Hilf Meinhard and Nettesheim Martin, *Das Recht der Europäischen Union, Band I EUV/AEUV* (Werkstand: 66. EL CH Beck 2019)

Hoeren Thomas, Sieber Ulrich and Holznagel Bern, *Handbuch Multimedia Recht* (48 Ergänzunglieferung CH Beck 2019)

Henssler Martin and Strohn Lutz, *Gesellschaftsrecht: Kommentar:* BGB-HGB-PartGG-GmbhG-AktG-GenG-UmwG-InsO-AnfgG-InGesR (4Aufl. CH Beck 2019)

Mestmäcker Ernst Joachim and Immenga Ulrich (eds.), *Wettbewerbsrecht, Band 1: EU. Kommentar zum Europäischen Kartellrecht* (6 Aufl. CH Beck 2019)

–, *Wettbewerbsrecht, Band 2 GWB/Teil 1: Kommentar zum Deutschen Kartellrecht* (6 Aufl. CH Beck 2019)

–, *Wettbewerbsrecht, Band 1/Teil 1* (5 Aufl. CH. Beck 2012)

–, *Wettbewerbsrecht, Band 2/Teil 1 und 2* (5 Aufl, CH Beck 2012)

Mestmäcker Ernst Joachim and Schweitzer Heike, *Europäisches Wettbewerbsrecht* (3Aufl CH Beck 2014)

Kapp Umnuß, *Corporate Compliance Checklisten Kapitel 9. Kartellrecht* (3 Aufl, CH Beck 2017)

Kamann Hans Georg, Ohlhoff Stefan and Völcker Sven B, *Kartellverfahren Und Kartellprozess: Handbuch* (CH Beck 2017)

Langen Eugen, Bunte Hermann Josef, Bahr Christian, *Kartellrecht: Kommentar* (12 Aufl. Luchterhand 2014)

Loewenheim Ulrich, Meessen Karl M., Lindemann Hans Jürgen Meyer, Riesenkampff Alexander, *Kartellrecht: Kommentar* (3 Aufl. CH Beck 2016)

Löwisch Manfred and Rieble Volker, *Tarifvertragsgesetz* (4. Aufl. CH Beck 2017)

Schulte Josef and Just Christoph (eds.) *Kartellrecht: GWB, Kartellvergaberecht, EU-Kartellrecht: Kommentar* (Carl Heymanns Verlag 2016)

Wiedemann Gerhard, *Handbuch des Kartellrechts* (3 Aufl. CH Beck 2016)

Journal Articles

Andreoli-Patrick Versbach and Franck J U, 'Econometric Evidence to Target Tacit Collusion in Oligopolistic Markets' '(Journal of Competition Law & Economics OUP 2013)

Muhammad Ali 'Penerapan Alat Bukti Petunjuk dalam Perkara Pidana' (Jurnal Hukum Bisnis 2013)

Anggraini Anna Maria Tri, 'Penggunaan Analisis Ekonomi Dalam Mendeteksi Kartel Berdasarkan Hukum Persaingan Usaha (Jurnal Hukum PRIORIS, Vol.3/Nr. 3 2013)

Caffarra C and Walker M, 'An Exploration into the Use of Economics before Courts in Europe' '(Journal of European Competition Law & Practice 2011)

Christiansen Arndt and Kerber Wolfgang 'Competition Policy with Optimally Differentiated Rules Instead of 'Per Se Rules Vs Rule of Reason'(Journal of Competition Law & Economics 2006)

Chowdhury A and Jenkins H, 'Inference or Evidence? The Uncertain Fate of Patent Settlement Agreements' (Journal of European Competition Law & Practice 2018)

Damgaard MT, Ramada P, Conlon G and Godel M, 'The Economics of Cartels: Incentives, Sanctions, Stability, and Effects' '(Journal of European Competition Law & Practice 2011)

Deng Ai, 'Cartel Detection and Monitoring: A Look Forward' '(Journal of Antitrust Enforcement 2017)

Capobianco Antonio. 'Information Exchange under EC Competition Law' (Common Market Law Review, Vol.41(5), 2015)

Chin W. 'Do Price Increases While Demand Is Falling Indicate Collusion?' (Journal of Competition Law & Economics 2011)

Damgaard MT, Ramada P, Conlon G and Godel M, 'The Economics of Cartels: Incentives, Sanctions, Stability, and Effects' (Journal of European Competition Law & Practice 2011)

Deng Ai, 'Cartel Detection and Monitoring: A Look Forward' '(Journal of Antitrust Enforcement 2017)

Engel Christopher How Much Collusion? A Meta-Analysis of Oligopoly Experiments (Journal of Competition Law & Economics, Vol.3/4 2007)

Frank N and Lademann R P, 'Economic Evidence in Private Damage Claims: What Lessons Can Be Learned from the German Cement Cartel Case?' (Journal of European Competition Law & Practice 2010)

Fung SS, Yu Y and Ridyard D, 'The Use of Economics in the Anti-Monopoly Law of China' (Journal of European Competition Law & Practice 2015)

Gavil AI, 'The Challenges of Economic Proof in a Decentralized and Privatized European Competition Policy System: Lessons from the American Experience' '(Journal of Competition Law & Economics 2008)

Greg, Shaffer 'Market-Share Contracts as Facilitating Practices' (RAND Journal of Economics Vol. 41 (4) 2010)

Ghezzi Federico and Maggiolino Mariateresa, 'Bridging EU Concerted Practices with U.S. Concerted Actions' (Journal of Competition Law & Economics Vol. 10/3 2014)

Ginsburg Douglas H, 'Comparing Antitrust Enforcement in the United States and Europe' (Journal of Competition Law & Economics 2005)

Harrington Joseph E, 'Posted Pricing as a Plus Factor' (Journal of Competition Law & Economics 2011)

Houwen Fred, European Court of Justice Clarifies Circumstances in Which Financial Institutions May Exchange Credit Information without Breaching Competition Law (Journal of Financial Regulation and Compliance Vol16 (1) 2008)

Hüschelrath Kai and Laitenberger Ulrich, 'The Settlement Procedure in the European Commission's Cartel Cases: An Early Evaluation' (Journal of Antitrust Enforcement 2017)

Junaidi Ahmad, 'Pembuktian Kartel dalam UU No.5/1999" (Jurnal Kompetisi, edisi 11 2008)

–,'Bukti Petunjuk dan Pembuktian Keadaan dalam Perkara Persaingan' (Jurnal Hukum Bisnis 2013)

Johnson JH and Leonard GK, 'Economics and the Rigorous Analysis of Class Certification in Antitrust Cases' (Journal of Competition Law & Economics 2007)

Kim N and Kim Y, 'Who Confesses for Leniency? Evidence from Korea' (Journal of Competition Law & Economics 2016)

Kaplow Louis 'On the Meaning of Horizontal Agreements in Competition Law' (Calif. L. Rev., Vol.99 2011)

Koki Arai 'Indirect Evidence in Japanese Cartel Control' (International Review of Intellectual Property and Competition Law Vol.46 2015)

Koenig Carsten, 'An Economic Analysis of the Single Economic Entity Doctrine in EU Competition Law' (Journal of Competition Law & Economics 2017)

Kovacic William E, Marshall Robert C, Marx Leslie M, White Halbert L. ,Plus Factors and agreement in Antitrust Law (Michigan Law Review Vol.110 (3) 2011)

Lubis Andi Fahmi, Analisis Ekonomi dalam Pembuktian Kartel (Jurnal Hukum Bisnis Vol. 32/5 2013)

Marx Leslie M., Mezzetti Claudio 'Effects of Antitrust Leniency on Concealment Effort by Colluding Firms' (Journal of Antitrust Enforcement 2014)

Petersen Niels 'Antitrust Law and the Promotion of Democracy and Economic Growth' (Journal of Competition Law & Economics 2013)

Ramos Alvaro, 'Exchange of Information as Restriction by Object? The STANPA Cases in Spain' (Journal of European Competition Law & Practice 2011)

Ritter Cyril, 'Presumptions in Eu Competition Law' (Journal of Antitrust Enforcement 2018)

Rusu CS, 'Eturas: Of Concerted Practices, Tacit Approval, and the Presumption of Innocence' (Journal of European Competition Law & Practice 2016)

Schinkel Maarten Pieter, 'Forensic Economics in Competition Law Enforcement' '(Journal of Competition Law & Economics 2008)

Sidak J Gregory, 'Court-Appointed Neutral Economic Experts' (Journal of Competition Law & Economics 2013)

Silalahi M. Udin. 'Indirect Evidence dalam Hukum Persaingan Usaha' (Jurnal Hukum Bisnis 2013)

Silalahi M. Udin and Parluhutan Dian. 'The Necessity of ASEAN Competition Law: Rethinking' (Hasanuddin Law Review 2017)

–, 'Circumstantial Evidence in the Substantiation Mechanism Against Cartel Infringements in Indonesia' (Jurnal Hukum Bisnis 2011)

Silalahi and I C Edgina, 'Pembuktian Perkara Kartel Di Indonesia Dengan Menggunakan Bukti Tidak Langsung (*Indirect Evidence*) Kajian Putusan KPPU Nomor 17/KPPU-I/2010 dan Nomor 08/KPPU-I/2014 serta Putusan Nomor 294 K/PDT.SUS/2012 dan Nomor 221 K/PDT.SUS-KPPU/2016' (Jurnal Yudisial Vol. 10 No. 3 Desember 2017)

Simbolon, A.P. 'Bukti Tidak Langsung dalam Menentukan Pelanggaran UU No.5 Tahun 1999: Studi Kasus Industri Minyak Goreng Sawit'(Jurnal Hukum Bisnis 2013)

Svirinas Daivis 'The Assessment of Information Exchange Agreements Between Competitors from the Perspective of Competition Law of the EU and of the Republic of Lithuania'(Jurisprudencija Vol. 19 2012)

Temple Lang J, 'The Strengths and Weaknesses of the DG Competition Manual of Procedure' (Journal of Antitrust Enforcement 2013)

Toha Kurnia,'Extraterritorial Applicability of Indonesia Business Competition Law as an Efforts Dealing ASEAN Single Market (Journal of Dinamika Hukum Vol.15 2015)

Veri Antoni. 'The Position of Indirect Evidence as Verification Tools in the Cartel Case.' (Mimbar Hukum Universitas Gadjah Mada 2014)

Vilaca Jose Luis da Cruz, 'The Intensity of Judicial Review in Complex Economic Matters -Recent Competition Law Judgments of the Court of Justice of the EU' '(Journal of Antitrust Enforcement 2018)

Whelan Peter, 'CISAC: How Difficult It Is to Prove a Concerted Practice' (Journal of European Competition Law & Practice 2013)

Wils WPJ, 'Antitrust Compliance Programmes and Optimal Antitrust Enforcement' (Journal of Antitrust Enforcement 2013)

National Competition Commission Document

The German Federal Cartel Office-*Bundeskartellamt,* 'Bekanntmachung Nr. 18/2007 des Bundeskartellamtes über die Nichtverfolgung von Kooperationsabreden mit geringer wettbewerbsbeschränkender Bedeutung („Bagatellbekanntmachung")' 13. März 2007

The German Federal Cartel Office -*Bundeskartellamt,*'*Sektoruntersuchung Kraftstoffe (B8-200/09) Abschlussbericht*' Mai 2011

The German Federal Cartel Office- *Bundeskartellamt,*'Jahresbericht 2017'

ASEAN Secretariat Document

ASEAN Secretariat, 'ASEAN Economic Community' (2008)

ASEAN Secretariat, 'ASEAN Economic Community Blueprint' (2008)

ASEAN Secretariat 'ASEAN Regional Guidelines on Competition Policy' (2010)

ASEAN Secretariat 'An ASEAN Competition Action Plan 2016–2025' (2016)

Theses and Dissertation

Sadhya Madhubanti, 'Concerted action in an oligopoly and the role of plus factors' (LL.M Thesis, West Bengal University of Juridical Science, India, 2012)

Arvidsson Klas, 'Re-Use of PSI and the Undertaking Concept in the EU Competition Law' (LL.M Thesis Law Faculty Stockholm University, 2014) 21–24.

Vereecken Bram 'Hub and Spoke Cartels in EU Competition Law' (LLM Thesis Faculty of Law Academic Year 2014–15 Universiteit Gent)

Zega Inggrid G, ‚Tinjauan Mengenai Indirect Evidence (Bukti Tidak Langsung) sebagai Alat Bukti Dalam Kasus Dugaan Kartel Fuel Surcharge Maskapai Penerbangan di Indonesia.*(*Tesis Magister Hukum, Pascasarjana Universitas Indonesia, Jakarta 2012)

S Johri 'Attribution of Price Parallelism as Cartels under the Competition Act, 2002' (Dissertation submitted to Competition Commission of India, Nirma University 2012)

Conference Papers and Presentations

Bailey David, 'Gas Insulated Switchgear' (Presentation Paper for the Workshop Milestone Judgement in Competition Law, States Network for Economic Development in Collaboration with the Barbados Fair Trading, 30–31 July 2012)

Gleave S, ‚*Benzinpreis – Marktmacht, Preissetzung und Konsequenzen*' (*Bundeskartellamt Sitzung des Arbeitskreises Kartellrecht* 6. Oktober 201)

Iwantono Sutrisno, 'Kartel Dalam Perspektif Pelaku Usaha di Indonesia' (UPH Law Faculty National Seminar "Eradicating Cartel Practices in Indonesia: The Challenges of Indirect Evidence", Lippo Karawaci, 20th January 2012)

Kekevi, H G 'Can Economics Help Us with Cartel Detection?' (Presentation to the International Competition Network Cartel Workshop Lisbon, Portugal October 28, 2008

Kirchhoff Wolfgang, 'Requirements of proof in court – the economic approach: Introductory Statement' (Judge, Federal Court of Justice, Germany IKK Berlin April 15, 2011

Parluhutan Dian, 'Analysis of Judicial Procedural Cooperation in *Antitrust Matters in the ASEAN Countries for Accelerating ASEAN Economic Community (AEC): Quo Vadis?* (Presentation 16th Asian Law Institute Conference Singapore June 2019)

Rizkiyana Rikrik and Iswanto Vovo, 'Eradicating Cartel: The Use of Indirect Evidence' (UPH Law Faculty National Seminar "Eradicating Cartel Practices in Indonesia: The Challenges of Indirect Evidence", Lippo Karawaci, 20th January 2012)

Ruky Inne Minara, 'Economic Evidence Dalam Pembuktian Kartel' (UPH Law Faculty National Seminar Eradicating Cartel Practices in Indonesia: The Challenges of Indirect Evidence, Lippo Karawaci, 20th January 2012)

Silalahi M Udin 'Circumstantial Evidence Dalam Memberantas Kartel Berdasarkan Hukum Persaingan Usaha' (UPH Law Faculty National Seminar Eradicating Cartel Practices in Indonesia: The Challenges of Indirect Evidence, Lippo Karawaci, 20th January 2012)

Slobodenjuk Dimitri 'Parallel Behaviour under EU Antitrust Law' (Presentation Paper, IBA Conference 1st CIS Competition Law, Clifford Chance, London 8–9 December 2011

Sirait Ningrum Natasya, 'Overview of the Indonesia Competition Law Number 5/1999 concerning Prohibition of Monopolistic Practices and Unfair Business Competition' (Presentation Paper, Law School University Sumatra Utara, 2015)

Competition Authority and Court Decisions

European Union (EU)

European Court of Justice (ECJ) Joined Cases C-2/01 P and C-3/01 P "Bayer AG v Commission of the European Communities"

European Court of Justice Joined Cases C-89/85, C-104/85, C-114/85, C-116/85, C-117/85 and C-125/85 to C-129/85 "*Ahlström Osakeyhtiö and others v Commission (Woodpulp Case)*"

European Court of Justice Case C-180/16 P, 'Toshiba Corp. v European Union Commission' ("Gas Insulated Switchgear-GIS Cartel Case")

Federal Republic of Germany

The German Supreme Court-*Bundesgerichtshof* Kartellsenat, KVR 3/82, 04.10.1983, *Gemeinschaftsunternehmen für Mineralölprodukte (Texaco-Zerssen)*

The German Supreme Court-*Bundesgerichtshof* Beschluss vom 6. Dezember 2011 - KVR 95/10, *Total/OMV Tankstelle*

Republic Indonesia

Judgement of the Indonesian Supreme Court (MARI) Number 221 K/Pdt.Sus-KP-PU/2016 Tahun 2016, PT. Bridgestone Tire Indonesia and Parties v. Indonesian Supervisory Commission for Business Competition (KPPU) ("Automotive Tire Cartel")

Judgement of the Indonesian Higher Court (Pengadilan Tinggi) 70/Pdt.Sus-KP-PU/2015/PN.Jkt.Pst, PT. Bridgestone Tire Indonesia and Parties v. Indonesian Supervisory Commission for Business Competition (KPPU) (Appeal Decision "Automotive Tire Cartel")

Decision of the Indonesian Supervisory Commission for Business Competition (KPPU) Number 08/KPPU- I/2014 on Automotive Tire Cartel ("Automotive Tire Cartel")

Decision of the Indonesian Supervisory Commission for Business Competition (KPPU) Number 17/KPPU-I/2010 on Amlodipine Anti- hypertension Pharmaceutical.

Decision of the Indonesian Supervisory Commission for Business Competition (KPPU) Number 01/KPPU-I/2010 on the Cement Loco Cartel.

Decision of the Indonesian Supervisory Commission for Business Competition (KPPU) Number 25/KPPU-I/2009 on the Domestic Flight Airline Fuel Surcharges.

Decision of the Indonesian Supervisory Commission for Business Competition (KPPU) Number 26/KPPU-I/2007 on the SMS Cellular Telecommunication.

Decision of the Indonesian Supervisory Commission for Business Competition (KPPU) Number 24/KPPU-I/2009 on Cooking Oil Cartels.

United States of America

US Court Judgement, 346 U.S. 537, *Theatre Enterprises, Inc.* v *Paramount Film Distributing* 541 (1954)

US Court Judgement, 384 U.S. 127, 142–143, *United States v General Motor Corp* (1966)

US Court Judgement, 465 U.S. 752, 768, *Monsanto Co.* v *Spray-Rite Servs. Corp.* (1984).

US Court Judgement, 475 U.S. 574, 588, *Matsushita Electronics Industries Co.* v *Zenith Radi* (1986).

US Court Judgement, 550 U.S. 544,*Bell Atlantic Corp. v. Twombly* (2007)

US Court Judgement, In re Text Messaging Antitrust Litigation No. 10–8037, 2010 U.S. App. (2010)

Legislations

European Union (EU)

Consolidated Version of the Treaty on European Union (2012 O.J. C 326/13)

Consolidated Version on the Treaty on the Functioning of the European Union (TFEU) and of the Treaty on European Union (TEU) (2012 O.J. C 326/47)

Council Regulation No 2821/71 on application of Article 85 (3) [now 81 (3)] of the Treaty to categories of agreements, decisions and concerted practices (Official Journal L 285, 29.12.1971)

Council Regulation (EC) No 1215/1999 of 10 June 1999 amending Regulation No 19/65/EEC on the application of Article 81(3) of the Treaty to certain categories of agreements and concerted practices (Oficial Journal L 148)

Council Regulation EC No 1/2003 of 16 December 2002 on the Implementation of the Rules on Competition Laid Down in Articles 81 and 82 of the Treaty (OJ L 1, 4.1.2003)

Commission Regulation 773/2004/EC of 7 April 2004 relating to the conduct of proceedings by the Commission pursuant to Articles 81 and 82 of the EC Treaty (OJ L 123/18, 27.4.2004) amended by Commission Regulation 1792/2006/EC of 23 October 2006 (OJ L 362/1, 20.12.2006) and by Commission Regulation 622/2008/EC of 30 June 2008 (OJ L 171/3, 1.7.2008)

Commission Regulation 330/2010 of 20 April 2010 on the application of Article 101(3) of the Treaty on the Functioning of the European Union to categories of vertical agreements and concerted practices (Official Journal L 102, 23.4.2010)

Decision 2011/695/EU of the President of the European Commission of 13 October 2011 on the function and terms of reference of the hearing officer in certain competition proceedings (OJ L 275/29, 20.10.2011)

Commission Notice on the co-operation between the Commission and the courts of the EU Member States in the application of Articles 81 and 82 EC (OJ C 101/54, 27.4.2004)

Commission Notice on the definition of relevant market for the purposes of Community competition law (OJ C 372, 9.12.1997)

Commission Notice on agreements of minor importance which do not appreciably restrict competition under Article 81(1) of the Treaty establishing the European Community (**de minimis**) (OJ C 368/13, 22.12.2001)

Commission Notice: Guidelines on the effect on trade concept contained in Articles 81 and 82 of the Treaty (OJ C 101/81, 27.4.2004)

Commission Notice: Guidelines on the application of Article 81(3) of the Treaty (OJ C 101/97, 27.4.2004)

Guidance on the Commission's enforcement priorities in applying Article 82 of the EC Treaty to abusive exclusionary conduct by dominant undertakings (OJ C 45/7, 24.2.2009)

Guidelines on the method of setting fines imposed pursuant to Article 23(2)(a) of Regulation 1/2003/EC (OJ C 210/2, 1.9.2006)

Commission Notice on the handling of complaints by the Commission under Articles 81 and 82 of the EC Treaty (OJ C 101/65, 27.4.2004)

Commission Notice on informal guidance relating to novel questions concerning Articles 81 and 82 of the EC Treaty that arise in individual cases (guidance letters) (OJ C 101/78, 27.4.2004)

Commission Notice on the rules for access to the Commission file in cases pursuant to Articles 81 and 82 of the EC Treaty, Articles 53, 54 and 57 of the EEA Agreement and Council Regulation (EC) No 139/2004, (OJ C 325/7, 22.12.2005)

Commission Notice on the conduct of settlement procedures in view of the adoption of Decisions pursuant to Article 7 and Article 23 of Council Regulation 1/2003/EC in cartel cases (OJ C 167/1, 2.7.2008)

Commission Notice on Immunity from fines and reduction of fines in cartel cases (OJ C 298/17, 8.12.2006)

Council Regulation EC No 1/2003 of 16 December 2002 on the Implementation of the Rules on Competition Laid Down in Articles 81 and 82 of the Treaty

Charter of Fundamental Rights of the European Union (O.J. C 326/391 2012)

Federal Republic of Germany

Gesetz gegen Wettbewerbsbeschränkungen in der Fassung der Bekanntmachung vom 26. Juni 2013 (BGBl. I S. 1750, 3245), das zuletzt durch Artikel 10 des Gesetzes vom 12. Juli 2018 (BGBl. I S. 1151) geändert worden ist

Strafprozeßordnung in der Fassung der Bekanntmachung vom 7. April 1987 (BGBl. I S. 1074, 1319), die zuletzt durch Artikel 12 des Gesetzes vom 18. Dezember 2018 (BGBl. I S. 2639) geändert worden ist

Bürgerliches Gesetzbuch in der Fassung der Bekanntmachung vom 2. Januar 2002 (BGBl. I S. 42, 2909; 2003 I S. 738), das zuletzt durch Artikel 4d des Gesetzes vom 18. Dezember 2018 (BGBl. I S. 2651) geändert worden ist

Zivilprozessordnung in der Fassung der Bekanntmachung vom 5. Dezember 2005 (BGBl. I S. 3202; 2006 I S. 431; 2007 I S. 1781), die zuletzt durch Artikel 11 des Gesetzes vom 18. Dezember 2018 (BGBl. I S. 2639) geändert worden ist

Verwaltungsverfahrensgesetz in der Fassung der Bekanntmachung vom 23. Januar 2003 (BGBl. I S. 102), das zuletzt durch Artikel 7 des Gesetzes vom 18. Dezember 2018 (BGBl. I S. 2639) geändert worden ist

Gesetz über Ordnungswidrigkeiten in der Fassung der Bekanntmachung vom 19. Februar 1987 (BGBl. I S. 602), das zuletzt durch Artikel 3 des Gesetzes vom 17. Dezember 2018 (BGBl. I S. 2571) geändert worden ist

Verwaltungsverfahrensgesetz in der Fassung der Bekanntmachung vom 23. Januar 2003 (BGBl. I S. 102), das zuletzt durch Artikel 7 des Gesetzes vom 18. Dezember 2018 (BGBl. I S. 2639) geändert worden ist

Vergabeverordnung vom 12. April 2016 (BGBl. I S. 624), die zuletzt durch Artikel 4 des Gesetzes vom 10. Juli 2018 (BGBl. I S. 1117) geändert worden ist

Gesetz gegen den unlauteren Wettbewerb in der Fassung der Bekanntmachung vom 3. März 2010 (BGBl. I S. 254), das zuletzt durch Artikel 4 des Gesetzes vom 17. Februar 2016 (BGBl. I S. 233) geändert worden ist

Bundeskartellamt, Notice no. 9/2006 on the immunity from and reduction of fines in cartel cases (Leniency Programme 7 March 2006)

Bundeskartellamt, Guidelines for the Setting of Fines in Cartel Administrative Offence Proceedings (25 June 2013)

Bundeskartellamt, Notice no. 18/2007 on the Non-Prosecution of Cooperation Agreements of Minor Importance1 ("de minimis Notice") of 13 March 2007

Republic Indonesia

The Law Number 5 year of 1999 concerning the Prohibition of Monopolistic Practices and Unfair Business Competition

The Indonesian Law Number 8 year of 1981 concerning Criminal Procedure (KUHAP)

The Indonesian Civil Code (*Burgerlijk Wetboek* 1847)

The Indonesian Law Number 19/2003 concerning the State-Owned Company (Badan Usaha Milik Negara)

The Indonesian Law Number 25/1992 concerning the Cooperative (Kooperasi)

The Indonesian Law Number 40/2007 concerning the Limited Liability Company (Perseroan Terbatas-PT)

The Indonesian Law Number 25/2000 concerning the Foundation (Yayasan)

Kitab Undang-undang Hukum Dagang (*Wetboek van Koophandel voor Indonesie* S. 1847–23)

The Government Regulation (Peraturan Pemerintah-PP) Number 75 year of 1999 concerning the Indonesian Supervisory Commission for Business Competition (KPPU)

The Indonesian Supreme Court (MARI) Regulation Number 03 year of 2005 on Procedures for Appeal of Law against the Decision of KPPU

The Indonesian Supervisory Commission for Business Competition (KPPU) Regulation Number 04/2010 concerning the Guideline for Implementing Article 11 on Cartels.

The Indonesian Supervisory Commission for Business Competition (KPPU) Regulation Number 01/2010 concerning the Procedure for Handling Competition Violation Cases.

The Indonesian Supervisory Commission for Business Competition (KPPU) Regulation Number 04/2009 concerning the Guideline for Administrative Sanction according to Article 47.

The Indonesian Supervisory Commission for Business Competition (KPPU) Regulation Number 01/2019 concerning the Guideline for Handling Antimonopoly and Unfair Business Practices Cases

United States of America

The Sherman Act 1890.

The Federal Trade Commission Act 1914.

The Clayton Act 1914.

FSC®
www.fsc.org
MIX
Papier | Fördert gute Waldnutzung
FSC® C083411

Kolibri 360 GmbH
Ferdinand-Jühlke-Straße 7
99095 Erfurt, Deutschland
produktsicherheit@kolibri360.de